# Reaffirming Legal Ethics

It has been over 30 years since the founding crises that birthed legal ethics as both a field of study and a discrete field of law. In that time thinking about the ethical dimension of legal practice has taken several turns: from justifications of zealous advocacy, to questions of process and connections to specific legal values, to more recent consideration of legal conduct as part of a wider field of virtue. Parallel to this dynamism of thought, there have also been significant changes in how legal professions, especially within those that possess a common law heritage, have been regulated and the values and conceptions of legitimate conduct that have informed this regulation.

This volume represents an opportunity for a comprehensive review of legal ethics as an international movement. Contributors include many of the key participants to the legal ethics field from the United States, Canada and Australia, including David Luban and Deborah Rhode, as well as many of the recognized emerging thinkers.

The theme of the book is taking stock of the last 30 years of legal ethics practice and scholarship. It is also a forum for new ideas and new thinking regarding the conduct of lawyers and the moral and social responsibility of the legal profession. The contributions also consider the topic of dynamism. Over the last decade significant developments in both the expectations of professional conduct and the regulation of the profession have been experienced in all jurisdictions, which has seen traditional, and once sacred, conceptions of lawyering challenged and reevaluated. The contributors also look at the theme of affirmation. Within an increasingly complex environment of change and dynamism, this volume reaffirms that there is value within the field of legal ethics as a legitimate and highly relevant field of inquiry.

*Reaffirming Legal Ethics* will be of great value for law students wanting an overview of the ethical dimension of contemporary legal practice, lawyers seeking a deeper and wider perspective on what it means to practise law, and researchers in the fields of ethics, legal ethics and the legal profession.

**Kieran Tranter** is a Senior Lecturer and Managing Editor of the Griffith Law Review at Griffith University, Australia.

**Francesca Bartlett** is a Lecturer T.C. Beirne School of Law, The University of Queensland, Australia.

**Lillian Corbin** is a Senior Lecturer and Acting-Head of School at Griffith University, Australia.

**Professor Reid Mortensen** is Professor of Law at the University of Southern Queensland, Australia.

**Professor Michael Robertson** is Professor and Head of the Law School at the University of Southern Queensland, Australia.

# Routledge Research in Legal Ethics

Forthcoming titles in this series include:

**Alternative Perspectives on Lawyers and Legal Ethics**
*Francesca Bartlett, Reid Mortensen and Kieran Tranter*

**The Ethics Project in Legal Education**
*Michael Robertson, Lillian Corbin, Kieran Tranter and Francesca Bartlett*

# Reaffirming Legal Ethics

Taking Stock and New Ideas

**Edited by**
**Kieran Tranter, Francesca Bartlett,**
**Lillian Corbin, Reid Mortensen**
**and Michael Robertson**

Routledge
Taylor & Francis Group

LONDON AND NEW YORK

First published 2010 by Routledge
2 Park Square, Milton Park, Abingdon, Oxon OX14 4RN

Simultaneously published in the USA and Canada
by Routledge
711 Third Avenue, New York, NY 10017

*Routledge is an imprint of the Taylor & Francis Group, an informa business*

First issued in paperback 2012

Typeset in Baskerville by Taylor & Francis Books

*British Library Cataloguing in Publication Data*
A catalogue record for this book is available from the British Library

*Library of Congress Cataloging in Publication Data*
Reaffirming legal ethics : taking stock and new ideas / edited by Kieran Tranter
... [et al.].
    p. cm.
  Includes index.
  1. Legal ethics–United States. I. Tranter, Kieran.
  K103.L44R43 2010
  174'.3–dc22
                        2009051974


ISBN 13: 978-0-415-54653-9 (hbk)
ISBN 13: 978-0-415-63155-6 (pbk)
ISBN 13: 978-0-203-84935-4 (ebk)

# Contents

# Preface

This book, the first of three, arises out of papers delivered at the Third International Legal Ethics Conference held at the Gold Coast, Queensland, Australia in July 2008. The conference was hosted jointly by Griffith Law School at Griffith University and the T.C. Beirne School of Law at The University of Queensland. This conference, building on the successes of the first two in the series – in Exeter, United Kingdom in 2004 and in Auckland, New Zealand in 2006 – was one of the largest specialist gatherings of legal ethicists in the new millennium.

For us, the privilege of working with the contributors in this book followed on from the success of the conference itself. It is fitting that our expressions of thanks extend to colleagues from many countries who assisted in making the conference and this volume possible. We would first like to thank Kim Economides and Julian Webb for their foundational work in establishing the international legal ethics conference series, and for their encouragement in organizing the third conference. We would also acknowledge Tim Dare's role in organizing the second conference, which provided the platform for the third. We owe a particular debt to Brad Wendel, Christine Parker, Adrian Evans and Neil Watt for their help and enthusiasm over the two years of planning for the Gold Coast conference. Our thanks are also due to our respective Deans and others who contributed to the resources needed to run the conference: Charles Rickett and Ross Grantham from the T.C. Beirne School of Law and Paula Baron and Richard Johnstone from Griffith Law School; and to Teola Marsh from the University of Queensland and Linda Brauns from Griffith University. Substantial financial support for the conference was also given by College of Law Queensland, for which we are especially grateful.

We extend our thanks to the contributors to this volume for their willingness to work with us and for their patience during the editing process. We would also like to thank Katie Carpenter and Khanam Virjee from Routledge for their support and encouragement. And a special mention must go to Griffith Law student Stevie Martin, who not only worked tirelessly as the administrator for the conference, but also joyfully undertook the task of helping to edit the manuscripts in her final year at law school.

Finally, we wish to express our heartfelt thanks to colleagues, friends and, most importantly, to our families for their faith and support over these past few years.

—Kieran Tranter,
Francesca Bartlett,
Lillian Corbin,
Reid Mortensen and
Michael Robertson
September 2009

# Contributors

**Francesca Bartlett** is a Lecturer at the T.C. Beirne School of Law, The University of Queensland, Brisbane.

**Lillian Corbin** is a Senior Lecturer and Acting Head of School at the Griffith Law School, Griffith University, Brisbane.

**Kath Hall** is a Senior Lecturer in Law at the Australian National University College of Law, Canberra.

**Lawrence K. Hellman** is Dean and Professor of Law at Oklahoma City University School of Law, Oklahoma City University.

**David Luban** is the University Professor and Professor of Law and Philosophy at Georgetown Law, Georgetown University, Washington, DC.

**Reid Mortensen** is the Foundation Professor of Law, School of Law, University of Southern Queensland, Toowoomba.

**Christine Parker** is Associate Professor and Reader, Melbourne Law School, University of Melbourne.

**Deborah Rhode** is the Ernest W. McFarland Professor of Law and Director of the Stanford Center on the Legal Profession at Stanford Law School, Stanford University, Palo Alto, CA.

**Michael Robertson** is Professor and Head of the School of Law, University of Southern Queensland, Toowoomba.

**Charles Sampford** is the Director of the Institute for Ethics, Governance and Law, a joint initiative of the United Nations University, Griffith University and Queensland University of Technology in association with the Australian National University and the Center for Asian Integrity.

**Lorne Sossin** is a Professor at the Faculty of Law, University of Toronto.

**Jocelyn Stacey** is a recent graduate from the Faculty of Law, University of Calgary.

**Kieran Tranter** is a Senior Lecturer at Griffith Law School, Griffith University, Brisbane.

**W. Brad Wendel** is a Professor of Law at Cornell Law School, Cornell University, Ithaca, NY.

**Alice Woolley** is an Associate Professor at the Faculty of Law, University of Calgary.

**Fred C. Zacharias** is the Herzog Research Professor of Law at the University of San Diego School of Law.

# 1 Introduction

*Kieran Tranter, Francesca Bartlett, Lillian Corbin,*
*Reid Mortensen and Mike Robertson*

## 1.1 Reaffirming legal ethics

The contributors to this book reaffirm legal ethics. In doing so, they enable us to take stock of current thinking about the conduct of lawyers. All of the contributors assert, in no uncertain terms, the ongoing importance of legal ethics both as a practical matter concerned with the conduct of lawyers and as an area of sustained and critical scholarly inquiry. Therefore, at least in the common law world, legal ethics is viewed as a two-sided enterprise. On one side are the 'laws of lawyering',[1] the rules, regulations and disciplinary procedures that govern the practice of law in various jurisdictions. On the other side is the academic activity dedicated to understanding, probing and questioning the rules and institutions concerned with lawyers' behaviour and to articulating a coherent moral grounding for the work of lawyers.

Legal ethics, as with the ethics of any ancient profession, has a long history that predates modern conceptual distinctions between law and morality. However, once we as moderns assume the two distinct sides of legal ethics, critical points of its contemporary development can be identified. The law of lawyering itself has multiple beginnings. The legal profession has enjoyed and long cherished a professional freedom to self-regulate. Indeed, 2008 marked the centenary of the American Bar Association's 1908 'Canons of Professional Ethics'.[2] In addition, the common law courts have exercised authority to regulate entry (and exit) to the rolls of the legal profession. Further, as Fred Zacharias reminds us in Chapter 11, lawyers have always been subject to the rule of law, accountable to the general law of fiduciary duties, agency, contract and the like. The other side of legal ethics has had an even more sporadic development in the modern era, but the 'primers' on ethical conduct that began to emerge in the nineteenth century also remind us of recurring concerns in the profession about 'what is just and right'.[3] Nevertheless, it was the Watergate scandal in the 1970s that gave critical impetus to this side of legal ethics.

Many commentators credit the modern development of the field of legal ethics as a practical and intellectual reaction to Watergate.[4] The early 1970s represented a time of questioning of institutional legitimacy, and the legal profession was being called increasingly to public account.[5] In this context, the partisan behaviour of the lawyers, and the legally trained, involved in the White House's illegal surveillance of political opponents and its attempt to cover up the 1972 break-ins at the Watergate Complex in Washington DC represented an internal crisis for the legal profession and also an external crisis in public confidence in the legal profession. For the moral philosopher Richard Wasserstrom, writing in 1975, the conduct of lawyers involved in Watergate could be explained by 'role differentiation': the idea that, once a person assumes a given social role, it is both appropriate and right for them to ignore moral standards that should not be ignored outside that role.[6] He regarded lawyering as an extreme example of role differentiation, to the point that – especially in litigation – the client's objectives should be promoted, regardless of the moral or political outcome: 'the lawyer as professional comes to inhabit a simplified universe which is strikingly amoral – which regards as morally irrelevant any number of factors which non-professional citizens might take to be important, if not decisive, in their everyday lives.'[7] Wasserstrom identified the central moral foundation behind lawyering in the common law world, which remained under-appreciated until Watergate: lawyers assumed that they were engaged for their technical competence, and viewed questions of moral responsibility as largely outside their purview.

Wasserstrom's identification and critique of 'role morality' represented a catalyst in the development of legal ethics as an area of law and a field of study. Post-Watergate, the American Bar Association's rules, which were restated in 1969, were again revised in 1983.[8] These expanded rules provided a clearer articulation of the freedoms and constraints that comprise the role of the lawyer, and the reform process spread to the professional rules of conduct issued by the organized profession in other jurisdictions. For the professional societies, role morality remained the touchstone in consideration of good lawyering, but it was a touchstone that needed to be expressly stated, justified and increasingly refined. This is still the case.

A factor that helped to ferment the articulation, justification, criticism and refinement of the rules of professional conduct was the emergence of legal ethics as a dedicated intellectual endeavour. Again, role morality was a touchstone for the growth of scholarship in the field. Wasserstrom's identification and critique of role morality challenged a generation of legal scholars to think more deeply about the morality and politics of the lawyer's role. Some scholars, like Charles Fried, met Wasserstrom's challenge directly and offered more sophisticated moral justifications for role morality.[9] Others echoed Wasserstrom's criticisms of role morality and suggested the need for alternative moral grounds for legal practice – at least in the hard cases where strong adherence to role morality would lead to morally repugnant outcomes. On this side of legal ethics, significant diversity became evident concerning the origins, legitimacy and acculturation of called-for alternative values. David Luban argued for common morality that lay within the wider community;[10] Thomas Shaffer argued for the virtue implicit in human potential;[11] Shaffer and Carrie Menkel-Meadow introduced ethics of care to the field;[12] and in the 1990s Anthony Kronman developed a strong Aristotelian theory of virtue ethics for lawyers.[13]

Legal ethics, in both of its senses, has been consolidated since the decade after Watergate when role morality was directly articulated and justified by professional societies, and when the modern foundational positions of the field as a scholarly enterprise were expressed. The reform process within the law of lawyering has continued. Successive scandals – especially lawyer complicity in corporate collapses[14] and dubious litigation[15] – and a consistently negative public image[16] have placed significant political pressure on lawyers for far-reaching reforms of the profession, climaxing with the partial loss of self-regulation for the profession in England and Wales and also in most Australian jurisdictions.[17] For scholarship on legal ethics, two concerns emerged. The first related to legal education questioning when and how legal ethics should be taught.[18] The second was a heightened awareness of the implications of departing from role morality for the rule of law. What was exposed was the relationship between fundamental values that are supposedly safeguarded by a technically neutral legal system, and the threat and dilution of those values when legal actors are encouraged to adopt some moral perspectives that are independent of the law. Following William Simon's argument that the values that should guide lawyers in professional conduct are values implicit within a functional legal system,[19] a subsequent generation of scholars, such as Brad Wendel, presented what amounted to political justifications for a refurbished and revitalized role morality.[20]

These two sides of legal ethics sometimes rub against each other. For instance, as reiterated in the 'roundtable' published in this volume (see Chapter 2), Deborah Rhode protests that Wendel's views amount to 'legal ethics without the ethics'. The field undoubtedly has its ambiguities, evident even when we are trying to define its boundaries. However, we suggest that the friction generated when the two sides of legal ethics confront each other has helped motivate the contributors to this volume to reaffirm the field's importance. All of the contributors also demonstrate and assume the importance of sustained and critical inquiry into lawyering. Within an increasingly complex environment of change and dynamism, what is affirmed is the value of the project of reflecting on the special, if not unique, conduct requirements of lawyers who simultaneously serve the needs of clients and their community. This explains the two themes that weave through these contributions. The first theme concerns the dynamism of the current and changing context of legal practice. The second concerns the ongoing relevance of legal ethics to third millennium lawyering.

## 1.2 The current and changing context of legal practice

Social scientific studies of lawyering from the 1960s and 1970s painted a picture of the form and structure of legal practice from the decades that contemporary legal ethics emerged. Despite the rise of the mega-firm over those decades, most lawyers in the common law world practised as sole practitioners or in traditionally structured firms comprising a handful of partners.[21] In this pattern of legal practice, lawyers served the discrete communities to which they belonged, and the lawyer–client relationship could be seen as a personal one.[22] Lawyers were still predominately male, white and middle class.[23]

This rather homogenous picture of who lawyers were and what they did presents a baseline from which the revolutions that have occurred in lawyering over the ensuing 30 years become clearer. Legal practice has become more specialized and stratified. The mega-firm with a national, and indeed international, presence has emerged to serve the legal needs of transnational corporations. Organized according to Fordist principles of repetition and standardization, these firms have arguably given rise to patterns of production line lawyering. This has also transformed the experience of lawyering for junior lawyers from one that was predominantly a personal relationship with clients to one that is often a depersonalized routine.[24] Furthermore, women have entered the legal profession in increasing numbers.[25] There are more law schools that are producing more graduates, so that old class and cultural prejudices that erected social barriers to entering the legal profession have been diluted.[26] Lawyers now must compete for work with other professions. Lawyering is seen increasingly as a business pursued for profit – or, perhaps even more challenging, just a job rather than a calling. This is a long way from the image of lawyering that underpinned early work on legal ethics.

However, in other respects the world of lawyers has not changed much at all. The profession still largely comprises private practitioners and, as has been the case since the reforms of the nineteenth century, they are necessarily motivated by a need to generate income. Lawyers are educated and trained through traditional university education. The legal profession nevertheless retains a basic orientation towards client needs, advice-giving and agency work, which itself sometimes leads to representation of clients in litigation. There are still professional associations, and lawyers – officers of the court – retain a formal affiliation with the justice system. To be a lawyer involves accreditation and meeting standards established by professional associations and the courts. Alice Woolley and Jocelyn Stacey's discussion in Chapter 10 demonstrates the significant power exercised by these professional and judicial communities in dictating qualification standards that are imbued with ethical meanings. While much has changed, and the extent and implications of the changes in the context of lawyering over the past 30 years should not be under-estimated, contemporary patterns of legal practice preserve some core continuities from the traditional picture of legal practice.

It is this tension between the changing context of lawyering and the traditional conception that is explored in many of the chapters in this volume. In Chapter 5, David Luban considers a particular change in lawyering: the rise and rise of in-house government counsel. Much legal work now occurs 'behind the scenes' in reports and memos by lawyers employed, directly or indirectly, by government and corporations. Luban, considering the now infamous 'torture memos' issued by the US Justice Department in 2004 that authorized certain interrogation techniques as lawful, suggests that the partisanship championed by role morality is misplaced when applied to in-house counsel. He argues that lawyers acting as in-house counsel must exercise informed and critically independent judgement when advising client/employers. Instead of producing partisan perspectives based on what the lawyer believes the client/employer wants, in-house counsel must maintain a sense of integrity of the law. Luban also charts the changed context of lawyering in the impact of international humanitarian law in operational planning by the US military, and the tension that arises from 'lawfare' – that is, the manipulating and selective interpretation of humanitarian law as another arena for combat.

In Chapter 6, Charles Sampford considers changes in lawyering due to the increasingly globalized nature of contemporary legal practice. Sampford has previously written about the importance of the institutionalization of ethical constraints in the practice of domestic law.[27] In this chapter, he begins with the historical recognition that the modern legal profession (like the profession of arms) is a product of the sovereign nation state. In the modern era, legal ethics has been considered a domestic matter concerning the domestic legal profession. However, Sampford reminds us that prior to the modern period, lawyers in Western Europe did not consider that sovereign boundaries determined how they should practise. Taking inspiration from this older ideal he argues that lawyers – like soldiers – are well placed to think and act as a global profession, and when doing so assist in globalizing the value of the rule of law.

Christine Parker in Chapter 7 addresses a perennial concern that some suggest corrupts a lawyer's understanding of legal ethics: the influence of commercialization on legal services. Taking as her case study the recent opportunity that Australian law firms have been given to incorporate, and the subsequent incorporation of the well-known Australian 'plaintiff' firm Slater and Gordon, Parker argues that incorporation need not be seen as a further step away from the ethical profession ideal. Indeed, she argues that requirements of reporting and accountability that attach to incorporation and public listing can be seen as encouraging responsible and ethical lawyer conduct in ways that more traditional firm structures have not done. Parker's chapter affirms the view that unethical conduct is more likely the product of a micro-level context of an immediate lawyer than resulting from macro-level factors concerning structure and ownership of a firm. Thus Parker points to the complexity of the social and legal environment in which lawyers work and, when considered with the Sampford thesis, the importance of diverse perspectives which account for the internal and external realities of lawyering.

Lawrence Hellman in Chapter 8 examines the tensions between the traditional and contemporary understandings of lawyers. He reaffirms a consistent theme in legal ethics: that law schools are key institutions in the formation of a more responsible and ethically aware profession. Taking as his starting point the influential 2007 report on legal education by the Carnegie Foundation, Hellman argues that Carnegie missed a fundamental stage in the professional development of new lawyers. The last 30 years have seen a significant body of social scientific research into ethics and the ethical formation of lawyers that suggests that a newly admitted lawyer's 'professional personality' is not firmly formed at law schools, but crystallizes over the first few years of practice. Further, the evidence from this research seems to suggest that early experiences in law firms shape how new lawyers define what is ethical and unethical. Faced with this empirical reality, Hellman sees law schools as needing help from the profession and its regulatory bodies in developing and maintaining an ethical profession. Yes, law schools should attempt to 'inoculate' law students against unethical conduct. But, lawyers in practice must be trained and expected to administer frequent 'booster shots' if the value and understandings sought to be instilled by the law schools are to remain potent. Lawyers who act as supervisors for new entrants to the profession particularly require this training.

In Chapter 9, Lorne Sossin deals with a question that is often discussed in contemporary thinking about legal ethics: how does ethics relate to access to lawyers?[28] For Sossin, it is clear that an ethical profession has obligations of working *pro bono publico*. However, the relationship is not as simplistic as some *pro bono* advocates suggest. Sossin examines the various justifications for *pro bono* work, emphasizing that the context behind the lawyer offering and a client seeking *pro bono* should be considered in any formal *pro bono* scheme. While reflecting on the Canadian situation, Sossin makes a significant general contribution to the development of *pro bono* schemes by offering a matrix through which possible *pro bono* relationships can be assessed.

In Chapter 10, Alice Woolley and Jocelyn Stacey consider another common question for legal ethics: the standards of conduct or morality that should be imposed on those wishing to join the profession. They observe that the profession has a long history of using the concept of 'good character' as a gatekeeping criterion. Controversially, they argue for the removal of the good character test. They base this claim on recent psychological research, which renders problematic the assumption that past conduct in one context is indicative of similar conduct in another context. It has not been proven that inappropriate conduct prior to seeking admission is predictive of unethical conduct as a lawyer. As such, they expose the good character requirement as a cover for prejudice. In conclusion, they argue that entry to the legal profession should be based on technical competencies and not character judgements.

Fred Zacharias examines the traditional concept in legal ethics of professional self-regulation in Chapter 11. His first step is to canvass the various meanings possessed by self-regulation. He argues that self-regulation in the United States tends to refer to the Bar's standard-setting and disciplinary powers, but that this emphasis on standards and discipline ignores the plethora of ways in which the contemporary profession is regulated by other laws, institutions and professional associations. In perpetuating the self-regulation misnomer – and Zacharias sees the American Bar Association as the chief culprit in this process – he suggests that there is an opportunity now to discuss the more important question of the appropriate method of regulating those in the legal profession.

Unifying these contributions is the tension between tradition and change, between the context of lawyering pertaining to when legal ethics was in its infancy and the myriad influences that render contemporary legal practice dynamic, changed and different. While Woolley and Stacey and Sossin argue for changes in the law of lawyering, Luban, Sampford, Hellman, Parker and Zacharias suggest that the changing context of lawyering should inspire academics to rethink the definition of legal ethics. Importantly, Luban and Sampford identify examples and lessons that lawyers can learn from another profession – the military. However, it is also important to note that a second theme or assumption runs through these chapters. The contributors very clearly adhere to the view that the foundations, nature and purposes of legal ethics that were identified in the 1970s *are as relevant now as they ever were*.

## 1.3 Continuing relevance of legal ethics

In many ways, the contributions in this volume remain quite fundamentally connected with some of the core ideas and questions that were clearly articulated by Wasserstrom, Fried and the others who influenced the development of legal ethics as a scholarly discipline in the 1970s. Although the current contributions have much to offer the existing body of scholarship in terms of fresh analysis and insights, they tend on the whole to grapple with the same challenging issues. For example, the question about whether a good lawyer can be a good person remains largely unresolved, or is at least still strenuously debated; and, depending on the personal views of lawyers, their view of legal ethics can leave them feeling either comfortable or perplexed by role morality and its implicit claims of dual morality or moral schizophrenia. The reality of achieving the goal of being a 'good lawyer' may require lawyers to make choices about how they will act. Sometimes the course a lawyer takes may be at odds with both the lawyer's own conscience and the moral standards of the wider community. Moreover, legal ethicists are still engaged with the question of whether ethical lawyering involves fidelity to law, or choices and actions that pay attention to extra-legal values, or somehow integrates the two. In relation to these tensions, legal ethicists are still compelled to assess whether the actual practice of fidelity to law is really possible – that is, whether the resources that the law and its system provide for lawyers are ever complete enough to obviate recourse to other sources of authority.

Deborah Rhode in Chapter 3 provides a catalogue of these continuing normative questions in legal ethics. Rhode argues that there are critical moments in professional practice when a lawyer should be independent. For Rhode, role morality's zealous pursuit of a client's interest is not sufficient to guide good lawyering. In contrast to the dual morality thesis, she argues that lawyers need to act with a wider sense of integrity. Furthermore, Rhode argues that the many reasons given by professional organizations and their scholarly supporters for the maintenance of the established view turn out to be based on self-interest rather than principle.

Brad Wendel, like Rhode, reaffirms the central dilemma for legal ethics of role morality versus independent morality in Chapter 4. However, in contrast to Rhode, Wendel argues that role morality should remain the ethical guide for lawyers. For Wendel, when lawyers start to claim independent moral agency they are endangering the legal system and the underlying political system. He argues that a lawyer's ethical conduct should be based on values internal to a legitimate legal system and not drawn from another external source. So long as the legal system that the lawyer is serving is functional, role morality remains, according to Wendel, the best guide to ethical decision-making in legal practice.

This foundational controversy with legal ethics is explored in more detail in the transcript of the roundtable held at the Third International Legal Ethics Conference on the Gold Coast, Australia in July 2008. The participants in the roundtable were Deborah Rhode, David Luban and Brad Wendel. Christine Parker chaired the session. The transcript suggests, paraphrasing Luban, that an examination of the meaning of ethical lawyering must inevitably involve scrutiny of one or more of the following elements: the actor, the act, and the outcomes of the act. As the participants' statements demonstrate, there is little shared understanding of whether the good lawyer needs to have any appreciation for these philosophical distinctions, and therefore what they might mean for the process of reflection and decision-making. Another point emphasized in the roundtable was that legal ethics is still confronted by the crucial question of how it is that lawyers learn or know how to be ethical lawyers. It is sobering to consider, especially in light of the evidence reviewed by Hellman in Chapter 8, whether legal education has made – or even has the capacity to make – a great deal of progress on this issue. Wendel defends the teaching of legal ethics in terms of a near-exclusive focus on the law of lawyering, justified largely by the need to equip future lawyers with the ability to stay out of trouble. In contrast, Luban and Rhode call for a role – albeit often an indirect one – for philosophical concepts in embedding good decision-making habits for future lawyering.

Another salient point of discussion from the roundtable concerns what it means to be a good lawyer when there is reason to doubt the reliability of legal procedures and standards that are supposed to lead to fair and just outcomes within the ordinary institutions of law. For Luban, an important initial observation is that the argument that the law can always come up with a good result 'is simply an over-estimation of what a wonderful thing the law is'. Luban also notes in the roundtable that a vitally important question is whether one begins 'from the point of view of an individual moral agent or from the viewpoint of the integrity of the legal system and the institutions within it'. For Wendel, following his roundtable comments, it is not a question of *whether* it is ever proper for a lawyer to opt out of formal role obligations, but one of *when* the circumstances justify doing so. As he emphasizes in Chapter 4, these opportunities are apparently few and far between, given the lawyer's underlying responsibility of fidelity to law.

Another theme from the roundtable relates to the necessity of considering legal ethics as involving moral theory or a more pragmatic project – best determined through an appreciation of the realities of contemporary lawyering. Wendel states: 'I don't think the word utilitarianism or deontology or Aristotelian has ever been uttered in my classroom.' In contrast, Luban suggests that 'philosophy is not just a bunch of results', but a 'set' of very detailed arguments and these sometimes contain what appear to be 'disabling foundational issues'.

These comments concerning the use of philosophy for legal ethics could be construed to mean that a purely normative approach to legal ethics has reached a terminal point of circulating around role and personal morality, and that it may have become more helpful to examine specific aspects of lawyer conduct. Put another way, maybe it is time for scholars to focus on an empirical examination of how lawyers actually practise, rather than on 'how should lawyers in general practise'.

An example of this approach to legal ethics is offered by Kath Hall in her chapter. Her concern is how principled and experienced practitioners come to rationalize unethical conduct. In looking at internal rationalizations of lawyer behaviour, Hall presents a contemporary take on this question. Instead, of drawing on moral theory, Hall delves into psychology to produce a more sophisticated map of how external contexts and pressures lead to rationalizations that minimize responsibility, or 'ethical blindness'. Hall's contribution is ultimately pragmatic. In mapping the process of rationalization that leads to ethical blindness, lawyers can be trained to identify and minimize such tendencies.

While drawing on psychological research is a relatively novel development in legal ethics, Hall's chapter reaffirms the core consideration that has animated legal ethics over the past 30 years: that a fundamental aspect of inquiry in the field is trying to understand why lawyers make unethical choices. Her critique of ethical blindness resonates with Luban's and Rhode's critical projects, and ultimately harks back to Wasserstrom's critique of the limited responsibilities offered by role morality. Further, Hall's final registry concerns education. Her chapter supports the idea that legal ethics is a twinned enterprise, as highlighted in the roundtable, concerned with both the normative question from the philosophical domain of what *should* be regarded as good lawyering, and also with the descriptive questions that ask what *is* lawyering.

Ultimately, what is reaffirmed in the volume is the project of legal ethics. One of the underlying arguments of the volume as a whole is that 'legal ethics' cannot simply be submerged within a broader field of applied philosophy, or management, or regulatory studies. This does not mean that opportunities do not exist for interdisciplinary engagement with philosophy, social science, politics or even law. It *does* mean that legal ethics remains a more or less discrete, legitimate and highly relevant field of inquiry for thinking about, and evaluating, the dynamic and changing nature of lawyering in this millennium.

## Notes

1 R.J. Kutak, 'The law of lawyering', *Washburn Law Journal*, 1983, vol. 22, 413.
2 See L.M. Niehoff, 'In the shadow of the shrine: Regulation and aspiration in the ABA Model Rules of Professional Conduct', *Wayne Law Review*, 2008, vol. 54, 3.
3 W. Simon, *The Practice of Justice: A Theory of Lawyers' Ethics*, Cambridge, MA: Harvard University Press, 1998, p. 3.
4 See K. Clark, 'The legacy of Watergate for legal ethics instruction', *Hastings Law Journal*, 2000, vol. 51, 673; G.C. Hazard Jr, 'Future of legal ethics', *Yale Law Journal*, 1991, vol. 100, 1239; T. Shaffer, *American Lawyers and Their Communities*, Notre Dame, IN: University of Notre Dame Press, 1991, pp. 1–3.

5 Hazard, 'Future of legal ethics', pp. 1260–63. Another event that acted as a lightning rod for the venting of public dissatisfaction with the legal profession was the *Garrow* case. See D. Luban, 'Freedom and constraint in legal ethics: Some mid-course corrections to lawyers and justice', *Maryland Law Review*, 1990, vol. 49, 424, pp. 425–28.

6 R. Wasserstrom, 'Lawyers as professionals: Some moral issues', *Human Rights*, 1975, vol. 5, 1, p. 3.

7 Ibid., p. 8.

8 See Niehoff, 'In the shadow of the shrine'.

9 C. Fried, 'The lawyer as friend: The moral foundations of the lawyer–client relationship', *Yale Law Journal*, 1976, vol. 85, 1060.

10 D. Luban, *Lawyers and Justice: An Ethical Case Study*, Princeton, NJ: Princeton University Press, 1988, pp. 105–12.

11 T. Shaffer, 'Moral theology in legal ethics', *Capital University Law Review*, 1982, vol. 12, 179.

12 T. Shaffer, *On Being a Christian and a Lawyer*, Provo, UT: Brigham Young University Press, 1981; C. Menkel-Meadow, 'Portia in a different voice: Speculations on a women's lawyering process', *Berkeley Women's Law Journal*, 1985, vol. 1, 39.

13 A. Kronman, *The Lost Lawyer: Failing Ideals of the Legal Profession*, Cambridge, MA: Belknap Press, 1993.

14 E. Wald, 'Lawyers and corporate scandals', *Legal Ethics*, 2004, vol. 7, 54; D.L. Rhode and P.D. Paton, 'Lawyers, ethics and Enron', *Stanford Journal of Law, Business and Finance*, 2002, vol. 8, 9.

15 C. Cameron and J. Liberman, 'Destruction of documents before proceedings commence: What is a court to do?', *Melbourne University Law Review*, 2003, vol. 27, 273; M. Harvey and S. Le Mire, 'Playing for keeps – tobacco litigation, document retention, corporate culture and legal ethics', *Monash University Law Review*, 2008, vol. 34, 163.

16 Hazard 'Future of legal ethics', pp. 126–3.

17 On the UK reforms, see J. Webb, 'Legal disciplinary practices: An ethical problem in the making?', *Legal Ethics*, 2005, vol. 8, 185. On the well-documented reforms in Queensland, Australia, see R. Mortensen and L. Haller, 'Legal profession reform in Queensland', *University of Queensland Law Journal*, 2004, vol. 23, 280; L. Haller, 'Imperfect practice under the *Legal Profession Act 2004* (Qld)', *University of Queensland Law Journal*, 2004, vol. 27, 411.

18 R.B. McKay, 'Legal education: Law, lawyers, and ethics', *DePaul Law Review*, 1974, vol. 23, 641. An overview of approaches to legal ethics education can be found in M. Robertson and K. Tranter, 'Grounding legal ethics learning in social scientific studies of lawyers at work', *Legal Ethics*, 2006, vol. 9, 211.

19 W.H. Simon, 'Ethical discretion in lawyering', *Harvard Law Review*, 1988, vol. 101, 1093; W.H. Simon, 'Lawyer advice and client autonomy: Mrs. Jones's Case', *Maryland Law Review*, 1991, vol. 50, 213.

20 See W.B. Wendel, 'Public values and professional responsibilities', *Notre Dame Law Review*, 1999, vol. 75, 1.

21 See J.E. Carlin, *Lawyers' Ethics: A Survey of the New York City Bar*, New York: Russell Sage Foundation, 1966; D.E. Rosenthal, *Lawyer and Client: Who's in Charge?* New Brunswick, NJ: Transaction Books, 1974; J.P. Heinz and E.O. Laumann, *Chicago Lawyers: The Social Structure of the Bar*, Evanston, IL: Northwestern University Press, 1982; M. Cain, 'The general practice of lawyer and the client', in R. Dingwall and P. Lewis (eds) *The Sociology of the Professions: Lawyers, Doctors and Others*, London: Macmillan, 1983.

22 A. Sarat and W.L. Felstiner, *Divorce Lawyers and Their Clients: Power and Meaning in the Legal Process*, New York: Oxford University Press, 1995; L. Mather, C.A. McEwen and R.J. Maiman, *Divorce Lawyers at Work: Varieties of Professionalism in Practice*, New York: Oxford University Press, 2001.

23 Menkel-Meadow, 'Portia in a different voice'; D.B. Wilkins, 'Fragmenting professionalism: Racial identity and the ideology of bleached-out lawyering', *International Journal of the Legal Profession*, 1998, vol. 5, 141.

24 C. Parker, A. Evans, L. Haller, S. Le Mire and R. Mortensen, 'The ethical infra-structure in legal practice in large law firms: Values, policy and behaviour', *University of New South Wales Law Journal*, 2008, vol. 31, 164.
25 D. Rhode, 'Gender and the Profession: An American Perspective', in U. Schultz and G. Shaw (eds) *Women in the World's Legal Professions*, Oxford: Hart Publishing, 2003, 4. H. Sommerlad, 'Women solicitors in a fractured profession: Intersections of gender and professionalism in England and Wales', *International Journal of the Legal Profession*, 2002, vol. 9, 213; Francesca Bartlett, 'Professional discipline against female lawyers in Queensland: A gendered analysis', *Griffith Law Review*, 2008, vol. 17, 311.
26 See K. Tranter, 'The different side of society: Street practice and Australian clinical legal education', *Griffith Law Review*, 2006, vol. 15, 1.
27 C. Sampford, 'What's a lawyer doing in a nice place like this? Lawyers and applied ethics', *Legal Ethics*, 1998, vol. 1, 35.
28 See Luban, *Lawyers and Justice: An Ethical Case Study*, pp. 277–88.

## Postscript

Fred C. Zacharias passed away on 8 November 2009. Professor Zacharias was an enthusiastic supporter of the conference and of this publication. We are honored to be able to publish his chapter as a testament to his commitment and contribution to legal ethics, both in the United States and throughout the world.

# 2 The philosophical foundations of legal ethics: a roundtable[1]

*Moderator: Associate Professor Christine Parker,*
*The University of Melbourne*

*Participants:*

*Professor David Luban, Georgetown University*

*Professor Deborah Rhode, Stanford University*

*Professor Brad Wendel, Cornell University*

## 2.1 Christine Parker

What we're going to do in this roundtable is to talk about the philosophical foundations of legal ethics, the need for philosophy in legal ethics or not, and the significance of philosophy and different philosophical approaches to legal ethics in addressing practical issues.

We have worked out a series of four or five issues or questions that David Luban (as a kind of Socrates of the group)[2] is going to pose. With each question, there is going to be some discussion amongst the group and then we'll ask for comments from the floor.

Professor Deborah Rhode serves as the integrator of the group, the philosophically informed and empirically grounded ethicist. Professor Brad Wendel may be playing Plato, representing the new-generation legal ethics philosopher (although he is probably too established and has made his mark too much for us to label him the new generation).

I'll hand over to Socrates.

## 2.2 David Luban

Socrates was also famous for his ugliness. [Laughter] We thought that one place to begin would be with a very basic question about whether legal ethics needs philosophical foundations. There's a story that the philosopher Gerald Dworkin tells: 'I was riding in a cab and the cabbie asked me what I do and I told him that I was a philosopher. He sat back in his seat and said, "Philosophy – it's kind of like dermatology. It's not going to do much for you but it's not going to kill you either." ' To go along with that, the legendary philosopher Sidney Morgenbesser, when asked what a philosopher does, replied: 'You draw a few distinctions, you clarify a few concepts. It's a living.'

There is in philosophy a long tradition of scepticism about foundational projects. Philosophy typically asks questions that raise very deep paradoxes. We all know that Descartes raised the possibility that we are dreaming right now, and used that challenge to undermine the certainty of empirical knowledge. There are other arguments within philosophy, deriving paradoxes in the foundations of mathematics, or in the foundations of quantum physics. Nevertheless, the fact is that physicists go along happily doing physics, mathematicians go along happily proving theorems, and all of us go along happily knowing things even though there are what appear to be disabling foundational issues.

There is an interesting diagnosis of these phenomena by Wittgenstein, in his discussion of paradoxes in the foundations of mathematics. He says that these foundational problems 'are no more the foundation of mathematics for us than the painted rock is the support of a painted tower'.[3] If somebody erased the rock, the painting of the tower would not collapse or fall down – but of course the picture would become a Magritte-like surrealist painting. By analogy with Wittgenstein's striking image, my question is whether we actually think we need philosophical foundations for the subject of legal ethics. When Charles Fried asks, 'Can a good lawyer be a good person?'[4] it's a deep challenge to the foundations of legal ethics. If you can't come up with a satisfactory answer, does that mean that the enterprise collapses? Or does it just mean that the painted tower now seems to lack a painted rock under it? What's the whole point of providing philosophical foundations for legal ethics? Do those who don't do it in either their research or in their teaching have anything to feel nervous about?

## 2.3 Brad Wendel

I'll pick up a couple of points from the first questions: one of them, the Wittgensteinian point, and the other, the distinction between teaching and scholarship. I think there are occasions when it's important to push back the foundations. I think there are questions that we ask ourselves – Can a good lawyer be a good person? – but more recently the question we've all being talking about – 'What's wrong with lawyers when they do such-and-such?' What exactly is bad about John Yoo?[5] What is wrong with advising the government that torture is permissible? Those are questions that lead to philosophical reflection, and I guess I'm sort of a half-baked philosopher, unlike David, so I don't get caught up in the paradoxical questions. But for me philosophy is the reflective activity of pushing back the foundations and trying to figure out what lies at the root of some practice of evaluating or criticizing or prescribing. And I think that, as scholars, we find ourselves on occasion reflecting on the deep foundational questions, and that's when philosophy is useful.

But as a teacher I think it may have a more limited utility, and this puts me at odds with the rest of my panel. I teach what is called 'legal ethics', but it's really a 'law governing lawyers' course. In my law school, I teach it to 140 people and I do hard-core doctrinal law governing lawyers and we don't mention philosophical concepts ever. I don't think the words 'utilitarianism' or 'deontology' or 'Aristotelian' have ever been uttered in my classroom. And there are some reasons for this. The American law governing lawyers is quite complicated, and not the sort of thing that you can muddle through without some background. So I think it's important that my students know this stuff. A lot of my students are going out in big law firms where they risk serious liability problems if they don't know what they're doing. And so I think it's important to learn this. I also think that there is a theoretical foundation that emerges from that class. I'm very taken by Ernie Weinrib's idea of the imminent rationality of law. I think any area of law kind of hangs together around certain evaluative concepts that give it structure. And I think that the law governing lawyers hangs together around ideas like the fiduciary nature of the lawyer–client relationship, and duties of candour and loyalty that are owed to third parties in courts and clients. And I think there are philosophical analogues for all of these concepts. They're rough analogues only. I think there are kind of idiosyncratic concepts like loyalty and candour that inform the lawyer–client relationship and the lawyer's role. They may not be precisely the same as these concepts as they exist in ordinary morality, but nevertheless they're there and they structure the class – they give it some kind of sense.

But I don't think that's different in kind from the imminent rationality of contracts or torts or administrative law or anything else that we teach. I think every class that we teach has some sort of framework that has evaluative content. And so I don't know that the philosophy of legal ethics that leads to the sense of the law governing lawyers is different from the philosophy of torts and contracts or administrative law. So I think teaching it may have limited utility but my co-panellists have different ways of bringing it in. But I tend to do the sort of thing that ethics teachers advise us not to do, which is to draw a fairly strict separation between theoretical ethics and the actual law. I do teach a seminar in philosophical legal ethics and we read all of the texts that we talk about here, but that is its own little enterprise and I don't really see that as informing my day-to-day teaching of the law governing lawyers. And again, this is a radical position and my co-panellists can disagree with me on that.

## 2.4 Deborah Rhode

Well, Brad has just described what I have elsewhere somewhat scornfully referred to as legal ethics without the ethics. And it's not my approach, but not because I disagree with Brad about being able to muddle through without Kant. I think you can do that perfectly well. And not because I don't think that there's plenty of law of lawyering out there to occupy a full course and that students need to know where the lines are before they're in a position to cross one. So I too spend time on the law of lawyering, and I'm aware that some of my students have concerns about passing the 'God help us' multiple-choice, multi-state Bar exam. I always start off by telling them that the course is neither necessary nor sufficient to that end, and if they just pick the second most ethical course of conduct when in doubt they will pass it with no difficulty.

Early in my teaching career, I made the mistake of trying to get a sense of what I was dealing with in terms of philosophical foundations among the students. I asked how many of them had encountered Kant at any point in the under-graduate curriculum. I think two or three hands went up in a class of 75. What I should have said, as David told me this morning, was something reassuring like, 'Well we're all post-Kantians now' and gone on. But instead what I said was: 'Well you know, that's great, but I do think that some brief discussion of moral frameworks is going to help us later on in resolving issues where there are strong competing values at stake.' So we did a little bit of introductory moral philosophy and then later on when it was relevant to particular problems, I had students work through those problems, taking a utilitarian perspective and taking a rights-oriented perspective. I think doing that kind of applied philosophy does give people tools to think more systemically and deeply about issues that otherwise would get just intuitive reactions. Moral philosophy also offers a window into some of the harder questions of legal ethics that are left, in the law of lawyering, to the lawyer's own discretion. What kind of cases are you willing to take? When do you decide that, as Kunstler said, maybe everybody's got a right to a lawyer but they don't have a right to me? Where do you draw certain lines if you're in a subordinate position in a law firm?

And I bring in not just philosophy for those questions but also organizational psychology, and law and economics. But philosophy is a framework that helps to give people a richer sense of these questions. I do it in part because there's a tendency to view legal ethics as a step-child, and sort of soft and mushy where everybody's view is as good as everybody else's. Very early on, I want to challenge people who hold that relativist view that there's not some kind of systematic 'hard' way to talk about 'hard cases'. I want them to see that there may not be one right answer, but that there are better ways of thinking about the questions and formulating the answer that satisfies them. My hope at the end of the course is that they've come out with something that gives them a sense of themselves and the profession that's different than what they get from the standard torts or contracts class. I must say, I've been much aided in this endeavour by one of the greatest gifts that was ever given to me. The person sitting to my right gave me finger puppets of Kant and Hegel. Actually, you can buy these on the internet. So now I have visual displays and they're very cute.

## 2.5 David Luban

For those who are interested, you can get the finger puppets on the web from the company that makes them, which is called the Unemployed Philosophers Guild. I did write to them once and asked why they didn't have finger puppets of women philosophers. They wrote back and said that they were having trouble getting permission from the estates of Hannah Arendt, Simone de Beauvoir and

Simone Weil, but maybe they'll work through those issues. What they need is a good lawyer![6]

I think I've been in all parts of the continuum about this in my own teaching. When I started working on legal ethics, I had been hired as a person with a philosophy degree and no law degree to help a dean teach an ethics course because he was frustrated by the fact that he had no training in philosophy. So I thought that my mission was to bring the 'powerful tools of modern philosophy' to bear on problems of legal ethics, and discovered after a while that this was really a mistake for my class.

The reason was very simple. Philosophy is not simply a bunch of results. It's a set of arguments, and they're pretty detailed. If you try to bring Kant in, you can ask people to read an entire book by Kant. That takes weeks to do properly, and no law teacher can afford to spend weeks on it in the ethics course, and the students would be going crazy trying to figure out why they need to know the exact relation between pure reason and pure practical reason, and all of the other details in Kant. If, on the other hand, you edit the *Groundwork of the Metaphysics of Morals* down to two paragraphs, you've turned Kant into a finger puppet. Nowadays I teach a course that's closer to Brad's.

But the difference is that in my own presentation of doctrinal material, my philosophical background helps to organize it, and every so often some philosophical theme emerges that it seems to make sense to discuss explicitly in class. So, for example, I teach a problem that's in our casebook about in-house lawyers working for Ford Motor Company, who discover that Ford's Pinto automobile explodes when it's hit from the back. They try to bring this to the attention of the company's executives who do a cost-benefit analysis and decide that it's worth going ahead with production, not recalling the car and paying off the tort claims. We talk about cost-benefit analysis as a way of thinking that is fundamentally utilitarian. A lot of students are bothered by this, and that turns out to be a point where if I just mention that Kant draws a distinction between things that have a dignity and things that have a price, students find it illuminating. Admittedly there's no argument being given there and this is not doing justice to Kant, but it seems to organize the discussion for students in a way that they find helpful. The philosophy, so to speak, creeps in. I hope that I'm doing more than sound bites or philosophical memes when I do it that way – but even if that's all that it is, these do seem to be useful organizing ideas. I think my own problem with going more systematically through 'here's how a consequentialist thinks about things, here's how a rights theorist thinks about things', is that I fear that turns the discussion into a relativist one where students respond: 'Well okay, I've got this smorgasbord of theories, they yield different answers. I guess I just get to choose whichever theory I like. And since I'm a consequentialist, I would go for the cost-benefit analysis.' It's a much longer story for somebody to explain why am I a consequentialist rather than a Kantian or vice versa, or why am I a virtue ethicist?

So for me the main approaches to moral philosophy should emerge naturally from the classroom dialogue about doctrine. These approaches, I take it, are roughly: one that focuses on the character of the actor; one that focuses on the nature of the act; and one that focuses on the outcomes of the act – in other words, virtue ethics, deontology and consequentialism. Clearly, all of these are important. But if you just present them as a smorgasbord, it makes it seem as if everything is up for grabs.

## 2.6 Floor comment by Steve Mark[7]

When I deal with complaints against lawyers, one of the things that I tend to find is that whether people have some sort of an idea of: (1) what the purpose of law is, and (2) why they're becoming a lawyer and whether the underlying premise that they chose to be a lawyer is really important in determining much of their later behaviour. And when I'm lecturing to the lawyers, I ask them those simple questions like 'Why did you become a lawyer and what do you hope to achieve?' I find that most of the students that I talk to have never been asked the question and they get really confused because of it. So they end up deferring to rules rather than values, and get lost in the rules. And so I'm kind of in favour of the philosophical underpinnings being taught or being approached in every course so that the students have some sort of a basis on which they can put their behaviour and understand who they are.

## 2.7 Deborah Rhode

I totally agree, and I often say in the concluding lecture that it's important to remember when you leave law school why you came, and to hold on to those aspirational norms. I remember giving a keynote lecture at some place in Ohio once and someone put up their hand and said: 'Professor Rhode, what's your philosophy of right and wrong?' He obviously expected a serious answer. I thought of all sorts of humorous ways of deflecting the question, but there was a kind of earnestness about the inquiry. So I fumbled around to try to leave him with something and said:

> Well, you know, there are a lot of great philosophers who have grappled with that question and you can think about some of what they've told us in those moments when you have to make a really quick decision. Sometimes when I've been in those moments, I think of the *60 Minutes* television broadcast test or the newspaper headline test. How would you feel if this conduct appeared as a profile on *60 Minutes* and your mother was watching, or on the front page of the *New York Times*?

And I added: 'Really, this is kind of a version of what Kant talked about. How would you feel if this conduct were generalized and everyone did that? Could you defend it in a public setting?' While you can't have students read the whole categorical imperative literature in a legal ethics class, you can distil a few key insights and give them ways to think about how it might hook up to conduct in the real world. So I think that sometimes the philosophical tools, if you put them in a framework that's accessible, can be really useful.

## 2.8 Brad Wendel

I'd like to just quickly disagree but I hope to explain why. I tell my students in my law governing lawyers class:

'Look this is a big, thick casebook with lots and lots of cases in which lawyers have gotten into a lot of trouble. And almost without exception, these aren't people who are crooks. These are people who genuinely were trying to do the right thing and they were often consulting their values. They were often using their moral compass. They were often trying to muddle through doing the best they could. But what they didn't do is open the casebook and read the cases and learn the law.'

I want the students to understand the difference between the critical application of values to their life as a lawyer. From a normative standpoint from which they can say 'What I'm doing has value or it doesn't', on the one hand. And on the other hand, those values as instantiated in binding law and those can be very different things. I tell them that the sure-fire way to end up in the next edition of the casebook is to say, 'Let's think, what's the right thing to do here?' when I'm trying to figure out whether I can get an advance waiver of this conflict or whether I can represent this client, having represented an adversary in the past. Figuring out what a good person would do in that case is likely to be a fiasco. What they should do is approach it as if they were advising a client about what the law requires in some other area, which means pull the books, read the cases, read the rules, be really careful to work through it as a legal problem. That's how to stay out of trouble.

Now Deborah is going to say, 'That's ethics without the ethics.' But this is trading on an ambiguity in the term 'legal ethics', and I'm fairly tedious about this but it matters to me that we clarify what we mean when we say legal ethics. And I think we can mean a bunch of different things. One of the things that we can mean is the critical application of values to decide whether our role and its requirements have any sort of normative significance. That's lovely and wonderful and I write about that; I've spent my whole career as a scholar doing that. But it's different from legal ethics in the sense of legal ethics as regulation, legal ethics as risk management, legal ethics as the law governing lawyers, substantive liability standards. The term is fine as long as we keep it in its appropriate context. But when we're doing legal ethics in that second sense, I think it's important not to assume that, whatever the values are, a critical reflective person would think about are necessarily instantiated in positive law. They may be, they may not be, and I think it's very important for people to be careful about that.

## 2.9 Deborah Rhode

Well, let me add just a footnote to that. One of the other reasons why I so dis-agree with that as the framework for the course is that it leaves out all the critical perspectives on the regulatory process and access to justice. Who should control the disciplinary system and what can we learn from other countries? None of that is in the cases and the doctrine. I like to think that I'm helping to educate the people who are going to be in a position to make the system function better in the future, and I want them to have the tools of critical analysis. I want them to step back and say, if this system were being run by not the profession but disinterested third parties, would it look like this? Would we have these rules, and if not how can we get ourselves to a place where we have a more sensible regulatory framework? So I really want to leave them with all sorts of stuff that's not going to be on the multiple-choice MPRE [Bar examination] and that is not going to prevent them from being a case in Brad's casebook. If one of my students ends up there, I may rethink this position. But for now, I spend a significant chunk of time in the course talking about the broader regulatory issues and access to justice and public service, and all those things that would get left out of a course that is legal ethics without the ethics.

## 2.10 Floor comment by Kim Economides[8]

The problem, I think, is that Brad is constructing a very elegant system, a very impressive and persuasive system, but one that ultimately I fear creates a split in the personality of the lawyer. They are very conscious of their role as a professional, which is separate from that of being a person. My interest in this field is largely inspired by the same motives as Deborah has just articulated. And the notion of fidelity to law, I think, also needs to be counterbalanced by, if you like, some conception of fidelity to humanity – and character ethics, I think, are important. And there is a role in legal education in strengthening the character of lawyers. So I think the debate needs to also focus at the level of motivation. Perhaps just one philosophical reflection is that of Bertrand Russell, who says: 'Remember your humanity and forget the rest.' That's not a bad *dictum* for some lawyers.

## 2.11 Brad Wendel

I think it's easy to think that I'm encouraging students to become automatons about reading the rules and I don't think that's what I'm out for. I do think there is a certain disposition that law school generally cultivates. I don't know that it is the ethics course in particular. I think there is a certain attitude toward rules discussed by my former colleague, Roger Cramton, in a wonderful article called 'The Ordinary Religion of the Law School Classroom' (which I read when I start to teach torts every year). He is right about the kinds of dispositions that are cultivated in legal education generally, and I don't think it's different in the law governing lawyers class. I'm going to add a gross *ad hominem* argument now and apologize for the sloppiness of this. But I think the sympathetic way to see some of the lawyers in the torture scandal is that they are doing exactly what you suggest lawyers should do, which is to say they are acting as they think the value of humanity demands. They're helping defend American lives in a time of terror. They're forgetting about the importance of law and legality. And so I don't think that legal education inculcates robotic compliance with rules but I do think it inculcates the disposition to take seriously the idea of rule-governed or law-governed ways of interacting with one another and taking the idea of legality seriously. And I think one of the things I react to in my own work is the quick resort to individual notions about what justice and humanity require. And I think everyone needs to think about that as part of their own personal engagement with being a professional. I think it's important for people to think about why am I doing this, why did I become a lawyer, what's the connection between my own values and this profession? I think that's hugely important. But I don't think that necessarily over-rides the obligation as a professional to represent clients within a framework of law, exercising fidelity to law. So if that is the disposition they come away with, I'm not terribly concerned about that. I think it's exactly what lawyers should be doing. But I do think it's possible to caricature what I'm saying as suggesting some kind of blind attitude of obedience, and that's not by any means what I think students should take away.

## 2.12 David Luban

Well, this is a perfect opportunity to segue into the next set of questions that we wanted to discuss, which is about whether the underlying philosophical views actually yield different results in particular cases. And we thought that we would talk about a few examples. The one that I'd like to begin with is something that came out in the *New York Times* about a month ago.[9] It was a very interesting case about a prosecutor. The situation was this. There had been a very high-profile double murder in which two men were convicted but there was afterwards some evidence that they were the wrong men. The prosecutor's office assigned Daniel Bibb, a very senior prosecutor in the office, to investigate the case. He did quite an exhaustive investigation. It lasted 21 months. He interviewed 50 witnesses in 12 US states and concluded that the evidence against the men was way too weak, that they were very likely not guilty. But he could not convince his superiors to drop the cases. In fact, they told him to go into court and try to uphold the convictions. He did not quit. He thought that if he quit then someone who was much less familiar with the case than he and much more committed to upholding the convictions would probably take over for him. Instead he, as he put it, threw the case. The way in which he threw the case was that first of all he alerted the defence – I think this was probably an obligation of his – to what the witnesses had said. But he also aided the defence by helping to talk the witnesses into showing up for the hearing. That is, the defence were somewhat under-resourced and didn't have a prior relationship with these witnesses. So it's quite possible that the witnesses wouldn't have showed up, except that the prosecutor made sure that the witnesses, who were going to be on the defence side, showed up. He also told everybody in advance what questions he was going to ask them on cross-examination.

Now one eminent ethics scholar, Steve Gillers, said that Bibb should be disciplined for throwing the case, and it would be very easy, I think, to make out a case for prosecuting him for misconduct. You could imagine that a private lawyer who's decided that her client's case is unjust and does the same thing would be smacked with a hefty lawsuit. The grounds would be, first of all, incompetence; second, conflict of interest; third, a lack of zeal on the client's behalf; and possibly, misuse of confidential information. Under US rules, there's an all-purpose 'thou shalt not deceive' rule,[10] and there seems to be deceit going on, so it would be very easy to make out the grievance. On the other side, there is an idea that prosecutors should be seeking justice not victory, but it's oftentimes difficult to tell what that means, and it isn't a formal rule. So Steve Gillers thought that Bibb should conceivably lose his licence. I thought Bibb should be given a medal.

Gillers wrote to me and said: 'I think this is a no-brainer.' I wrote back and said: 'Absolutely, I agree this is a no-brainer.' It occurs to me that my reaction might be because I come to legal ethics from the standpoint of ethics in a broad non-legal sense. That approach asks: 'What does the good person do here?' And it seemed to me that the no-brainer was that the good person doesn't allow two innocent men to spend the next 25 years of their lives in prison. Most of my colleagues said the prosecutor should withdraw. You don't subvert the case, you withdraw. I think this is the second most ethical choice and therefore (as an old joke would have it) the correct answer on the multiple-choice Bar exam.

## 2.13 Brad Wendel

I will just very quickly put in a point here. I'm the fidelity to law guy. So my view is that the prosecutor should be doing justice but should be doing justice within a framework of institutions and procedures. And one of the things that these procedures are set up to do is to figure out things like what it means to do justice. And going through channels in a prosecutor's office is what someone does when there's some problem. Notice also what the philosophers do. And I'm a philosopher too by training and scholarship, so I'm kind of thinking of myself here. But notice how the term got changed from 'people suspected to be innocent' to 'two innocent men'. So David starts out by saying, well you know, the prosecutor was concerned that there may not be enough evidence to convict, but by the end we have two innocent men.

So I want to say: 'How do we know we have two innocent men?' And the way we have two innocent men is that we have all sorts of procedures to figure that out. We have both litigation and advocacy procedures but we also have internal office procedures. We have structures of authority and supervisory and subordinate lawyers within offices in order to work these questions out. We also have rules governing when subordinate lawyers should defer to the reasonable judgements of their supervisors. The reason for this presumably is that the institution as a whole is generally more reliable at making these decisions than individuals. I also don't want to valorize what the lawyer did in this case and then turn around and criticize the lawyers in cases like Enron and the torture memos for going freelance. One of the things that people always say about … let's just say John Yoo and Daniel Bibb and those guys in the Defence Department Working Group … is that they froze out all of the other people who can serve as effective internal checks on their legal reasoning and judgement. Well, if the problem there is that those guys went, let's not valorize the guy here who decided to go off on his own and not run this thing through the internal office procedures. So my criticism of him from the standpoint of fidelity to law is he didn't go through the internal procedures of his office, which the prosecutor's office is set up in order to figure out what the duty to do justice means in a particular case. So I don't think we should praise him for going off half-cocked here when we think that an essential part of being a good lawyer is working with others to make sure that one's judgement is as reliable as it can be.

## 2.14 Deborah Rhode

My natural law professor's instinct is to fight the question and ask for more facts. I think it would be useful to know exactly what he did internally, why he was convinced that he couldn't convince his superiors. I take Brad's point about freelancing but at the end of the day what I at least would want students to think about with a case like this is what it means to do justice in a second-best world. In that world perhaps office procedures don't get you where you want and perhaps a trial with incompetent defence counsel wouldn't get the result that you are convinced is the one that the justice system would want in this particular case.

The other hard case on which Brad and I have somewhat different views is the welfare client who is committing fraud. I talk about this case in my book *The Interests of Justice* as a 'hard case' because it was the first case that I encountered in which I had a real professional ethics dilemma. I was working as a law student in a legal aid programme in New Haven and we were representing a client who had unreported income. She was almost at the point of finishing a dental hygienist training programme that would allow her to get off the welfare rolls but she wasn't there yet. The welfare system in Connecticut at that point, like everywhere else, provided nothing close to a subsistence-level income. So everybody had unreported income and the way you ran a welfare clinic was to avoid finding that out. But I didn't know that – I was a first-year law student. So I came in with this problem to the supervisor in the clinic. He said: 'Well, you know that's a very hard case.' I knew that – what I wanted to know was what to do. About 20 years later when we encountered each other at an ethics conference, once again I related this incident to him and I said: 'I've been waiting 20 years, Steve, for the right answer to this one. And he said, "Well, you know I'm going to stand by my original statement." '

What I said in talking about this case is a little bit different than the view of my former colleague, William Simon (and we've taught this case together), and what Brad presented is Bill's position. [Brad asserted that] if your view is that you 'do justice' then you bend the rules in a case like this where the system is fundamentally flawed. I have a problem with that for some of the same reasons that Brad has a problem with that. In a world where usually there's a huge difference between what passes for justice among the haves and the have nots, the role of the lawyer is not to come in and just reverse the beneficiaries so you have a double standard of ethics that benefits the poor and oppressed. What I do think, though, is that in contexts like the welfare case there's a role for selective ignorance that's different than when you're representing the wealthy corporation that's trying to escape appropriate tax liability. When you've got the welfare client who's attempting to escape welfare, which is what she ought to be doing, and you're a temporary way station for assistance, I think that that's a moment where you learn to avert your eyes. I don't see that as a perfect solution but we don't live in a perfect world. I don't think you sign off on a fraudulent form. I don't think you present fraudulent evidence and I sure don't think that as a teacher in a clinic you leave the student adrift at what the right response is in the face of very pressing needs and rules that don't seem to make a lot of sense. I think you need to give future practitioners some systematic way of grappling with those issues.

There are a lot of different ways to talk about these cases. These are ones where you can get students to engage at deep levels about what they would do and then to step back and ask what could you do to affect the system. And one of the reasons why I think just the pure legality approach doesn't work is, well sure, there are ways to fix the welfare system but pending the revolution this client's got to eat. So that's why I think you want to try to give students a way to think more systematically about how they would resolve the tough cases. And I do think philosophical frameworks can help there.

## 2.15 David Luban

Well, I think before throwing open these cases for discussion in the group it might be helpful to try to make explicit what, if any, philosophical issues the cases raise because that might help us figure out whether thinking philosophically is going to yield value added over the casuistry of the cases. Like a tennis player, all I want to do is put a second serve on the other side of the net to get the conversation going. It seems to me that in the first case one of the big issues philosophically is roughly whether we are starting from the point of view of an individual moral agent or from the viewpoint of the integrity of the legal system and the institutions within it (which I thought was the view that Brad was pressing just now).

In the welfare case, I think that one of the interesting jurisprudential issues is raised by Simon. He tends to back off from saying you should settle these things by appeals to morality, moral principle, moral theory; instead, you should settle them by principles of legality. But he's got a broad natural law view of what legality is. He avoids the word 'natural law'; instead, he uses the word 'substantivism', but I think it works out to be the same. So it turns out that the reason that you can violate the regulation and not report the welfare client is because you are actually realizing deeper values within the legal system. I think that my view is that that's probably – as a matter of legal construction and fidelity to the law – not correct. The legal system can be stretched but it can't be stretched to encompass all good things. I think that an argument that says you can get every good result out of the law itself is simply an over-estimation of what a wonderful thing the law is. My basic approach to the problem would be to say that there's always a question when you're confronted by a law, about whether you obey it or not. That's a question of conscience.

Here I think I really will put on the improbable hat of Socrates for a moment. There's a place in Plato's *Apology* where Socrates, standing before the Athenians on trial for his life, is talking about what a great guy he has been for his entire life. He says: 'At one point when we had the Thirty Tyrants in charge of Athens they called a number of us from my tribe to come forward and then they told us to go off and arrest Leon the Salaminian.' He gives us to understand that this was an unjust tyrannical arrest. And of course, what the tyrants were trying to do was implicate as many ordinary Athenians in their crimes as possible. This is what tyrannies always do: they spread the blame among as many ordinary citizens as possible. And Socrates says: 'I've got a *daimon*, an inner voice that never tells me what to do but sometimes tells me what not to do. And it spoke. The others went off to arrest Leon. I went home. Had the tyrants not been overthrown I would be toast.' (I'm not sure what the Greek is for 'toast'.)

It's not as extreme as arresting Leon the Salaminian, but I think both Daniel Bibb and Deborah in this welfare case might say: 'It's not what the law says but I'm going to do it anyway because the law doesn't exhaust morality.' To me, the Bibb example is a little bit more complicated when I think about what he did to throw the case. He made sure the truthful witnesses showed up at court and he told people what his cross-examination questions were going to be so that they lost the element of surprise, which might get them to make fools of themselves. So he actually was ensuring a more truthful outcome by violating basic principles of adversary advocacy. It strikes me that that raises the philosophical question about how good the adversary system is.

## 2.16 Brad Wendel

I think this is a great example of a case where if there is a place where philosophy is needed it is this. All these questions are philosophical questions and I think the analysis of both cases has two steps. The first step is, is there a jurisprudential issue at all? In other words, you have to take some position on the obligation creating force of law. Does the law create obligations? Are they merely *prima face*? Are they not *prima face* at all? It seems to me the default position among political philosophers is whether there is an obligation to obey the law. David is right that the law does not exhaust morality, but there may be some moral reason to respect the law. So you have to take a position on that case. If you conclude that there is an obligation or a duty to respect the law, then the second philosophical question kicks in, which is: What's the jurisprudential approach? How does one understand what the content of law is? And it might be as substantive as a natural law position; it might be a positivist position. But I think both of these are core philosophical issues and I'm not entirely sure, despite being a big fan of doctrinal law teaching, of how to approach these issues without some philosophy.

## 2.17 Deborah Rhode

As I look at the conduct that's at issue, this isn't a case where he deliberately didn't put forward the evidence for the government that he had. He simply removed elements of surprise. He helped convince people who had exculpatory evidence to show up. He was helping the system to get to the right result. It seems to me that even if that's a result that his superiors didn't want, he was certainly acting within the scope of the law and the scope of the ethical obligations of a prosecutor. It's not a career-advancing move. But I think that's probably where the hard choice comes in for the prosecutor. This is one where it seems to me you certainly have some room to manoeuvre.

## 2.18 Brad Wendel

I should just emphasize too that this hopefully has been implicit in what I've been saying but the duty of fidelity to law arises only in reasonably just and well-functioning institutions. I'm talking about an objective reading of the facts here and this case arose within the Manhattan Defence Attorney's office in New York City, which is a pretty good office. Now if this was some small town prosecutor's office in Texas (I grew up in Texas, so I can make fun of Texas), a prosecutor's office which is well known for racially biased prosecutions in death cases, the prosecutor there [might not be] inclined to listen to reasonable presentations about the evidence, and [might be inclined to be] the kind of person who will unreasonably order subordinate lawyers to stay in a case even if there's no probable cause. That's a very different dilemma than the lawyer faces in the Manhattan Defence Attorney's office. So you know, I understand that someone like me now has to come up with an account of when you can opt out of these role obligations. But at least as a general matter the role obligations that I'm talking about attach when someone is working within a reasonably just, well-functioning institution, understanding that all those terms need to be defined. That's part of my problem. It is also important to emphasize that we're talking here about lawyers acting within role. I at least don't have a view about the way lawyers ought to act outside their role. I think one might say that lawyers who have information from the inside about the injustice of institutions or arguable injustice or ways the institutions can be reformed might then be motivated *qua* person to come outside the role and seek to reform the institutions or to become a lobbyist. David mentioned in his talk a number of military lawyers who had been involved in the tribunals in Guantánamo Bay who are now outside of their role, who have retired from the military and are now tireless critics of the military tribunal process.[11] I think lawyers are very well positioned to do that sort of thing. But I just want to emphasize that all this about deliberative priorities or fidelity to law only exists within the role when a lawyer is acting in a representative capacity.

## 2.19 David Luban

To conclude the discussion, we would like to very briefly discuss our own sense of what the future, the near future, holds for the philosophical foundations of legal ethics – what we think the issues are, what's unsettled, what's settled. To kick this off, I will offer a brief historical overview. There was an initial burst of interest in the philosophical, theoretical side of legal ethics that really began in the late 1970s with Richard Wasserstrom's paper[12] and Bill Simon's paper, 'The ideology of advocacy',[13] and Gerry Postema's paper on professional roles.[14] That conversation went on for a number of years. In recent years, it seems to me that the action on the research side of legal ethics has switched more and more to various pieces of the empirical study of the legal profession – for example, the use of social psychology and organization theory in understanding the dynamics of moral decision-making in law firms; economic models, both of regulation and studies of the economics of law firms and the incentives that they create for lawyer behaviour; and finally, ethnographic studies and demographic studies of the legal profession. It seems to me that the philosophical debate was still going on but was a subordinate strand and maybe a little bit dormant. But now we are seeing a new flowering of interest in the philosophical side. Brad's forthcoming book, *Lawyers and Fidelity to Law*, Tim Dare's book, *The Counsel of Rogues? A Defence of the Standard Conception of the Lawyer's Role*,[15] and a book by Daniel Markovits from Yale Law School, *A Modern Legal Ethics: Adversary Advocacy in a Democratic Age*,[16] are extremely sophisticated philosophical treatments of issues in legal ethics. I think these are coming more from the standpoint of political theory and jurisprudence than moral philosophy. I'm looking forward to a renaissance of research in the philosophical side of legal ethics. But I don't know what direction it's going in, and at this point I just want to ask my colleagues where they think the action is. And then we can call it a good day's work.

## 2.20 Brad Wendel

I'm developing a course now on ethical cultures with the Professor of Business Ethics at the Johnson School at Cornell. Our kind of working subtitle is 'Why do good people do bad things?' We're drawing from a lot of the social psychology and organizational theory literature, and I actually think it's a hugely important project for teaching, for figuring out how to teach people about Deborah's point – how our students may end up going out and designing institutions and how they might design them to work better. And second, how do you work within institutions? How do you figure out whether an institution is dysfunctional? How do you figure out whether it's slanting your decision-making in a predacious way? How do you know when you're in an Enron versus a healthy functioning organization? How do you work within an Enron if you find yourself there? So I think that, despite my own research interest in philosophy, I'm very interested in being a consumer – not a producer by any means – of the organization of social psychology literature and figuring out how to apply that to teaching. Because I think it's huge. And so we'll see how this course goes with law and business students jointly. But we intend to do it in a business school case method kind of way where we put the students together and have them work out problems and figure out what aspects of their environment and their organizational culture make it more or less conducive to making good ethical decisions.

## Notes

1 The following is an edited transcript of a roundtable forum conducted during the Third International Legal Ethics Conference at the Gold Coast, Queensland, Australia, on 16 July 2008. The transcript has been edited for reasons of clarity and context. In this process, a number of comments made by conference participants have been omitted or placed in a different order within the discussion.
2 To which Professor Luban replied that he did not even drink hemlock. Christine Parker responded that there was hemlock available if he went over time.
3 L. Wittgenstein, *Remarks on the Foundations of Mathematics*, 2nd ed., eds G.H. von Wright, Rush Rhees, G. E. M. Anscombe, trans. G. E. M. Anscombe, Cambridge, MA: MIT Press, 1967, p. 171.
4 C. Fried, 'The lawyer as friend: The moral foundation of the lawyer–client relation', *Yale Law Journal*, 1976, vol. 85, 1060.
5 Professor John Yoo, Office of Legal Counsel lawyer and Berkeley Professor of Law, and author of the infamous so-called 'torture memos'. See Chapter 5 of this volume.
6 The Unemployed Philosophers Guild now offers a Hannah Arendt finger puppet. See www.philosophersguild.com/index.lasso?page_mode=home&category=magnetic&sortby=Alpha (accessed 7 September 2009).
7 Legal Services Commissioner, New South Wales, Australia.
8 The University of Otago, New Zealand.
9 B. Weiser, 'Doubting case, a prosecutor helped the defense', *New York Times*, 23 June 2008. See www.nytimes.com/2008/06/23/nyregion/23da.html (accessed 7 September 2009).
10 American Bar Association Model Rules of Professional Conduct, Rule 8.4(c): 'It is professional misconduct for a lawyer to engage in conduct involving dishonesty, fraud, deceit or misrepresentation.'
11 See Chapter 5 of this volume.
12 R. Wasserstrom, 'Lawyers as professionals: Some moral issues', *Human* Rights, 1975, vol. 5, 1.
13 W. Simon, 'Ideology of advocacy: Procedural justice and professional ethics – the commentary', *Wisconsin Law Review*, 1978, vol. 29, 30.
14 G. Postema, 'Moral responsibility in professional ethics', *New York University Law Review*, 1980, vol. 55, 63; Fried 'The lawyer as friend'.
15 T. Dare, *The Counsel of Rogues? A Defence of the Standard Conception of the Lawyer's Role*, Abingdon: Ashgate, 2009.
16 D. Markovits, *A Modern Legal Ethics: Adversary Advocacy in a Democratic Age*, Princetown, NJ: Princetown University Press, 2008.

# 3  Personal integrity and professional ethics

*Deborah L. Rhode*

## 3.1 Introduction

Some years ago, en route to an international meeting on legal ethics, I had a spectacularly unsuccessful interchange on the topic at the passport control desk. It was a slow evening, and an obviously bored Canadian official launched a series of questions about the 'business purpose' of my trip. Where was I giving a lecture? On what? Who had squandered Canadian taxpayers' dollars on a subject as futile as legal ethics? 'Bit of an oxymoron, don't you think?'

This did not seem a particularly promising forum for my views on lawyers' integrity, so I let the question pass as rhetorical. Yet the incident did aptly capture one discomfiting by-product of the Bar's failure to take more seriously certain ethical dimensions of the professional role. Too often, when lawyers come together to address broad themes like integrity, the tone resembles that captured in a classic *New Yorker* cartoon. It features two monks gliding through cloisters, with one protesting, 'I am too holier than thou.' The American Bar Association's recent campaign for a Renaissance of Idealism was a classic case in point, with public relations billboards, exhortatory resolutions, and 'I am an Idealist' buttons.[1]

Integrity deserves better. Publications like this, which bring together legal ethics experts from across the globe, offer opportunities for more self-critical reflection. To that end, the discussion that follows will focus on what integrity demands of lawyers, and what stands in the way. The first section of this chapter focuses on definitions. In essence, my argument is that what integrity demands of lawyers is personal accountability for the consequences of their professional actions. The following section explores what this entails in the context of client representation. A third section examines lawyers' responsibility for the performance of regulatory structures, including their impact on access to legal services. Part of what distinguishes professions from other occupations is their claim to act in the public interest in establishing ethical rules, roles and regulatory structures. If, as subsequent discussion suggests, those governance institutions have fallen short, then members of the profession bear some individual as well as collective responsibility for helping to set them right. Legal educators are not exempt from this responsibility, and the final section of the chapter concludes with some thoughts about what integrity requires in academic contexts.

## 3.2 Definitions of integrity: personal accountability for professional conduct

Discussions of integrity are not charting untraveled ground. A search on Amazon.com yields over 200,000 titles including integrity and a search on Google generates over 92 million websites. As philosophers also note, integrity is not only one of the most important and oft-cited ethical concepts, it is one of the most ambiguous.[2] In common usage, 'integrity' often functions as an all-purpose term of moral approval. In philosophical discussions, the concept connotes a more specific set of qualities that make for an integrated self. At a minimum, integrity demands practices that are consistent with principles, even in the face of strong countervailing pressures.[3] Yet the term also implies something more than steadfastness. Fanatics may be loyal to their values, but we do not praise them for integrity. What earns our respect is a willingness to adhere to principles that satisfy certain basic demands, such as reasoned deliberation, internal consistency, generalizability and concern for others.[4]

For lawyers, those principles would demand more than simple compliance with Bar ethical codes. Such codes set only a baseline of conduct that a self-interested group is willing to accept for purposes of professional liability; they do not exhaust the values that reasoned deliberation would reveal as necessary to an effective governance system. Indeed, the Bar's codes often recognize as much. For example, the Preamble to the ABA's Model Rules of Professional Conduct declares: 'A lawyer as a member of the legal profession is a representative of clients, an officer of the legal system and a public citizen having special responsibilities for the quality of justice.'

Implicit in such definitions is the concept of personal accountability for the consequences of professional action. When acting as attorneys, individuals should assess their decisions under the same kind of consistent, disinterested and generalizable principles that are applicable in other settings. These moral principles can, of course, recognize the distinctive needs of lawyers' occupational role. Ethically responsible decision-making always takes into account the context and capacity in which a person acts. But where this framework departs from more conventional conceptions of professional role is the insistence on personal accountability for social consequences and Bar governance structures.

## 3.3 Accountability in client representation

At its core, the relationship between lawyers and clients is one of agency, which imposes fiduciary obligations of competence, confidentiality and loyalty. Yet these obligations do not always trump competing concerns. Lawyers also need to consider the potential harms to other affected parties, and core values such as honesty, fairness and good faith on which any effective justice system depends.

In accommodating these interests, lawyers should, of course, be guided by relevant legal authority and Bar regulatory codes. Respect for law is a fundamental value, particularly among those sworn to uphold it. Adherence to generally accepted rules also serves as a check against lawyers' own biases and self-interest. But most ethical dilemmas arise in contexts in which the applicable rules leave room for discretion, so that reference to broader moral principles is necessary. Whether to accept or withdraw from representation, what tactics to pursue and how to address suspected client misconduct generally are matters calling for individual judgement. In resolving those questions, lawyers of integrity need to consider the social context and consequences of their choices. They cannot evade responsibility by deferring to some idealized model of adversarial and law-making processes in which all interests are adequately represented. Rather, lawyers need to assess their actions against a realistic backdrop, in which wealth, power and information are unequally distributed. Not all interests are adequately represented, and most legal issues will never reach a neutral tribunal. The less confidence attorneys have in the legal system's capacity to deliver justice in a particular case, the greater their own responsibility to attempt some corrective.

Such demands of moral accountability generally provoke three major objections. The first involves ambiguity. According to many lawyers, terms like 'justice,' 'fairness' and 'good faith' are too vague to serve as the basis for moral or legal responsibility; lawyers have no special ethical expertise to determine what these mandates require. Such humility is, however, highly selective. The Bar frequently claims expert knowledge about where justice lies when regulations governing its own conduct are at stake. When acting in legislative, judicial or administrative capacities, lawyers also tend to assume that others should be liable for failing to meet such standards. The legal system routinely requires prosecutors to pursue 'justice', judges to determine 'fairness' and businesses to act in 'good faith'. Lawyers charge substantial fees for interpreting such requirements; the interpretative process is no different when their own actions are involved.[5] In any case, professional appeals to humility, however well founded, are ultimately beside the point. The rationale for moral accountability is not that lawyers have special moral expertise, but rather that they deserve no special moral exemption from what integrity requires of any decision-maker.

The Bar's second objection to heightened responsibility is that, even if attorneys are able to determine what standards like justice or fairness require, it is not their role to do so. Their obligations run to clients, whose lives, liberty and property are at issue. The justness of those clients' causes should be determined by judges or juries with due process safeguards, not by individual attorneys with no procedural protections. Clarence Darrow, one of America's most distinguished trial lawyers, put the point directly: 'my job is not to judge a man ... [but to] defend him.'[6]

Often, this argument proceeds without further elaboration, as if its force were self-evident. But the claim that 'it is not my role' begs the question at issue, which is what that role *should* be. After all, attorneys have considerable autonomy, individually and collectively, to determine the appropriate scope of their professional obligations. The deference to judges and juries ignores the reality of most legal representation, which occurs in the absence of such trial safeguards.

A more sophisticated variation on this argument rests not on neutral decision-makers, but rather on client autonomy. Bradley Wendel argues that: 'We do not want to constrain individual choices by channeling legal advice through lawyers who are free to substitute their own value judgments ... Only law, not lawyers, set justifiable limits on liberty.'[7] Yet, in our market-driven legal system, it is money as much as law that sets limits on liberty. Individual choices are highly constrained, along the lines well captured in a *New Yorker* cartoon. There, a well-heeled lawyer peers out at his client and notes: 'You have a pretty good case, Mr Pitkin. How much justice *can* you afford?'[8]

Moreover, as philosophers including David Luban have noted, autonomy does not hold intrinsic value; its importance rests on the other values it fosters, such as initiative and social responsibility.[9] If a particular client's project does little to promote such values, or does so only at great cost to innocent third parties, a lawyer's undivided allegiance hardly serves the 'quality of justice'. From a moral standpoint, why should the rights of clients trump all others whose health, welfare and livelihood are directly implicated and inadequately represented? As Wendel himself has noted on other occasions, 'the real scandal of differential access to lawyers is that wealth, not the morality of the prospective client's projects, determines whether a lawyer will be willing to accept the representation.'[10] An ethic of undivided loyalty to those who can afford it has involved lawyers in some of the most socially costly enterprises in recent memory. In the United States, these include the distribution of asbestos, the suppression of health information about tobacco, and the moral meltdowns of financial institutions and corporations like Enron et al. Under these circumstances, lawyers' exaltation of client loyalty may evoke reactions similar to Ralph Waldo Emerson's: 'The louder he spoke of his honor, the faster we counted our spoons.'

A final objection to moral accountability is pragmatic. If lawyers refuse assistance rather than participate in actions that appear unjust, then legal ethics experts such as Geoffrey Hazard worry that the effect might be counter-productive. The result may be replacement by 'a less high minded successor ... [thus] insulating the client from conscientious advisors in the future'.[11] Other commentators worry that imposing third-party responsibilities on lawyers will erode client trust and candour, and leave lawyers out of the loop of confidential information necessary for effective representation and compliance counselling.

Such concerns are not without force, but neither are they as compelling as many practitioners assume. It is by no means clear how often a moral stand by lawyers will pave the way for someone worse. When attorneys are prepared to refuse assistance for ethical reasons, they raise the stakes, both financial and psychological, for colleagues and clients. In some cases, the costs of educating a new lawyer will prompt individuals to rethink their objectives rather than find a replacement. In other contexts, where withholding assistance would clearly have little impact on clients' or colleagues' decision-making, lawyers are entitled to consider that fact in weighing their responsibilities. An ethically reflective and contextualized decision will take into account not only the magnitude and likelihood of harms resulting from client conduct, but also the attorney's capacity to affect them and the personal costs of attempting to do so. In some circumstances, lawyers' limited leverage and access to information, together with the adverse effects of jeopardizing client or collegial relationships, will justify suspension of judgement. But where the ethical stakes are substantial, lawyers may have an obligation to refuse assistance whatever the other consequences. We do not normally absolve individuals of moral responsibility on the ground that their successor could be worse.

Neither should we assume that a greater sense of social responsibility among lawyers would necessarily undermine client relationships. Historical, cross-cultural and cross-professional research makes clear that practitioners have provided assistance on confidential matters without the undivided client loyalty that American lawyers now assert.[12] As many commentators have noted, even if the result of greater public obligations for lawyers might be somewhat less candour from clients, there is reason to believe that the social benefits would outweigh the costs.[13]

What stands in the way of a more ethically demanding professional role has little to do with principle and much to do with self-interest. This should come as no surprise. Integrity sometimes comes at a price, which is precisely why it commands respect. If we are serious about encouraging a morally satisfying conception of professional responsibility, we need to address the institutional and psychological pressures that push in the opposite direction. Although traditional moral philosophy tends to present integrity as a fixed character trait, con-temporary moral psychology suggests otherwise. Ethical conduct often reflects intuitive responses to situational influences and cognitive biases.

The most obvious influence is, of course, money. As American judge Marvin Frankel put it: 'Why should the client pay for loyalties divided between himself and [justice]?'[14] Integrity is a quality that everyone wants in other people's law-yers, but it is not always what clients are looking for in their own. The contexts in which individuals need legal assistance do not always bring out the best in human nature, so advocates who will push the envelope are often in demand. Increased competition has also exerted increased pressure to satisfy client objectives despite their social costs. Corporate clients are parcelling out more work based on bottom-line considerations rather than long-term relationships. That, in turn, has compromised lawyers' ability to provide unwelcome messages about what legal rules and social responsibilities require.[15]

Competition has compounded the problem. Advancement, status and com-pensation increasingly depend on attorneys' capacity to attract and retain lucrative clients. That makes it correspondingly harder to decline, or to withdraw from, representation on ethical grounds. In-house counsel also face corresponding pressures to demonstrate 'value added' by facilitating short-term profits, irrespec-tive of broader concerns.[16] In a culture where income has become a crucial measure of status, the market for morality is bound to suffer. 'Virtue,' Mark Twain once observed, 'never has been as respectable as money.'[17] Corporate America's recent moral meltdowns provide all too many unbecoming examples of that mindset at work.

Organizational cultures can also undermine ethical decision-making. Research on group loyalty and peer pressure demonstrates their potential for corrosive impact, particularly in workplaces that place a premium on team players.[18] Socialization to expedient norms can readily 'protect people from their own consciences'.[19] In highly profit-oriented settings, a worldly cynicism can take hold, and conventional morality can come to seem relevant only as a 'public relations stance'.[20]

Diffusion of responsibility can also skew a professional's moral compass. A wide array of studies finds that individuals in group settings are less inclined to act morally than they would in contexts in which they feel personally accountable.[21] The impact of diffuse or deflected responsibility is readily apparent in legal settings. One well-known example involves the failure of Salomon Brothers to take corrective action against a trader who submitted false auction bids. Four top executives, including the general counsel, knew of the misconduct and failed to act for several months. According to findings by the Securities and Exchange Commission, each of these officials 'placed responsibility for investigating [and curbing the trader's] conduct … on someone else'.[22] Similar dynamics were apparent in widely publicized scandals involving Australian wheat exports, and fraudulent investigative techniques by the American computer corporation Hewlett Packard. The Australian debacle involved millions of dollars in kickbacks to Iraq in violation of United Nations restrictions on the international 'Oil For Food Programme'. In-house counsel for AWB Ltd, the nation's exclusive wheat exporter, 'pushed [the relevant decisions] upstairs to business managers' and disclaimed accountability for the legal, financial and public relations disasters that resulted.[23] In the Hewlett Packard case, the CEO, chair of the board, outside counsel, inside counsel and ethics compliance officer all were aware of fraudulent 'pretexting' by investigators seeking to trace a corporate board leak; all placed blame for allowing such conduct everywhere and anywhere else.[24]

Cognitive bias adds further challenges. Social psychology research confirms what common sense and common experience suggest. People have a natural inclination to view conduct that is personally advantageous as ethically sound and socially just.[25] Self-interest often skews intuitive value judgements that are not products of deliberative reasoning.[26] Commitment to such unreflective decisions then can entrap individuals in an escalating series of ethically indefensible acts. An incremental slide into ever more dubious conduct produces what psychologists label 'the boiled frog' problem. A frog thrown into boiling water will jump out of the pot. A frog placed in tepid water that gradually becomes hotter will calmly boil to death.[27]

When decision-makers compromise their ethical standards in response to situational pressures, a desire to reduce cognitive dissonance often kicks in, and standards change to justify the behaviour.[28] A related dynamic involves 'ethical fading'. In order to avoid a conflict between their interests and principles, individuals are drawn to strategies that bleach out the moral content of their choices. Tendencies such as adopting euphemistic labels for injurious conduct or remaining wilfully ignorant or understating responsibility for failures to act all allow the ethical dimensions of decision-making to fade from view.[29]

There are, to be sure, some countervailing incentives. Virtue is not always its own reward; it often pays off in tangible forms for both lawyers and clients. In relatively small communities of repeat players, a reputation for candour and fair dealing can generate credibility with opposing counsel, courts and regulatory authorities.[30] Lawyers of integrity can also prompt clients to rethink conduct that works against their better instincts and long-term interests.[31] As American statesman Elihu Root once famously put it: 'About half the practice of a decent lawyer consists in telling would-be clients that they are damned fools and should stop.'[32] Integrity can also be a source of substantial psychic income. According to American Bar Association surveys, young lawyers' greatest source of career dissatisfaction is a 'lack of contribution to the social good'.[33] Expanding opportunities for that contribution can significantly enhance professional satisfaction.

It can also serve societal interests. Frankel's question – Why should clients pay for loyalties divided between themselves and justice? – is obviously intended as rhetorical. But the answer is not self-evident. Clients *should* pay because, over the long term, clients collectively benefit from advocates who encourage efficient and equitable dispute resolution, and who seek to prevent financial debacles that destabilize markets. Equally to the point, clients *will* pay for qualified allegiance when that is part of the expected professional role.

To that end, the Bar needs to do more to reward and reinforce integrity in practice, not just in principle. Strengthening lawyers' social responsibilities through ethical rules, gatekeeper regulations and civil liability structures could help prevent a race to the bottom, so would building ethical infrastructures in law firms and corporate counsel office through more effective oversight structures.[34] Informal reputational sanctions should also play a greater role. George Sharswood, one of America's first legal ethics scholars, warned lawyers to 'shun most carefully the reputation of a sharp practitioner'.[35] Today, such a reputation too often becomes a career asset. One of the nation's most notoriously uncivil practitioners, Jo Jamail, has a net worth estimated at $1.5 billion, and a pavilion, legal research centre and several statues in his honour at his alma mater.[36]

Legal education also needs to do a better job of educating lawyers about the cognitive processes and organizational pressures that compromise ethical judgement. As moral psychologist John Doris notes, people typically have a 'rather tenuous grasp' on their own reasoning dynamics; they need to place less faith in moral 'character' and design more correctives for corrosive influences.[37]

## 3.4 Personal accountability for professional regulation and access to legal services

A second dimension of integrity involves responsibility for professional regulatory structures, including those that affect access to justice. The Bar has long asserted authority over its own governance and, in countries like the United States, it has succeeded in maintaining considerable control. American courts have asserted inherent power to regulate the practice of law, and state judges have typically been deferential to the Bar, whose support is critical for their reputation, election and advance. So too, the dominant role of lawyers in legislative and administrative arenas makes it difficult for those bodies to impose a significant check on professional autonomy. This lack of accountability has perpetuated a regulatory structure that is often more responsive to professional than public interests.[38]

The failures are apparent along multiple dimensions. The US system of Bar discipline is a case in point. Although lawyers generally have a duty to report serious professional misconduct to regulatory authorities, such reports are rare, and discipline for failure to report is rarer still. A recent two-decade survey found only four reported cases involving such discipline.[39] Of complaints that are made, generally by aggrieved clients, the vast majority are dismissed; only 4 per cent result in public sanctions.[40] Part of the reason is that most disciplinary agencies are under-staffed and under-funded, and decline to exercise jurisdiction over minor grievances, such as neglect, negligence and fee disputes. In theory, civil remedies or alternative dispute-resolution (ADR) processes are available for these matters. Yet many ADR processes are voluntary and lack remedies that respond to the sources of complaints or ensure adequate compensation. Except in one state, American lawyers are not required to carry malpractice insurance, so many consumer grievances go unredressed.[41] And because courts and disciplinary systems are generally reluctant to jeopardize a practitioner's livelihood, they require clear and compelling evidence of misconduct, and seldom impose stringent sanctions that could more effectively deter misconduct.[42] Not surprisingly, what limited data are available indicate that only about one-third of Americans think that the Bar does a good job disciplining lawyers.[43]

Inadequacies persist partly because they lack visibility. In over 90 per cent of jurisdictions, the Bar will not disclose complaints unless it has found a disciplinary violation or probable cause to believe that one has occurred.[44] Lawyers with as many as 20 complaints pending have received a clean bill of health when a consumer asked for information about their records.[45] Even when complaints or sanctions are made public, consumers lack a ready way to discover them. Not all states publish disciplinary information, few have data banks that are readily accessible, and fewer still disclose any information about the effectiveness of disciplinary and ADR systems in preventing future violations.[46]

Although lawyers would be among the first to challenge such inadequacies in any other regulatory system, few show interest in reforming their own. In nations like the United Kingdom and Australia, which have made significant changes, the impetus has come from outside the Bar.[47] In the United States, proposals for independent oversight have met with sustained and successful resistance. According to the Preamble of the ABA's Model Rules, self-regulation serves to 'maintain the legal profession's independence from government domination. An independent legal profession is an important force in preserving government under law; for abuse of legal authority is more readily challenged by a profession whose

members are not dependent on government for the right to practice.'
Yet jurisdictions that have an external regulatory structure, such as Sweden and
parts of Australia, have not experienced threats of government domination or
interference with lawyers' challenges to the state.[48]

Moreover, professional autonomy has come at a cost. If, as a history of the
ABA once put it, Bar organizations are 'not the same sort of thing as a retail
grocers' association', self-regulation brings out more of the similarities than the
differences.[49] No vocational group, however well intentioned, can make unbiased
assessments of the public interest on issues that place its own status, reputation
and income directly at risk. The greater an occupation's autonomy, the greater
are the risks of tunnel vision. The Anglo-American Bar's record on self-regulation
is no exception.

Improvements are possible not only through external oversight, but also
through co-regulatory systems in which the Bar shares authority with an independent board or commission, often headed by a non-lawyer. England, New
South Wales and Queensland all have such systems, which are designed to be
more responsive to complaints than the professionally controlled structures that
preceded them.[50] For example, in Queensland, problems of competence
and diligence can result in discipline, the standard is a consumer's reasonable
expectations of competence, and all judgements are published and electronically
available.[51]

As these examples suggest, many countries, including the United States, could
improve their Bar governance processes. The jurisdiction of disciplinary agencies
should be broad enough to include concerns of negligence, neglect and fees.
Resources and remedial powers should be sufficient to meet client concerns.
Lawyers should be required to carry malpractice insurance and the standard for
misconduct should reflect reasonable client expectations and normal burdens of
proof, not compelling evidence. Disciplinary systems should be public and should
include a readily accessible data bank with information about disciplinary, judicial
and civil liability sanctions. Regulatory structures should be subject to oversight
by a body independent of the group to be regulated. If, as the profession
acknowledges, its governance processes must be conceived 'in the public interest',
they should be subject to more public accountability.[52]

Similar points are applicable to the distribution of legal services. All lawyers,
according to the ABA's Model Rules, should be 'mindful of deficiencies in the
administration of justice ... and should devote time and resources and use civic
influence to ensure equal access to our system of justice for all those who ...
cannot afford or secure adequate legal counsel'. Yet, here again, the American
Bar's performance reveals a dispiriting disjuncture between principle and practice. 'Equal justice under law' often appears over courthouse doors, but it comes
nowhere close to describing what occurs inside them. Millions of individuals
lack any access to that system, let alone equal access. For example, an estimated
four-fifths of the legal needs of low-income Americans, and two-thirds of moder-
ate-income Americans, remain unmet.[53] Unlike most other industrialized nations,
the United States recognizes no right to legal assistance for civil matters, and

courts have exercised their discretion to appoint counsel in only a narrow category of cases.[54] It is a shameful irony that the nation with the world's highest concentration of lawyers has one of the least adequate systems for making legal services accessible. The record in many other nations should be the source of similar embarrassment.[55]

Part of the reason is the inadequacy of lawyers' pro bono assistance and their resistance to non-lawyer alternatives. Although the American Bar Association's Model Rules set an aspirational standard of 50 hours a year of pro bono service, liberally defined, the vast majority of lawyers fail to meet even that minimal standard. Although precise estimates are impossible to come by, the best available data indicate that the average pro bono contribution for lawyers is still less than half a dollar a day and half an hour a week.[56] Contributions are shamefully low, even among those lawyers who could most readily afford more. Only about two-fifths of lawyers in the nation's 200 most profitable firms have contributed at least 20 hours a year.[57] Yet proposals to require some minimal level of assistance have met with overwhelming resistance. Only seven states even demand reporting of pro bono contributions, and almost no effort is made to evaluate their quality.[58] In other countries, the situation generally is no better.[59]

The Bar's 'civic' responsibility concerning alternatives to lawyers is equally undistinguished. In some countries, including Great Britain, it has taken government intervention to curtail the professional monopoly in areas like conveyancing. In other nations, including the United States, the Bar has been more successful in restricting access to non-lawyers, which has helped to price law out of reach for millions of low- and middle-income individuals.[60] Although the profession attempts to cast its restrictions as consumer protection, other countries generally allow non-lawyers to provide routine legal advice, and the evidence available reveals no significant ill-effects. In fact, the American Bar's own commissions, as well as almost all independent experts in the field, have supported greater access to non-lawyer specialists.[61] Yet the profession's rank and file have repeatedly rejected such proposals.[62]

A more principled approach to access to justice must build on different premises. For lawyers of integrity, significant pro bono contributions in time or money should be a professional obligation. As Marian Wright Edelman once noted, 'service is the rent each of us pays for living'.[63] That is especially true for members of the Bar, who serve as gatekeepers to justice. Pro bono work is critical, not only in protecting fundamental rights, but also in exposing lawyers to how the legal system functions, or fails to function, for the have-nots. Public service is also a way of building practitioners' skills, contacts and 'connection to the social good', and enabling them to express values that led them to law in the first instance.

To that end, lawyers need not just exhortation but enforceable expectations of assistance, imposed by courts, Bar associations or legal employers.[64] More information should be widely available about lawyers' contributions, and the quality of service provided. Requiring attorneys to report hours and financial contributions, ranking large firms on hourly commitments, and profiling high performers and 'cellar dwellers' can lead to substantial increases.[65] Enlisting law students, clients and legal publications in the demand for better pro bono records should be a high priority.[66]

Making justice accessible will also require less expensive alternatives to lawyers for routine needs. Procedural simplification, self-help assistance and qualified lay services are obvious strategies. In 'poor people's' courts' that handle housing, bankruptcy, small claims and family matters, parties without lawyers are less the exception than the rule.[67] Yet the system in which these parties operate has been designed by and for lawyers. The challenge is to make it more responsive to everyone else, and to enlist the profession in that enterprise.

## 3.5 Accountability in legal education

Law faculty share these professional responsibilities, and they need to give them greater priority in legal education. In too many institutions, issues of legal ethics and access to justice are missing from or marginal in the core curriculum. Most American law schools relegate the subject to a single required course, which focuses largely on the minimum requirements of the Bar's Model Rules of Professional Conduct. The result is often legal ethics without the ethics. The same is true in other countries, which treat such issues almost exclusively in skills training.

Moreover, few law schools pay significant attention to access to justice and the performance of regulatory structures. The Carnegie Foundation's recent overview of American legal education found that issues such as social justice, along with lawyers responsibilities to promote them, rarely received significant curricular coverage; when the issues arose, 'they were almost always treated as addenda'.[68] In my own national survey on pro bono service, only 1 per cent of lawyers reported that their school addressed the issue, even in professional responsibility courses; only 3 per cent reported that it received visible support from faculty.[69] Fewer than half of students participate in pro bono work while in law school.[70] If legal educators are serious about reinforcing professional responsibility, they cannot continue to treat these issues as someone else's responsibility.

Yet efforts to give values a more respectable position in the academic landscape have met with considerable scepticism. In the view of many academics, professional integrity, 'like politeness on subways … or fidelity in marriage' is beyond the capacity of legal education.[71] American judge Richard Posner puts a common assumption with uncommon candour: 'As for the task of instilling ethics in law students at … law schools, I can think of few things more futile than attempting to teach people to be good.'[72] Yet this characterization both over-states the objectives of professional responsibility courses and under-states their influence. In three decades of teaching in this field, I have yet to encounter a colleague whose mission was 'teaching people to be good'. Neither does the evidence available suggest that less grandiose objectives of making students more informed and reflective about professional responsibilities are similarly futile. Research on ethics education finds that individuals' moral views and strategies change significantly during early adulthood, and that well-designed courses can improve capacities for moral reasoning.[73] Many Bar regulatory issues call for conventional techniques of policy analysis that are not distinctive to courses on ethics.

At its best, a focus on integrity throughout the curricula can encourage future lawyers to think more deeply about the kind of life they want to lead, the profession they want to serve and how both can contribute to their vision of a just society. The point is not for professors to pontificate about virtue, or lead a death march through great works of moral philosophy. The task, rather, is to build students' own capacities for reflective judgement.[74] By confronting actual dilemmas against a realistic social backdrop, future practitioners can wrestle with decisions where peer pressures, client loyalties, financial considerations and moral convictions tug in different directions. There is much to be said for having individuals address such questions before they have a vested interest in coming out one way rather than another. Enabling students to recognize the cognitive and structural forces that compromise moral judgement can do more than just inform their individual decision-making; it can also assist them in their future roles as lawyers, regulators and policy-makers when it comes to designing ways to counter those corrosive influences.

Of equal importance is ensuring that all students have some well-designed pro bono or clinical experience. Such an experience can both lay the foundations for later service and expose individuals to what passes for justice among those who cannot afford it. Pro bono opportunities in law school can also remind future practitioners of the opportunities and obligations that come with a profession. Lawyers have many ways to leave their workplace and their world somewhat better than they found it, and legal education can underscore the importance of making that effort.

Law professors have similar responsibilities. For legal academics, integrity demands accountability for the consequences of professional actions, and for the performance of educational institutions. At a minimum, that requires faculty members to practise what they preach and to model concern for ethics in all their courses, as well as a commitment to public service in their own careers. Students learn from sub-texts as well as texts, and faculty members' own commitments inevitably become part of the educational process. Those who profess on professional responsibility have a special obligation to live up to the standards that the profession aims to inspire.

## 3.6 Conclusion

In commenting on America's recent economic crisis, and the public's desire for retribution, President Obama underscored the limits of legal sanctions. 'Here's the dirty little secret ... Most of the stuff that got us into trouble was perfectly legal.'[75] If anyone needed reminding, the ripples from that 'stuff' underscore the need for gatekeepers who are conscious of broader obligations than the minimums established by law. As officers of the legal system, lawyers also have special responsibilities for the quality of justice and regulatory institutions. That entails personal accountability for the social consequences of professional action, and for client conduct that puts public interests at risk. Whether certain conduct is legal or satisfies Bar disciplinary standards only begins the analysis. As *New York Times* columnist William Safire put it, 'the right to do something does not mean that doing it is right.'[76] Integrity demands more, including adherence to the core values on which any just society depends.

## Notes

1 Commission on Renaissance of Idealism in the Legal Profession, *Renaissance of Idealism in the Legal Profession*, Washington: American Bar Association, 2006, p. 20.
2 D. Cox, M. La Caze and M. Levine, 'Integrity', in E. Zalta (ed.), *The Stanford Encyclopedia of Philosophy*, Fall 2008 Edition, Online. Available from http://Plato.stanford.edu/archives/fall2008/entries/integrity (accessed 31 March 2009).
3 For definitions of integrity, see L. McFall, 'Integrity', *Ethics*, 1987, vol. 98, 7; D. Putnam, 'Integrity and moral development', *Journal of Value Inquiry*, 1996, vol. 30, 242; N. Schauber, 'Integrity, commitment and the concept of a person', *American Philosophical Quarterly*, 1996, vol. 33, 120; G. Taylor, 'Integrity', *Proceedings of the Aristotelian Society*, 1981, vol. 55, 148.
4 M. Halfon, *Integrity: A Philosophical Inquiry*, Philadelphia, PA: Temple University Press, 1998, pp. 32–33, 133–36; J. Graham, 'Does integrity require moral goodness?' *Ratio*, 2001, vol. 14, 244; N. Bews and G. Rossouw, 'A role for business ethics in facilitating trustworthiness', *Journal of Business Ethics*, 2002, vol. 39, 381; B. Husted, 'The ethical limits of trust in business relations', *Business Ethics Quarterly*, 1998, vol. 8, 233. For an overview of various positions on whether integrity is content free or implies some commitment to broadly shared values, see S. Dolovich, 'Ethical lawyering and the possibility of integrity', *Fordham Law Review*, 2002, vol. 70, 1629, pp. 1654–56.
5 W. Simon, *The Practice of Justice: A Theory of Lawyers' Ethics*, Cambridge, MA: Harvard University Press, 2000.
6 Clarence Darrow, quoted in J. Basten, 'Control and the lawyer–client relationship', *Journal of the Legal Profession*, 1981, vol. 6, 15.
7 W.B. Wendel, 'Public values and professional responsibility', *Notre Dame Law Review*, 1999, vol. 75, 1, pp. 51–52.
8 Cartoon by J. Handelsman, *The New Yorker*, 24 December 1973.
9 D. Luban, 'The Lysistratian prerogative: A reply to Stephen Pepper', *American Bar Foundation Research Journal*, 1986, 639. See also J. Raz, *The Morality of Freedom*, New York: Oxford University Press, 1986, p. 381.
10 W.B. Wendel, 'Institutional and individual justification in legal ethics: The problem of client selection', *Hofstra Law Review*, 2006, vol. 34, 1008.
11 G. Hazard Jr, *Ethics in the Practice of Law*, New Haven, CT: Yale University Press, 1976, pp. 143–46.
12 See sources cited in D.L. Rhode, *In the Interests of Justice: Reforming the Legal Profession*, New York: Oxford University Press, 1999, p. 111.
13 W. Simon, 'After confidentiality: Rethinking the professional responsibility of the business lawyer', *Fordham Law Review*, 2005, vol. 75, 1453; J. Bankman, 'The tax shelter battle', in H. Aaron and J. Slemrod (eds), *The Crisis in Tax Administration*, Washington: Brookings Institution Press, 2004, p. 9; R. Gordon, 'A new role for lawyers? The corporate counselor after Enron', *Connecticut Law Review*, 2003 vol. 35, 1185; and sources cited in D.L. Rhode, 'Moral counseling', *Fordham Law Review*, 2006, vol. 75, 1332.
14 M. Frankel, 'The search for truth: An umpireal view', *University of Pennsylvania Law Review*, 1975, vol. 123, 1031, p. 1056.
15 Rhode, *In the Interests of Justice*, p. 30; G. Miller, 'From club to market: The evolving role of business lawyers', *Fordham Law Review*, 2005, vol. 74, 1105,

pp. 1107–18, 1121–26. For lawyers' sense that the market rewards aggression, not ethics, see R. Nelson, 'The discovery process as a circle of blame: Institutional, professional, and socio-economic factors that contribute to unreasonable, inefficient, and amoral behavior in corporate litigation', *Fordham Law Review*, 1998, vol. 67, 773, pp. 778–79.

16  S. Kim, 'The banality of fraud: Resituating inside counsel as gatekeeper', *Fordham Law Review*, 2005, vol. 73, 983, p. 1016; Miller, 'From club to market', p. 1123; R.E. Rosen, 'Risk management and corporate governance: The case of Enron', *Connecticut Law Review*, 2003, vol. 35, 1157, p. 1169; R. Nelson and L. Nielson, 'Cops, counsel, and entrepreneurs: Constructing the role of inside counsel in large corporations', *Law & Society Review*, 2000, vol. 34, 457, p. 466.

17  M. Twain, *The Innocents Abroad*, New York: Oxford University Press, 1996, p. 590.

18  D. Messick and M. Bazerman, 'Ethical leadership and the psychology of decision making', *Sloan Management Review*, 1996, vol. 37, 9; M. Banaji, M. Bazerman and D. Chugh, 'How (unethical) are you?', *Harvard Business Review*, 2003, vol. 81, 856, p. 864; J. Darley, 'The cognitive and social psychology of contagious organizational corruption', *Brooklyn Law Review*, 2005, vol. 70, 1177; D. Luban, 'Integrity: Its causes and cures', *Fordham Law Review*, 2003, vol. 72, 279, p. 283.

19  J. Braithwaite, *Crime, Shame, and Reintegration*, New York: Cambridge University Press, 1989.

20  R. Jackall, *Moral Mazes: The World of Corporate Managers*, New York: Oxford University Press, 1988, p. 6; see Kim, 'Banality of Fraud', pp. 1011, 1019.

21  B. Latanae and J. Darley, *The Unresponsive Bystander: Why Doesn't He Help?* New York: Appleton-Century-Crofts, 1970; J. Armstrong, 'Social irresponsibility in management', *Journal of Business Research*, 1977, vol. 5, 185.

22  In *Re Gutfreund*, 51 S.E.C. 93, 98 (3 December 1992).

23  K. Hall and V. Holmes, 'The power of rationalisation to influence lawyers' decisions to act unethically', *Legal Ethics*, 2008, vol. 11, 137, p. 150 (quoting General Counsel Cooper).

24  J. Stewart, 'The Kona files: Hewlett Packard's surveillance scandal', *The New Yorker*, 19 and 26 February 2007, p. 152; S. Reisinger and D. Baskins, 'See no evil at HP?', *Corporate Counsel*, 18 December 2006 (discussing responses of in-house counsel and compliance officer); L. Hurley, 'Congress asks HP where were the lawyers', *San Francisco Daily Journal*, 29 September 2006, pp. 1, 9 (quoting Larry Sonsini, outside counsel, stating that he did not give a 'legal opinion'); P. Waldman and D. Clark, 'Probing the pretexters', *Wall Street Journal*, 25 September 2006, p. B1 (quoting Board Chair Patricia Dunn stating that 'I do not accept personal responsibility for what happened').

25  Kim, 'Banality of fraud', pp. 1030–31; Z. Kunda, 'The case for motivated reasoning', *Psychological Bulletin*, 1990, vol. 108, 480, p. 485; Messick and Bazerman, 'Ethical leadership', pp. 10, 99–100.

26  Darley, 'The cognitive and social psychology', pp. 1181–84; D. Kahneman, 'A perspective on judgment and choice: Mapping bounded rationality', *American Psychologist*, 2003, vol. 58, 697.

27  J. Kroger, 'Enron, fraud, and securities reform: An Enron prosecutor's perspective', *University of Colorado Law Review*, 2005, vol. 76, 57, p. 93.

28  M. Metzger, 'Bridging the gaps: Cognitive constraints on corporate control and ethics education', *University of Florida Journal of Law & Public Policy*, 2005, vol. 16, 435, p. 467. For classic accounts, see L. Festinger, *A Theory of Cognitive Dissonance*, Stanford, CA: Stanford University Press, 1962; E. Aronson, *The Social Animal*, San Francisco: W. H. Freeman, 1972, p. 108.

29  A. Tenbrunsel and D. Messick, 'Ethical fading: The role of self-deception in unethical behavior', *Social Justice Research*, 2004, vol. 17, 223, p. 224.

30  F. Zacharias, 'Effects of reputation on the legal profession', *Washington & Lee Law Review*, 2008, vol. 65, 173, pp. 181–82; W.B. Wendel, 'Nonlegal regulation of the legal

profession: Social norms in professional communities', *Vanderbilt Law Review*, 2001, 54; W.B. Wendel, 'Informal methods of enhancing the accountability of lawyers', *South Carolina Law Review*, 2002, vol. 54, 967, pp. 970, 976; M.C. Regan, Jr, 'Professional reputation: Looking for the good lawyer', *South Texas Law Review*, 1998, vol. 39, 549, pp. 555, 561; R. Gilson and R. Mnookin, 'Disputing through agents: Cooperation and conflict between lawyers in litigation', *Columbia Law Review*, 1994, vol. 94, 509, p. 551.

31  Rhode, 'Moral counseling', pp. 13–20, 25.
32  P. Jessup, *Elihu Root (Vol 1)*, New York: Dodd Mead, 1938, p. 133.
33  Young Lawyers Division, *Career Satisfaction Survey 28*, Washington: American Bar Association, 2000.
34  E. Chambliss and D. Wilkins, 'Promoting effective ethical infrastructure in large law firms', *Hofstra Law Review*, 2002, vol. 30, 691.
35  G. Sharswood, *An Essay on Professional Ethics*, 6th edn, Philadelphia: George T. Bisel, 1930, p. 73.
36  J. Macey, 'Occupation Code 541110: Lawyer self regulation and the idea of a profession', *Fordham Law Review*, 2005, vol. 74, 1081, pp. 1088–89; J. Jamail, 'Keeping it simple', *ABA Journal*, 2009, March, 95.
37  J. Doris, *Lack of Character: Psychology and Moral Behavior*, New York: Cambridge University Press, 2002, pp. 139–46.
38  See the discussion and sources cited in Rhode, *In the Interests of Justice*, pp. 19–20.
39  L. Rogers, 'Conference panelists call for clarification of obligation to report peer misconduct', *AA/BNA Lawyers' Manual Professional Conduct*, 2007, vol. 23.
40  Center for Professional Responsibility, *Survey on Lawyer Discipline Systems, Charts 1 and 2*, Washington: American Bar Association, 2007.
41  D.L. Rhode and D. Luban, *Legal Ethics*, 5th edn, New York: Thomson Reuters/Foundation Press, 2009.
42  Rhode, *In the Interests of Justice*, p. 160; J. O'Sullivan, 'Professional discipline for law firms: A response to Professor Schneyer', *Georgetown Journal of Legal Ethics*, 2004, vol. 16, 3, p. 55; M.S. Frisch, 'No stone left unturned: The failure of attorney regulation in the District of Columbia', *Georgetown Journal Legal Ethics*, 2005, vol. 18, 1713.
43  Rhode, *In the Interests of Justice*, p. 158. For dissatisfaction with alternative grievance processes, see Rhode and Luban, *Legal Ethics*, p. 983, n. 19.
44  Rhode and Luban, *Legal Ethics*, p. 984.
45  Rhode, *In the Interests of Justice*, pp. 159–60; L.C. Levin, 'The case for less secrecy in lawyer discipline', *Georgetown Journal Legal Ethics*, 2007, vol. 20, 1, pp. 2, 19.
46  V. Jaksic, 'Attorney discipline web data uneven', *National Law Journal*, 10 September 2007, 10, pp. 1, 7; Levin, 'The case for less secrecy', pp. 20–21.
47  C. Parker and A. Evans, *Inside Lawyers' Ethics*, Melbourne: Cambridge University Press, 2007; R. Parnham, 'The Clementi reforms in a European context – are the proposals really that radical?', *Legal Ethics*, 2007, vol. 8, 195.
48  Parker and Evans, *Inside Lawyers' Ethics*, pp. 47, 60.
49  R. Pound, *The Lawyer from Antiquity to Modern Times*, St Paul, MN: West Publishing Company, 1953, p. 7.
50  For examples, see Great Britain's *Legal Profession Act* (2007); Parnham, 'The Clementi reforms'; Parker and Evans, *Inside Lawyers' Ethics*, pp. 47–50; L.C. Levin, 'Building a better lawyer discipline system: The Queensland experience', *Legal Ethics*, 2006, vol. 9, 167, pp. 193–94.
51  Levin, 'Building a better lawyer discipline system', pp. 193–95.
52  ABA Model Rules of Professional Conduct, Preamble.
53  For low-income Americans, see Legal Services Corporation, *Documenting the Justice Gaps in America: The Current Unmet Civil Legal Needs of Low-Income Americans*, Washington, DC: Legal Services Corporation, 2005, pp. 11–18. For middle-income Americans, see D.L. Rhode, *Access to Justice*, New York: Oxford University Press, 2004, p. 79.

54 The test is whether, under the due process clause of the US Constitution, the proceeding would prove 'fundamentally unfair' without appointed counsel: *Lassiter v Department of Social Services*, 452 U.S. 18 (1981). For the narrow interpretation of this ruling, see Rhode, *Access to Justice*, p. 9.

55 D.L. Rhode, *Pro Bono in Principle and in Practice*, Stanford, CA: Stanford University Press, 2005, p. 103; D.L. Rhode, 'In the interests of justice: A comparative perspective on access to legal services and accountability of the legal profession', *Current Legal Problems*, 2003, vol. 56, 114. For challenges in New South Wales, see C. Courmarelos, Z. Wei and A.Z. Zhou, *Justice Made to Measure: New South Wales Legal Needs Survey in Disadvantaged Areas*, Sydney: Law and Justice Foundation of New South Wales, 2006. Available from www.lawfoundation.net.au/report/survey2006 (accessed 31 March 2009); Legal Services Agency, *Report on the National Survey of Unmet Legal Needs and Access to Services*, Wellington, New Zealand: Legal Services Agency, 2006.

56 Rhode, *Pro Bono*, p. 20. ABA survey results finding that two-thirds of lawyers report doing some pro bono work are not inconsistent with this estimate, given that the average hourly contribution of lawyers who offered pro bono assistance needs to be adjusted for the numbers who did not, and for those whose contributions involved activities such as Bar Association service. See Standing Commission on Pro Bono and Public Service, *Supporting Justice: A Report on the Pro Bono Work of America's Lawyers*, Chicago, IL: American Bar Association, 2005.

57 A. Press, 'In house', *American Lawyer*, July 2008, p. 13; N. Raymond, 'A silver lining', *American Lawyer*, July 2008, 100.

58 ABA State by State Pro Bono Service Rules. Available from www.abanet.org/legal-services/probono/stateethicsrules.html (accessed 31 March 2009). On the absence of quality data, see Rhode, *Pro Bono*, p. 174.

59 Rhode, *Pro Bono*, pp. 100–124; F. McKleay, 'The legal profession's beautiful myth: Surveying the justifications for the lawyer's obligation to perform pro bono work', *International Journal of the Legal Profession*, 2008, vol. 15, 24, p. 252 (noting Australian average of 23 hours per year); M. Twomey and J. Corker, 'Pro bono at work: Report on the pro bono legal work of 25 large Australian law firms', *Legal Ethics*, 2009, vol. 11, 255, p. 258 (finding a median for Australian lawyers of 21 hours per year).

60 Rhode, *In the Interests of Justice*, pp. 135–40. For a historical overview, *see* Rhode, *Access to Justice*, pp. 75–76.

61 Rhode, *Access to Justice*, pp. 88–90; H. Kritzer, *Legal Advocacy: Lawyers and Nonlawyers at Work*, Ann Arbor, MI: University of Michigan Press, 1998, pp. 193–203; Commission on NonLawyer Practice, *NonLawyer Activity in Law-Related Situations: A Report with Recommendations*, Washington, DC: American Bar Association, 1995.

62 Over four-fifths of lawyers support prosecution of lay competitors, and the ABA has voted to strengthen enforcement efforts. Rhode, *Access to Justice*, p. 88; P. Mason, 'Target unauthorized practice, ABA urges', *Chicago Law Bulletin*, 14 February 2000, p. 1.

63 M.W. Edelman, *I Can Make a Difference: A Treasury to Inspire Our Children*, New York: HarperCollins, 2006, p. 6.

64 Rhode, *Pro Bono*, pp. 167–69.

65 For increases as a result of reporting requirements, see Standing Committee on Pro Bono Legal Service, *Report to the Supreme Court of Florida, the Florida Bar and the Florida Bar Foundation on the Voluntary Pro Bono Attorney Plan*, Tallahassee, FL: Florida Pro Bono Resource Centre, 2006. For the influence of media rankings, see B. Hallman, 'Starting at the top', *American Lawyer*, July 2007, pp. 92, 95; B. Hallman, 'A first for Orrick: Stronger pro bono scores help the firm make its A-list debut', *American Lawyer*, July 2007.

66 Rhode, *Pro Bono*, pp. 167–69. One such initiative is 'Building a Better Legal Profession', a database grading firms on their diversity and pro bono records. Available from www.betterlegalprofession.org/leadership.php (accessed 7 September 2009); A. Liptak,

'In students' eyes, look-alike lawyers don't make the grade', *New York Times*, 28 October 2007, p. A10.

67 Rhode, *Access to Justice*, pp. 81–86.

68 W. Sullivan, A. Colby, J.W. Wegner, L. Bond, and L.S. Shulman, *Educating Lawyers: Preparation for the Profession of Law*, San Francisco: Jossey-Bass, 2007, p. 187.

69 Rhode, *Pro Bono*, p. 162.

70 National Center for Post-Secondary Research, *Law School Survey of Student Engagement, 2004 National Survey Results, Student Engagement in Law Schools*, Bloomington, IN: Indiana University Press, 2004.

71 E. Schnapper, 'The myth of legal ethics', *ABA Journal*, 1978, vol. 64, 202, p. 205.

72 R.A. Posner, 'The deprofessionalization of legal teaching and scholarship', *Michigan Law Review*, 1993, vol. 91, 1921, pp. 1921, 1924. For similar views, see P. Steinfels, 'Mixing morals with education?', *New York Times*, 19 June 2004 (quoting Stanley Fish's comment to his university colleagues that 'You can't make ... [students] into good people and you shouldn't try').

73 *See* M. Mentkowski and Associates, *Learning that Lasts: Integrating Learning, Development and Performance in College and Beyond*, San Francisco: Jossey-Bass, 2000, pp. 120–21; M. Bebeau, 'Promoting ethical development and professionalism: Insights from educational research in the professions', *University of Saint Thomas Law Journal*, 5, 2008, vol. 5, 366, pp. 384–85; D.L. Rhode, 'Ethics by the pervasive method', *Journal of Legal Education*, 1992, vol. 42, 31, p. 46; M. Browne, C. Williamson and L. Barkas, 'The purported rigidity of an attorney's personality: Can legal ethics be acquired?', *Journal of the Legal Profession*, 30, 2006, vol. 30, 55; R.G. Pearce, 'Teaching ethics seriously: Legal ethics as the most important subject in law school', *Loyola University Chicago Law Journal*, 1998, vol. 29, 719, pp. 719, 734; S. Hartwell, 'Promoting moral development through experiential education', *Clinical Law Review*, 1995, vol. 1, 505.

74 D. Luban and M. Millemann, 'Good judgment: Ethics teaching in dark times', *Georgetown Journal of Legal Ethics*, 1995, vol. 9, 31; R. Granfield and T. Koenig, 'It's hard to be a human being and lawyer: Young attorneys and the confrontation with ethical ambiguity in legal practice', *West Virginia Law Review*, 2003, vol. 105, 495, p. 520.

75 B. Obama, Transcript of *Tonight with Jay Leno*, 19 March 2009. Available from www.whitehouse.gov/the_press_office/Interview-of-the-President-by-Jay-Leno-on-the-Tonight-Show-3-19-09 (accessed 31 March 2009).

76 W. Safire, 'Face down in the mud', *New York Times*, 22 December 1986, p. A23.

# 4  Legal advising and the rule of law

*W. Bradley Wendel*

## 4.1 Introduction

The fundamental question for a theory of legal ethics is what ends, functions and values give content to the lawyer's role, underwrite specific normative principles telling lawyers how to act, and ground criticism in ethical terms of lawyers who engage in wrongdoing. The question is well known in Charles Fried's famous formulation, 'Can a good lawyer be a good person?'[1] Stated that way, the issue is presented in terms of the problem of role-differentiated morality. That is, one's professional role as a lawyer requires or permits actions that would be deemed wrongful by ordinary moral standards. In the advocacy context, these role-acts include things like cross-examining a truthful witness to discredit her testimony, or using some procedural device, such as the statute of limitations, to avoid a judgement on the merits of a claim. The problem of role-differentiated morality arises when one understands these acts in ordinary moral terms under descriptions like 'lying' or 'cheating'.[2] It is no answer to say that the acts can also be described in role-specific terms, such as 'cross-examination' or 'filing a motion' because the descriptions in ordinary moral terms persist.[3] Arguing for a result contrary to what the lawyer knows to be true is still 'deception', even if it can also be described as 'zealous advocacy' or 'putting the other side to its proof'. Because of the persistence of description in ordinary moral terms, there arises a demand for justification, in the terms that one would ordinarily be expected to offer for what is *prima facie* an interference with the rights of others.

The response typically given to this demand has been aptly named the 'adversary system excuse' by David Luban.[4] Lawyers claim they are not morally accountable for committing acts of deception or cheating because they work within an institutional framework that is designed to accomplish some valuable social end, and realizing this end requires the lawyer to perform certain acts that would otherwise be morally wrong, but for the institutions and procedures of the adversary system. Thus, the description in ordinary moral terms is sort of beside the point, just as describing money as little green pieces of paper (if you're an American) misses the point of money as a placeholder for value that facilitates exchanges. This is the sort of 'institutional fact' that arises only as a result of a complicated set of formal and informal norms respecting how properties of objects in the natural world, such as green pieces of paper with pictures of dead presidents on them, should be treated.[5]

As Luban notes, however, the adversary system excuse turns on the tightness of the connection between the acts that lawyers claim to be permitted to engage in, and the social end for which the adversary system is constituted.[6] If it turns out that this end can be achieved without lawyers committing the acts in question – lying, cheating, and so on – then the adversary system fails to relieve lawyers of moral accountability. For whatever end is posited, however – such as protecting legal rights or ascertaining the truth about some factual dispute – it is usually not a difficult matter to show that the adversary system is not necessary for achieving it. Individual rights are protected at least as well in many civil law systems, for example, in which lawyers do not have the same duties of partisan advocacy as lawyers in the United States, including stringent obligations of confidentiality and permission to make 'creative and aggressive' legal arguments. Even within the American legal system, if lawyers acted on the basis of ordinary moral obligations, in violation of their professional duties, the harm that would accrue to the effective functioning of the system would typically be slight. This relatively insignificant marginal harm would almost always be outweighed by the marginal benefit of increased compliance with the demands of morality.[7]

If we accept the arguments against the adversary system excuse, it would appear that vast swathes of the daily practices of lawyers are without moral justification. If the legal system is comprehensively unjustified – or, as Luban claims, only weakly pragmatically justified – then morally conscientious lawyers would appear to be acting in bad faith, getting up and going to work every morning thinking they are participating in an enterprise with real social value, but being insufficiently critical to realize that the normative foundation of the practice is actually shifting sands. Rather than thinking that the entire profession is massively in error, I tend to think that lawyers properly should have a different way of conceiving of the relationship between moral agency and professional roles. A professional role might, for good moral reasons, require someone to act on the basis of less than the full range of reasons that would otherwise apply to someone outside the role. Lawyers do things that may seem like lying or cheating in ordinary moral terms, but their role instructs them to do it anyway. In other words, the role creates *exclusionary* reasons, telling lawyers to ignore what would otherwise be moral reasons not to do something.[8] My argument here is an attempt to justify the exclusionary character of the lawyer's role, and to explain why lawyers have a moral reason to act on a restricted set of reasons or values when acting in a professional capacity.

In particular, I want to defend the claim that when lawyers are representing clients, they should give advice based on a good faith interpretation of positive law, not based on what the lawyer believes the client morally ought to do. The context is important here, because the usual all-purpose statement of lawyers' duties, 'zealous advocacy within the bounds of the law', is inapposite as applied to lawyers counselling their clients on compliance with the law. Lawyers representing clients in litigated matters may be permitted to advance less well-supported interpretations of the law, because there are procedures to check the effects of excessive partisanship. When counselling clients on what the law permits or requires, however, lawyers are effectively private lawgivers with respect to their clients. The lawyer's advice may be challenged subsequently if there is litigation, but a great deal of legal advice is confidential and never made the subject of adversarial litigation. As a result, legal advising should be considered a political act, like lawmaking in a legislature or adjudication, not an essentially private matter like giving moral advice to a friend. The relevant values that inform the lawyer's role are therefore values associated with the rule of law, not ordinary morality.

## 4.2 Legitimacy and moral agency as the foundation of legal ethics

The important thing to notice about the standard debate in theoretical legal ethics is that it is framed in terms of the sorts of evaluative considerations that would inform the deliberations of persons acting as ordinary moral agents. As Deborah Rhode writes in *In the Interests of Justice*: 'Attorneys should make decisions as advocates in the same way that morally reflective individuals make any ethical decision … and to respect core values such as honesty, fairness, and good faith on which the system depends.'[9] In other words, the way to approach the question of being a good person and a good lawyer is from the standpoint of a good person – the good lawyer bit should be sacrificed to the demands of personal moral agency if the demands of being a good lawyer come into conflict with personal integrity and conscience. This structure is why lawyers' professional obligations always seem to end up less weighty than ordinary morality – what could be more important than individual moral agency and integrity?

The trouble with seeing it in this way is that the legal system – with all its associated institutions and roles – is designed, among other things, to handle the predicament of people living together in a community who disagree over what integrity and moral agency require. People disagree in good faith about how their competing claims of rights should be resolved. Talk by political philosophers about moral pluralism and disagreement often focuses on high-profile controversies like abortion and affirmative action, but the most mundane issues handled by the law can involve intractable disagreement. William Simon and Deborah Rhode each offer a version of an example of a lawyer advising the recipient of welfare assistance about whether she should report free lodging with a family member as in-kind income, thereby reducing the cash assistance to which she is entitled.[10] Alternatively, the lawyer might recommend a way to evade the reporting requirement – a loophole to exploit, if you like – by advising the client to make a nominal payment to her family member so that the housing is no longer free.

Although Simon labours to read the applicable American law on welfare benefits in such a way that the client has a legal entitlement to the full cash benefit, not reduced to take account of the free housing, it is clear that Simon's real objection is that it would be substantively *unjust* to provide inadequate welfare benefits. The lawyer 'might be justified in disregarding [the law] if she thought it problematic', he writes, and defines 'problematic' law as that which has purposes which 'endanger fundamental values'.[11] But the conclusion that the result would be unjust, as a matter of fundamental values, is contestable. Not only are there many political conservatives who oppose welfare benefits entirely, but even those who accept that some level of cash assistance is desirable may disagree about how benefits should be allocated among various categories of recipients. There may be a reasonable argument to be made that the client in Simon's example is less deserving of the full amount of benefits than another recipient who does not have free housing. It may also be the case that the welfare system as a whole could and should be better funded, but this implicates many more questions about which there is good faith disagreement over how the benefits and burdens of living together in society should be distributed.

The point of this example is that I am not sure how a lawyer should act if the basic message of legal ethics is that one should make the decision exactly as an ordinarily reflective person would make any decision, respecting core values such as honesty and fairness. Deborah Rhode goes on to qualify her position, in the passage I quoted previously, to note that an ordinarily reflective individual must 'take account of the distinctive needs of their occupational roles'.[12] But that just pushes the problem of pluralism back a level or two. What a value like fair distribution of resources requires in a case like this is exactly what people are likely to disagree about. We do have institutions and procedures for dealing with that sort of disagreement, but that means only that an ordinarily reflective individual has to decide not only first-order questions of whether a reduction in benefits is fair, but must also deal with second-order questions of the fairness of procedures for dealing with disagreements about substantive fairness. A lawyer may have their own view on how these questions should be answered, but they are just that – the lawyer's own view – unless there is sufficient support in the materials of the community's law to justify the claim that this position is more than one person's judgement about justice and fairness, but is the stance of the community as a whole.

Because of the persistence of disagreement within ordinary morality, I believe that legal ethics should be understood as making a demand for justification in political terms – that is, calling for a defence of lawyering norms in terms of the *legitimacy* of institutions and their associated roles. These values relate to properties of states of affairs and relations among persons that are constituted and regulated by social and political institutions. Political values are those that are associated with the problems and possibilities of living together in communities – they are the sorts of values that are inherent in there being such a thing as politics.[13] To take an example from one of the classic works of political philosophy, Hobbes begins his argument in *Leviathan* with the observation that people are approximately equal in strength and have a tendency to compete for resources and glory.[14] Significantly, Hobbes says that certain evaluative considerations do not apply in the state of nature: 'To this war of every man against every man, this also is consequent: that nothing can be unjust. The notions of right and wrong, justice and injustice, have there no place.'[15]

While one might quibble with Hobbes' claim that there can be no such thing as right or wrong in the state of nature, his methodological claim appears sound: there are certain evaluative concepts, like justice, that attach only to relations among persons that are mediated through some sort of structure of government. Values associated with these sorts of facts about human communities form the starting point of political, not moral theories. This does not mean they are detached from ordinary moral considerations, only that they are not directly reducible to the sorts of values that inform the deliberation of moral agents outside the context of relationships with others in a political community. For example, the notion of legitimacy has no real parallel in ordinary morality, yet it is one of the central evaluative concepts in political philosophy, measuring as it does the moral worth of political institutions. In general, politics – being a purposive activity engaged in by reflective humans for intelligible reasons – carries with it internal evaluative standards. Legitimacy is another way of saying success in light of those standards – political institutions are legitimate if, at a minimum, there are reasons beyond brute power and intimidation for the subjects of these institutions to act in accordance with their directives.[16] These reasons must make sense in light of a whole range of moral, social, cultural, historical and interpretive concepts,[17] but that does not mean they can be reduced straightforwardly to a morally reflective individual making decisions outside the context of some complex, normatively significant set of institutions and practices.

In contrast with the usual understanding that legal ethics is basically applied moral philosophy, I contend that the particular political evaluative standards that are the starting point for reflection on lawyers' ethics are those concerned with the ideal of the rule of law. I realize the concept of the rule of law has a lot of baggage associated with it. Lawyers trained in the United Kingdom and Canada tend to associate it with Dicey's insistence on parliamentary supremacy over administrative agencies, and an implicit hostility to the regulatory state.[18] More recently, the rule of law has been invoked in connection with neo-liberal economic development programmes, involving the wholesale export of Western (usually American) institutions and practices into transitional and developing countries, usually without much success.[19] The notion of the rule of law thus carries a connotation of imperialism, because of the appropriation of the term 'rule of law' to identify a highly contestable conception of a fair distribution of rights and resources. But there is a core, and I hope less freighted, concept underlying these various conceptions of the rule of law, which is essential to understanding legal ethics in terms of institutional and political values.

The classic ideal of the rule of law is that 'all persons and authorities within the state, whether public or private, should be bound by and entitled to the benefit of laws publicly and prospectively promulgated and publicly administered by the courts.'[20] Legal institutions can therefore be designed and criticized with reference to the ideal of acting according to pre-established rules and standards that are applicable to everyone, including state actors themselves. This core concept of the rule of law – what we might call the value of *legality* – emphasizes constraint on the arbitrary exercise of power.[21] Philosophers who have given content to this core notion, including Joseph Raz, John Finnis and Lon Fuller, have argued that the law and legal institutions must have certain formal features if they are to perform well their function of safeguarding against the arbitrary exercise of power.[22] (Interestingly, there always seem to be eight enumerated criteria, the number eight apparently having a deep mystical connection with the rule of law.) While these criteria vary somewhat, I think the most important aspects, for the purposes of legal ethics, can be boiled down to a distinction between power as such and *lawful* power. The point of the law is to differentiate between *de facto* power, which might be possessed by the state or by private actors, and the exercise of power that is legitimated somehow by the community as a whole.

The implication for legal ethics is that the role of lawyers should be understood in terms of the values associated with the social achievement represented by legality.[23] In my view, the most general obligation of all lawyers is to exhibit fidelity to enacted, positive law when representing clients. The reason the law deserves respect is that it represents a recognizable moral good of some sort.[24] However, being a moral good is not the same thing as being an *ordinary* moral good – the sort of thing that conscientious reflective people take into account in deciding how to act. Rather, the normative significance of law is related to the legitimacy of legal institutions and procedures, and this in turn is a matter of how responsive they are to the needs of people living together in communities, who require some means by which they can treat one another with respect, deep and persistent disagreement notwithstanding. This is why the lawyer in Simon's example should not decide for herself what justice requires. We all have views about what justice requires, but to the extent that we seek to act under a claim of right – asserting that what we are doing has been authorized in the name of the community as a whole – we are constrained to refer to the output of procedures that have been established for resolving competing claims about justice.

One might object to this whole line of argument by pointing out that the rule of law may be observed by some pretty horrific governments 'procedurally "correct" repression is perfectly compatible with legalism.'[25] No sensible philosopher writing about the rule of law denies this, but it is important to distinguish between an abuse of the form of legality and the virtue of legality as it pertains to the normative foundations of the lawyers' role. Joseph Raz has a helpful example: It may be the case that a sharp knife can do harm, but that does not mean that being sharp is not a good-making characteristic of knives.[26] A good knife is, among other things, a sharp knife, but that good quality does not prevent its being used for bad ends. Similarly, the forms of general, impartial government can be abused. However, that does not mean that the moral goodness of the rule of law does not reside in qualities such as the capacity of legal systems to safeguard against the abuse of power, and to enable people to give a justification for their actions that refers to considerations that have been adopted using tolerably fair procedures in the name of the community as a whole. This capacity of the law has value, and it is this value that underpins the lawyer's role and gives it normative significance. As David Luban observes, lawyers object to the establishment of the law-free zone at Guantánamo Bay as a 'standing affront to a political order that gives their profession meaning'.[27] That is exactly what I am trying to capture with the notion of a political morality of lawyering. When lawyers are representing clients within a reasonably just political system, their role partakes of the positive value of the rule of law.

## 4.3 The rule of law and the craft of lawyering

The historian E.P. Thompson argues that, historically speaking, law has been understood as 'something more than ... a pliant medium to be twisted this way and that by whichever interests already possess effective power'.[28] We need not endorse Thompson's controversial conclusion that the rule of law is an 'unqualified human good' to appreciate the point that citizens are able to perceive a difference between arbitrary power and the rule of law.[29] Thompson states this rather acidly when he says:

> people are not as stupid as some structuralist philosophers suppose them to be. They will not be mystified by the first man who puts on a wig. It is inherent in the especial character of law ... that it shall apply logical criteria with reference to standards of universality and equity ... If the law is evidently partial and unjust, then it will mask nothing, legitimize nothing, contribute nothing to any class's hegemony. The essential precondition for the effectiveness of law, in its function as ideology, is that it shall display an independence from gross manipulation and shall seem to be just.[30]

This well-known passage describes well the response to many of the recent legal ethics scandals in the United States and elsewhere. It is significant that many recent cases involving accusations of wrongdoing by lawyers involve abuses of power by public and private institutions – financial reporting failures by large corporations like Enron, abusive tax avoidance schemes marketed by accounting firms such as KPMG, and, of course, the Bush administration's attitude toward the treatment of detainees.

The critical response to these sorts of abuses has frequently been to assert values associated with legality, not ordinary moral values. When internal government memoranda were disclosed which purported to justify the use of torture in interrogation, the public outcry was not based only on the immorality of torture. Rather, people seemed particularly upset that government *lawyers* were trying to claim that torture was legally permitted. This criticism is different in kind from that which would be directed at executive branch officials who urged that American policy should be to permit torture, or even from the revulsion we would feel toward one of the frontline soldiers or CIA officers who actually did the torturing. This shows that there is an evaluative framework that is specific to the work lawyers do in advising clients about their legal obligations, and it is on the basis of these standards that we can say the lawyers advising the government, or Enron, or the accounting firms engaged in dodgy tax transactions, have acted unethically. Specifically, they acted unethically because they regarded the law as merely an inconvenient obstacle standing in the way of their clients' freedom of action. But recall E.P. Thompson's observation that historically citizens have been able to resist the unjust exercise of power by asserting that the law is not just a pliant medium, to be twisted this way and that way by whatever interests already have power. That's something, and it gives us, as lawyers and legal ethics scholars, the normative resources to push back against powerful clients who demand that lawyers give them the blessing of the ascription of legality on their conduct.

We can make this more difficult by considering an example from the predicament of government lawyers advising the Bush administration. The *Washington Post* in 2005 reported a comment by Michael Hayden, then the Deputy Director of National Intelligence, now Director of the CIA. Hayden described the attitude that he wanted lawyers to take toward the law. (This is with respect, by the way, to the NSA warrantless wiretapping program.) He said: 'We're going to live on the edge ... My spikes will have chalk on them ... We're pretty aggressive within the law. As a professional, I'm troubled if I'm not using the full authority allowed by the law.'[31] Although this comes off as a typical American cowboy attitude, I want to ask a serious question: what's wrong with being creative and pushing the boundaries of the law? Isn't that what lawyers do?

The answer to this question builds on the agency structure of the lawyer–client relationship. By this I mean to refer to something that is a feature of the common law of agency, namely the idea that the agent's powers are entirely derivative of the principal's legal entitlements. In agency law, this is expressed in terms of the distinction between power and authority. Agents have the power to do a lot of things, such as make their principal vicariously liable for their torts, but that doesn't mean they have the authority to do those things. Authority is, basically, lawful power. The scope of the legitimate authority of lawyers to do anything for their clients is therefore given by their clients' legal entitlements, not by some standard external to the law, such as client interests or moral rights. That's what the rule of law means, as applied to the activities of lawyers – laws impartially applied, without regard to whether the client thinks the laws are inconvenient, anachronistic, inefficient, unjust or just plain stupid.

When lawyers act in an advisory capacity, by definition they are trying to determine the content of their clients' entitlements. Metaphorically, entitlements fix a boundary between the freedom of action of one person and that of another. When lawyers talk about pushing on the boundaries of the law, or getting chalk on their spikes, what they are saying is that the client is claiming the right to invade someone else's sphere of legally protected entitlements. The client may have de facto power to do that, but it's not the legitimate exercise of power if the law doesn't actually permit it. As Daniel Markovits nicely puts it, the law permits people to transform brute demands into claims of right.[32] Without a genuine legal entitlement backing up their advice, lawyers cannot accomplish this transformation, and the client's interest remains as a brute demand. Lawyers who are excessively creative or aggressive in advising clients are therefore purporting to engage in alchemy, converting de facto power into lawful power.

But this response begs the question, unless there were some way to ascertain the boundary between lawful action and de facto power in an objective manner. It works well enough in addressing the abstract question of legitimacy versus moral agency to talk about the law in these schematic terms – 'the law permits X' or 'the law says you can't do Y' or whatever. But lawyers know this will only go so far, and in practice it is necessary to dig deeper into statements in that form. The interesting cases for lawyers, as opposed to political philosophers, are those in which the law might permit X, but it might not. There might be some chance that a court could be persuaded to conclude that the law permits X, but there might be a risk of a decision going the other way. The authorities may be mixed, so that the best a lawyer could advise a client is that there is some support for the client's entitlement to do X, but nothing can be said with any certainty. And once we admit that the law underdetermines legal judgements to some extent, the door seems to be opened to the exploitation of this indeterminacy by powerful clients – the directive to get chalk on one's spikes no longer seems abusive, but is rather a reminder to lawyers that they shouldn't be the ones standing between the client and its ability to act based only on their subjective views about how the law should be interpreted.

It is not part of my argument to assert that the law is perfectly determinate – that is, it yields only one right answer in hard cases. There is room for reasonable disagreement about what the law permits or requires in many interesting cases, and there is nothing wrong with lawyers pushing for their clients' preferred outcomes within this range of reasonable interpretations. In the litigation context, this problem really does not arise, at least not in a way that goes to the heart of a theory of legal ethics, because there is a procedural, or institutional, solution to the problem of indeterminacy. Opposing counsel are permitted to argue for their preferred interpretation, and the mechanism of adversary briefing, oral argument and appeals, as well as the intervention of judges and law clerks, all ensure that by and large the law is not distorted by creative and aggressive interpretation. But one must confront directly the problem of distortion of the law in the legal advising context, where there is no procedural checking of aggressive interpretations.

The response to this problem is to fall back on a notion that is a bit out of fashion, but should receive renewed attention: the idea of the craft of lawyering. The distinction between legal alchemy – purporting to convert a client interest into a legal entitlement – and fidelity to law is something that lawyers appreciate intuitively, but it is difficult to theorize. There is no single methodology that represents the right way to read cases, statutes and regulations, and deal with all sorts of non-textual interpretive principles. Ultimately, the standards governing the legitimacy of an interpretation are not reducible to rules or meta-rules. Rather, they are largely tacit standards of acceptability of an interpretation to a professional community of lawyers, judges and scholars.[33] Professional communities are close to the foundation of this account of interpretation, but they are not the bedrock. There is still a constraint on what counts as a legitimate interpretive community, one whose tacit norms regulating interpretation are reliable guides to the content of the law. This constraint is provided by the ideal of the rule of law. The rule of law in this case is mostly a negative value, ruling out certain interpretive moves as illegitimate.[34] When we criticize lawyers for providing abusive, aggressive or too-clever legal advice, what we are saying is that the arguments in support do not withstand scrutiny, keeping in mind rule of law values such as generality, impartiality and publicity.

## 4.4 Conclusion

The complaint from the point of view of lawyering craft and jurisprudence, when lawyers create dodgy tax transactions or advise that it is permissible to torture detainees, is that the result is arbitrary in a way that is antithetical to the rule of law. It is not enough to simply assert this; one must demonstrate it. But the way one demonstrates it is not through theoretical argument. Rather, it is by engaging directly with the legal positions themselves, unpacking and criticizing them exactly as law students are trained to do from the very first day of law school. My claim here is that evaluating lawyers as having done well or poorly by virtue of the internal craft standards of lawyering is a substantial part of the task of legal ethics. If law deserves respect from a moral point of view because it is more than de facto power,[35] then lawyers should expect to come in for criticism when they attempt to subvert the law in the service of power. The line between subversion and fidelity to law is not one that can be given as the pat conclusion to an argument like this. Rather, this argument is meant to suggest that our task as lawyers and legal ethics scholars is to go out and assess lawyering from the inside, from the point of view of someone seeking to demonstrate that a client's actions are legally authorized. So I'll end by disclaiming much of a role for theory in legal ethics. If there is moral value in legality, then there is legal ethics in legal analysis.

## Notes

1 C. Fried, 'The lawyer as friend: The moral foundation of the lawyer–client relation', *Yale Law Journal*, 1976, vol. 85, 1060, p. 1060.
2 D. Markovits, *Between Self and State*, Princeton, NJ: Princeton University Press, 2008.
3 A. Applebaum, *Ethics for Adversaries*, Princeton, NJ: Princeton University Press, 1999, Ch. 5.
4 D. Luban, *Legal Ethics and Human Dignity*, Cambridge: Cambridge University Press, 2007, Ch. 1; D. Luban, 'The adversary system excuse', in D. Luban (ed.), *The Good Lawyer*, Totowa, NJ: Rowman & Allanheld, 1983.
5 The example of money is familiar from J.R. Searle, *The Construction of Social Reality*, New York: Free Press, 1995. For a recent application of Searle's ideas to legal theory, see N. MacCormick, *Institutions of Law*, Oxford: Oxford University Press, 2007.
6 Luban, 'The adversary system excuse', pp. 26, 31.
7 D. Luban, 'Freedom and constraint in legal ethics: Some mid-course corrections to *Lawyers and Justice*', *Maryland Law Review*, 1990, vol. 49, 424, pp. 430–31. ('the marginal harms to the system that result from violating one's professional duty typically are slight in a single case. On the other side of the ledger, the marginal benefits of following [ordinary] morality rather than professional duty may be great.')

8 For a careful analysis of the exclusionary effect of professional roles, see T. Dare, *The Counsel of Rogues? A Defence of the Standard Conception of the Lawyer's Role*, Farnham: Ashgate, 2009, Ch. 3.

9 D.L. Rhode, *In the Interests of Justice: Reforming the Legal Profession*, New York: Oxford University Press, 2000, p. 67.

10 W.H. Simon, 'Ethical discretion in lawyering', *Harvard Law Review*, 1988, vol. 101, 1083, pp. 1105–6; Rhode, *In the Interests of Justice*, pp. 76–79.

11 Simon, 'Ethical discretion', p. 1106.

12 Rhode, 'Personal integrity and professional ethics'.

13 B. Williams, 'Realism and moralism in political theory', in G. Hawthorn (ed.), *In the Beginning Was the Deed: Realism and Moralism in Political Argument*, Princeton, NJ: Princeton University Press, 2005, p. 1.

14 T. Hobbes, *Leviathan*, ed. Edwin Curley, Indianapolis: Hackett, 1994, Ch. XIII.

15 Hobbes, *Leviathan*, Ch. XIII, para. [13].

16 Williams, 'Realism and moralism', p. 11. ('This requires ... that there is a legitimation offered which goes beyond the assertion of power'.)

17 Ibid.

18 See, for example, D. Dyzenhaus, 'Dicey's shadow', *University of Toronto Law Review*, 1993, vol. 43, 127. Thanks to Alice Woolley for this reference and for helpful conversations about the concept of the rule of law in Canadian administrative law.

19 Bob Gordon nicely summarizes an immense literature in a recent unpublished paper. See R.W. Gordon, 'Lawyers and liberalization – lessons from Western experience for projects to export the "rule of law"', presented at the Fordham University School of Law Legal Ethics Schmooze, New York, 2 June–3 June 2008.

20 T. Bingham (Baron of Cornhill), 'The rule of law', *Cambridge Law Journal*, 2007, vol. 66, 67.

21 J. Raz, 'The rule of law and its virtue', in J. Raz, *The Authority of Law: Essays on Law and Morality*, Oxford: Clarendon Press, 1979, p. 219.

22 Bingham, 'The rule of law', pp. 69–82; Raz, 'The rule of law', pp. 210–29; J. Finnis, *Natural Law and Natural Rights*, Oxford: Clarendon Press, 1980, pp. 270–76; L.L. Fuller, *The Morality of Law*, New Haven: Yale University Press, 2nd edn, 1964, pp. 33–91.

23 L.L. Fuller, 'Positivism and fidelity to law: A reply to Professor Hart', *Harvard Law Review*, 1958, vol. 71, 630.

24 Ibid., p. 631 ('Law, as something deserving loyalty, must represent a human achievement; it cannot be a simple fiat of power or a repetitive pattern discernable in the behavior of state officials.').

25 J. Shklar, *Legalism*, Cambridge, MA: Harvard University Press, 1964, p. 17.

26 Raz, 'The rule of law', p. 225.

27 See Luban, Chapter 5, this volume.

28 E.P. Thompson, *Whigs and Hunters: The Origin of the Black Act*, New York: Pantheon, 1975, p. 262.

29 Ibid., p. 266.

30 Ibid. pp. 262–63.

31 Quoted in D. Priest, 'Covert CIA program withstands new furor', *Washington Post*, 30 December 2005, p. A01.

32 D. Markovits, 'Adversary advocacy and the authority of adjudication', *Fordham Law Review*, 2006, vol. 75, 1367.

33 W.B. Wendel, 'Professionalism as interpretation', *Northwestern University Law Review*, 2005, vol. 99, 1167.

34 Raz, 'The rule of law', p. 224.

35 Fuller, 'Positivism and fidelity', p. 631.

# 5 Tales of terror: lessons for lawyers from the 'war on terrorism'

*David Luban*

## 5.1 Introduction

An astonishing feature of the so-called 'global war on terrorism' (GWOT) waged by the United States and its allies against Al Qaeda is the prominent role played by lawyers, civilian and military, representing both the US government and the people it has captured.[1] The conduct of these lawyers has been a topic of interest to many, both in and out of the legal profession, since the first so-called 'torture memos' were released in 2004. It is a subject of international, not merely parochial, interest; as I write these words, a Spanish investigating magistrate is considering whether to proceed with an indictment of the 'Bush Six' – six high-ranking lawyers in the Bush administration who, it is alleged, enabled the torture of Spanish nationals by contriving advice that stripped prisoners of legal protections. I will discuss the 'torture lawyers', but also lawyers who represent the prisoners.[2] Although most of these are Americans, not all of them are. Some of the leading Guantánamo defence lawyers come from the London-based organization, Reprieve. One lawyer I will discuss, US Marine Major Dan Mori, became a minor celebrity in Australia through his representation of David Hicks. The laws at issue in these cases are by and large international law, and of course Guantánamo has become an international symbol of the rule of law and its absence, a point central to the debate. In any case, the lessons I draw from looking at these lawyers are quite general and, I trust, of use to legal ethicists with no special interest in the US torture debate.

## 5.2 Background

In 1975, Richard Wasserstrom published a paper that arguably inaugurated the modern philosophical discussion of legal ethics. The paper was titled 'Lawyers as professionals: some moral issues', and it began with the striking assertion that 'at best the lawyer's world is a simplified moral world; often it is an amoral one; and more than occasionally, perhaps an overtly immoral one'.[3]

Wasserstrom illustrated his point with an anecdote from the then-recent Watergate scandal that brought down the Nixon presidency. Nixon's White House counsel John Dean was asked about a list of Watergate participants he had kept. Some had asterisks in front of their names, and the questioner wanted to know what the asterisks signified. Membership in some further conspiracy? Decision-making authority? Dean responded that the asterisks simply singled out the participants who were lawyers. He had been struck by how many there were. Dean wondered 'whether there was some reason why lawyers might have been more inclined than other persons to have been so willing to do the things that were done' in Watergate and its cover-up.[4] Wasserstrom wondered the same thing. He concluded that what makes lawyers particularly vulnerable to sins of excessive partisanship is the unique role morality of the profession, according to which lawyers should do everything possible to advance the interests of their clients, and bear no moral responsibility for the rightness or wrongness of what the client wants. Of course, Wasserstrom's observation about the curious tension between extreme partisanship and moral detachment was hardly a novelty. A century before, the English historian Macaulay asked rhetorically why a lawyer 'with a wig on his head, and a band round his neck, [would] do for a guinea what, without those appendages, he would think it wicked and infamous to do for an empire'.[5] Wasserstrom analyzed the problem as a clash between common morality and lawyers' role morality, a lead taken up a few years later by other legal ethicists, including Alan Goldman, Gerald Postema and myself.[6]

I was reminded of Wasserstrom's paper recently while reading Philippe Sands' book *The Torture Team*.[7] Sands is a British human rights lawyer, and he set out to discover the decision-making that went into Bush administration policies about torture, interrogation and Guantánamo. Sands' is not the only such book – by this time there is a small library of them – but Sands somehow persuaded a large number of the principals who formulated these policies to talk to him.[8]

By now you will have guessed what comes next. Going down the list of *dramatis personae* that Sands provides at the start of his book, I marked the lawyers with asterisks, and the number is astonishing. Half the members of the 'torture team' were lawyers.[9] These included not only those who wrote the various torture memos, but also the highest-ranked legal officers of the US government: the President's counsel, the Vice-President's counsel, the Attorney General, and the Defense Department's general counsel. Several of these met regularly as a self-styled 'War Council'.[10] The lawyers included, as well, a Defense Department Undersecretary who urged that the Geneva Conventions should not apply to GWOT captives.[11] And they included the first task force commander of the Guantánamo prison – a reserve army general who in civilian life is a state court judge, and who shared in the initial devising of the harsh new interrogation techniques used at Guantánamo.[12]

## 5.3 Lawyers waging lawfare

In one way, it was inevitable that lawyers would be deeply involved in decisions about the detention and interrogation of detainees. To a remarkable degree, contemporary armed conflict takes place amidst a dense network of laws and treaties, called the 'law of armed conflict' by military lawyers and 'humanitarian law' by human rights organizations. More than a generation of US military officers have been trained in these laws, and the official policy of the United States has been one of enthusiastic support for them. Ironically, it takes considerable legal ingenuity to unwind all this law. This meant that moving away from the law of armed conflict, or humanitarian law, required intensive activity on the part of lawyers.

The War Council consisted of lawyers who were deeply suspicious of humanitarian law, for a variety of reasons. Some were enthusiasts for boundless executive power, and reject the idea that law can bind the president, particularly in a military emergency.[13] Some of them were so-called 'new sovereigntists' – sceptics about international law who insist that it takes a back seat to domestic law and who regard international law's champions as an undemocratic elite who aim to chip away at US sovereignty.[14] Some adhered to the theory that has come to be known as 'lawfare':[15] the suspicion that America's enemies use humanitarian law strategically as a way to advance their own military interests by tying American hands – a view that appeared officially in the 2002 and 2005 National Defense Strategy of the United States, an official document prepared in the Pentagon.[16] And, to be fair, all of them were operating in an environment of intense fear that another Al Qaeda attack might happen around the anniversary of 9/11, and that their prisoners might have important information about the attack. General Richard Myers, who chaired the Joint Chiefs of Staff at the time, recalled that '[t]here was a sense of urgency that in my forty years of military experience hadn't existed in other contingencies.'[17] Indeed, when the Office of Legal Counsel (OLC) of the Department of Justice repudiated several of these opinions in January 2009, it explained how they came to be written by noting the 'extraordinary historical context,' when 'in the wake of the atrocities of 9/11, ... policy makers, fearing that additional catastrophic terrorist attacks were imminent, strived to employ all lawful means to protect the Nation' – the implication being that the OLC responded to that demand through opinions that were overbroad and ultimately thought to be wrongheaded enough that the OLC retracted them.[18]

Some of the reasons behind the adoption of a lawfare mentality by the War Council may have been unique to the legal outlook of the Bush administration and the legal theorists they recruited to staff their offices. However, I do want to note that the 'lawfare' theory comes naturally to lawyers schooled in the adversary system. The idea that parties might use law designed for peaceful purposes tactically in order to confound their enemies is simply Litigation Tactics 101. The litigator's mission has always included beating plowshares into swords. It is common knowledge both within the legal profession and the academy that some litigators delay litigation to drive up the adversary's expenses; others try to get opposing counsel disqualified for a conflict of interest; many do whatever they can to obstruct the adversary's access to essential information. The novelty of the lawfare theory lies only in the fact that before it was formulated, few people thought specifically of the laws of war as weapons. But the thought comes naturally to lawyers within the adversary system, and it is no surprise that the military theorist who popularized the lawfare theory is a lawyer – at this moment, the number two military lawyer in the US Air Force.[19]

The torture team demolished humanitarian law's protections of GWOT prisoners in three steps. The first step was the decision to use Guantánamo as a prison. In part, Guantánamo was chosen because its remoteness made it ideal from a security standpoint. But the decision was also influenced by the fact that Guantánamo would be outside the jurisdiction of US courts. Eventually, the US Supreme Court concluded that this was not so.[20] But the tactic of choosing Guantánamo and fighting bitterly in court against jurisdiction bought at least two years of freedom from law and law's scrutiny.

The second step was to strip Geneva Convention protections away from the detainees. The task fell to the Office of Legal Counsel, an elite unit of 20 lawyers within the Justice Department whose job is to provide legal advice to the executive branch of government. In a series of memos written in early 2002, OLC lawyers interpreted the Geneva Conventions to apply only to a narrow category of conflicts that excluded the GWOT.[21] The memos were also remarkable for proclaiming that customary international law has no purchase on American law, and for a bizarre argument that Afghanistan is not really a state.[22] Although the State Department's lawyer objected strenuously that the reasoning in these memos was preposterous, he lost his internal battle, and the President issued a finding that the detainees were unprotected by Geneva.[23]

With their Geneva protections gone, the third step was to consider whether the international Convention Against Torture protected the prisoners from harsh interrogation. Here, the OLC did the fundamental work for the torture team, crafting at least six memos that lowered the bar on what counts as torture so that more than a dozen previously prohibited techniques could pass muster.[24] One of the first acts of President Barack Obama was to disavow all the OLC memos on detainee treatment from 9/11 up until Obama's inauguration.

One of them, written by OLC lawyer and Berkeley law professor John Yoo (but issued under the name of then OLC head, Jay S. Bybee), has become famous and iconic because of the extremity of its conclusions and the boldness of its legal arguments.[25] As noted above, the 'Bybee memo' claimed authority for the President to override law in wartime. The memo sketched out the criminal defences that could be available to interrogators accused of torture. Further, the memo defined 'severe pain', a legal criterion for torture, by drawing on a health-care statute's definition of a medical emergency. The health-care statute includes the unsurprising statement that severe pain can be a symptom of a medical emergency. However, in the memo, the statute was reversed so that only the equivalent of a medical emergency counted as severe pain. On the Bybee memo's analysis, that meant that nothing short of the pain associated with organ failure or death was counted as 'severe' – an argument that one critic aptly called 'textual interpretation run amok – not "lawyering as usual," but the work of some bizarre literary deconstructionist'.[26] Even Harvard law professor Jack Goldsmith, who was to work for the Bush administration, describes the memos as 'get-out-of-jail-free cards' for torturers, and believes that the torture memo's 'conclusion [about executive power] has no foundation in prior OLC opinions, or in judicial decisions, or in any other source of law'.[27] This is an amazing assessment, because shortly after Yoo wrote the memo, Goldsmith became the head of the OLC. In his view, the Bybee memo 'lacked the tenor of detachment and caution that usually characterizes OLC work, and that is so central to the legitimacy of OLC.'[28]

In the wake of Abu Ghraib, the OLC repudiated the Bybee memo and replaced it.[29] Indeed, it was Jack Goldsmith, as the head of the OLC, who made this decision. The substitute memo no longer discussed presidential power or criminal defences, and it criticized and repudiated the 'organ failure' definition of severe pain. John Yoo, in his 2006 book *War by Other Means* insists that replacing his memo was a political rather than legal decision, and he points out that the substitute memo still approves all the interrogation tactics he approved.[30] My own assessment is that Yoo is more right than not about this, and that the substitute memo differs more cosmetically than substantively from the Bybee memo.[31] While the lawyer who wrote the substitute memo reportedly had himself waterboarded to see what it felt like,[32] the substitute memo nevertheless presented a novel requirement with no basis in the statutory language, which appears to permit waterboarding.[33]

## 5.4 The jurisprudence of legal advice

Are there lessons that lawyers can learn from this episode? The crucial lesson has to do with the ethical obligations of lawyers in their role as confidential counsellors, or legal advisers, to their clients. Let me set aside for a moment the most fundamental criticism of the Bybee memo, namely, that it enabled torture. The more general criticisms of the memo are two: first, it stretched and distorted the law to reach the outcome that the client wanted; and second, it nowhere indicated that its interpretations were outside the mainstream.[34] The principles behind these criticisms apply to lawyers in private practice as well as government lawyers.

They are noteworthy criticisms, because they highlight the ethical distortion that results when lawyers bring the neutral partisan role morality of courtroom advocates into the counselling role. After all, stretching the law to reach the client's desired outcome, and disguising the fact that stretching is going on, are exactly what advocates do every day in litigation and brief-writing. The major point, then, is that the role of the counsellor and that of the advocate are fundamentally different. In the words of current US ethics rules, the counsellor is supposed to provide clients with independent and candid advice – telling the client what the law requires even if that is not what the client wants.[35] The reason for sharply distinguishing the advocate's pro-client tilt in stating the law from the counsellor's more objective stance is straightforward. In adversary litigation, whatever exaggerations a lawyer introduces in presenting the law can be countered by the lawyer on the other side, and an impartial decision-maker will choose between the arguments. In a counselling situation, it is just the lawyers and their clients, with no adversary and no impartial adjudicator. The institutional setting that justifies an advocate's one-sided partisanship in setting forth the law is absent in the counselling role.[36]

For that reason, the counsellor's rule of thumb should be different from the one-sided partisanship of the advocate. It is to make your description of the law more or less the same as it would be if your client wanted the opposite result from the one you know your client wants.[37] That should be the litmus test of whether your advice is truly independent, rather than result-driven by what you know your client wants. It seems clear that the torture memos failed this test.

What should legal opinion writers do when they believe they have the law right and the mainstream has it wrong? Here, it seems to me, the rule of thumb should be this: if your view of the law is out of the mainstream, but you believe you're right, you have the responsibility to tell your client both those things: what the law, on your own best understanding, requires; *and* the fact that your own best understanding is not one that the legal interpretive community would accept.[38]

The Bybee memo on this argument may have done the first but did not do the second.[39] In not meeting the second condition, Yoo and Bybee can be seen as exceeding the bounds of a legal counsellor by, essentially, rewriting the law. Of course, the change was in a direction the client fervently desired, but here my point of emphasis is somewhat different: it is that a lawyer owes a duty to disclose to the client where his advice deviates from the mainstream – whether or not the client wants to hear this news.

No doubt the ability of OLC lawyers to turn their theories of what the law should be into opinions binding the entire executive branch, makes the role unique. But here too, the lessons generalize to other law practice. That is because *every* lawyer who provides a client with confidential legal opinions on which the client relies is, in effect, a mini-legislator. Literally millions of lawyer–client conversations occur every week, in which a lawyer advises a client on what the client must or must not do to comply with the law. Think of these conversations as individual mosaic tiles. Put the tiles together and the result is what the realists called the 'law in action'. Only a tiny fraction of such legal advice will ever be tested in a court of law, and in this respect the lawyer giving the advice is the highest legal authority the client has. That is why I call the lawyer-advisor a mini-legislator. The case of OLC lawyers, whose client is the mightiest branch of the national government, dramatically demonstrates the point – it is in macrocosm what every lawyer's legal advice on which a client relies represents in microcosm.[40]

The fact that OLC advice was delivered in secret, without an adversarial voice presenting alternative views, in what had become an echo-chamber of like-minded lawyers, is deeply troubling. It is more troubling because we now know, through the investigative efforts of Philippe Sands and Jane Mayer, that the lawyers in the 'War Council' deliberately froze out of the process the military lawyers who were likely to object, and who reacted with outrage when the memo was made public.[41]

But on a lesser scale, the same phenomenon is no less troubling when a tax adviser, or a corporate compliance counsellor, delivers a contestable legal opinion safe in the knowledge that it will never be audited or tested by outside authorities.

In a phrase, that lawyer is creating secret law. No doubt that is inevitable as long as lawyers advise clients about the law in confidential conversations. What makes this prospect bearable, it seems, is that the lawyers offering their secret advice adhere to certain standards. W. Bradley Wendel has described the operative standard as a matter of their fidelity to the law, and I find that a useful way to think about it.[42] Rather than focusing on the meaning of fidelity to law, I wish to offer two theoretical points about lawyers as micro-level lawmakers.

The first is a jurisprudential point. As we all know, the realists were impatient with the law in books.[43] For them, what matters is what officials – and particularly judges – do with the law: for the realists, the only real law is the law 'in action'. Holmes writes that 'prophecies of what the courts will do in fact, and nothing more pretentious, are what I mean by the law'.[44] As for the law in books, Holmes' friend John Chipman Gray went so far as to hold that statutes are not law, merely sources of law. They become law only when the judge applies them.

Later realists broadened and refined the thesis. Llewellyn and Cook pointed out that realism, rightly understood, should look not just at judges, but at other officials as well – sheriffs and police, for example.[45] After all, the judge's order, without police to enforce it, is simply more law on paper. But the underlying theory is the same: official actions, not words in a book, are the law.

Viewed in these terms, my claim about lawyers is that, millions of times a week, the lawyer advising the client is the point where the law in books gets translated into the law in action. When I refer to lawyers in their advisory role as mini-legislators, the reader might regard this as a fundamentally realist point – a deviant strand of realism because I relocate the lawmaking authority from judges and officials to lawyers, but realist nonetheless.

It is in a way. But I see it somewhat differently. There is a well-known objection to the realists' predictive theory of law that prevents us from simply redefining law as the law in action rather than the law in books. The objection, which has been posed by writers as varied in outlook as Felix Cohen, H.L.A. Hart and Lon Fuller, is that the predictive theory, which seems like the plainest common sense to lawyers who analyze the law by asking what courts are likely to do, is perfectly useless from the judge's point of view.[46] If a judge is honestly puzzled about a legal question, it will do no good at all to think, 'The law is whatever I say it is!' You can't figure out what the law is by predicting your own answer to the question 'What's the law here?' The problem is not that you cannot get it right – it's that you cannot get it wrong.

An exactly analogous problem arises for a lawyer advising a client. We outside observers of the legal system may understand that the law in action is very largely the mosaic of thousands of lawyers advising their clients. But if you are the lawyer trying to figure out what advice to give, you cannot simply predict your own behaviour. You must look without, not within. You must look at the sources of law – the law in books. That, it seems to me, is why Wendel's notion of lawyerly fidelity to the law is so important. Without external constraint on powers of invention, there is the dangers of hubris and usurpation – of turning idiosyncratic theories into the law.

My second observation about viewing lawyers as micro-legislators concerns the moral rule of thumb they should follow when they write their secret law. The rule I have in mind comes straight out of Immanuel Kant. I am not referring to Kant's categorical imperative, but to a principle that he called (in his typically understated way) the 'transcendental formula of public law'. It says: 'All actions relating to the rights of other human beings are wrong if their maxim is incompatible with publicity.'[47] Call this the *publicity principle* for short. Kant argued that the publicity principle provides what he labels an 'experiment of pure reason', which political actors perform by asking themselves, roughly: 'Could I get away with this if my action and my reason for performing it were made public?' The test, in Kant's words, will rule out 'a maxim which I may not declare openly without thereby frustrating my own intention'.[48] That certainly encompasses lawyers who give, let us say, far-fetched tax advice, relying on the fact that it will probably not be disclosed. It encompasses the torture lawyers. And it encompasses, I think, all lawyers in the counselling role.

So, by examining the work of the OLC lawyers, we arrive at three rules of thumb for lawyers in their advisory role: asking whether your legal opinion would be the same if your client wanted the opposite result from the one you know your client wants; offering both your best interpretation of the law and an honest statement of where it deviates from mainstream understandings; and the publicity principle.

## 5.5 Lawyers talking torture

At this point, I want to resume the story of the lawyers in the 'war on terrorism'. John Yoo wrote the famous torture memo in August 2002. Two months later, a group of intelligence officers met in Guantánamo to discuss interrogation techniques. Present at the meeting were two lawyers – the Staff Judge Advocate to the task force commander at Guantánamo, and the chief counsel to the CIA's counter-terrorism centre.

For obvious reasons, we very seldom find out what lawyers say to clients in confidential meetings. This one is an exception. Detailed minutes of the meeting exist, and in summer 2008 a US Senator released those minutes.[49] They offer a rare window into the legal counselling process. And they are, as we shall see, disturbing.

Before proceeding to discuss them, I wish to note that one of the lawyers participating in the meeting – the CIA lawyer – has protested that he did not say what the minutes report him as saying.[50] I will nevertheless use the minutes, for three reasons. First, none of the other participants in the meeting has denied the veracity of the minutes. Second, the lawyer's protest came in a letter written six years after the meeting. Common sense suggests that no one, even with the best faith in the world, can be certain about what they did *not* say in a meeting six years earlier. Third, a careful reading of the lawyer's letter of protest shows that he does not actually deny most of the things attributed to him in the minutes. Because of his protest, however, I will refrain from using the names of the participants in the meeting, instead identifying them by their roles ('Staff Judge Advocate', 'CIA lawyer').

For example, we find the Staff Judge Advocate saying to the group: 'We may need to curb the harsher operations while the [International Red Cross] is around. It is better not to expose them to any controversial techniques.' At that point, the CIA lawyer helpfully adds that: 'In the past when the [Red Cross] has made a big deal about certain detainees, the [Defense Department] has "moved" them away.'

He then goes on to provide a brief exposition of the law against torture. I quote: 'torture has been prohibited under international law, but the language of the statutes is written vaguely. Severe mental and physical pain is prohibited. The mental part is explained as poorly as the physical.'

Pause for a moment. So far, it seems to me, the CIA lawyer is on solid ground. He has correctly stated the legal test, and his complaints about vagueness are entirely fair. He continues:

> Severe physical pain [is] described as anything causing permanent physical damage to major organs or body parts. Mental torture [is] described as anything leading to permanent, profound damage to the senses or personality.

Pause again. Here, we find him paraphrasing the Bybee memo almost verbatim, as though it is the actual wording of the statute. Then comes the money line, as he adds his own gloss to the Bybee memo's analysis: 'It is basically subject to perception. If the detainee dies you're doing it wrong.'[51]

Later, when asked about waterboarding, the CIA lawyer explains: 'If a well-trained individual is used to perform this technique it can feel like you're drowning. The lymphatic system will react as if you're suffocating, but your body will not cease to function.' Then he moves to other techniques: 'It is very effective to identify phobias and use them (i.e. insects, snakes, claustrophobia).' The Staff Judge Advocate asks about 'imminent threats of death' – a phrase that may have stuck in her mind because the US torture statute singles it out as a form of mental torture. And the CIA lawyer replies that it should be handled on a case-by-case basis. But then he adds: 'Mock executions don't work as well as friendly approaches, like letting someone write a letter home, or providing them with an extra book.'

At this point one of the intelligence officers pipes up: 'I like the part about ambient noise.'[52] Soon after that, the meeting ends. This incredible script largely speaks for itself; but a few remarks are useful.

First, notice the way in which the OLC torture memo percolated down through the CIA counter-terrorism counsel in Guantánamo, to the Judge Advocate who would advise the commander, to the intelligence officers who, as it happens, would very shortly start torturing a detainee named Mohammed Al Qahtani for eight weeks. The CIA counsel reproduced the Bybee memo's analysis of severe pain and suffering with fair accuracy, but in his telling it develops into 'anything goes as long as the detainee doesn't die'. A few moments' thought will show that 'anything goes as long as the detainee doesn't die' is the operational version of the Bybee memo's 'organ failure or death' test of torture. Ideas have consequences. Lawyers may believe that they bear no moral responsibility for what use their advice is put to, but even if you are not interested in moral responsibility, moral responsibility is interested in you.

Second, from the minutes it seems rather clear that the two lawyers in the room have internalized the outlook of their clients: the Staff Judge Advocate and the CIA lawyer frankly discuss methods for evading Red Cross inspectors; the CIA lawyer discusses with an undertaker's equanimity waterboarding, snakes and mock executions. In the minutes these threats seem to be all on a par with rapport-building techniques such as giving detainees a book to read. Although he is a lawyer and not an interrogator, the CIA counsel offers recommendations about which tactics are most effective (which is, of course, *not* legal advice). If their clients were looking for the two lawyers to provide an independent perspective, then they have come to the wrong lawyers.

Three weeks later, a criminal investigator in the Pentagon read these minutes. He quickly emailed another official, 'This looks like the kinds of stuff Congressional hearings are made of'[53] – a rather prescient comment, given that the minutes were released at a Congressional hearing. He flagged the Judge Advocate's comments about cover-ups and the CIA lawyer's about torture, and described them as 'beyond the bounds of legal propriety'. Concerning the comments about how the lymphatic system reacts to waterboarding, he wrote, 'would in my opinion shock the conscience of any legal body'. And he concludes: 'Someone needs to be considering how history will look back at this.'

The author of this email is a career criminal investigator, not a lawyer, but his choice of words make clear that he is as well trained in the legal tests of permissible interrogation as any lawyer. In any event, it seems that his outsider's perspective enabled him to perceive what the Staff Judge Advocate and CIA lawyer apparently could not: that their professional independence had been compromised through excessive identification with the goals and aims of their clients.

Wasserstrom feared that lawyers inhabit a simplified moral world – one that is often amoral and occasionally immoral.[54] He believed that this phenomenon results from the neutral-partisan role morality of lawyers.[55] However, in the Bybee memo and the minutes of the 2002 intelligence officer meeting at Guantánamo, we see something a bit different from Wassertrom's concern with role morality. While partisanship clearly has its place, the simplified moral world of the partisan advocate does not belong in the counsellor's role. For lawyers acting as counsellors conceiving the role as a partisan advocate is too likely to distort the lawyer's judgement and blur the line between lawyer and client. The problem is the confusion of roles, not the advocate's role itself.

## 5.6 The rule of law in the world-view of the Guantánamo Defence Bar

At this point, I turn to the lawyers who represented detainees at Guantánamo. The detainees have been represented by both civilian and military lawyers. The 500 or so civilian lawyers include professional public-interest lawyers as well as hundreds of volunteers from large American law firms, many of whom consider it a badge of honour to represent Guantánamo inmates seeking *habeas corpus*. One of my colleagues, who studies the American criminal justice system, finds it frustrating that there is so much enthusiasm and pro bono legal work for the Guantánamo cases and so little for the tens of thousands of inmates enduring worse conditions in American prisons.

The fact is that Guantánamo has taken on significance far greater than itself, precisely because of the government's legal strategy in creating it as a law-free zone.[56] Symbolically, the legal profession of a liberal-democratic state – a *Rechtsstaat* – cannot tolerate the existence of a state-created law-free zone. If the state can create one, the thought runs, then a *Rechtsstaat* is at its core nothing more than a hollow mocking promise of a system that deserves our moral and political allegiance. It is this threat to the *Rechtsstaat* that seemed to have motivated lawyers to represent Guantánamo inmates. In doing so the legal profession was trying to show that it is not the priesthood of a false god.

To be sure, all this loads an enormous amount of symbolic freight onto Guantánamo – perhaps more than it deserves. I have interviewed a dozen of the Guantánamo defenders and these interviews convince me that all conceive what is at stake in Guantánamo in the elevated terms just described: somehow, their professional identity is deeply bound up with Guantánamo. Guantánamo is more than a prison camp – in the eyes of the defence lawyers, it is a standing affront to the political order that gives their profession meaning.[57] That, more than any political view about the Bush administration or the detainees, is what drives so many lawyers to volunteer their time and energy to represent the prisoners.

One of the most remarkable phenomena is the role of military lawyers representing detainees, and I want to conclude by discussing them. The military lawyers, called 'judge advocates' and known as JAGs, have been appointed to defend the detainees charged with war crimes before military commissions. The JAG defenders are mostly political conservatives (as, indeed, most US military officers are according to survey data). David Hicks' lawyer Dan Mori described himself to me as a 'pretty conservative guy'. Navy Cmdr. William Kuebler told a reporter that he has never voted for a Democrat in his life, and a fellow officer described him by saying 'Take the average conservative guy in the street and multiply that by a million.'[58]

And yet the JAG defenders have turned out to be among the fieriest critics of the military commissions and the government that created them. Consider a closing argument made in June 2008 by Major David Frakt, representing Mohammad Jawad, a teenage prisoner who had been subjected to the 'frequent flyer' programme of intense sleep deprivation. Maj. Frakt spoke bitterly about 'the civilian political appointees of this administration', who 'intentionally cut out the real experts on the law of armed conflict, the uniformed military lawyers, the JAGs ... for fear that their devotion to the Geneva Conventions might pose an obstacle to their intended course of action'.[59] He described the torture memos as 'now disgraced, disavowed, and relegated to the scrapheap of history where they belong'.[60] He praised by name the handful of lawyers within the administration and the military who opposed the strategy of detainee abuse. And then, he described the 'enablers of torture'[61] as war criminals of the 'home-grown variety'.[62] He then listed nine of them by name: the Vice President and Secretary of Defense of the United States, and seven lawyers: three from the OLC; two from the Defense Department; the Vice President's counsel; and the former Attorney General of the United States.[63] These are remarkable accusations from a major in the US Air Force, voiced in a military court to a military judge.

In the same vein, Marine Corps Major Dan Mori, David Hicks' lawyer, who made eight visits to Australia, gave passionate speeches against the fairness of the military commissions and Hicks' treatment. Mori and his civilian co-counsel Joshua Dratel had concluded that the only way Hicks would ever get out of Guantánamo would be through political pressure on the Australian government to cut a deal, and Mori gave his speeches to increase that pressure. Furthermore, as Dratel explained to me, both of the lawyers felt it necessary 'to put David in a positive light in Australia. We knew it was likely that he would serve some time there, and we worried about how the Australians would view him when he returned in custody. We needed to help his re-entry to Australia.'[64] In other words, Mori and Dratel were thinking about the case and their client in the way a sophisticated white-collar defender does.

Nevertheless, Dan Mori unexpectedly found himself threatened by the prosecutor because of his Australian speeches. Under US military law, it is a criminal offence for an officer to speak contemptuously about the civilian leadership of the country. Suddenly, Mori found himself face to face with an intense conflict between his role as a military officer, sworn to duty to his government, and his role as a defence lawyer who, in the famous words of Lord Brougham, must 'separate[e] the duty of a patriot from that of an advocate, [and] go on reckless of consequences'.[65] Of course, if military defenders could be stopped from criticizing the military commissions by threat of court martial, they would all face a disabling conflict of interest, and none of them could ethically represent detainees. Sensing the stakes, Mori filed a motion to have the prosecutor disqualified for improperly coercing a defence lawyer. The issue was never resolved because the Hicks case was successfully plea-bargained before the judge ruled on Mori's motion.[66]

In a parallel case, Air Force Major Yvonne Bradley, representing Binyam Mohammed, was given a direct order by a military judge who outranked her to proceed at a hearing when she believed she had a disabling conflict of interest. Like Mori, her role as a lawyer and her role as an officer were on a collision course. Bradley resolved the conflict in a startling way: she invoked her own right against self-incrimination, on the theory that if she disobeyed the order she would face charges, but if she obeyed it she would betray her ethics as a lawyer.[67]

In both Bradley's case and Mori's, we can see something very interesting and important. Faced with a conflict between their role as officers and their role as lawyers, it would seem that Mori and Bradley in effect opted for their role as lawyers. Or so I thought when I interviewed them.

Mori, however, doesn't see it that way. When I asked him whether he perceived a role conflict, he replied: 'I didn't have any conflict. Saying someone deserves a fair trial is what being an American and a military officer is all about.'[68] Although at the time I thought the role conflict was greater than Mori believed, on reflection it now seems that Mori had in mind exactly the threat to the *Rechtsstaat* described above – the sense among many lawyers that Guantánamo poses a standing challenge to the rule-of-law values that in their eyes define the constitutional order. As Major Frakt put it in the speech I quoted previously:

> America is a nation founded on a reverence for the rule of law. We should never forget that when we take an oath to enlist or be commissioned as an officer in the United States Armed Forces, we do not swear to defend the United States, we swear 'to support and defend the Constitution of the United States against all enemies, foreign and domestic'.[69]

There is no role conflict because, in the eyes of these military lawyers, the country they swore to defend as officers is defined by the rule of law to which their profession as lawyers commits them.

This defence of the rule of law is a significant lesson from the lawyers in the 'war on terrorism'. Earlier, I focused on the integrity of the role of legal advisor and counsellor, its differences from the role of advocate, and the threat that extreme partisanship poses to it. When it comes to the defence lawyers, their basic role is that of partisan advocates, and the conflict is between that role and others they might occupy – those of military officer or patriotic American. They resolve the conflict by identifying their country with its constitution, the constitution with the rule of law, and their own identities – both as soldiers and as lawyers – with being guardians of the rule of law. Some might criticize this chain of identifications as being overly simplistic, and political philosophers may dispute the thought that political community can be reduced to the single value of legality.

Yet it seems to me importantly true that the *Rechtsstaat* represents a distinctive and worthy political order. Further, it is importantly true that lawyers play a constitutive role in defining and maintaining the *Rechtsstaat*. Even if the equation of country with constitution and constitution with legality is untrue, it is a noble lie in something very close to Plato's sense: a myth that defines the legal profession as a distinctive calling. If we are looking for the source of moral steadfastness in the legal profession, we could do worse than start here.

# Notes

1 For convenience, I will occasionally use the military abbreviation 'GWOT' (pronounced 'jee-wot'). In 2009, the administration of President Barack Obama abandoned the use of the 'war on terrorism' terminology, although it remains to be seen whether the new President has also abandoned the legal doctrines based on the theory that the struggle with Al Qaeda is an armed conflict. I wrote this paper as the keynote address to the Third International Legal Ethics Conference, held on the Gold Coast, Australia on 14 July 2008. Although I have rewritten the paper somewhat, I have retained the style of the spoken address.

2 I have discussed at greater length the ethical difficulties facing these lawyers in D. Luban, 'Lawfare and legal ethics in Guantánamo', *Stanford Law Review*, 2008, vol. 60, 1981.

3 R. Wasserstrom, 'Lawyers as professionals: Some moral issues', *Human Rights*, 1975, vol. 5, 18.

4 Ibid., p. 2.

5 T. Macaulay, 'Macaulay's essay on Bacon', in G. Trevelyan (ed.), *The Works of Lord Macaulay*, 6th edn, London: Longman, Green and Co, 1866, p. 163.

6 A. Goldman, *The Moral Foundations of Professional Ethics*, Lanham, NJ: Rowman & Littlefield, 1980; G. Postema, 'Moral responsibility in professional ethics', *New York University Law Review*, 1980, vol. 55, 63; D. Luban, *Lawyers and Justice: An Ethical Study*, Princeton, NJ: Princeton University Press, 1988.

7 P. Sands, *Torture Team: Rumsfeld's Memo and the Betrayal of American Values*, New York: Palgrave Macmillan, 2008.

8 Shortly after Sands' book appeared, Jane Mayer published a magnificent book about US torture, J. Mayer, *The Dark Side: The Inside Story of How the War on Terror Turned into a War on American Ideals*, New York: Doubleday, 2008.

9 Sands, *Torture Team*, pp. xii–xiv.

10 J. Goldsmith, *The Terror Presidency: Law and Judgment Inside the Bush Administration*, New York: Norton, 2007, pp. 22–23.

11 Sands, *Torture Team*, p. 31.

12 Ibid., pp. 43–48.

13 Notably, the 1 August 2002 'torture memorandum', written by John Yoo and signed by Jay Bybee, argued for such executive predominance. Readily available on the internet, it is reprinted in K. Greenberg (ed.), *The Torture Debate in America*, New York: Cambridge University Press, 2006, as well as in D. Cole (ed.), *The Torture Memos*, New York: New Press, 2009. I cite to the Greenberg volume, where the arguments on executive power appear on pp. 344–51.

14 Ibid., p. 172.

15 On these positions as based in lawfare see Luban, 'Lawfare and legal ethics in Guantánamo', pp. 2020–21.

16 Goldsmith, *The Terror Presidency*, pp. 58–63. The lawfare idea also promotes the idea that the United States can use law as its own weapon. The National Defense Strategy warned that 'Our strength as a nation state will continue to be challenged by those who employ a strategy of the weak using international fora, judicial processes, and terrorism,' lumping international fora and judicial processes together with terrorism, and identifying all of them as a form of strategy. The National Defense Strategy of the United States of America may be found at www.globalsecurity.org/military/library/policy/dod/nds-usa_mar2005_ib.htm.

17 Sands, *The Torture Team*, p. 88.

18 Steven G. Bradbury, Deputy Assistant Attorney General, 'Memorandum for the Files *Re: Status of Certain OLC Opinions Issued in the Aftermath of the Terrorist Attacks of September 11, 2001*', 15 January 2009, available at www.justice.gov/olc/docs/memostatusolcopinions 01152009.pdf.

19 Major General Charles J. Dunlap, Jr has been widely credited with populizing the term 'lawfare' in a 2001 paper. C. Dunlap Jr, 'Law and military interventions: Preserving humanitarian values in 21st century conflicts', Cambridge: CARR Centre for Human Rights and Policy, Harvard Kennedy School, 2001. Available at www.hks.harvard. edu/cchrp/Web%20Working%20Papers/Use%20of%20Force/Dunlap2001.pdf. (accessed 26 June 2009). On Dunlap and lawfare see T. Yin 'Boumediene and lawfare', *University of Richmond Law Review*, 2009, vol. 43, 865, p. 868.

20 *Rasul v Bush*, 542 U.S. 466 (2004).

21 These and other crucial legal memoranda and reports are reproduced in K. Greenberg and J. Dratel (eds), *The Torture Papers: The Road to Abu Ghraib*, New York: Cambridge University Press, 2005. See Memo 4, pp. 38–79 (John Yoo to William J. Haynes II, 9 January 2002); Memo 6, pp. 81–117 (Jay S. Bybee to Alberto R. Gonzales, 22 January 2002); and Memo 12, pp. 136–43 (Jay S. Bybee to Alberto R. Gonzales, 7 February 2002).

22 Memo 4 (Yoo to Haynes), pp. 53–58, 71–76.

23 See Memo from William Howard Taft IV to John Yoo, 11 January 2002. Available at www.cartoonbank.com/newyorker/slideshows/01TaftMemo.pdf (accessed 7 September 2009); Memo from George W. Bush to the Vice President et al., 7 February 2002, in Greenberg and Dratel, *The Torture Papers*, pp. 134–35.

24 All these memoranda are reprinted and analyzed in Cole, *The Torture Memos*. The OLC subsequently withdrew all the memos that had not already been withdrawn by the Bush administration. David J. Barron, Acting Assistant Attorney General, 'Withdrawal of Office of Legal Counsel CIA Interrogation Memos', 15 April 2009, available at www.justice.gov/olc/2009/withdrawalofficelegalcounsel.pdf.

25 The memo appears as Memo 14 in K. Greenberg and J. Dratel, *The Torture Papers*, pp. 172–217. On the controversy triggered by the memo see for example J. Angell 'Ethic, torture, and the marginal memoranda at the DOJ Office of Legal Counsel', *Georgetown Journal of Legal Ethics*, 2005, vol. 18, 557; J. Radack, 'Tortured legal ethics: The role of the government advisor in the War on Terrorism', *University of Colorado Law Review*, 2006, vol. 77, 1; W. Wendell, 'Legal ethics and the separation of law and morals', *Cornell Law Review*, 2005, vol. 91, 61; J. Waldron 'Torture and positive law: Jurisprudence for the White House', *Columbia Law Review*, 2005, vol. 105, 1681.

26 P. Brooks, 'The plain meaning of torture?', *Slate*, 9 February 2005.

27 Goldsmith, *The Terror Presidency*, pp. 97, 149.

28 Ibid., p. 149.

29 The replacement ('Levin') memo may be found in K. Greenberg (ed.), *The Torture Debate in America*, New York: Cambridge University Press, 2006, pp. 361–76, as well as on the Office of Legal Counsel website, available at www.usdoj.gov/olc/18usc23402340a2.htm (accessed 7 September 2009). Abu Ghraib is, of course, a prison in Iraq where US troops tortured and humiliated Iraqi captives; it was subject to worldwide notoriety after photos of the abuse became public in April 2004.

30 J. Yoo, *War by Other Means: An Insider's Account of the War on Terror*, New York: Atlantic Monthly Press, 2006, pp. 182–83. See the Levin memo, footnote 8, in Greenberg, *The Torture Debate in America*, p. 362.

31 So I have argued in D. Luban, 'Liberalism, torture, and the ticking bomb', in Greenberg, *The Torture Debate in America*, p. 72; Luban, *Legal Ethics and Human Dignity*, pp. 180–82.

32 Waterboarding is a form of water torture in which water is poured through a cloth covering the victim's nose and mouth; it stops before the victim drowns, but the experience of drowning begins in the first few seconds.

33 Luban, *Legal Ethics and Human Dignity*, pp. 181–82. The first to note this point is M. Lederman, 'Yes, it's a no-brainer: Waterboarding *is* torture', Balkanization blog, 28 October 2006. Available at http://balkin.blogspot.com/2006/10/yes-its-no-brainer-waterboarding-is.html (accessed 7 September 2009).

34 Luban, *Legal Ethics and Human Dignity*, pp. 194–200; see also Angell 'Ethic, torture, and the marginal memoranda'; Radack, 'Tortured legal ethics'.
35 ABA Model Rules of Professional Conduct, Rule 2.1. Online. Available at www. abanet.org/cpr/mrpc/rule_2_1.html (accessed 7 September 2009). See Comment [1], www.abanet.org/cpr/mrpc/rule_2_1_comm.html (accessed 7 September 2009).
36 See Luban, *Legal Ethics and Human Dignity*, pp. 153–57, 201–3.
37 Ibid., p. 198.
38 Ibid., p. 199.
39 Indeed, in a second Bybee memo of 1 August 2002, which approved a grim list of CIA interrogation techniques – the list included waterboarding and sleep deprivation of up to 180 consecutive hours – the authors stated, 'We wish to emphasize that this is our best reading of the law.' Jay S. Bybee, 'Memorandum for John Rizzo, Acting General Counsel of the Central Intelligence Agency, Interrogation of al Qaeda Agent', 1 August 2002, p. 18, available at www.washingtonpost.com/wp-srv/nation/pdf/OfficeofLegalCounsel_Aug2Memo_041609.pdf (accessed 3 February 2010). This memo is reprinted in Cole, *The Torture Memos*.
40 On this point, see ibid., pp. 131–61.
41 See especially Mayer, *The Dark Side*, pp. 213–37. See also the letters from the Judge Advocate Generals of the US Army, Navy, and Air Force, reproduced in Greenberg, *The Torture Debate in America*, pp. 377–91.
42 W. Wendel, 'Professionalism as interpretation', *Northwestern University Law Review*, 2005, vol. 3, 99.
43 K. Llewellyn 'Some realism about realism', *Harvard Law Review*, 1931, vol. 44, 1221.
44 O. Holmes Jr, 'The path of the law', *Harvard Law Review*, 1897, vol. 10, 461.
45 K. Llewellyn, 'A realistic jurisprudence – the next step', *Columbia Law Review*, 1930, vol. 30, 431, p. 450 n. 16; W. Cook, '"Substance" and "procedure" in the conflict of laws', *Yale Law Journal*, 1933, vol. 42, 333, p. 348.
46 L. Fuller, *The Law in Quest of Itself*, Chicago: Foundation Press, 1940, pp. 94–95; H.L.A. Hart, *The Concept of Law*, Oxford: Clarendon, 1964, p. 10; F. Cohen, 'The problems of a functional jurisprudence', *Modern Law Review*, 1937, vol. 1, 5, p. 17. See also R. Summers, *Instrumentalism and American Legal Theory*, New York: Cornell University Press, 1982, pp. 101–15; Y. Rogat, 'The judge as spectator', *University of Chicago Law Review*, 1964, vol. 31, 213, pp. 248–49; Luban, *Lawyers and Justice*, pp. 22–24.
47 I. Kant, 'Perpetual peace: A philosophical sketch', in H. Reiss (ed.), *Kant's Political Writings*, Cambridge: Cambridge University Press, 1970, p. 126. I have slightly altered the translation. For analysis and discussion, see D. Luban, 'The publicity principle', in R. Goodin (ed.), *Theories of Institutional Design*, Cambridge: Cambridge University Press, 1995, pp. 154–98.
48 Ibid.
49 The document is available at http://levin.senate.gov/newsroom/supporting/2008/Documents.SASC.061708.pdf, Tab 7 (accessed 7 September 2009). All quotations are from this document.
50 Kara Rowland, 'Lawyer's letter counters torture report', *Washington Times*, May 4, 2009, available at www.washingtontimes.com/news/2009/may/04/lawyers-letter-counters-torture-report/ (accessed 3 February 2010). I have a PDF copy of the lawyer's letter on file.
51 I note that the CIA lawyer denies that he said that it is basically subject to perception. He writes (in the letter referred to earlier):

> 'I also emphasized that the requirements of the statute are not, and cannot be, a matter for individual perception. The question of whether specific conduct would be torture, for example, and therefore criminal under the anti-torture statute cannot depend upon whether any particular officer believes that the proposed conduct would or would not produce "severe pain or suffering" or, instead, would

simply produce some lesser degree of discomfort. In light of the importance of the issue, CIA sought an authoritative statement of Federal law from the Department of Justice, whose Office of Legal Counsel provides the legal advice which is binding upon all Federal departments, agencies, and employees. We did so specifically to *avoid* having the anti-torture statute misinterpreted as in any way subject to an individual's particular perception.'

This paragraph deserves careful reflection. As we know, the Bybee memo's advice is that pain becomes 'severe' when it is 'equivalent in intensity to the pain accompanying serious physical injury, such as organ failure, impairment of bodily function, or even death.' Bybee memo, in Greenberg, *The Torture Debate in America*, p. 317. Under this test, which the CIA lawyer apparently explained to the meeting – because the minute-taker accurately summarizes it – an interrogator must determine whether the pain has reached this point. Such judgement is 'subject to perception' in the sense that no objective way of carrying out this comparison exists. The interrogator must adjudge how much pain the victim is feeling, guess what the pain of organ failure or death feels like, and match the two. The minute-taker who summarized this test as 'subject to perception' has not misspoken. And the CIA lawyer, who is certain that he did not use the phrase 'subject to perception', *is* certain that he explained the OLC's view, which is hard to understand any other way.

52  Prisoners were frequently bombarded with noise: ear-splitting rock music, round-the-clock hissing sounds, and so on.
53  Mark Fallon quoted in J. Warrick, 'CIA played larger role in advising Pentagon: Harsh interrogation methods defended', *Washington Post*, 18 June 2008 available at wwwwa-shingtonpost.com/wp-dyn/content/article/2008/06/17/AR200806170286.html?hpid=topnews (accessed 30 September 2009).
54  Wasserstrom, 'Lawyers as professionals', p. 8.
55  Ibid., pp. 12–15.
56  See for example, M. Ratner, 'Guantánamo and the lawyer as hero: 500 and counting', *Northeastern University Law Journal*, 2009, vol. 1, pp. 6–7.
57  D. Luban, 'Lawfare and legal ethics in Guantánamo'.
58  W. Glaberson, 'An unlikely antagonist in detainee's corner', *New York Times*, 19 June 2008.
59  D. Frakt, 'Closing argument at Guantanamo: The torture of Mohammed Jawad', *Harvard Human Rights Journal*, 2009, vol. 22. p. 10. Outraged letters from the four TJAGs (heads of the JAG Corps) when they learned after the fact about the Bybee memo are reprinted in Greenberg, *The Torture Debate in America*, pp. 377–91.
60  Frakt, 'Closing argument at Guantanamo', p. 11.
61  Ibid., p. 19.
62  Ibid.
63  Ibid.
64  Luban, 'Lawfare and legal ethics in Guantánamo', p. 2016.
65  2 *Trial of Queen Caroline* 8 (J. Nightingale ed., J. Robins & Co., Albion Press, 1820–21).
66  Luban, 'Lawfare and legal ethics in Guantánamo', pp. 2014–18. For a vigorous critique of my claim of role conflict, see C. Dunlap Jr and L. Letendre, 'Military lawyering and professional independence in the war on terror: A response to David Luban', *Stanford Law Review*, 2008, vol. 61, 417, pp. 438–40.
67  I have described this incident in Luban, 'Lawfare and legal ethics in Guantánamo', pp. 2007–14. For a fuller description, see C. Stafford Smith, *Eight O'Clock Ferry to the Windward Side*, New York: Nation Books, 2007, pp. 124–27.
68  Ibid., p. 2004.
69  Frakt, 'Closing argument at Guantanamo', p. 14.

# 6 Legal ethics in a post-Westphalian world: building the international rule of law and other tasks

*Charles Sampford*

## 6.1 Introduction

> The time has come for mankind to make the rule of law in international affairs as normal as it is now in domestic affairs. Of course the structure of such law must be patiently built, stone by stone. The cost will be a great deal of hard work, both in and out of government particularly in the universities of the world. Plainly one foundation stone of this structure is the International Court of Justice ... [and] the obligatory jurisdiction of that Court ... One final thought on rule of law between nations: we will all have to remind ourselves that under this system of law one will sometimes lose as well as win. But ... if an international controversy leads to armed conflict, everyone loses.
>
> President Dwight D. Eisenhower[1]

Those who believe that good governance should start at home and extend abroad will easily agree but may be surprised at the source of the quote and be more optimistic about its achievement. In this chapter, I argue that the emergence of strong sovereign states after the Treaty of Westphalia turned two of the most cosmopolitan professions, the law and the military, into the least cosmopolitan. Sovereign states determined the content of the law within their borders – including what elements of ecclesiastical law, law merchant and international law applied. Similarly, states sought to ensure that all military force was at their disposal in national armies. The erosion of sovereignty in a post-Westphalian world may significantly reverse this process.

The erosion of sovereignty is likely to have profound consequences for the legal profession and the ethics of how, and for what ends, it is practised. Lawyers have played a major role in the civilization of sovereign states through the articulation and institutionalization of key governance values – starting with the rule of law. An increasingly global profession must take on similar tasks – and may find unexpected allies within the profession of arms. This chapter reviews the concept of an international rule of law and its relationship with domestic conceptions, and outlines the task of building the international rule of law and the role that lawyers can and should play in it.[2]

## 6.2 Westphalian states and two cosmopolitan professions

### 6.2.1 Pepo and Bologna

The gradual evolution of the institutions that gave rise to universities means that there is no precise date for when particular institutions became 'universities' and which can claim the mantle of the 'first'.[3] Some ancient bodies might claim as much right to call themselves 'universities' as the eleventh- and twelfth-century European centres of learning in Bologna, Paris and Oxford. China's Nanjing (c. 200), Morocco's Al-karouine (859) and Egypt's Al Azar (975) could claim to be the oldest continuing universities, while India's Odantapuri (c. 550 BC to c. 1040 AD) and Jalandhar (c. 450 BC to 1193 AD) have respectable claim to be the earliest institutions that could be called universities. Although predated by a medical school at Salerno, the institution with the claim to be the first university in Europe is the University of Bologna, and there is evidence of law lectures being given by the monk Pepo in 1076.[4] Universities and university law teaching thus predated the modern state by at least five centuries. They were originally among the most cosmopolitan of institutions.

The students of the time learnt Roman Law, Canon Law and, as it developed, the Law Merchant.[5] Such law was not made by territorial sovereigns but was developed by jurists, priests and traders, and covered most of Western Europe. Indeed, the re-emergence of international trade involved issues which the existing local laws were not equipped to address but which the preserved Roman law could. Accordingly, the legal education gained by students at Bologna, and later Paris, Oxford and other mediaeval universities, allowed them to work for any of the Princes of Western Europe and to argue in many courts – making the profession of law highly cosmopolitan. Indeed, most professions were cosmopolitan. This applied not only to medicine and law but also the profession of arms, where there was a claimed transnational affinity between knights and a code of chivalry setting out how one could and could not fight. Most soldiers did not fight directly for kings but for local lords or 'captains' of 'military bands' or 'military companies'. They might be part of armies organized by kings. But they might also fight against kings or in civil wars – or for foreign princes as individuals or groups who would fight in return for land or money.

However, the rise of strong sovereign states in the seventeenth century turned these two most cosmopolitan professions into two of the least cosmopolitan. Those who like a convenient date look to the Treaty of Westphalia in 1648, which provided the basis for state sovereignty and was reflected in later treaties such as the Treaty of Paris 1763 and Treaty of Versailles 1919. These transitions arguably commenced long before Westphalia and were never fully completed 300 years later when the United Nations (UN) Charter enshrined key aspects of the Westphalian system but also incorporated a recognition of rights that created the potential for the undermining of Westphalian sovereignty.[6]

### 6.2.2 The legal profession

The claim of sovereign states to determine the content of the law within their borders – including which, if any, ecclesiastical laws, what form of economic regulation and what, if any, international law were to apply – meant that those who sought to study law would study the law of a particular sovereign state. Admission to practice was determined by domestic institutions – courts, inns of court and various forms of apprenticeship and professional examination. In common law countries, universities were not initially engaged in educating lawyers for such practice. English law was not even taught at Oxford until 1758. However, after six centuries, even Oxford came around to teaching primarily English laws.

Two other developments profoundly affected the law and lawyering:

1.   The rise of printing, which allowed legislation and case law to be disseminated more widely and in far greater detail than had ever been possible.
2.   The decline of feudal land tenure, the gradual decline in the importance of land in European economies and the extension of the market led to the idea that landholding typically involved an 'owner' with sole dominion over it.[7]

Over some 300 years, these developments came to be seen as so entrenched that they were perceived to be natural, and the legal pluralism of pre-Westphalian Europe seemed contrary to the very nature of law. However, the last decade and a half has seen the emergence of trends that involve profound challenges to the nature of law in Westphalian sovereign states. The challenges to sovereignty include the rise of transnational law – including international law, free-trade treaties, the extra territorial reach of US law and the development of universal jurisdiction.

The rise of international and transnational organizations in the public, corporate and voluntary sectors has also increased the move towards pluralism. The growth of the United Nations and the other pillars of the UN system (the International Monetary Fund and World Bank) have led to a profusion of international organizations for global public purposes. The International Court of Justice (ICJ), the International Criminal Court (ICC) and now the World Trade Organization (WTO) are international judicial institutions capable of enforcing an increasing volume of international law, and the growth of universal jurisdiction allows domestic courts to apply international law in certain circumstances. While the WTO has real 'teeth', the growth of transnational supply chains and global corporations has led to calls to establish internationally acceptable norms to bind corporations to international human rights norms. In response to the growth of corporations and their increased recognition as actors under public international law, the UN established the Global Compact.[8] The Global Compact is a corporate social responsibility scheme where corporations agree to be bound by ten principles in return for the perception of being a good corporate citizen. This scheme is the largest corporate citizenship in the world, with approximately

40,000 stakeholders across 100 nations.[9] Despite the current limitations on the enforcement of international law, states have created regulatory vehicles to hold non-state actors accountable for unethical business practices. The Organization for Economic Cooperation and Development (OECD) Guidelines, for example, provide voluntary guidance for corporations in their international affairs and are enforced by member states.[10] While these guidelines have limited impact on many corporations to which those guidelines are directed, they do represent moves by states to impose universal standards across jurisdictions.[11] There is no barrier to OECD member states agreeing to implement similar ethical guidelines for the way in which lawyers conduct themselves in international affairs, and they should be encouraged to do so.

In the not-for-profit sector, the growth of international and transnational non-governmental organizations (NGOs) from the Red Cross to Greenpeace and Transparency International has given such NGOs a larger place in the global community than in most sovereign states. By way of contrast, institutionalized religion has a more limited place than in pre-Westphalian Europe, despite attempts by fundamentalists in the 'Middle East' and 'Mid-West' whose aspirations for states dominated by particular religions are distinctly pre-Westphalian.[12]

More generally, the challenges of globalization, involving the movement of people, goods, services and ideas across boundaries, have increased the growth of a global community. One important aspect of this is the emergence of the internet, which has created substantial difficulties for states that desire to regulate their citizens' access to information.[13]

The issue of sovereignty has been substantially challenged by the environmental problems facing the global community. Arguably, the greater ease of movement of organisms that damage flora, fauna and people, and the unintended effects on the environment of human activity, are leading to an awareness that the land is, once again, too important to be the subject of the private dominion of individual citizens. The perception that the environment should be regarded as a global issue arguably gained traction with the Convention on Climate Change and has obtained increased recognition with the Kyoto Protocol.[14] The Kyoto Protocol 'creates significant responsibilities for the participating countries, and brings together many of the most industrialized countries of the world to limit gas emissions in an unprecedented way'.[15]

Most of these trends will intensify over the next few decades and could lead to fundamental changes to the nature, practice, structure and content of law over the professional lifetimes of those students we are currently teaching. By the time students entering law schools in 2010 retire in the mid-twenty-first century, the law and the legal profession may be as different from its Westphalian sovereign paradigm as that paradigm was to the world of Pepo's students.

### 6.2.3 *The profession of arms*

The profession of arms was also transformed by the rise of the nation state. The European feudal system involved direct loyalty to local lords rather than to princes, kings or, in the Holy Roman Empire, the Emperor. Outside the feudal system, mercenaries had been a common feature[16] – particularly in pre-Westphalian Europe where soldiers' loyalties were often to their immediate captain rather than to a sovereign.

The growth of sovereign states resulted in standing armies that claimed the loyalties of their soldiers directly, rather then through their lords or captains. States claimed a monopoly of legitimate violence. If the soldiers' loyalty and duty were to the nation state, it was inappropriate for them to give their loyalty to, and fight for, one part of the state against another, risking the newly established order which it was the prime responsibility of the state to engender for the protection of its citizenry. Professional soldiers saw themselves as maintaining order rather than contributing to disorder. Similarly, it was also totally inappropriate for a soldier to fight for another state. These principles were not always followed. Occasionally, the military would break up and join opposing sides in a civil war – something that was seen as the ultimate tragedy for a professional military force. More often, the military would remain unified in suppressing insurgency – or unified in overthrowing governments in *coups d'état* – one of the curses of the modern state. On the external front, some states continued to recruit mercenaries, but they were generally looked down upon as not real soldiers.[17] The use of mercenaries became less popular, and in the twentieth century there were national and international steps taken to outlaw the use of private military forces.[18]

The last two decades have seen the rise of private military forces associated with the US military, corporations and criminal gangs. The largest remaining forms of private military forces exist in private military companies (PMCs). These PMCs can provide training, security or direct military support. The 'Sandline affair' involved an attempt to bypass the Papua New Guinea military in suppressing a secessionist movement.[19] Where PMCs perpetrate human rights abuses within a sovereign state on behalf of that state or an invading state, these forces have largely been immune from prosecution. More recently, the international community has been examining vehicles to hold PMCs responsible under international law.[20]

The forces of globalization are changing the profession of arms as surely as they are the profession of law. While the monopoly of legitimate force was a matter of definition, in most states, most of the time, the military forces of the state could prevail over any and all other coercive forces ranged against them. For mainstream military forces, the development of the laws of war has entrenched codes of behaviour that can now be enforced by the International Criminal Court. The increasing range and intensity of cooperation between military forces through participation in each other's training programmes, joint exercises and UN deployments are reinforcing the sense that soldiers are part of a common global profession of arms. Accordingly, the military are developing as a global profession similar to lawyers. Indeed, their common code of conduct is far more advanced, being distilled into a number of international agreements – with the four Geneva Conventions and the three amendment protocols the most significant.[21]

## 6.3 Building global professions as important institutions in a globalizing world

### 6.3.1 Global values and global institutions

The trends towards globalizing the legal and military professions and others are important. Indeed, given the absence of any equivalent to national governments within the international order, such professions may need to play a disproportionate role in building and sustaining that international order. The basis for this argument is a narrative that has much influenced my thinking over the last 10 years. Good governance requires the articulation of governance values (for example, liberty, equality, citizenship, community, democracy, human rights, the rule of law and environmental sustainability)[22] and the institutions that can realize those values. Since the seventeenth century, governance debates have centred on sovereign states rather than relations between them. Late seventeenth-century states were generally highly authoritarian and justified as such. Hobbes argued that rational people would mutually agree to subject themselves to an all-powerful sovereign to avoid a 'state of nature' in which the life of man would be 'poor, nasty, brutish and short'.[23]

Once internal order had been restored, this social contract did not seem such a good bargain. The eighteenth-century Enlightenment sought to civilize these authoritarian states by holding them to a set of more refined and ambitious values – notably, liberty, equality, citizenship, human rights, democracy and the rule of law. Some of these values were adaptations of classical city state ideals to the much larger polities of the time. Nineteenth-century thinkers extended the range of rights championed and added concern for environment and for practical and social equality.

Values are rarely self-implementing: they require institutions to realize them. Institutional innovations included an independent judiciary exercising judicial review of the executive, representative institutions, bicameral parliaments, federal division of functions, government and civil society watchdogs, universal education, questioning media and 'responsible' (or 'parliamentary') government.[24] This development of governance values and the institutions to realize them can be seen as an 'enlightenment project'.

Debates have rightly continued over the precise meaning and relative importance of these governance values and the best institutional means of achieving them. However, the centre of gravity in governance debates has remained the sovereign state with the 'enlightenment project' becoming a 'UN project' in which all the peoples of the world become members of strong sovereign states securing their citizen's universal human rights.

This 'UN project' has been shaken by the 'globalizing' flow of ideas, people, goods and services flooding over international borders and weakening many sovereign states. Liberal democratic values were formed *in and for* strong states. Citizenship, democracy, welfare and community have clear meaning *within* sovereign states, but lack apparent application in a broader, more diffuse globalized world. The institutions that sustain, promote and realize those values are very much state-based. The rights, duties and 'sense of belonging' that citizenship carries are attached to state institutions. Democracy is realized through citizen participation in national and sub-national legislatures – and loses mileage if the real power and range of choice open to those legislatures is restricted. Welfare rights like education and health care are only implemented through the institutions of strong, sovereign (and wealthy) states – and even their capacity to do so is increasingly questioned.

Two common responses are to abandon inconvenient governance values such as democracy and welfare or to resist globalization and strengthen the state. I have long argued for a third approach because globalization exposes a flaw in the 'enlightenment project' and later 'UN project'.[25] How can universal rights be secured by geographically limited entities? Why should the welfare rights of the citizens of some states be a tiny fraction of the welfare rights of others? This approach suggests a fundamental rethink of our governance values and the mix of institutions that can achieve them – a 'global enlightenment' in which, as in the eighteenth century, the ideals will come first and the practical institutional solutions will come later.[26] As in the eighteenth century, when city-state values and institutions were reworked and recombined for nation states, sovereign state values and institutions may need reworking and recombining.

I have argued that the institutional arrangements that are most likely to emerge and are most likely to secure such values will not resemble 'sovereign states writ large'. States and multilateral institutions will be important but other institutions – corporations, superannuation funds,[27] professions and NGOs may play a larger role.[28] In this light, I will be considering the roles of the legal and soldierly professions in a future order, and I will suggest that lawyers and the military should see themselves as part of an international profession, respecting international values.

### 6.3.2 Towards global professions

I suggest that the legal profession is, and should be, breaking free of their Westphalian shackles. Professions are not bound by their employers, let alone their states. This principle is the whole point of an independent profession.[29] The concept of a profession involves a group which develops and deploys a body of knowledge and skills for a public purpose. Such knowledge and skills can be used for good or ill – put to work for the ostensible purpose which justifies the powers and privileges of the relevant profession or abused for other purposes. As argued elsewhere,[30] the justification of a profession (indeed, institutions generally) should be in terms of the values it furthers on behalf of the community in which it operates. Those values provide the core for ethical standard-setting (both aspirational and disciplinary), legal regulation and institutional reform.

The importance of ethical guidelines is axiomatic in the case of the military – whose knowledge and skills are in the deployment of organized deadly force against other states in defiance of international law or deployed against the state itself (and generally the human rights of its citizens) in a *coup d'état*. The oft-asked question about the difference between a government and a band of robbers is repeated in asking the difference between the army and an organized group of violent gangsters. The answer cannot simply lie in following orders of the civilian 'commander in chief' as to which groups of people are to be killed *en masse*, as that does not guarantee that the military is more than a reliable accomplice. The answer must lie in the values the military forces claim to espouse, the codes of honour and ethics they develop to realize those values, the commitment to that code and the institutional means that they provide in order to make that realization probable – including mechanisms for reviewing the actions of soldiers and applying appropriate sanctions.

While lawyers cannot directly deploy lethal force, if they are not bound by ethical restraints they can provide advice, which can result in spectacular individual and social harm. Where lawyers give advice on the legality of wars or torture, the consequences can be catastrophic for those who suffer invasion and/ or torture. The fact that those who sought selective legal advice may leave office with their reputations shattered is small consolation and an insufficient deterrent.

While the abuse of the knowledge and skills of lawyers is not as spectacular as the deployment of military force, it is potentially insidious if the knowledge and skills of lawyers are used to deny justice. Sometimes globalization makes this task easier – when lawyers forum-shop for jurisdictions wherein their clients can engage in lawful practices, which would be regarded as criminal in their home state.[31] A similar question arises with regard to the difference between a lawyer and a 'spin doctor' – saying whatever suits the client's interest and, in effect, making lawyers figuratively rather than literally 'guns for hire'. I have previously argued that, where the client refuses to have disputes heard in a court of competent jurisdiction, there is a temptation for clients to seek, and lawyers to give, advice they want to hear. Under such conditions, they are not acting as lawyers but as spin doctors, no better than the much-despised Jamie Shea who was lent by Prime Minister Blair to NATO during the Kosovo conflict. Egregious examples include some of those who provided opinions to governments on the legality of the Kosovo and Iraq wars[32] and the treatment of prisoners.[33] As with the military, the answer for lawyers must lie in values, ethics, commitment and the institutional means for keeping lawyers to their task.

In both cases, the professionals act, with very few exceptions, on instructions by the commander-in-chief or client. However, they do so in an institutional context designed to further the core values of that profession and reduce the likelihood that the professionals' knowledge and skills will be abused. In the case of the military in Western states, the core values are the protection of the civil population and constitutional authority from external attack and, rarely, internal insurrection. For lawyers, the core values are the rule of law, due process, and human rights – sometimes packaged under an overall value of doing justice according to law. For the military, it is civilian control by constitutional authority (only using force when legally permitted), and that force should be used against citizens only under very strict rules and specific safeguards. However, there is considerable overlap. The core values of the military reflect core values of lawyers.

Likewise, the rule of law and human rights can be central to some conceptions of the role of the military. The Hon. Mike Kelly, Parliamentary Secretary for Defence, had argued that the military would be more likely to be successful if it subjected itself to the rule of law in interventions because others knew when force would be used and when it would not.[34] In a workshop on 'Reconceiving the Rule of Law in a Globalizing World' in 2001, he argued that the Australian army was the largest human rights organization in Australia because it did more to further human rights through its peacekeeping operations than any other organization.

I emphasize *furthering* core values of the relevant profession. It is not sufficient for a profession to avoid actions that compromise their core values. Professions take a lead role in promoting certain values. Lawyers were critical in developing and proselytizing the rule of law and the institutional mechanisms to make it effective within strong sovereign states. The military has taken a lead role in the strongest democracies in emphasizing its subordination to the Constitution, to law and to constitutional authority. Lawyers and soldiers should now do the same in international affairs, recognizing that the profession of arms may be an ally. The rest of the chapter discusses how this concept might be understood and refined, and how it might be strengthened.

## 6.4 Refining our understanding of the rule of law in international affairs

### 6.4.1 The 'domestic' rule of law: a contested concept with multiple dimensions

The rule of law is a majestic phrase with many largely reinforcing and supportive meanings. It stands for a fundamental value or ideal, an ethic for lawyers and officials, the basic principles of constitutionalism and a set of institutions supporting its attainment. While these multiple meanings and dimensions may occasionally serve to confuse, each of them is vital in achieving the others. The partial achievement of each supports the fuller achievement of all.

Some of the most popular definitions mix an expression of the normative ideal with the institutional prerequisites for the achievement of that ideal. Developing ideas found in Hayek, Fuller and others, Joseph Raz listed eight basic principles: (1) laws should be prospective, open and clear; (2) laws should be relatively stable; (3) lawmaking should be guided by open, stable, clear and general rules; (4) independence of the judiciary must be guaranteed; (5) principles of natural justice should be observed; (6) courts should have review powers (of the exercise of power by others); (7) courts should be easily accessible; and (8) discretion of crime-policing agencies should not be perverted.[35]

#### 6.4.1.1 The rule of law as a fundamental governance value

The rule of law is now seen as one of the fundamental values underlying modern states – along with human rights, democracy and the famous trinity of *liberté, egalité, fraternité.* It was not always so. The Treaty of Westphalia was, in many senses, a tyrants' charter – made by and for the absolutist rulers of the day. It recognized a set of formally independent and equal states whose sovereigns were recognized on the basis of their ability to effectively control the territory of a state. Their brutal suppression of the former rulers they displaced and others who did not accept their right to rule was an indication of sovereignty rather than a disqualification for it. As discussed above, *philosophes*, lawyers and revolutionaries sought to impose a series of enlightened governance values on authoritarian states. The rule of law was the first of these values, and many states were substantially *Rechstaats* long before they saw even a modicum of democracy and human rights. The rule of law is not only the longest standing of enlightenment values; it is generally the least controversial.

### 6.4.1.2 The rule of law as an ethic for officials

The rule of law is a central ethical principle for judges and the legal profession more generally. The profession's central goal is the effective operation of law so that official power is exercised predictably and according to predetermined rules. The rule of law is also central to most officials, including civil servants, the military and, at root, elected officials – power is held in trust to be used only to the extent permitted and for the purposes authorized.

The rule of law has an illustrious history in Europe, the United States and many Commonwealth countries. The recent lack of support by the United States and the United Kingdom[36] may cause concern for some, but it is important to recognize that the United States, similar to most P5 members, has a very high degree of compliance with treaties and has been pressing for an enforceable rules-based system in global trade. While more politicians openly argue that the United States should ignore international law in the use of force, the legality of American interventions is strongly asserted – indicating that the United States seems to think this is important politically and in the court of public opinion.

### 6.4.1.3 The rule of law as a basic constitutional principle

The rule of law underlies and is supported by basic constitutional principles such as constitutional rule and the separation of powers. However, it does not require a formal or written constitution, and the concept clearly predates such instruments. What the rule of law does seem to require is a separation of judicial power from legislative and executive power and a means of determining what texts are recognized as laws.

### 6.4.1.4 The rule of law as a set of institutions

Those who value the rule of law recognize that it can never operate effectively as a purely normative phenomenon (be it value, ethic or principle). It requires institutions to make it effective:

1. If we are to know what law must rule, it is necessary to have an institution or set of institutions that are sources for authoritative texts. Legislatures are the most common but *Grundnorms* can, and generally do, recognize other sources.
2. There is a need for an institution that provides authoritative interpretations of the meaning of those texts in particular circumstances.

Other institutions that can reinforce the rule of law include an independent Bar, independent prosecutorial services and, to an extent, police forces. Institutions such as ombudsmen and independent commissions against corruption can make the laws more effective and ensure that powers are used for the purposes for which they are entrusted.

### 6.4.1.5 The rule of law and nascent integrity systems

Since the late 1990s, it has become increasingly accepted that the way to avoid corruption and other abuses of power is through an 'integrity system' – a set of norms (formal and informal), institutions and practices that serve to promote integrity and inhibit corruption. All effective integrity systems involve some basic institutional arrangements associated with the rule of law – especially courts and a legal profession that are not indebted to the holders of political power and can review the actions of powerful institutions to determine whether or not they are within power. These institutions are the oldest and longest-standing elements of the integrity systems of Western states.

These meanings are now well developed, widely supported and generally achieved in the domestic affairs of most modern democracies and several autocracies. They are mutually supportive so that the partial achievement of each supports the fuller achievement of all. They are far less developed in international affairs and face obstacles that lead some to doubt the possibility of an international rule of law or international law itself.

### 6.4.2 Apparent difficulties in developing and operationalizing an international rule of law

There are many difficulties in achieving the above meanings and dimensions of the rule of law in the international sphere. I will not go into detail of previous conceptual work done by myself and my colleagues on reconceiving the rule of law in a more global world; much of this can be found in a collection of essays and the last chapter of my most recent monograph.[37] The general conclusion of this work is that the rule of law transfers conceptually very well across cultures and into the international sphere. Chesterman set out three possible meanings of the international rule of law: the application of rule of law principles to states and other subjects of international law; priority of international law over other forms of law; and the direct application of international law to individuals.[38] I have adopted the first mentioned.

### 6.4.2.1 Fundamental values

The concept of the rule of law used here is derived from the domestic law, and the differences between domestic and international law may lead some to query its applicability. The problem is not so much one of conceptualization but of commitment. Low expectations about the effectiveness of international law may undermine its perceived legitimacy and the willingness of international actors to take it seriously. In particular, concern is expressed about the commitment of the United States and its allies to international law over the last 20 years. Despite recent aberrations, Australia and the United States have long been supporters of a rules-based international system on a bipartisan basis. The quotation from President Eisenhower cited at the beginning of this chapter is more representative of the long-term views of Australians and Americans than the 24 years from Reagan's repudiation of the ICJ to the electorate's repudiation of George W. Bush. Even during those 24 years, the United States claimed to act in conformity with international law, and some of us have argued that it is in their interests to do so. With the greater realization of the limits of American military and economic power, unilateral action in contravention of international law may become more difficult and less attractive. The alternate view is that the United States should seek to rebuild and then strengthen international law as insurance for the time when its military power is equalled or surpassed.

### 6.4.2.2 Ethics for officials

The above problems of commitment to the international rule of law lessen the likelihood that international law will be at the forefront of the ethical considerations of lawyers and officials. Lawyers' ethics, formed around the laws and institutions of nation states, may not show the same respect for international law as domestic law. Indeed, Anglo-Saxon systems of legal ethics are based on the duties to courts.[39] Where that domestic law reflects and advances other important ideals, lawyers may have much greater attachment to domestic law.

### 6.4.2.3 Constitutional principles

The limited reach and scope of international law mean that some may doubt the applicability of familiar constitutional principles on the United Nations. This aspect is reinforced by the lack of familiar institutions such as legislatures and executives, and the fact that the institutions which operate internationally are often hybrids, compromises and historical oddities.

### 6.4.2.4 The limitations of international law

International law emerges via different means (there is no real equivalent to a legislature), applies to states rather than citizens, has a radically different extent and lacks an all-powerful sovereign body to enforce it. However, most international law is followed most of the time despite the lack of a sovereign power with the monopoly of legitimate force. In fact, all laws are followed for a number of reasons – of which the nature and certainty of sanctions for breach represent but one, and for most actors not the primary one.

### 6.4.2.5 *Institutions*

The largest problems for the international rule of law lie in the lack of institutions that create, interpret and enforce international law. This lack of effective institutionalization inhibits the development of the rule of law in its other senses. The lack of a legislature is not a fundamental problem for the rule of law. It makes change difficult, but all that is needed is a set of clearly agreed sources, the means by which those sources generate authoritative legal texts and the hierarchy of sources in cases of conflict.

There is a court that can provide authoritative interpretations of those texts and of any conflicts between them. What is more, the ICJ is harder to stack than the highest courts of any other jurisdiction in the world. The problem is, of course, the lack of compulsory jurisdiction and the limited number of cases that can therefore be heard before it.[40] This makes it much harder for the law to give clear guidance to those who want to be bound. The lack of an effective court that sits regularly also makes it difficult to develop and enforce ethical codes for international lawyers.

Despite these problems, lawyers have attempted to develop voluntary international codes of ethics. One such effort was finalized on 10 October 2008 by the International Bar Association's Anti-Money Laundering Legislation Implementation Group in consultation with members of the American Bar Association and the Council of Bars and Law Societies of Europe. The international anti-money laundering guidance issued for the legal profession sets out voluntary guidance on adopting a risk-based approach to managing the occurrence of money laundering, including monitoring processes and training for lawyers. The International Bar Association has a two-page 'International Code of Ethics'[41] and the Union Internationale des Avocats has developed the 'Turin Principles for the Legal Profession in the 21st Century' (2002). The only area with developed codes that are authorized and (in theory at least) enforced by courts are in the ICJ and the various ad hoc criminal tribunals for Rwanda, Sierra Leone and the Former Yugoslavia. During 2008, two more ambitious projects were commenced. One is led by Philippe Sands and supported by the NYU/UCL Project on International Courts and Tribunals (PICT).[42] It aims to develop a code of ethics for lawyers engaged in the practice of international law, and its first meeting was held in London on 12 June 2009.[43] The other project, entitled 'Building the Rule of Law in International Affairs', is led by Professors Thakur, Chesterman and myself, supported by the Institute for Ethics, Governance and Law, the Center for International Governance Innovation (CIGI) and the United Nations University (UNU) and funded by an Australian Research Council Linkage grant. The first workshop was held in October 2009 and examined ethical supports for building the rule of law in international affairs. The two projects are collaborating, with the leaders of each project being invited to the workshops run by the other.

## 6.5 Role of the legal profession in developing the international rule of law

One could conclude that, in many areas where the rule of law seems most needed, it is as distant as it would have seemed to those living under the largely absolutist regimes that emerged in Western Europe after the Treaty of Westphalia. The fact that the heroic efforts by lawyers and revolutionaries over several centuries led to a remarkable transformation in those states may offer little comfort. The international community cannot wait that long and cannot sustain the violent struggles that were often necessary for the rule of law to emerge domestically. However, the rule of law is a very strong domestic ideal on which we can build and which we can support – an ideal that is not only endorsed, but in many cases sincerely so, by various leaders' summits. To make the attainment of an international rule of law realistic, there needs to be coordinated action to address some of the institutional limitations of international law. Lawyers can and should take a lead in such action – just as they did in the development of the domestic rule of law and the institutions that underpin it. This is not the time or place to set out a comprehensive strategy for building the rule of law in international affairs to match the rule of law in domestic affairs (something we hope to be closer to at the end of the above-mentioned projects). However, I will suggest some things lawyers may do and the reasons why they may find unexpected allies in the military.

### 6.5.1 Developing and promoting the rule of law as a fundamental governance value in international affairs

Just as lawyers were major contributors to the development and promotion of the rule of law in domestic affairs, so they should be in international affairs. However, they should not be so as narrow lawyers, but rather as lawyers who understand the philosophical, political and economic issues it raises. Indeed, they should recognize that the rule of law was developed at a time when those disciplines had not yet become distinct. While mastering these disciplines in their entirety is not a realistic goal for individuals, it is for groups of lawyers who respect those disciplines and bring their insights to bear.

If the rule of law becomes a fundamental value of the profession and a value that it uses to justify the profession, lawyers need to reflect carefully and debate publicly its meaning, value and relationship to the nature of the profession and its work to a global community.

### 6.5.2 Ethical standard-setting through codes

Lawyers can contribute to the articulation of more specific codes for lawyers and others – not least the military, who are, as we have seen, potential allies in building the international rule of law. Lawyers should begin by developing a code of ethics for international lawyers and lawyers operating across borders. However, this should not be done in isolation. One of the most important underpinnings of the rule of law in modern states is the importance it plays in the ethics of key participants. Lawyers have 'duties to the court' or, more generally, to 'the law' or 'justice'. Civil servants are concerned with ensuring that all action taken in the name of the state has legal authority. More generally, the rule of law is an ethic for the wielders of power – to exercise powers they have for the purposes that are entrusted to them. Codes need to be developed for:

- international lawyers; international judges and tribunal members; and international civil servants. Such codes cover a variety of issues but centrally concern how entrusted power is handled and a commitment to international law and the rule of law in international as well as national affairs;
- member states and their delegates to General Assembly (GA), United Nations Security Council (UNSC) and international bodies (analogous to codes of ethics for parliamentarians in domestic systems);
- military forces acting under UN authority and military forces engaging in international action – reflecting the same kind of respect for international law, and particularly the UN Charter, that they are expected to show for domestic laws and domestic constitutions.

The nature of the code development would vary depending on the work already undertaken and completed by others. In all cases, the code development should consider the dilemmas, apparent and real conflicts of duties, as well as the pressures and temptations of practice that may lead participants to 'read down' their ethical duties. However, the focus of the work will vary depending on the codes and principles already in place, and the degree to which those codes and principles are controversial. For example:

- where there are rival codes or principles, it is very important to tease out the reasons for disagreement and make suggestions; and
- where most of the relevant ethics codes are domestic (for example, practising lawyers and, to a lesser extent, judges), it is important to deal with issues involving the extension of existing codes, potential conflict between codes, the relationship between the duties to domestic courts and clients and relevant duties to international courts and clients.

In all cases, the relationships between the codes must be considered carefully by examining the ways in which they may unintentionally conflict and ways in which they may be mutually supportive (for example, in the complementarity of the ethics of judges and advocates).

Once relevant international codes for lawyers acting and advising in international matters are developed, their principles should be incorporated into domestic legal ethics codes so that respect for international law and the rule of law in international affairs is built into the codes by which most lawyers practise. Similar domestic implementation should be followed in professional civil service codes and military ethics.

### 6.5.3 Other forms of ethical standard-setting

The creation of codes is a high priority for a number of reasons:

- There is a current opportunity to do so with the Project on International Courts and Tribunals (PICT) project, and there is a great deal of disquiet about the 'torture memos' discussed elsewhere in this volume.
- The creation of an international code will emphasize the responsibilities of international lawyers to the international legal system separately from their responsibilities as lawyers within their domestic jurisdictions.
- Such codes can provide inputs for those who want to reform the domestic legal ethics codes following the torture memos.

While the creation of codes is a high priority and is a natural activity for lawyers, it should be recognized that this does not exhaust the ethics of this or any other profession. If legal ethics were coextensive with codes of ethics, two counter-intuitive consequences would follow. First, it would mean that there would be no sense in complimenting or criticizing the ethics codes. Second, it would make no sense to criticize the ethics of some and praise others. It would be pointless to compliment Lord Goldsmith for the first advice and to criticize him for the second advice. It would also be pointless to refer to the temptation for clients to seek, and lawyers to give, the advice the client wants to hear rather than the advice the client should hear if they are facing court. If the client has no intention of accepting the jurisdiction of a court of competent jurisdiction, they should make it clear that they will not give such advice or, if they do, they will not be acting as lawyers and there should be no privilege.

Before there are codes, people can debate what kind of conduct they admire as ethical and which they criticize as unethical. They can advocate new rules to bolster these normative claims. Even where there are codes in place, they generally set minimum standards of behaviour. There is room to articulate and practise according to what the proponents believe to be higher standards. These will help set standards even while they are supererogatory. While they may affect code development, there will always be room for such higher standards, and they are part of a dynamic profession.

## 6.6 Legal regulation and institutional development

In all cases, the pressures for and against compliance should be considered. While the initial focus of code development would involve the clarification of ethical standards for those subject to the pressure, and those who may be applying the pressure, suggestions would also be made for institutional changes that remove or reduce dilemmas, temptations and pressures for unethical behaviour.

Simultaneously, the legal profession should be actively involved in strengthening institutions that will support the international rule of law and the participation of all states in it. Lawyers made tremendous contributions to the institutionalization of the rule of law domestically – not always succeeding and sometimes risking occasional death or imprisonment.

Some of the institutional changes to be pressed for include:

1. Urging all countries to (re-)commit to compulsory jurisdiction of the ICJ provided that the other national litigant has accepted compulsory jurisdiction before filing.[44]
2. Urging all states to commit to the use of force only subject to international law, with countries only going to war if there is a public statement by the most senior relevant legal authority (for example, Attorney-General or Solicitor-General) that, in their independent judgement, the war is legal and the government is prepared to accept the compulsory jurisdiction of the ICJ in any case brought against it.
3. Moving to define the crime of aggression under the Rome Statute so that politicians who start wars are as liable for breaches of *ius ad bellam* as soldiers are for breaches of *ius in bello*.
4. Controlling private military companies – setting out enforceable rules for their operation and criminalizing those who do not commit to them.
5. Campaigning for the Security Council to subject itself to judicial review in the ICJ.
6. Urging international tribunals to require those who appear before them to abide by codes of ethics for lawyers engaging in international practice and advice – disbarring them from appearance before international tribunals and declaring that they are not entitled to refer to themselves as international lawyers. In so doing, international tribunals start to take on the kind of supervisory role assumed by domestic courts in Anglo-Saxon systems.
7. Referring any substandard advice on going to war, torture, and so on to relevant professional tribunals and the courts which oversee the ethics of lawyers in their own jurisdictions.
8. Developing formal legal rules to ensure civil and criminal accountability for at least the worst such examples.
9. Possibly placing restrictions on professional negligence cover.
10. Potentially erasing lawyer–client confidentiality where the government is not prepared to defend its action in the ICJ – especially where it is likely to attack the court. The lawyer's duty to law and the system of justice mean that they must report the planned commission of a crime. Note that it is hard to see any argument for privilege if the client does not intend that the matter go to a court of competent, given that the point of privilege is to determine what may not be discovered or heard in court.

11.  Refusing to accept lawyers or judges in serious breach of their ethical duties to international conferences or other gatherings of the profession – a matter of naming and shaming.
12.  Following a similar practice with military leaders who breach their ethical duties.[45]

While most of these goals require the action of politicians, lawyers should take the lead in identifying the legal and institutional changes required. In many cases, the relevant leaders will be lawyer-politicians.

## 6.7 Role of the military in developing the international rule of law

As emphasized throughout this chapter, lawyers should seek suitable allies within the military. During the lead-up to the Iraq war, two of those most implicated in what seems to most international lawyers to be a serious breach of international law were lawyers turned prime ministers. Prime Minister Blair appears to have been instrumental in persuading Lord Goldsmith to produce a short and misleading opinion claiming the proposed war would be legal, omitting the caveats in his original advice.[46] On 6 March 2003, Prime Minister Howard told the Australian parliament that there was ample legal authority for the war although virtually no legal authorities supported it.[47] Some members of the military behaved much more creditably. Admiral Sir Michael Boyce, the Chief of the UK armed forces, refused to cross the Kuwait border with written legal advice that the war was legal.[48] If the lawyers providing written advice for public consumption had been prepared to acknowledge the limited support their arguments had, and the unlikelihood of being able to succeed in a court of competent jurisdiction, the British military may have stopped the war.

Later in the Iraq war, it was serving soldiers who first reported and then leaked what had happened at Abu Ghraib.

While soldiers who are also lawyers may play an important role in this, it is the respect for international law by other soldiers that is determinative. In the Kosovo and Iraq wars, Judge Advocate General (JAG) officers in the armed forces advised against some targeting. The differential responses of different militaries indicate the importance of their role and the extent to which the adherence to international law is built into their ethics and the way they see themselves serving their countries. In the Iraq war, this respect for JAG advice could have been motivated by an awareness of the ICC and the possibility of criminal conviction. However, the differential response in the Kosovo war indicates a difference in ethics of different militaries.

The idea of professional obligation is deeply entrenched in the military – so deep that they are prepared to die for it, something other professions are rarely called on to do. But this is cross-fertilized by the fact that a number of military officers are members of two professions – with engineers and doctors being more numerous than lawyers. While being a member of two professions may be potentially confusing, it is more likely to help them develop codes in under-developed areas. Some cross-fertilization between professions in the military may assist.

## 6.8 Conclusion

This chapter endorses the idea that the rule of law should become as fundamental a governance value within the international community as it is within sovereign states. The legal profession should take a lead in developing our understanding of that value and the ethical and institutional means of realizing that value. The military are a potential ally and Americans have traditionally been, and hopefully will again become, natural allies in this process. Our good work in the twentieth century has been tarnished by a poor start to the twenty-first century. However, those who are either unduly optimistic or pessimistic about major institutional change might do well to recognize that history is a 'long game'.

## Notes

1 D. Eisenhower, *Remarks Upon Receiving an Honorary Degree of Doctor of Laws at Delhi University*, 11 December 1959, available from www.eisenhowermemorial.org/speeches/1959 (accessed 7 September 2009). Those who are surprised by the source of the quote should recall that this soldier turned politician used federal troops to protect a black student in Little Rock and warned of the military industrial complex. In Delhi, the old warrior who had masterminded the 6 June Normandy landings of the 'United Nations' (a phrase used in newspapers on that day) made his plea for law not war.

2 In so doing, it will expand on views expressed in C. Sampford, 'Challenges to the concepts of "sovereignty" and "intervention"', closing keynote, 19th World Congress on Legal and Social Philosophy, United Nations, New York, June 1999, published in T. Campbell and B.M. Leiser (eds), *Human Rights in Philosophy and Practice*, Aldershot: Ashgate, 2001, pp. 335–91; C. Sampford, 'What's a lawyer doing in a nice place like this? Lawyers and applied ethics', *Legal Ethics*, 1998, vol. 1, 35; C. Sampford, 'Get new lawyers', *Legal Ethics*, 2003, vol. 6, 185; C. Sampford, 'More and more lawyers but still no judges', *Legal Ethics*, 2005, vol. 8, 221; and C. Sampford, *Retrospectivity and the Rule of Law*, Oxford: Oxford University Press, 2006.

3 See http://en.wikipedia.org/wiki/List_of_oldest_universities_in_continuous_operation for Wikipedia's discussion of the issue with the claims of Nanjing and Academy of Gundishapur in Iran as well as University of Al-Karaouine in Morocco and Al Azar in Cairo.

4 C. Phillipson, 'Andrea Alciati and his predecessors', *Journal of the Society of Comparative Legislation*, 1913, vol. 13, n.p.

5 For a discussion generally, see W. Mitchell, *An Essay on the Early History of the Law Merchant*, Cambridge: Cambridge University Press, 1904.

6 For example, Chapter 1, Article 2, principles 1 and 7: 'The Organization is based on the principle of the sovereign equality of all its Members' and 'Nothing contained in the present Charter shall authorize the United Nations to intervene in matters which are essentially within the domestic jurisdiction of any state or shall require the Members to submit such matters to settlement under the present Charter; but this principle shall not prejudice the application of enforcement measures under Chapter VII.' The concept of universal standards provided increased support for the human rights instruments which accompanied the Charter. The preamble of the *Universal Declaration*

*of Human Rights* (UDHR), G.A. res. 217A (III), U.N. Doc A/810 71 (1948), explains that human rights are a 'common standard of achievement for all peoples and all nations'. Article II of the UDHR explains the universal application of human rights by stating: 'Everyone is entitled to all the rights and freedoms set forth in this Declaration, without distinction of any kind, such as race, colour, sex, language, religion, political or other opinion, national or social origin, property, birth or other status. Furthermore, no distinction shall be made on the basis of the political, jurisdictional or international status of the State or territory to which a person belongs, whether it is independent, trust, non-self-governing or under any other limitation of sovereignty.' The *International Covenant on Civil and Political Rights* (ICCPR) and the *International Covenant on Economic, Social and Cultural Rights* (ICESCR) both support the notion of universality in their preambles when they state that nations are obliged to give 'universal respect for, and observance of, human rights and freedoms'.

7 This development is in sharp contrast to feudal law when land was at the centre of life and likely to be subject to a range of rights. In a sense, it was 'too important' to simply be owned by one person.

8 The UN General Assembly on 5 December 2007 unanimously adopted a Resolution which supported the work of the UNGC Office: United Nations General Assembly, 62nd session, 3 December 2007, Agenda item 61, Res Towards Global Partnerships; United Nations Global Compact; 'UN General Assembly renews and strengthens global compact mandate', *Compact Quarterly*, 2007, vol. 12. See for a comprehensive discussion, A. Rasche, 'A necessary supplement – what the United Nations Global Compact is and is not', *Business & Society*, 2009, vol. 48, 347.

9 United Nations Global Compact, *Annual Review 2006*, 2007, vol. 2. The UN General Assembly on 5 December 2007 unanimously adopted a Resolution which supported the work of the UNGC Office: United Nations General Assembly, 62nd session, 3 December 2007, Agenda item 61, Res *Towards Global Partnerships; United Nations Global Compact*; 'UN General Assembly renews and strengthens'.

10 S. Cooney, 'Improving regulatory strategies for dealing with endemic labour abuses', JSD, Columbia University, 2005, pp. 155–58; S. Cooney, 'A broader role for the Commonwealth in eradicating foreign sweatshops?', *Melbourne University Law Review*, 2004, vol. 28, 291, pp. 315–16.

11 For a criticism of the OECD Guidelines for Multi-National Enterprises (2000), see J. Ruggie, 'Protect, respect and remedy: A framework for business and human rights', report of the Special Representative of the Secretary-General on the issue of Human Rights and Transnational Corporations and Other Business Enterprises, presented to the Human Rights Council, 2008.

12 The caliphate predated Westphalia by 800 years and the establishment of religiously defined colonies predated it by 30 years.

13 See for a discussion on attempts to regulate the internet, S. Deva, 'Corporate complicity in internet censorship in China: Who cares for the Global Compact or the global online freedom act?', *George Washington International Law Review*, 2007, vol. 39, 255.

14 United Nations Framework Convention on Climate Change, opened for signature on 4 June 1992, 31 ILM 849 (entered into force on 21 March 1994); Kyoto Protocol to the United Nations Framework Convention on Climate Change, opened for signature 16 March 1998 (entered into force on 16 February 2005). See for discussion of the impact, D.G. Victor, *The Collapse of the Kyoto Protocol and the Struggle to Slow Global Warming*, Princeton, NJ: Princeton University Press, 2001.

15 H.D. Shumaker, 'The economic effects of the European Union Carbon Dioxide Emission Quota on the new member states of the European Union: Can they become equal economic partners of the European Union while complying with the 2008–12 quota?', *Pennsylvania State Environmental Law Review*, 2008, n.p.

16 D. Stinnett, 'Regulating the privatization of war: How to stop private military firms from committing human rights abuses', *Boston College International and Comparative Law*

*Review*, 2005, vol. 28, 211, pp. 213–16; the main instruments banning mercenary activities are the Additional Protocols to the Geneva Conventions of 12 August 1949 (Protocol I) 42 and the International Convention against the Recruitment, Use, Financing and Training of Mercenaries (UN Mercenary Convention) U.N. GAOR, 44th Sess., Supp. No. 43, U.N. Doc. A/RES/44/34 (1989) (entered into force 20 October 2001).

17 While some would argue that the Ghurkas are a potentially contradictory example, there were attempts to avoid considering them as mercenaries and their rights were never as extensive as Britain's citizen soldiers.

18 W. Singer, 'Corporate warriors: The rise of the privatized military industry and its ramifications for international security', *International Security*, 2001/2002, vol. 26, 186, pp. 188–89, 191.

19 S. Dinnen, R. May and A. Regan (eds), *Challenging the State: The Sandline Affair in Papua New Guinea*, Canberra: NCDS and Department of Political and Social Change, RSPAS, 1997; S. Dorney, *The Sandline Affair: Politics and Mercenaries and the Bougainville Crisis*, Sydney: ABC Books, 1998.

20 D. Morgan, 'Professional military firms under international law', *Chicago Journal of International Law*, 2008, vol. 9, n.p.; D. Ridlon, 'Contractors or illegal combatants? The status of armed contractors in Iraq', *The Air Force Law Review*, 2008, vol. 62, 199.

21 First Geneva Convention 'for the Amelioration of the Condition of the Wounded and Sick in Armed Forces in the Field' (first adopted in 1864, last revision in 1949); Second Geneva Convention 'for the Amelioration of the Condition of Wounded, Sick and Shipwrecked Members of Armed Forces at Sea' (first adopted in 1906); Third Geneva Convention 'relative to the Treatment of Prisoners of War' (first adopted in 1929, last revision in 1949); Fourth Geneva Convention 'relative to the Protection of Civilian Persons in Time of War' (first adopted in 1949, based on parts of the 1907 Hague Convention IV); Protocol I (1977): Protocol Additional to the Geneva Conventions of 12 August 1949, relating to the Protection of Victims of International Armed Conflicts; Protocol II (1977): Protocol Additional to the Geneva Conventions of 12 August 1949, relating to the Protection of Victims of Non-International Armed Conflicts; Protocol III (2005): Protocol Additional to the Geneva Conventions of 12 August 1949, relating to the Adoption of an Additional Distinctive Emblem.

22 Though not as recently as might be imagined, nineteenth-century environmentalists sought to clean up the Thames and protect the countryside via the National Trust.

23 T. Hobbes, *Leviathan*, Cambridge: Cambridge University Press, 1991, p. 89.

24 A feature shared by all long-standing democracies other than the United States.

25 Sampford, 'Challenges', pp. 335–91.

26 While deferring the institutional issues, I would emphasize that this does not amount to an argument for global government – the sovereign state writ large. A more likely result is a mix of institutions reflecting both pre-Westphalian Europe and the modern ideal of an integrity system made up of public, corporate and NGO bodies.

27 Especially if driven to engage in sustainable investment that meets the values and interests of their unit holders who have longer-term interests than the investment managers.

28 There is also likely to be a place for unions or faith-based organizations – though I am not sure that their role will be larger or smaller. It is relevant to observe that faith-based NGOs have been involved in pressuring corporations to date on good corporate citizenship: L. Allen, 'Religion and corporate social responsibility: the Interfaith Centre on Corporate Responsibility and the corporate withdrawal movement from Burma', PhD Thesis, Boston University, 2003.

29 In describing the profession as 'independent', this does not mean that it is entirely self-regulating. Zacharias' chapter in this volume (Chapter 11) points out the central role played by legislation, and especially the judiciary. However, the main impetus for enunciating and developing legal ethics and the structure and role of the profession

comes from lawyers with many of the regulatory and most of the disciplinary decisions in the hands of the judicial branch of the profession.

30 See C. Sampford, 'Law, institutions and the public–private divide', invited keynote address at the Australasian Law Teachers Association Conference, Canberra, September 1990; C. Sampford and C. Parker, 'Legal ethics: Legal regulation, ethical standard setting and institutional design', in S. Parker and C. Sampford (eds), *Legal Ethics and Legal Practice: Contemporary Issues*, Oxford: Oxford University Press, 1995, p. 11.

31 For a discussion of where this has occurred in relation to bribery and medical trials, see P. Ala'i, 'The legacy of geographical morality and colonialism: A historical assessment of the current crusade against corruption', *Vanderbilt Journal of Transnational Law*, 2000, vol. 33, 4; D. Fidler, '"Geographical morality" revisited: International relations, international law, and the controversy over placebo-controlled HIV clinical trials in developing countries', *Harvard International Law Journal*, 2001, vol. 42, 299.

32 See C. Sampford, 'Get new lawyers', *Legal Ethics*, 2003, vol. 6, 185; C. Sampford, 'More and more lawyers but still no judges', *Legal Ethics*, 2005, vol. 8, 221.

33 The subject of numerous papers in the 2006 and 2008 International Legal Ethics Conferences.

34 Discussions with the then Lt Col Kelly in Canberra over 1999 during our work on an ARC linkage grant on 'Preserving and Restoring the Rule of Law in the Asia Pacific.'

35 J. Raz, *The Authority of Law: Essays on Law and Morality*, Oxford: Clarendon Press, 1979; Chesterman summarizes these eight principles into three broad principles: S. Chesterman, 'An international rule of law?', *The American Journal of Comparative Law*, 2008, vol. 56, 331, p. 342. M. Aronson and B. Dyer, *Judicial Review of Administrative Action*, 2nd edn, Sydney: Law Book Company, 2000, Ch. 1.

36 From the US termination of, and refusal to accept, the compulsory jurisdiction of the International Court of Justice in 1986 to the British engagement in the Iraq war despite the clearest advice from their most senior international lawyers. On the United States, see Luban, Chapter 5 in this volume.

37 S. Zifcak (ed.), *Reconceiving the Rule of Law*, London: Routledge, 2005, especially the lead essay, C. Sampford, 'Reconceiving the rule of law for a globalizing world', and the last chapter of C. Sampford, *Retrospectivity and the Rule of Law*, Oxford: Oxford University Press, 2006.

38 S. Chesterman, 'An international rule of law?', *The American Journal of Comparative Law*, 2008, vol. 56, 331, p. 342.

39 While duties to clients are important, both kinds of duty are determined by courts and a lawyer's ethical duties are based on being 'officers of the court'. As the duty to client is ultimately determined by the court, it is not surprising that duties to court take priority over duties to clients to the extent that there is a conflict. To me, there should be no conflict if the relevant duties are properly construed. In my view, the duty to the client is part of the lawyer's duty to courts and the administration of justice. Lawyers representing clients in an adversary system are doing their duty to the court by ensuring that justice is done via a vigorous contestation of issues in front of that court. See Sampford and Parker, 'Legal ethics'.

40 If states do not agree to be bound by the ICJ, then the ICJ has no jurisdiction, even over such crimes as genocide. The voluntary nature of the ICJ even over breaches of *Jus Cogens* was emphasized by *Democratic Republic of the Congo v Rwanda (2002), request for the indication of provisional measures order*, ICJ 12610, 40. In this case, the parties accepted the *Genocide Convention* stated laws of the *jus cogens*. The majority held that genocide enjoyed peremptory status; nevertheless, they held the ICJ Justice did not have jurisdiction to consider an action against a State which had not agreed to be subject to the court's jurisdiction, pp. 71–72.

41 First adopted in 1956, last amended in 1988.

42 See www.pict.org (accessed 7 September 2009).

43 The meeting was attended by Professors Philippe Sands, Laurence de Chazournes (co-chairs), Judge Jean-Pierre Cot, Lord Jonathan Mance, Alexis Martinez, Judge Thomas Mensah, Professor Charles Sampford and Professor Alfred H. Soons.
44 As had the American Bar Association on several occasions.
45 This list incorporates most of the suggestions made in Sampford, 'Get new lawyers'.
46 R. Whitaker, 'The Crawford deal: Did Blair sign up for war at Bush's Texas ranch in April 2002?', *The Independent*, 27 February 2005.
47 Sampford 'More and more lawyers but still no judges'.
48 A. Barnett and M. Bright, 'British military chief reveals new legal fears over Iraq war', *Observer*, 1 May 2005.

# 7 An opportunity for the ethical maturation of the law firm: the ethical implications of incorporated and listed law firms

*Christine Parker[1]*

## 7.1 Introduction

On 21 May 2007, the incorporated law firm Slater and Gordon listed on the Australian Securities Exchange with a fully subscribed offer of $35 million dollars worth of A$1 shares – the first law firm in the world to go public.[2] Slater and Gordon was able to do this because Australia is the first place in the world where legal practices are allowed to incorporate under the ordinary corporations law without restriction on the members of the firm or the business of the firm. Other common law jurisdictions, including Canada, New Zealand and the United States, currently allow only limited liability partnerships or very restricted forms of incorporation, not the full, unrestricted incorporation allowed now in Australia.[3] Soon, full incorporation – and consequently public listing – of legal practices will also be permitted in the United Kingdom when 'alternative business structures' for legal practice are allowed.[4] Other jurisdictions may follow Australia and the United Kingdom.[5]

Some commentators on ethics in the profession believe that full incorporation and listing of law firms is a dire threat – the final step that might tip the noble profession of the law over the ethical precipice into the grubby, greedy world of business. This chapter argues that there are indeed temptations and pressures implicit in the full incorporation and listing of law firms that pose great ethical dangers. However, incorporation and listing are also providing a new – and long overdue – opportunity for the profession and its regulators to recognize the ethical responsibilities of law firms as firms and businesses. Because incorporation and listing make obvious the organizational and commercial aspects of law firms, they are also forcing the profession and its regulators to recognize that law firms need to develop organization-level 'ethical infrastructures' that encourage and nurture individual ethical responsibility in the face of corporate and competitive pressures.[6]

First, the chapter sets out the reasons why some Australian law firms are choosing to incorporate and even list, and the main two ethical dangers they are likely to face in doing so – managerialism (the use of generic management structures to provide legal services rather than individualized professional service) and commercialism (an excessive emphasis on financial profit).

Second, the chapter uses the story of one of Slater and Gordon's most high-profile pieces of litigation – the *McCabe* tobacco litigation – to show that the ethical dangers of managerialism and commercialism that commentators worry *will* come with incorporation and listing represent a formalization and accentuation of *existing* ethical pressures on legal practice, rather than a fundamental change in those pressures.[7]

Third, the chapter argues that, paradoxically, there is an opportunity to improve ethical practice in law firms through the advent of laws allowing alternative business structures for law firms. This is because in Australia and the United Kingdom these laws also mandate the adoption of an 'ethical infrastructure' as a condition of incorporation. The chapter concludes by critically assessing the potential of Australia's governance framework for 'meta-regulating' law firms' ethical infrastructure to address the organizational and business aspects of law practice.

## 7.2 The ethical dangers of incorporation and listing

### 7.2.1 Incorporation and listing of legal practices in Australia

The full incorporation of law firms – under the ordinary company law and without any restrictions on who may own shares or what type of business can be carried on – is now allowed in seven of Australia's eight states and territories.[8] These laws also effectively allow multidisciplinary practice and external investment because they remove all restrictions on incorporated legal practices.

Table 7.1 provides a state-by-state breakdown of when incorporation was first allowed in each state, and the number of incorporated legal practices where that information is available. Incorporation has been allowed in New South Wales, the home of almost half of Australia's lawyers, since 2001. Almost 20 per cent of the firms in that state have now incorporated. In Victoria and Western Australia, the proportions are similarly high. In Queensland, incorporation was only allowed in the middle of 2007, but by the middle of 2008 almost 10 per cent of legal practices were incorporated. Only two firms in Australia have listed so far.[9]

The vast majority of practices in Australia are still small practices with a single principal (with or without employee lawyers)[10] – and the vast majority of incorporated legal practices are too: 612 (78 per cent) of 790 incorporated legal practices in New South Wales have only one principal.[11] But proportionately, incorporation is most popular with medium-sized practices (three to five principals): 32 per cent of legal practices of this size are incorporated in New South Wales compared with 18 per cent of legal practices overall. Two-principal practices are also proportionally more likely to incorporate than single-principal practices, with 28 per cent of these practices incorporated.

The very largest practices (20+ principals) have mostly not yet (as of February 2009) incorporated. The main reason is that was only in 2007 that the four largest states all allowed incorporation, and it is still not the case that all states allow

*Table 7.1* Year in which incorporation first allowed, and number and proportion of incorporated legal practices by state and territory, 2008*

| State | Date full incorporation allowed | Number of incorporated legal practices | ILPs as % of total legal practices (total in brackets) |
| --- | --- | --- | --- |
| New South Wales | July 2001 | 800 (March 2008) | 18%(4341) |
| Northern Territory | May 2004 | Not known | Not known (approx. 56) |
| Western Australia | June 2004 | 173 | Approx. 27% (approx. 649) |
| Victoria | December 2004 | 520 | Approx. 21% (approx. 2430) |
| Australian Capital Territory | July 2006 | Not known | Not known (approx. 133) |
| Queensland | July 2007 | 106 | 8% (1294) |
| Tasmania | December 2008 | Not known | Not known (approx. 116) |
| South Australia | Reforms in progress | NA | NA (approx. 413) |

* New South Wales figure for ILPs at 1 March 2008, obtained from Law Society of New South Wales. Total New South Wales practices figure at 2 May 2007, obtained from Law Society of New South Wales. Western Australia figure for ILPs at February 2008 obtained from Legal Practice Board Western Australia. Victorian figures at 30 June 2008, obtained from Victorian Legal Services Board. Queensland figure for ILPs at 30 June 2008, and total practices at 30 June 2007, obtained from Queensland Legal Services Commissioner. Approximate total numbers of legal practices for Northern Territory, Western Australia, Victoria, Australian Capital Territory, South Australia and Tasmania are based on 2002 figures reported in Australian Bureau of Statistics, *8667.0 – Legal Practices, Australia, 2001–02*, Canberra: Australian Bureau of Statistics, p. 20. The actual numbers of practices in each state/territory to date are not available but are probably greater.

incorporation.[12] Previously it would have been inconvenient for the largest, multi-state, Australian law firms to incorporate in some states and not others. For larger firms, there may also be significant capital gains tax liabilities to be paid on the transfer of the business to the newly incorporated entity. This provides a disincentive for incorporation.[13] Reportedly, many larger firms are waiting for clarification from the Australian Tax Office about how goodwill will be valued and taxed in relation to capital gains tax rules before seriously considering whether to incorporate, and potentially list.[14] It has also been widely reported that very large firms see the public reporting requirements that would come with incorporation, and even more so with listing, as unattractive.[15]

## 7.3 Reasons for incorporation and listing

A review of the 'trade' literature on the pros and cons of legal practices incorporating in Australia suggests those firms that do incorporate are probably doing so primarily in the belief that they will be able to organize their finances so that most of their income can be taxed at the company rate (which is lower than the personal rate that applies to partners' income),[16] or because they see incorporation as a good way of managing retirement and succession (since it makes the legal practice easier to transfer to younger colleagues or sell to another practice).[17]

The policy intention, however, was that firms would use incorporation to make themselves more competitive and efficient, and that this would strengthen the Australian economy and improve access to justice.[18] Indeed, full incorporation of legal practices was introduced throughout Australia because it was recommended as part of Australia's National Competition Policy Review process.[19] It was seen as 'a key means of enabling legal practices to raise capital for expansion to facilitate competition in domestic and international markets' and also to 'allow legal practitioners to compete with other service providers, such as banks and retailers'. In particular, it was intended to encourage multidisciplinary practices that would be 'one-stop shops' that increased 'competition and efficiency, thereby reducing costs for consumers'.[20] Full incorporation of legal practices was also supported by at least parts of the profession because in the late 1990s larger law firms in Australia were worried about the increasing amount of legal work being done by the big accounting firms.[21]

There are five main ways in which incorporation is intended to give legal practices the opportunity to become more efficient and competitive:[22] first, it can help firms streamline governance and management arrangements by providing the possibility of a corporate management structure rather than the more unwieldy partnership structure (e.g. firms can differentiate between the duties and powers of partners and management and formalize decision-making powers in an appropriately accountable board of directors and corporate officers).[23] This may be especially attractive for larger firms. Second, incorporation makes it easier to reinvest profits in the business rather than partners taking the profits out at the end of each year. Third, incorporation gives firms the opportunity to reward both lawyer and non-lawyer staff with employee share ownership plans, rather than only lawyers having the opportunity of partnership. Fourth, the corporate governance structure and non-lawyer ownership of the incorporated firm is supposed to provide a more solid basis for multidisciplinary practice. It allows the different aspects of a multidisciplinary firm to be integrated in one structure rather than operating through less formal alliances, or with non-lawyers being minor players compared to lawyers.[24] Fifth, the corporate form is also a more flexible way of dealing with admission and resignation of partners, since ownership interests in the firm are easily transferred and the firm has its own continuity of existence, which is not dependent on its individual members. This makes it easier to enter into contracts and other commercial relationships, including groupings of practices (e.g. through franchise-type arrangements or corporate groups).[25]

The most significant way in which incorporation can assist with competitiveness is that with full incorporation comes the possibility of public fundraising. It has been suggested that, on the whole, the business of legal practice is not especially capital-intensive, and that most legal practices operate satisfactorily with assets worth less than one year's income and borrowing as required.[26] This implies that incorporation and listing will make little difference. However, there are some areas of practice, such as personal injuries, in which the ability to raise capital from the public might be very important in building a competitive, efficient business – because of the upfront expenses involved in making an income.[27] Debt recovery and real estate practice are two other areas regularly mentioned as areas in which significant capital investment might be helpful.[28] Where a big investment in information technology could lead to the more efficient processing of volume or innovation in the whole way legal services are delivered, then incorporation and listing in order to get that upfront capital might also make sense.[29] Finally, any law firm that wants to expand might also find public fundraising valuable to get the capital to acquire other firms and to give the option of using the issue of shares as part of the acquisition price.[30] Even the very largest law firms might find this attractive in order to fend off encroachments and attacks from global law firms and multidisciplinary investment banks and accounting firms.

The listing of Slater and Gordon provides a good illustration of these reasons for incorporation and listing. Slater and Gordon is one of the most recognizable names in the legal industry in Australia – its prospectus claims 80 per cent brand recognition in its home state of Victoria and 60 per cent nationally, mainly because of its involvement in many of the most high-profile class actions and personal injuries test cases in Australia, its relationship with unions and its advertising of no-win, no-fee plaintiff litigation.[31] Personal injuries is not a highly profitable sector of the legal services market at present in Australia. Indeed, the market for personal injuries work in Australia is highly fragmented and generally considered to have shrunk in recent years due to legislative and insurance changes restricting liability.[32] Profits of the magnitude available in North America are not available in personal injuries in Australia since Australian lawyers are not allowed to recover contingency fees.[33] Nevertheless, Slater and Gordon is a business success: it has about 10 per cent of the national market for personal injuries and is increasing its market share, geographical reach and profitability.[34]

Nevertheless, when Slater and Gordon listed in 2007, it was carrying at least A$15 million in short-term debt.[35] It listed because its management wanted to grow the firm off a solid financial base, did not want to continue to rely on debt to fund its growth, and wanted to provide a sustainable future for the firm and its employees – even when the existing partners sought to leave and wanted to take their capital with them. It sought external investment through the securities exchange in order to acquire other firms, fund litigation, advertise its services and acquire shares back from the partners and lawyers who were the original shareholders in the incorporated firm.[36] These are the same sorts of reason why thousands and thousands of other businesses have listed over the last 300 years.

### 7.3.1 Ethical dangers of full incorporation and listing of legal practices

Australian legislators are allowing full incorporation of legal practices and multidisciplinary practice because they see it as no longer 'appropriate to use business structures as a way to regulate legal practice. Responsibility to maintain professional and ethical rules should be placed solely with individual solicitors, who should be free to choose the business structures which suit them.'[37]

In Australia, Britain, Canada and the United States, the practice of law by incorporated entities was traditionally completely banned. Only individual professionals could practise law – either as sole practitioners or in partnership. This was because the professional skills, moral character and ethical responsibility of each and every individual lawyer was seen as the only appropriate foundation for the ethical conduct of the profession as a whole. The very concept of an ethically responsible legal professional working in an incorporated legal practice was a non-sequitur for two main reasons.[38]

First, incorporation degrades the personal moral judgement and responsibility of individual legal professionals. In a partnership, individual partners share personal liability for each other's negligence and breaches. They therefore have an incentive to monitor the quality and honesty of their own and each other's work, to assist one another, and to train and mentor the new recruits who will become their partners in the future.

Incorporation puts the firm and its governance structures in the place of the individual partner. The board of directors makes decisions for the firm, which is now owned by shareholders – and neither the directors nor the shareholders have personal liability for the way the firm runs it business. The shareholders, of course, are only liable to pay for their shares, while the directors do have responsibility for the overall control and monitoring of the firm, but not necessarily for the individual mistakes and frauds of its employees.

The danger is that 'managerialism' or bureaucracy in the collective entity of the corporation will replace professional responsibility and collegiality in the day-to-day running of the firm. Lawyers might have little incentive to develop their own ethical and professional judgement or to encourage others to do so. Rather, they will just perform their role in the hierarchy. Even the language reflects this change: a 'head of practice area' or 'director' sounds less ethically responsible for the firm than a 'partner'.

Second, incorporation privileges 'commercialism' or profit-orientation over ethical responsibilities to the law, the court, access to justice and loyalty to individual clients. Incorporated firms can have non-lawyer investors, officers and employees who do not share legal professionals' commitment to prioritizing ethics over profit.[39] The very creation of an incorporated firm means that the firm now acquires its own legal personality and its own interests and reputation. The danger is that a listed firm, in particular, will be oriented solely to making profit, since this is the very basis on which the securities market operates. It is what investors and analysts expect of a listed firm – they have no metric or incentive for valuing the ethical judgement of the individual lawyers who make up the firm. Incorporated legal practices will greedily seek profits by seeking to please profitable clients at the expense of their duties to the law, the court and access to justice for all.

Moreover, external investment will create a whole new range of conflicts of interest when the shareholders in an incorporated legal practice (ILP) include businesses and individuals whose commercial or legal interests are at odds with those of clients.[40] What would Slater and Gordon do if the next big securities class action it could take on for a client were against one of its own institutional investors? Is there a danger that some of Slater's most likely corporate foes will purposely protect themselves from the risk of litigation by buying shares in Slater and Gordon to conflict the firm out of acting against them? External investment also creates conflicts between lawyers' traditional obligation to do pro bono work and the need to justify how the activities of the firm will lead to profit. How will Slater and Gordon explain to its shareholders why it is 'sinking' a million dollars or more in a pro bono class action case the next time it takes on an Australian company with operations in some Third World country that have harmed local inhabitants who could never hope to pay their legal fees themselves? Will the obligation to report to shareholders stop some of these cases?

Incorporation and listing indubitably do increase the ethical pressures on lawyers working in law firms. The degradation of personal moral responsibility and the temptation to put profits above ethics are very serious threats to legal professionalism. But incorporation and listing represent an accentuation and formalization of these threats – a quantitative more than a qualitative shift in the ethical dangers of legal practice. A listed law firm like Slater and Gordon might be balanced very precariously on the ethical precipice between profession and business – but so are many, many other law firms, as the next part of this chapter shows.

## 7.4 Comparing ethical dangers of commercialism and managerialism in incorporated and unincorporated law firms

### 7.4.1 Comparing ethical dangers in incorporated and unincorporated law firms: the McCabe tobacco litigation

One of Slater and Gordon's high-profile pieces of litigation – the *McCabe* tobacco litigation – illustrates the ways in which commercialism and managerialism are already intertwined with professionalism, individual ethical judgement and justice values in law firm practice.[41] On one side of this litigation was Slater and Gordon, an incorporated firm of about 150 lawyers, acting for Rolah McCabe, a dying woman who had started smoking in 1959 when she was 9 years old. On the other side was an army of in-house corporate lawyers and external commercial law firm lawyers – including, most prominently, lawyers from the unincorporated law firm Clayton Utz, a firm of about 800 lawyers, and the fourth largest firm in Australia. The ethical values demonstrated in the behaviour of each of these two firms – the incorporated Slater and Gordon and the unincorporated Clayton Utz – illustrate the ways in which commercialism and managerialism can be just as relevant and dangerous for firms structured as partnerships as for firms that have chosen to incorporate. The lawyer behaviour in this case also shows that it is quite possible for a firm that is incorporated to maintain strong ethical values and social justice commitments after incorporation. Unethical behaviour does not automatically go along with incorporation and listing, just as commitment to the core ethical values of the legal profession is not guaranteed by a traditional partnership structure. In both types of firm, ethical commitments and behaviours will depend on the individual lawyers in the firm and, crucially, the ethical character of the firm as a whole.

Briefly, McCabe's was the first case outside the United States in which a plaintiff won a judgement against a tobacco company for cancer caused by smoking.[42] In 2002, a single judge of the Victorian Supreme Court found that the solicitors for the defendant tobacco company had advised the company on a 'document-retention policy' that intentionally resulted in the destruction of thousands of documents, as part of the preparation for an anticipated wave of litigation against the tobacco industry.[43] The court also found that the defendant and its legal advisers had misled the plaintiff and the court about the fact and the extent of their document destruction. The trial judge struck out the defendant's defence and ordered judgement in the amount of $700,000 for McCabe without a trial because the destruction of documents had been done with the 'deliberate intention of denying a fair trial to the plaintiff'.[44] Rolah McCabe died six months later. It is unlikely her case would have got to trial before she died if this extraordinary judgement had not been made. The defendant tobacco company, however, appealed successfully.[45] The full court of the Supreme Court of Victoria overturned the judgement in favour of McCabe on the basis that the trial judge had applied the wrong test in entering summary judgement, and that the defence should only be struck out if the defendant had intentionally acted to pervert the course of justice or in contempt of court. The Court of Appeal found there was not sufficient evidence of this.

The actions and attitudes of both Slater and Gordon and Clayton Utz in this litigation illustrate the dangers of commercialism and managerialism in contemporary legal practice, and also what is required to avoid them.

### 7.4.2 Testing the moral character of an incorporated firm: Slater and Gordon

By the time of the appeal judgement, Rolah McCabe had already passed away. Her family was then left with a bill for the other side's costs – A$2 million. (In Australia, costs generally follow the event.) Slater and Gordon were left with the dilemma of whether to keep fighting an extremely risky case on behalf of a deceased plaintiff. It is at this point that the moral character of Slater and Gordon as a firm becomes obvious.[46]

For Slater and Gordon, there was now little direct commercial benefit to be gained from pursuing the *McCabe* case – bearing in mind that there would never be any contingency fee windfall to compensate it for this risk.[47] Nevertheless, and despite the fact that it was an incorporated and listed law firm, Slater and Gordon continued to pursue the case. Presumably this is out of a sense of loyalty to the deceased client and her family, the firm's commitment to social justice (which Slater and Gordon is clear is a central mission of the firm), and the lawyers' own personal emotional and professional investment in the case. The result is that, for the first time in the Australian courts, tobacco companies and their litigation strategies are very slowly and painfully being made legally accountable. Even if *McCabe*'s case is ultimately found to be unmeritorious on the facts, some of the facts of the tobacco company's practices and knowledge are coming out. Previous cases have all been settled or stymied before they got anywhere close to a trial.[48]

There is even a sense in which Slater and Gordon's commercial orientation has probably supported its professional and ethical commitments in this case. This is a hugely costly and risky piece of litigation for the firm, and for the individuals involved in it. Even with pro bono assistance from barristers, this particular piece of litigation would have financially and professionally exhausted most smaller, less profitable firms. Few firms would have had the social justice commitment combined with the capital necessary to run a case like this without the firm collapsing.[49]

This is not to say that the listed Slater and Gordon company will not have many ethical temptations. But the competing pressures and obligations at stake are not fundamentally any different now than they were *before* incorporation and listing. They include the competing pressures to remain true to the client commitments and social justice values that comprise the firm's fundamental ethical and brand identity, while maintaining a healthy enough balance sheet to provide reasonable prospects of ongoing employment and remuneration for each of the individual lawyers who put their hearts and souls into the firm's cases, and at the same time invest enough back into the firm to provide a buffer against the risk of loss in litigation and grow a future for the firm. In other words, it was equally important before the firm was listed and incorporated as it was afterwards that the firm be profitable. The difference is that now external investors will be formally voicing that expectation.

Large commercial law firms may not feel any great need to seek external investment because of their regular billings from rich and highly liquid corporate clients. But there is a strong argument that incorporation and listing provide a useful pathway for those firms that serve individual clients of modest means to develop their businesses to a scale and management model that would allow them to serve these clients reliably, efficiently and affordably. In other words, as with the legal profession's former ban on advertising, there is an argument that the ban on incorporation and listing disproportionately affects the sort of firms that serve individual clients – and that it therefore helps maintain unequal access to justice.

Slater and Gordon's prospectus and public statements certainly make it clear that the firm believes that its incorporation and listing were important steps in consolidating the market for personal injuries lawyering in Australia – and therefore making those services more widely available at a high level of quality and affordable price – as well as providing a financial basis for broader social-justice lawyering. Bear in mind that since there are no contingency fees in

Australia, there is little prospect of firms like Slater and Gordon making the huge profits that would allow them to sustain their practices for several years from one successful case, and also none of the ethical dilemmas that go with contingency fees. Similarly, the other firm that has listed in Australia, Integrated Legal Holdings, has done so as part of a (less successful) attempt to deliver services more efficiently and affordably to individuals via a franchising strategy.

The third part of the chapter will discuss the safeguards that Slater and Gordon and other firms are putting in place to try to make sure that incorporation and listing do provide a basis for ethical practice, rather than subverting the whole enterprise of access to justice. But first we turn to one of the prominent firms on the other side of the *McCabe* litigation, Clayton Utz.

### 7.4.3 The ethical temptations of commercialized legal practice in unincorporated firms: Clayton Utz

It is on the Clayton Utz side of the *McCabe* litigation that the corporate and business pressures on ethical practice are most obvious. Clayton Utz's tobacco company client may not have been a *shareholder* in the firm, but Clayton Utz's lawyers appear to have been sufficiently aware of the tobacco industry's investment in the firm's profitability – by way of monthly fees – to create a conflict of interest and duty.

The precise legal obligations and ethical responsibilities that applied to this particular situation remain a topic of legal debate.[50] But the public and media reaction to the case indicated that ordinary members of the public considered Clayton Utz's advice on the tobacco company's document-'retention' policy to be at least unethical, if not illegal.[51] Certainly the destruction of documents with the purpose of making it difficult or impossible for meritorious plaintiffs to prove their case, and the fact that the defendants did not at first reveal the intentional destruction of those documents during the discovery process, could both amount to a breach of the ethical duty to the administration of justice.[52] That duty is supposed to over-ride lawyers' duties to their clients. A government report recommended that the law in Victoria, where the case occurred, should make it unambiguously clear that such actions are unlawful,[53] and there is now a maximum five-year jail term for wilful document destruction.[54]

Clayton Utz has now dropped its tobacco litigation practice – although the reason for doing so was framed in terms of a 'business' decision about wanting to foster work from other important clients (especially government clients), not an ethical decision as such.[55]

Since the tobacco company's successful appeal of the judgement against it, a number of new facts have also come to light. A former in-house counsel to the tobacco company has now come forward and provided compelling evidence that the tobacco company and its law firm had participated in a 'contrivance' to hide evidence behind client legal privilege.[56] The tobacco company would give its law firm copies of its documents, ostensibly for legal advice. The originals would be destroyed under the document retention policy while the law firm kept the copies, but claimed that they were protected by privilege. This may mean that the McCabe family and Slater and Gordon can get access to previously privileged tobacco company documents that will allow them to reopen the original *McCabe* case.[57]

Also, a former partner at Clayton Utz has come forward and leaked to Slater and Gordon and *The Age* newspaper the report of an internal Clayton Utz investigation into whether any misconduct occurred inside the firm in relation to the document destruction.[58] This indicated that, at the time of the investigation, Clayton Utz itself believed that two of its own lawyers acting for the tobacco company had engaged in serious professional misconduct and, in one case, potentially perjury. One of the two senior lawyers involved in the conduct had reportedly been told to leave, and another had also left, although other lawyers named in the original judgement are still at the firm. Neither of the two lawyers identified in the Clayton Utz report has faced any official regulatory action, as far as can be seen from the public record.[59] Neither, as far as we can tell, was this internal investigation disclosed to the independent regulators of the legal profession in the relevant states – even though they were known to be attempting to investigate whether any misconduct had taken place.

With these two new sets of evidence, the Director of Public Prosecutions (DPP) in Victoria has now referred the whole matter to the Australian Crime Commission with a strong recommendation that both the law firm and the tobacco company be investigated for misconduct, including perjury and conspiracy to pervert the course of justice.[60] The DPP probably referred the matter to the Australian Crime Commission because the latter is the only body with sufficient powers to compel production of the relevant documents and evidence from the firm and its (now former) client.[61]

### 7.4.4 Commercialism and managerialism in incorporated legal practices as an accentuation and formalization of ethical dangers in commercial practice in unincorporated firms

The behaviour of the Clayton Utz lawyers in the *McCabe* litigation is a good example of the commercialism and profit-orientation of contemporary legal practice. This occurred in a commercial, businesslike but unincorporated law firm. The ethical environment in which lawyers in this particular firm apparently disregarded their own, and their client's, duty to the court is similar to that in many other large law firms around the world.[62] (In fact, a number of Australia's largest law firms had also advised on different aspects of the tobacco company's document-'retention' policy at different times, and the tobacco company is now represented by another one of these firms.[63]) The firm-level factors that probably contributed to this conduct show that the sort of ethical evils – related to commercialism and managerialism – that we fear will come with incorporation and listing are already thriving in at least some corners of contemporary legal practice.

*7.4.4.1 Commercialism in unincorporated law firms*

We have seen that it is feared incorporation and listing will privilege commercialism and profit-orientation over ethical responsibilities to the law, the court,
access to justice and loyalty to individual clients. Yet law firm partnerships are
also, of course, run for profit. The partners draw down the profits each year, and
in many large law firms partners and employees are painfully aware of the extent
to which they are contributing to profits on a monthly or even weekly basis.[64] It is
very common now in Australian law firms for employee lawyers to receive a
weekly printout of the number of billable hours they and their colleagues have
worked that clearly shows their place in the race to bill more hours. The relative
rates at which different lawyers are charged out to clients also indicates their
place in the profit-making hierarchy of the law firm. And the partners know who
among them have brought in new work or organized their teams to leverage
more billing out of existing clients – with these metrics used in many firms to
decide how profits and various perks will be divvied up between partners and
their work teams.

There was a case several years before the *McCabe* litigation in which the senior
partner in Clayton Utz's family law division was disciplined for forging the evidence required to sue her client for half a million dollars in fees for her divorce
and property settlement.[65] It turned out that Clayton Utz had told this lawyer
that the family law section was going to be closed down unless she could start
delivering the same sort of regular fees and profitability that the firm was making
from one of its most long-standing clients – the Tobacco Institute! Despite heavy
judicial criticism of firms' charging culture and policies, the court made no finding of gross over-charging in this case. A complaint of gross over-charging could
only be sustained if the lawyer's charges were grossly in excess compared with
other similar lawyers, and there is no legal or regulatory capacity to call a firm to
account for the way in which its management policies and decisions probably
contributed to over-charging and misconduct. Only individual lawyers can be
disciplined, not firms.

The pressure to prioritize profit over ethical obligations has deepened in recent
years as the market for legal services has become more competitive and fragmented. Big companies (and also government departments) now shop around
more for the right legal advice at the right price. They have unbundled their legal
services so that no one firm, not even their own in-house legal department, is
necessarily guaranteed a steady flow of legal work, or is aware of all legal matters
in which the company is involved. At the same time, there is also more demand
for commercial lawyers to be embedded in (employed by, or seconded to) business sub-units within corporate clients so that they can provide commercially
realistic advice and anticipate, avoid or resolve legal problems.[66] So there is
demand for a closer relationship between lawyers and business, but that relationship is also less secure for the lawyer – lawyers can easily be sacked if their
advice does not suit. In this environment, we can expect lawyers to come under
increasing pressure to please individual managers, executives or work teams (who

control the purse strings), rather than consider their obligation to the corporate client as a whole, let alone any duty to the law or the public interest.

This environment also creates a dynamic not unlike the securities market: firms and lawyers are constantly competing with each other to attract and retain income streams from the sorts of clients who will pay very large fees regularly. There have been many cases where larger law firms have dropped one client they perceive to be less profitable in order to take on the legal work of a bigger, richer client with opposing commercial or legal interests to their original client.[67] Clayton Utz's eventual closure of its tobacco litigation practice can be construed in these terms: they feared the loss of government and other work due to the bad publicity associated with the *McCabe* decision. There have also been many cases of larger law firms deciding they could unilaterally 'manage' a conflict of interest with information barriers because they want to keep the income streams from two clients on opposite sides of a deal – regardless of whether the two clients are happy with this arrangement or not.[68] Often this has occurred where a large firm has grown by swallowing a smaller firm (and its clients) whole.

If one of the defendants being sued by Slater and Gordon buys some of its shares, then it will be far from the first time that a law firm has accepted an 'investment' in its business from someone with opposing interests to its existing clients and has had to work out how to handle the consequential conflicts. Clayton Utz's closeness to, and financial dependence on, its tobacco company client was likely a big factor in its disregard for its duty to the court.[69]

### 7.4.4.2 Managerialism in unincorporated law firms

The ethical dangers posed by businesses' increasingly commercial and profit-oriented approach to legal advice are compounded by the fact that law firms themselves are also being managed more and more like large business corporations. We have seen that it is feared managerialism stemming from incorporation and listing will degrade the personal moral judgement and responsibility of individual legal professionals. But the increasing size and organizational complexity of much of contemporary legal practice is already degrading lawyers' personal moral judgement. An increasing number of lawyers today work as employees subject to detailed direction and supervision in large national and international law firms and in-house corporate legal departments. Individual employee lawyers often do not even meet the client. They do not have an opportunity to understand how the work that they are doing relates to the client's overall aims or what ethical ramifications it may have. Employed lawyers in law firms and in-house legal departments must answer to whichever partner is their boss on each case. Kimberly Kirkland's in-depth interview research in large US firms has shown that this means young lawyers learn to not only second-guess the legal style of each different supervising partner with whom they work, but also their ethical norms. They come to see ethics as contingent on the demands of their supervisor and client – rather than having their own sense of personal ethical responsibility nurtured and sustained.[70]

It has also been suggested by empirical research that about 150 people is the largest number who can work together in a community with shared ethical and other norms.[71] Once a firm expands beyond this size, there will inevitably be sub-communities that might have quite different ethical norms. Or there might be an overall sense of alienation and 'normlessness', which makes people feel that they do not have any particular ethical standards in responsibility for their own work – they just have to do what their boss tells them.

The work team within Clayton Utz that represented tobacco companies probably had developed its own norms in response to law firm billing policies and the fact that team members spent so much time with one client and its in-house lawyers. The reported facts indicate that the Australian lawyers in the case were essentially following the litigation tactics developed by the tobacco industry and its lawyers in the United States and, to a lesser extent, the United Kingdom. They may not have exercised independent individual judgement about the propriety of what they were doing at all.

This is not an atypical story. There have recently been a number of corporate scandals in which external lawyers have failed to show the sort of independent ethical judgement that we might expect of a professional lawyer.[72] In the collapse of Enron, a number of lawyers have been criticized for exactly this sort of failure precisely for the same reason – getting too close to clients on whom they were financially dependent.[73] Similarly, another of Slater and Gordon's arch litigation foes, James Hardie, a major Australian company that previously produced asbestos, recently devised a scheme, with the help of its in-house lawyer, in which it was able to quarantine its asbestos liabilities in a couple of orphaned subsidiaries while the parent decamped to the Netherlands – leaving the subsidiaries with inadequate funds to properly compensate all the known James Hardie asbestos cases. James Hardie's external lawyers were heavily criticized in the report of a public inquiry into this incident for completely failing to provide the sort of independent ethical advice that might have stopped this from happening.[74]

## 7.5 The ethical opportunity in incorporation and listing

### 7.5.1 Moral panic and moral opportunity

There are always those who say that, whatever the latest development in professional practice may be, it always marks the point at which legal practice has finally lost the ethical ideas of professionalism and careened over the precipice.[75] This sense of 'moral panic' is a completely natural defensive reaction to apparently radical new developments – such as the listing of a law firm. Moral panics are usually directed at some obvious, discrete behaviour that people believe can easily be reversed or eradicated. Most often, however, the real moral issues that need to be addressed are entrenched, enculturated and systemic. They are difficult to perceive, let alone effectively address. The particular behaviour that prompts the moral panic is often just a manifestation of a problem that has been festering below the surface for some time.

The incorporation and listing of law firms accentuate and bring into focus certain ethical issues, but it is not incorporation and listing as such that are the main problem. Law is already a business as well as a profession, and has been so for a very long time. The ethical issues that come with incorporation and listing already exist – at least among the largest firms and those that aspire to be like them. The real issue with ethics in law firm practice that must be urgently addressed is the historic failure of law firm leaders, professional associations, independent regulators and academic ethicists to adequately recognize that law is both a business and a profession, and that it is carried on by commercial firms, not just professionally qualified individuals.

Individual professionals have traditionally been seen as the only, or main, focus of ethical responsibility and regulation. This is not sustainable in a world where firms and work teams within firms significantly influence individuals' ethical judgements and behaviours.[76] Firms have the power to either prevent or encourage ethical or unethical behaviour by individual lawyers – and to prevent individual lawyers ever being held to account for their behaviour. Yet they are generally still not the subject of the regulatory system,[77] and rarely even of ethical discussion. Historically, the business aspects of legal practice have been denied and deemed illegitimate, rather than acknowledged and addressed as legitimate objects of ethical deliberation and regulation. We tend to assume that individual lawyers in law firms should not feel, let alone succumb to, the ordinary ethical pressures of business. And so we have not done enough to identify what those pressures are and how we might ethically manage them.

In Australia, the advent of incorporation and listing have prompted both law firms and legal profession regulators towards some initiatives that begin to address these problems. As the Australian experience shows, along with the ethical dangers of incorporation and listing, there is also an opportunity that regulators and the profession can take advantage of – to address and improve the moral character of law firms as firms and businesses.

For example, as part of its listing, Slater and Gordon started an extensive and continuing process of identifying all its ethical and legal obligations and values – and then working out what policies, practices and structures it needed within the firm to make sure those obligations and norms were implemented. This was partly voluntary – in response to the Australian Securities Exchange's Listing Rules, which include the requirement for each listed company to disclose the extent of its compliance with the voluntary Australian Corporate Governance Principles.[78] But it was also partly compulsory – to ensure compliance with the Australian requirements for incorporated firms, explained further below. Much of it is consistent with what other well-governed, socially responsible listed businesses do in order to maintain and strengthen their ethical culture.[79] But for a law firm, it is particularly important that some ethical obligations to law and justice over-ride the financial bottom line in all circumstances.

Slater and Gordon therefore included prominently in its prospectus and in its constitutional documents a very clear statement that one of the risks for an investor of investing in the firm's business was that:

Lawyers have a primary duty to the courts and a secondary duty to their clients. These duties are paramount given the nature of the Company's business as an Incorporated Legal Practice. There could be circumstances in which the lawyers of Slater & Gordon are required to act in accordance with these duties and contrary to other corporate responsibilities and against the interests of Shareholders or the short-term profitability of the Company.[80]

This wording was developed in consultation with the relevant corporate and legal professional regulators[81] – along with other more specific provisions making it clear that investors cannot interfere with the running of the firm and its cases.[82] These provisions directly address the problem of the conflict created by having a shareholder in the firm whose interests are at odds with those of a client. It is clear that client interests come before the shareholder's, and that the duty to the court is paramount over both clients and shareholders.

### 7.5.2 Ethical infrastructure for incorporated legal practice

A firm's 'ethical infrastructure' is its formal and informal management policies, procedures and controls, and, importantly, habits of interaction and practice that support and encourage ethical behaviour.[83] It recognizes that firms above a certain size cannot rely on the natural functioning of informal collegial relations among the partners to ensure consistent ethical norms are transmitted throughout the work teams that make up the firm – and that junior lawyers develop their own sense of individual ethical judgement and responsibility. As firms become larger and more bureaucratic in the way they organize their business activities,[84] they will also need to become more intentional about designing ethics into their organizational structures.[85] At the moment, we rely too much on individual lawyers to act professionally and ethically in organizational contexts that put tremendous pressure on them to act unethically.

Most law firms, especially the larger ones, already recognize that some aspects of ethical infrastructure are desirable and necessary in some areas as a matter of good practice, although they may not have thought of what they do as 'implementing an ethical infrastructure'. For example, most law firms in Australia and elsewhere already recognize the need to have systems in place to check for potential conflicts of interest before taking on a new client.

These conflicts systems have often involved appointing a conflicts partner or conflicts committee to decide how obligations to avoid conflicts should be complied with in specific cases.[86] After the *McCabe* case, some Australian legal professional associations also encouraged law firms to appoint ethics partners and put in place more general measures to promote ethical discussion and 'reporting up' of potential ethical problems.[87] In the United States over the last 10 years, many larger law firms have begun to appoint ethics partners and ethics committees to be specially responsible for monitoring compliance with professional ethical obligations more broadly, and to act as a point of contact for advice and discussion about ethical issues.[88] In some US firms, this is a full-time, specifically compensated position.[89] Having a compensated ethics partner position, and appropriate timesheet options for raising, discussing and receiving advice on ethical problems, could be an important way for a firm to show how serious it is about ethical behaviour. If firm managers want lawyers to have the capacity to see ethical issues, and the opportunity to make and act on ethical judgements, then the firm needs to provide the time, resources and incentives for lawyers to be able to do so.

Some Australian law firms have also hired external ethics consultants to audit their ethical infrastructure and suggest changes. Clayton Utz did this in direct response to the criticism of its behaviour in the *McCabe* case – and is now considered a leader in this area.[90] Slater and Gordon, as we have seen, is also doing it as part of its listing and ongoing governance arrangements.

For incorporated law firms in Australia, intentionally designing an ethical infrastructure is not an optional extra – it is a regulatory requirement that goes along with incorporation. The Australian law requires that all incorporated legal practices must have 'appropriate management systems' in place to ensure that the firm, its directors and employees comply with all their legal and professional ethical obligations. Each incorporated legal practice must have at least one director who is a legal practitioner and whose nominated job it is to make sure that appropriate management systems are in place to enable the provision of legal services by the practice according to professional conduct obligations. The legal practitioner director must also take all reasonable steps to ensure that breaches of professional obligations do not occur and that, if they do, appropriate remedial action is taken.[91] The legal practitioner director can be liable for disciplinary action if the provisions quoted above are breached. These are additional responsibilities on incorporated legal practices that are intended to complement and supplement the continuing professional conduct and duty of care obligations of all legal practitioners employed by the firm.[92] In other words, a degree of firm-level corporate responsibility has been added on to the existing individual responsibility system. Similar requirements are to be placed on law firms operating as alternative business structures in the United Kingdom, when they are allowed.[93]

The various regulatory requirements on ILPs and their officers are to be supervised and enforced by the ordinary professional conduct regulators (such as the Legal Services Commissioners in each state, the tribunals that decide professional conduct matters and the self-regulatory professional associations). These regulators are given powers to audit the compliance with regulatory obligations of ILPs, their officers and employees, as well as their management of the provision of legal services (including the way they supervise officers and employees). These audits may be conducted whether or not a complaint has been made about the ILP's provision of legal services. They may be taken into account in disciplinary proceedings against a legal practitioner director or other persons, and in decisions about the grant, renewal, amendment, cancellation or suspension of a practising certificate.[94]

The New South Wales and Queensland Legal Services Commissioners (independent regulators of the legal profession in those states) have adopted a list of 10 objectives to be addressed by 'appropriate management systems' (shown in Table 7.2).[95] These Commissioners are requiring incorporated firms to assess themselves as to how well they have achieved each of these 10 objectives throughout the firm on a five-point scale – and report the results back to the independent regulators.[96] They are also developing a programme for further monitoring, assessment and external auditing of these appropriate management systems.[97] External audits by the regulator are triggered by events such as a referral from a Law Society trusts account inspector, a failure to respond to the request for self-assessment or ratings less than 'compliant' on the self-assessment form. An empirical evaluation of the impact of this self-assessment scheme in New South Wales has suggested that it is incredibly effective: incorporated law firms that have been through the self-assessment process have on average only one-third the number of complaints per practitioner per year made to the independent Legal Services Commissioner as other firms.[98]

*Table 7.2* Ten areas to be addressed to demonstrate 'appropriate management systems' for incorporated law firms in New South Wales and Queensland

| | | |
|---|---|---|
| 1. | Negligence | Competent work practices |
| 2. | Communication | Effective, timely and courteous communication |
| 3. | Delay | Timely review, delivery and follow-up of legal services |
| 4. | Liens/file transfers | Timely resolution of document/file transfers |
| 5. | Cost disclosure/billing practices/termination of retainer | Shared understanding and appropriate documentation on commencement and termination of retainer along with appropriate billing practices during the retainer |
| 6. | Conflict of interests | Timely identification and resolution of 'conflict of interests', including when acting for both parties or acting against previous clients as well as potential conflicts which may arise in relationships with debt collectors and mercantile agencies, or conducting another business, referral fees and commissions, etc. |
| 7. | Records management | Minimizing the likelihood of loss or destruction of correspondence and documents through appropriate document retention, filing, archiving, etc., and providing for compliance with requirements regarding registers of files, safe custody, financial interests |
| 8. | Undertakings | Undertakings to be given, monitoring of compliance and timely compliance with notices, orders, rulings, directions or other requirements of regulatory authorities such as the Office of the Legal Services Commissioner, courts, costs assessors |
| 9. | Supervision of practice and staff | Compliance with statutory obligations covering licence and practising certificate conditions, employment of persons and providing; quality assurance of work outputs and performance of legal, paralegal and non-legal staff involved in the delivery of legal services |
| 10. | Trust account regulations | Compliance with Part 3.1 Division 2 of the *Legal Profession Act* (concerning trust accounting obligations) and proper accounting procedures |

### 7.5.3 Critical assessment of Australian meta-regulation of law firm ethical infrastructure

Schneyer has argued that law firms, not just individual legal practitioners, ought to be the subject of discipline, and that the primary purpose of this regulation and discipline should be to promote ethical infrastructures within firms. Otherwise, he argues, firm policies and procedures can create economic and social incentives for individual conduct that are distinct from and prior to individual bad acts.[99] For similar reasons, Chambliss and Wilkins have argued that law firms ought to be required to at least have an in-house compliance specialist employed in each firm.[100] The Australian requirements for incorporated legal practices to have appropriate management systems in place are directed at this same goal. They seek to ensure that law firms have in place internal systems and cultures that ensure compliance with professional conduct obligations – and, obversely, to make sure they do not have in place systems and cultures that are likely to discourage employees' and officers' ethical conduct. Indeed, there was some suggestion at the time these requirements were introduced for New South Wales incorporated legal practices that they should be applied to all legal practices, not just those that were incorporated.[101] It appears that in the United Kingdom these types of provision will be applied to all firms.[102]

These Australian requirements begin to take into account the historical failure of ethical regulation of legal practice to address the commercial and organizational aspects of law firms as firms, rather than just concentrating on individuals. But the Australian approach is just a beginning, and raises a number of issues and questions about how expectations for law firm ethical infrastructure should develop in the future.

First, the current regulatory assessment of whether incorporated firms are implementing and maintaining appropriate management systems is based mainly on self-assessments by the firms themselves. It is quite appropriate that in the first instance professional services firms should engage in their own 'self-regulated' process of planning and implementation of appropriate management systems to meet ethical values in the way that bests suits their own contexts.[103] But there must also be capacity for external regulatory monitoring and enforcement in order for the requirement to implement appropriate management systems to be taken seriously. The New South Wales and Queensland Legal Services Commissioners are both committed to auditing incorporated legal practices that either receive a lot of complaints or which have inadequate self-assessment processes in place, and are developing further strategies for monitoring and audit.[104] However, legal profession regulators face the underlying problem that they are not adequately resourced to proactively monitor all incorporated legal practices, let alone all practices (if requirements for ethical infrastructure spread). Moreover, they have traditionally used a mainly reactive style of regulation (in the technical sense that they react to complaints rather than engaging in proactive inspections and monitoring), so taking on responsibilities for monitoring management systems to ensure professionally competent and ethical practice requires new skills and ways of thinking about the regulatory role.

Second, there is a danger that ethical infrastructure initiatives will be narrowly designed to enforce compliance only with lawyers' clearest and most visible legal obligations – duties to the client, rather than duties to the court and the legal system as a whole – and that they will focus on trust accounting duties in particular. This bias is already evident in the way the 10 objectives (see Table 7.2) have been framed. They clearly focus mostly on obligations to client. Moreover, since legal profession regulators have generally been mainly reactive regulators, and most complaints are received from clients, the orientation towards duties to clients is likely to continue. It is very important to protect duties to clients, but it is possible that duties to the court and the law will be neglected. The regulators are unlikely to receive complaints from clients about their own lawyers failing to fulfil their duty to the court, since this is often in the interests of those very clients. Moreover, third parties who are damaged by such conduct and the community at large do not necessarily know about it. Therefore, regulators cannot use complaints to monitor how well appropriate management systems are working to prevent breaches of duty to the court that damage third parties and the overall functioning of the legal system. Moreover, ethical pressures to breach the duty to court in litigation may exist in law firms despite formal policies that value ethics. This is because informal work team cultures and incentives might promote aggressive adversarialism to advance client interests.[105]

Even in relation to duties to clients, there is a danger of a legalistic focus in appropriate management systems. For example, in relation to billing, mere compliance with legal obligations and contractual principles is not enough to inculcate ethical behaviour. The law is mainly aimed at making sure that the client understands and agrees to the fees to be charged so that the lawyer can legally recover those fees if the client later does not pay up. But an ethical law firm would want to make sure the fees it charged were not only authorized by a properly constituted contract with the client after full disclosure, but also that the fees were actually reasonable in all the circumstances. This would require regular, ethically sensitive bill review or double-checking procedures, and attention to what 'padding' conventions existed within the firm. A firm concerned with ethical billing, and not providing ethical disincentives to its lawyers, might even reconsider the need for hourly billing in all circumstances given its ethical implications, and would set billable hours targets for lawyers with a view to them being achievable without padding or unreasonable working hours.[106]

A third limitation of the current Australian legislation regulating incorporated legal practices is the fact that it is the one 'legal practitioner director' who bears the burden on behalf of the whole practice for making sure appropriate management systems are in place. It is probably useful to require a nominated person to have a specific responsibility in this area,[107] but why is the obligation not also shared by the practice as a whole? That one lawyer can be responsible for the misconduct of every member of the firm and every member of the board is much more onerous than the responsibilities which would fall on a similarly appointed person in a corporation. The only sanction available against the firm for failure to have appropriate management systems in place or for substantive breaches of professional responsibility requirements is the possibility that the relevant Supreme Court can disqualify a corporation from providing legal services in the jurisdiction. (The court can also disqualify a particular person from managing an ILP.)[108]

The fourth and most challenging limitation is the danger that regulators and law firm management will be satisfied with formalistic ethics management initiatives that do not make any difference to everyday actions and behaviours, and are not supported by commitment to ethical values by lawyers throughout each firm. In particular, they might fail to support or encourage the development of individual lawyers' awareness of their own ethical values and ethical judgement as to how to apply them in practice.

There is the danger that legislators and regulators will fall into the trap of thinking that law firms that incorporate operate in practice as purely hierarchical, command and control structures in which ethics can easily be legislated from above by the executive via appropriate management systems. There is a danger that an 'ethical infrastructure' will implicitly be thought of as an optional accessory that slots neatly into the corporate form and works instantly – just like you can choose to add a DVD player or hot pink leather seat covers to your new car. But just because a legal practice is incorporated does not necessarily mean that the lawyers and other staff in the firm itself work and organize themselves in a hierarchical, goal-oriented way and that ethics can be value added through a command and control ethical infrastructure. Some incorporated legal practices – such as listed Australian law firm Integrated Legal Holdings' 'franchise model' business – may not be very hierarchic at all. They might be more like a set of contracts and relationships linking various individuals and practice units.[109] Careful thinking about what makes for 'appropriate' management systems for legal practices that are organized in different ways will be necessary. The most robust way of institutionalizing ethics in an organization is likely to be through creating a 'moral community' that is not hierarchical, but more dialogic.[110] The application of moral theory to lawyers' ethics suggests that a crucial aspect of individual lawyers' expression of their own ethical values and judgement should be a law firm context in which lawyers are encouraged and empowered to individually and together deliberate over what ethics requires of them in different situations – and then, importantly, to put the outcomes of those deliberations into practice. Formal policies must support this – for example, by allowing timesheet options for ethical discussion – but cannot create such a culture. Only imaginative leadership can do this.

## 7.6 Conclusion

Incorporation and listing of law firms may have a few access-to-justice advantages for some kinds of legal practice. But there are also plenty of ethical dangers to go along with them. What is encouraging about the advent of incorporated law firms in Australia is that regulators, professionals and ethics academics are now discussing what it means for the ethics, governance and management of legal practice for law to be both a profession and a business. The increasing

organizational complexity and commercialism of legal practice have already sub-
verted traditional individual ethical responsibility in *substance*. But the fact that
legal practice has up to now maintained the *form* of a profession has made it seem
unnecessary to develop new ways of supporting ethics in the business of law. This
is dangerous. The community rightly expects the legal profession to continue to
safeguard the rule of law above private client interests. The profession therefore
needs to support the vast majority of individual lawyers who want to be able
to take pride in the ethical practice of their professional skills – but find it
increasingly difficult to do so in the law factories and in-house situations in which
they find themselves practising.

As lawyers, regulators and legal ethicists, the incorporation and listing of law
firms has prompted us to take the first steps towards working out how to design
twenty-first-century commercial legal practices – whether in law firms, multidisciplinary practices or in-house – where individuals can develop and exercise
their own ethical judgement and responsibility in partnership with others.

Many commercial lawyers have considerable expertise in advising their corporate clients on how to comply with the spirit of the law – and run a successful
business at the same time. We might hope that these lawyers can bring their
expertise and ingenuity to marrying their own particular legal and ethical
responsibilities with the successful running of legal businesses. There is even some
hope that this might have a flow-on effect to other businesses, making it clear that
the general duty to make a profit for shareholders is always subject to other more
specific legal obligations (e.g. environmental regulation, occupational health
and safety standards, competition and consumer protection law, and so on) and
ethical standards.

## Notes

1 Earlier versions of this chapter were presented as the J. Donald Mawhinney Lecture in
Professional Ethics for the University of British Columbia Law School on 12 February
2008 and at The Future of the Global Law Firm Symposium at Georgetown Law
Center, Center for the Study of the Legal Profession on 17–18 April 2008. I am
grateful for helpful discussions at those events and with Mitt Regan, Greg Restall and
Rob Rosen, and for discussions and support from my colleagues in the Ethical Infrastructure in Large Commercialised Law Firms Project – Adrian Evans, Linda Haller,
Suzanne LeMire and Reid Mortensen. I am also grateful to Di Bates, Tahlia Gordon
and Scott McLean for supplying information about incorporation, Peter Gordon
and Andrew Grech for talking with me about their experiences at Slater and Gordon, and
to Sharyn Broomhead and Susie Sugden for very helpful research assistance.
2 Information about Slater and Gordon's listing and share price can be found by
searching Slater and Gordon (coded 'SGH') on the Australian Securities Exchange
webpage: www.asx.com.au
3 See S. Fortney, 'Tales of two regimes for regulating limited liability law firms in the
U.S. and Australia: Client protection and risk management lessons', *Legal Ethics*,
2008, vol. 11, 230; B. Wright, 'Incorporated law firms: The practical and ethical
considerations', *Auckland University Law Review*, 2007, vol. 13, 47.
4 Under the *Legal Services Act* 2007 (UK), 'alternative business structures' with non-lawyers
and external investment are likely to be allowed in 2011 or 2012 after a new regulator,

the Legal Services Board, has been set up. See Solicitors Regulatory Authority, *Legal Services Act: New Forms of Practice and Regulation* (November 2007); C. Edmond, 'Private equity firm first to openly target legal services in U.K.', *Legal Week*, 6 March 2008; J. Flood, 'Future directions in the UK legal profession: Life after the *Legal Services Act*', presentation at the 'Future of Global Law Firm' Symposium, Georgetown University Law Center, Center for the Study of the Legal Profession, 17–18 April, 2008.

5 Some commentators have suggested that once full incorporation is allowed in the United Kingdom, there will be pressure on US jurisdictions to allow incorporation so that US firms can compete with cashed up 'Magic Circle' firms in Asia: C. Mondics, 'Buy stock in a law firm? There's talk again', *The Philadelphia Inquirer*, 12 August 2007, p. D01. Contrariwise, there has also been reported scepticism about whether the very big UK City law firms would find any advantage in incorporation and listing: J. Rozenberg, 'It's tempting, but the Magic Circle is unlikely to go public', *The Evening Standard* (London), 16 October 2007, p. B30; A. Spence and J. Rossiter, 'Investors give thumbs up to world's first law firm flotation', *The Times* (London), 21 May 2007 (online edition). See also W. Li-en, 'Major law firms express interest in going public: UK's Upper House passes Bill to let British law firms list on stock exchange', *The Business Times Singapore*, 29 October 2007 (online edition).

6 The term 'ethical infrastructure' is further explained below at the discussion accompanying n. 84 and following. The term was coined by T. Schneyer, 'A tale of four systems: Reflections on how law influences the "ethical infrastructure" of law firms', *South Texas Law Review*, 1998, vol. 39, 245. See also T. Schneyer, 'Professional discipline for law firms', *Cornell Law Review*, 1991, vol. 77, 1. It was further developed by E. Chambliss and D. Wilkins, 'A new framework for law firm discipline', *Georgetown Journal of Legal Ethics*, 2003, vol. 16, 335; and E. Chambliss and D. Wilkins, 'Promoting effective ethical infrastructure in large law firms: A call for research and reporting', *Hofstra Law Review*, 2002, vol. 30, 691. See also C. Parker, A. Evans, L. Haller, S. LeMire and R. Mortensen, 'The ethical infrastructure of legal practice in larger law firms: Values, policy and behaviour', *University of New South Wales Law Journal*, 2008, vol. 31, 158; M.C. Regan Jr, *Eat What You Kill: The Fall of a Wall Street Lawyer*, Ann Arbor: University of Michigan Press, 2004, pp. 358–61.

7 For a similar argument, see E. Chambliss, 'The Nirvana fallacy in law firm regulation debates', *Fordham Urban Law Journal*, 2005, vol. 33, 119. See also J. Faulconbridge and D. Muzio, 'Organizational professionalism in globalizing law firms', *Work, Employment and Society*, 2007, vol. 22, 281.

8 See the *National Legal Profession Model Bill* ('Model Laws') Part 2.7. Available from www. lawcouncil.asn.au/natpractice/currentstatus.html (accessed 18 July 2008). (The Model Laws were agreed by the Attorneys General of the states and territories of Australia, as well as the Law Council of Australia, the peak organization representing Australian legal professional associations and lawyers. The Bill sets out core model provisions for state legislation governing the legal profession and most states have now implemented legislation in line with the Model Laws.) The provisions allowing full incorporation of legal practices in the states and territories that allow it are as follows: *Legal Profession Act* 2006 (ACT) Part 2.6 (commenced 1 July 2006); *Legal Profession Act* 2004 (NSW) Part 2.6, ss. 135–64 (commenced 1 October 2005); *Legal Practitioners Act* 2006 (NT) Part 2.6 (commenced 31 March 2007, replacing *Legal Practitioners Amendment (Incorporated Legal Practices & Multidisciplinary Partnerships) Act* 2003 (NT), commenced 1 May 2004); *Legal Profession Act* 2007 (Tas) Part 2.5 (commenced 31 December 2008); *Legal Profession Act* 2004 (Vic) Part 2.7, ss. 2.7.4 to 2.7.35 (commenced 12 December 2005); *Legal Practice Act* 2003 (WA) ss. 45–74 (commenced 1 January 2004); *Legal Profession Act* 2007 (Qld) Part 2.7 (provisions were originally inserted in 2003 but only came into effect when the 2007 Act commenced on 1 July 2007). Similar legislation is in progress in South Australia but has stalled for other reasons: *Legal Profession Bill* 2007 (SA) Part 5 (third reading speech 26 February 2008). The rest of this chapter will refer to the relevant

provisions in the Model Laws where relevant, rather than each of the state laws. For further discussion of these provisions, see C. Parker, 'Law firms incorporated: How incorporation could and should make firms more ethically responsible', *University of Queensland Law Journal*, 2004, vol. 23, 347; J. Shaw, 'Incorporation of legal practices under the Corporations Law', *Law Society Journal*, 1999, vol. 37, 67.

9 After Slater and Gordon had listed, a second Australian firm, Integrated Legal Holdings, listed on 17 August 2007. Previously in March 2004 another Australian law firm, Noyce Legal, spun off and listed its residential mortgage processing division on the ASX as National Lending Services Ltd. Previously the British Murgitroyd Group, a holding company that operates subsidiary intellectual property advisory services, had also publicly listed: see V. Burrow with M. Moncrief, 'Legal eagles soar on day one', *The Age Business Day* (Melbourne), 22 May 2007, p. 1. A third firm, Sparke Helmore, the twelfth largest firm in Australia (by number of lawyers), is reportedly looking into incorporation and listing: J. Eyers and R. Nickless, 'Hearsay', *The Australian Financial Review* (Sydney), 14 March 2008, p. 61.

10 The largest five law firms in Australia each have around 200 principals and 800–801,000 lawyers (including principals) nationally, with numbers dropping rapidly after that. Only 100 or fewer firms in Australia have 10 or more principals: see Australian Bureau of Statistics, *Legal Practices*, p. 21. (Data collated by the author from the various state bodies about the largest firms in 2007 confirm that this is still the case.) According to the ABS in 2002, about 70 per cent of Australian solicitors' firms had single principals/proprietors.

11 Based on information about ILPs at 1 March 2008 and total practices at 1 May 2007 supplied by Law Society of New South Wales. Does not include six ILPs with zero principals. 'Number of principals' is counted as number of partners in partnership or in incorporated legal practice number of solicitors holding principal practising certificate. Note that the figures in Table 7.2 give only numbers of principals and lawyers in the New South Wales office of national firms.

12 South Australia has not yet passed the model laws for the legal profession (as of February 2009).

13 There are exemptions available for smaller businesses. See M. Priest, 'Lawyers Inc to beat taxman', *The Australian Financial Review*, 29 June 2005, pp. 1, 4.

14 Eyers and Nickless, 'Hearsay'.

15 Incorporated firms with any two of $10 million or more annual turnover; $5 million or more in assets; or 50 or more employees are required to file annual financial statements under Australian company law. Note that all top 25 firms in Australia would satisfy at least the first and last of these criteria. These would need to comply with Australian Accounting Standards, meaning a profit and loss statement would be required. Guy Templeton, the managing director of one of Australia's largest law firms, Minter Ellison, has stated: 'Minter Ellison is a large firm, and we just can't see a reason to list. We simply don't need the capital and we want to share our profits only with those that make a difference to serving our clients and that's our legal partners. We could certainly live without the onus of stock market regulation and the need to report to the stock market quarterly.' Transcript of ABC Radio National, *The World Today*, 'Legal firm lists on stock market', 21 May 2007. Available from www.abc.net. au/worldtoday/content/2007/s1928472.htm (accessed 7 September 2009).

16 It can also provide tax advantages by distributing income to non-lawyer employees or relatives.

17 See N. Berkovic, 'Company structure can be poison' and 'Is public listing worth the bother?', *The Australian* (Sydney), 31 August 2007, p. 37; K. Harpley, 'Practice simplified', *Lawyers Weekly Magazine*, 24 March 2006 (online edition); K. Harvey and A. Tang, 'Making it your business', *Law Institute Journal*, 2005, vol. 79, 62; P. King, 'Should your firm incorporate?', *Law Society Journal*, 2001, vol. 39, 44; Law Society of Western Australia, *Position Paper: Flexible Practice Structures for Lawyers*, Perth: Law

Society, 1999; J. Lewis, 'In good company', *Law Society Journal*, 2007, vol. 45, 22; J. Lewis, 'Board games: NSW law firms embrace incorporation part 1', *Law Society of SA Bulletin*, 2007, vol. 29, 8; and J. Lewis, 'Part 2', *Law Society of SA Bulletin*, 2007, vol. 29, 12; M. Mahon, 'The role of ILPs, service trusts and other entities', *Proctor*, December 2005; M. Northeast, 'Legal practice structuring: Making the right selection', *Law Institute Journal*, 2007, vol. 81, 34; M. Wasilewicz and G. Beaton, 'Undressing Incorporation', *Law Institute Journal*, 2006, vol. 80, 40.

18 According to the second reading speech for the New South Wales legislation: 'The Bill will allow incorporated companies to expand and complete with other occupational business. The flexible corporate structure will allow Australia to become the legal hub for the provision of legal services in the Asia-Pacific region.' Legal Profession Amendment (Incorporated Legal Practices) Bill Second Reading, NSW Legislative Council, *Hansard*, 12 October 2000, p. 9152; see also R. Evans and M. Trebilcock (eds), *Lawyers and the Consumer Interest*, Toronto: Butterworths, 1982; G. Hadfield, 'Legal barriers to innovation: The growing economic cost of professional control over corporate legal markets', *University of Southern California Law School, Law and Economics Working Paper Series*, Paper 76, 2008.

19 The Australian federal government's National Competition Policy Review process required all states and territories to review all legislation and practices for competition implications. Regulation of the professions, especially the legal profession was a particular priority for competition reform: see F. Hilmer, M. Rayner and G. Taperell, *National Competition Policy (The Hilmer Report)*, Canberra: Australian Government Publishing Service, 1993. The regime introduced in New South Wales to allow ILPs was introduced as a direct result of the 1998 New South Wales *National Competition Policy Review of the Legal Profession Act* 1987. See also Trade Practices Commission, *Study of the Professions: Legal, Final Report*, Canberra: Trade Practices Commission, 1994; E. Shinnick, F. Bruinsma and C. Parker, 'Aspects of regulatory reform in the legal profession: Australia, Ireland and the Netherlands', *International Journal of the Legal Profession*, 2003, vol. 10, 237.

20 Quotations from Victorian Attorney-General Robert Hull's *Second Reading Speech – Legal Profession Bill*, Victorian *Hansard*, 16 November 2004, p. 1546.

21 C. Merritt, 'Lawyers look at survival plan', *The Australian Financial Review* (Sydney), 3 February 1997, p. 5.

22 See the references at n. 18 above.

23 See J. Story, 'Incorporation of legal practices', *Proctor*, November 1999, p. 16. Mayson suggests that there is a natural limit on the size of a fully effective partnership because of the need to monitor against the risks of moral opportunism and moral hazard and the need for the partnership to be built on trust and susceptibility to peer pressure: S. Mayson, *Making Sense of Law Firms: Strategy, Structure and Ownership*, London: Blackstone, 1997, pp. 138–39.

24 The first justification given for allowing full incorporation in the New South Wales Second Reading Speech was that, although practice in multidisciplinary practices was already allowed, it had 'not widely occurred because solicitor companies have unlimited liability and restrictions on membership prevent fundraising from the public': Legal Profession Amendment (Incorporated Legal Practices) Bill Second Reading, NSW Legislative Council, *Hansard*, 12 October 2000, p. 9152. Firms that have in the past formed informal alliances with financial, technical or other providers can properly integrate those businesses using the corporate structure. See also J. Quinn, 'Multidisciplinary legal services and preventive regulation', in R. Evans and M. Trebilcock (eds), *Lawyers and the Consumer Interest*, Toronto: Butterworths, 1982, p. 329 (on the benefits to consumers of multidisciplinary practice); C. Parker, *Just Lawyers*, Oxford: Oxford University Press, 1999, pp. 38–41. Contrast M. Wasilewicz and G. Beaton, 'Undressing incorporation', *Law Institute Journal*, 2006, vol. 80, 40 (arguing that the corporate structure of a firm is much less important than good governance and culture and that the supposed advantages of incorporation in creating value from human capital can be realized just as easily within partnerships).

25 According to 'Hearsay', *Australian Financial Review* (Sydney), 16 April 2004, p. 57, in New South Wales: 'One medium-sized law firm has now incorporated its Sydney office, and then franchised its regional legal practices. Another legal practice incorporated and created several subsidiary companies.'

26 R. Brealey and J. Franks, 'The organisational structure of legal firms: A discussion of the recommendations of the 2004 Review of the Regulatory Framework for Legal Services in England and Wales', paper prepared for UK Department of Constitutional Affairs, 13 July 2005, p. 10.

27 Ibid.

28 See also R. Lloyd, 'British firms watch Australia's law firm IPOs with interest', *The American Lawyer*, 6 June 2007 (online edition).

29 D. Mountain, 'Disrupting conventional law firm business models using document assembly', *International Journal of Law and Information Technology*, 2007, vol. 15, 170.

30 Integrated Legal Holdings, the other law firm listed in Australia, sought listing for this reason and to fund investment in technology.

31 Slater and Gordon Limited, *Prospectus*, 13 April 2007, p. 25. Available from www.slatergordon.com.au/pages/reports_presentations.aspx (accessed 27 February 2008).

32 See S. Clarke, C. Loveday and G. Williams, 'The future for product liability law in Australia', *Australian Product Liability Reporter*, 2005, vol. 16, 129; E. Pearson, 'Insurer profitability and the impact of tort reform', *Precedent*, 2005, vol. 70, 40; J. Spigelman, 'Tort Law Reform: An Overview', *Tort Law Review*, 2006, vol. 14, 5; and E. Wright, 'National trends in personal injury litigation: Before and after Ipp', *Brief*, August 2006, p. 6.

33 Model Laws, cl. 1025. In Australia, lawyers are allowed to enter into 'conditional costs agreements' with clients in which the lawyer can only recover a fee from the client if the client is successful. Under a conditional costs agreement lawyers are allowed to charge an 'uplift' on their normal fee of up to 25 per cent of their normal fee in addition to the normal fee if their client is successful: Model Laws, cl. 1024. (See n. 8 above for an explanation of the Model Laws.)

34 Slater and Gordon Limited, *Prospectus*, p. 24.

35 According to the Slater and Gordon *Prospectus*, p. 44, $15 million of the capital raised was to be used to 'reduce' existing debt. According to the balance sheet in the *Prospectus* (p. 46), Slater and Gordon had approximately $15 million in short-term borrowings and $6 million in long-term borrowings at the end of 2006. The notes to the balance sheet show that there was also an additional $14 million in debt that was retired some time between December 2006 and April 2007.

36 See the Slater and Gordon *Prospectus* and also Bruce MacEwen's interview with Andrew Grech (Managing Director of Slater and Gordon) (August 2007). Available from www.bmacewen.com/blog/archives/2007/08 (accessed 6 March 2008). Contrast the more sceptical view of some commentators that the Slater and Gordon float was just a way to deal with the firm's debt and allow the most senior partners to get their money out of the firm: C. Batt, 'Law firm's float raises cash and eyebrows', *The West Australian* (Perth), 14 April 2007, p. 70.

37 Shaw, 'Incorporation of legal practices', p. 68. See also L. Ribstein, 'Law firms as firms', paper presented at the 'Future of the Global Law Firm' Symposium, Georgetown University Center for the Study of the Legal Profession, 17 April 2008; A. von Nordenflycht, 'The demise of the professional partnership? The emergence and diffusion of publicly traded professional service firms', paper presented at the 'Future of the Global Law Firm' Symposium, Georgetown University Center for the Study of the Legal Profession, 17 April 2008.

38 The author has previously published a more detailed analysis of the arguments against incorporation: Parker, 'Law firms incorporated'. Since then, there have also been a number of more nuanced analyses of the likely ethical pressures and counter-productive incentives that incorporation and listing will provide: Brealey and Franks,

'Organizational structure'; B. MacEwan, M. Regan and L. Ribstein, 'Law firms, ethics, and equity capital', *Georgetown Journal of Legal Ethics*, 2008, vol. 21, 61; S. Mark, 'The corporatisation of law firms – conflicts of interests for publicly listed law firms', paper presented to Australian Lawyers Alliance National Conference, 2007. Available from www.lawlink.nsw.gov.au/lawlink/olsc/ll_olsc.nsf/pages/OLSC_speeches (accessed 26 February 2008); M. Regan, 'Commentary: Nonlawyer ownership of law firms might not cause the sky to fall', *The American Lawyer*, 14 August 2007 (online edition); J. Vidal, I. Jewitt and C. Leaver, 'Legal disciplinary practices: A discussion of the Clementi proposals', paper prepared for the UK Department of Constitutional Affairs, 2005. Available from www.dca.gov.uk/legalsys/blanes-i-vidal-leaver-jewitt.pdf (accessed 26 February 2008).

39 But note that lawyers have already found various ingenious ways around the prohibition on sharing profits with non-lawyers. For example, firms commonly use 'service entities' (most commonly trusts) to minimize tax. The service entity is controlled by the firm, which pays it in exchange for the provision of services: clerical, administrative support, catering, and so on. This payment is then claimed by the firm as a deduction for business expenses, but the profits of the service entity go to the partners (or their family members). There are several reasons why this occurs, including tax savings and de facto profit-sharing: see K. Harvey and A. Tang, 'Making it your business', *Law Institute Journal*, 2005, vol. 79, 62, pp. 64–65; M. Northeast, 'Legal practice structuring: Making the right selection', *Law Institute Journal*, 2007, vol. 81, 34, p. 35.

40 Steve Mark, the New South Wales Legal Services Commissioner, was quoted as saying in 2004: 'My tentative view is that where an ILP becomes publicly listed, the duty of an ILP solicitor-director to the court and to clients will inevitably conflict with the duty of a solicitor-director to the ILP and its shareholders. Furthermore I believe that such conflict is irreconcilable … While the perceived conflict between professional ethics and profit is an ongoing concern in the regulation of at least some present partnerships, in publicly listed ILPs, shareholder pressure for commercial gain will introduce a dynamic for solicitor-directors which was non-existent in partnership structures.' Quoted by M. Priest, 'Hearsay', *Australian Financial Review* (Sydney), 16 April 2004, p. 57. In 2007, Steve Mark stated: 'Apparently, however, my fears about law firms adopting unethical practices appear to be largely unwarranted.' Mark, 'Corporatisation of Law Firms', p. 11. Note also s. 2.7.12(4) Model Laws, which allows ILPs to engage in pro bono services without breach of duties to shareholders. ('The directors of an incorporated legal practice do not breach their duties as directors merely because legal services are provided without fee or reward by the Australian legal practitioners employed by the practice.')

41 Citations to the various judgements and other developments in this case are given below as relevant. The author has previously written about aspects of this case as a case study for teaching and learning legal ethics with Adrian Evans in C. Parker and A. Evans, *Inside Lawyers' Ethics*, Melbourne: Cambridge University Press, 2007, pp. 15–16, 67, 213, and in relation to incorporation of law firms in Parker, 'Law firms incorporated', pp. 362–64. See also C. Cameron, 'Hired guns and smoking guns: *McCabe v British American Tobacco Australia Ltd*', *University of New South Wales Law Journal*, 2002, vol. 25, 768; P. Spender, '*McCabe*: Unresolved questions about truth and justice', *Torts Law Journal*, 2004, vol. 12, 155.

42 L. Cameron, '*McCabe v Goliath*: The Case Against British American Tobacco Australia Services Ltd', *University of Queensland Law Journal*, 2002, vol. 22, 124, p. 124.

43 *McCabe v British American Tobacco Australia Services Ltd* [2002] VSC 73 (Unreported, Eames J, 22 March 2002).

44 *McCabe v British American Tobacco Australia Services Ltd* [2002] VSC 73 (Unreported, Eames J, 22 March 2002) at 385.

45 *British American Tobacco Australia Services Ltd v Cowell* (2002) 7 VR 524. The High Court of Australia refused special leave for a further appeal: *Cowell v British American Tobacco Australia Services Ltd* [2003] HCA Trans 384.

46 This section is based on the author's reading of media coverage of the McCabe litigation and other material publicly available on the case as footnoted below, and the author's conversations with Peter Gordon and Andrew Grech of Slater and Gordon in 2008.

47 See above n. 34.

48 For an investigative journalist's account of the ways in which this had happened pre-*McCabe*, see the episode of *Four Corners* (the Australian Broadcasting Corporation's in-depth investigative journalism programme) broadcast on 10 June 2002 and titled 'Beyond the Brief' (Reporter: Ticky Fullerton, Producer: Linda Larsen).

49 Consider the account in the novel and movie, *A Civil Action* (J. Harr, *A Civil Action*, New York: Random House, 1995; *A Civil Action*, Touchstone Pictures, 1998) of the way in which litigation on a similar scale causes the collapse of a legal practice and the nervous collapse of the main lawyer involved in running the case. See also discussion in Vidal et al., 'Legal disciplinary practices', p. 24.

50 See C. Cameron and J. Liberman, 'Destruction of documents before proceedings commence: What is a court to d?', *Melbourne University Law Review*, 2003, vol. 3, 273; Spender, 'McCabe: Unresolved Questions'.

51 This is evident from the titles of newspaper articles reporting the case such as A. Keenan and J. Fife-Yeomans, 'Lawyers choking in their own smoke', *The Weekend Australian* (Sydney), 13–14 April 2002, pp. 1, 4; C. Merritt, 'Call for ethics debate after BAT case', *The Australian Financial Review* (Sydney), 2 August 2002, p. 55.

52 Cameron, 'Hired guns'.

53 P. Sallman, 'Document destruction and civil litigation in Victoria', Paper AU2004 submitted to the Center for Tobacco Control, Research and Education, University of California, San Francisco. Available from http://repositories.cdlib.org/tc/reports/AU2004.

54 *Crimes (Document Destruction) Act* 2006 (Vic) s. 3, amending *Crimes Act* 1958 (Vic) ss. 253–55. A professional conduct rule to similar effect was also introduced in New South Wales: *Legal Profession Regulation* 2005 (NSW) reg. 177.

55 Clayton Utz Media Release, 'Clayton Utz to close tobacco claims litigation practice', 18 July 2002. The media release states: 'Clayton Utz Chief Executive Partner David Fagan today announced that Clayton Utz will close its tobacco claims litigation practice, effective immediately. Mr Fagan said the Board of Clayton Utz had decided that tobacco claims litigation did not fit with Clayton Utz's positioning as a key strategic adviser to Government and Corporate Australia and was no longer compatible with the firm's long-term national business interests. "The tobacco claims litigation practice is a small Sydney based practice area, representing less than 1% of the firm's business," Mr Fagan said. "For instance, this is substantially less than our pro bono practice, which has a value of $5M per annum." He said the decision removed any potential incompatibility with Clayton Utz's strongly growing public sector practice, and was also in the interests of its thriving corporate business. Mr Fagan said today's announcement related to the firm's business strategy. He said that the review into various aspects of the McCabe judgment was continuing but it was inappropriate to finalize that review until after the McCabe vs BATA appeal and the investigation by the NSW Legal Services Commissioner.'

56 See *(Re Mowbray) Brambles Australia Ltd v British American Tobacco Australia Services Ltd* [2006] NSW Dust Diseases Tribunal 15 (Unreported, Curtis J, 30 May 2006) (rejecting a claim by BAT for legal privilege on the grounds that its document retention policy was 'in furtherance of the commission of a fraud' at 57 and set up under the 'pretence of a rational non-selective housekeeping policy' at 44). See also E. Sexton, 'Ifs, butts and big bucks', *The Age* (Melbourne), 3 June 2006, p. 4; E. Sexton, 'Tobacco giant sidesteps claim it destroyed damaging records', *Sydney Morning Herald* (Sydney), 6 July 2006 (online edition).

57 An initial decision to this effect in favour of Slater and Gordon and the McCabe family was made in December 2007 in the Victorian Court of Appeal: *Cowell & Ors v*

*British American Tobacco Australia Services Ltd & Ors* [2007] VSCA 301 (Unreported, Warren CJ, Chernov JA, Nettle JA, 14 December 2007). Note that because of the fact that Slater and Gordon itself has been subject to legal action from BAT, Slater and Gordon has now become a litigant and both Slater and Gordon and the McCabe family are now represented by another law firm, Arnold Bloch Liebler. This decision is now subject to appeal: W. Birnbauer, 'McCabe rollercoaster hits a high as saga rolls on', *The Sunday Age* (Melbourne), 16 December 2007, p. 9.

58 'How lawyers set out to defeat a dying woman', *The Age* (Melbourne), 29 October 2006 (online edition); W. Birnbauer, 'Cheated by the law', *The Age* (Melbourne), 29 October 2006 (online edition). Subsequently, British American Tobacco sought orders to prevent the publication of the documents against the newspapers, the Cancer Council and Slater and Gordon: W. Birnbauer, 'Tobacco giant sends in big huns', *The Age* (Melbourne), 3 December 2006 (online edition); N. McKenzie, 'Tobacco giant gags Cancer Council', *The Age* (Melbourne), 9 December 2006 (online edition).

59 The legal profession regulators have been rather vague about the outcomes of their inquiries. Presumably they are leaving themselves the option open of being able to reopen those inquiries if more evidence becomes available.

60 W. Birnbauer, 'Top lawyers face scrutiny', *The Age* (Melbourne), 19 August 2007 (online edition). (Reportedly this was in a 'letter' to the Attorney-General from the DPP in August 2007 that was presumably leaked to the newspaper.)

61 See explanation of referral by W. Birnbauer, 'Smoking gun aimed at big tobacco', *The Sunday Age* (Melbourne), 19 August 2007, p. 4.

62 For summaries of evidence about the commercialism, profit orientation and ethical culture of contemporary legal practice in larger law firms, see J. Conley and S. Baker, 'Fall from grace or business as usual? A retrospective look at lawyers on Wall Street and Main Street', *Law & Social Inquiry*, 2005, vol. 30, 783; Parker et al., 'Ethical infrastructure'; Parker and Evans, *Inside Lawyers' Ethics*, pp. 216–24; M. Regan and J.D. Bauman, *Legal Ethics and Corporate Practice*, Eagan, MN: West Group, 2005.

63 See the original judgement: *McCabe v British American Tobacco Australia Services Ltd* [2002] VSC 73 (Unreported, Eames J, 22 March 2002).

64 See L. Corbin, 'How "firm" are lawyers' perceptions of professionalism?', *Legal Ethics*, 2005, vol. 8, 265; S. Fortney, 'Soul for sale: An empirical study of associate satisfaction, law firm culture, and the effects of billable hour requirements', *University of Missouri-Kansas City Law Review*, 2000, vol. 69, 239; S. Fortney, 'The billable hours derby: Empirical data on the problems and pressure points', *Fordham Urban Law Journal*, 2005, vol. 33, 171; L. Lerman, 'Blue-chip billing: Regulation of billing and expense fraud by lawyers', *Georgetown Journal of Legal Ethics*, 1999, vol. 12, 205, pp. 241, 266; L. Lerman 'A double standard for lawyer dishonesty: Billing fraud versus misappropriation', *Hofstra Law Review*, 2006, vol. 34, 847; W. Ross, 'Kicking the unethical billing habit', *Rutgers Law Review*, 1998, vol. 50, 2199; W. Ross, 'The ethics of hourly billing by attorneys', *Rutgers Law Review*, 1991, vol. 44, 1. Cf. H. Kritzer, 'Lawyer fees and lawyer behavior in litigation: What does the empirical literature really say?', *Texas Law Review*, 2002, vol. 80, 1943.

65 *Law Society of New South Wales v Foreman* (1994) 34 NSWLR 408. See also more detailed discussions of this case in A. Daniel, 'Chapter Four: The cost of justice', in A. Daniel, *Scapegoats for a Profession*, Amsterdam: Harwood Academic, 1998, p. 71; Parker, 'Law firms incorporated', pp. 358–61; Parker and Evans, *Inside Lawyers' Ethics*, pp. 209–10.

66 See R. Rosen, '"We're all consultants now": How change in client organizational strategies influences change in the organization of corporate legal services', *Arizona Law Review*, 2002, vol. 44, 637. See also A. Bruck and A. Canter, 'Why the center will not hold: How supply-side and demand-side market forces are changing the economics of large law firms', *Stanford Law Review*, 2008, vol. 60, 2087.

67 See Parker and Evans, *Inside Lawyers' Ethics*, pp. 161, 172–73; J. Griffiths-Baker, *Serving Two Masters: Conflicts of Interest in the Modern Law Firm*, Oxford: Hart, 2002; S. Shapiro,

*Tangled Loyalties: Conflicts of Interest in Legal Practice*, Ann Arbor, MI: University of Michigan Press, 2002.

68 See Regan, *Eat What You Kill*.

69 See *McCabe v British American Tobacco Australia Services Ltd* [2002] VSC 73 (Unreported, Eames J, 22 March 2002) at 62, 284–86. ('One outstanding feature of this case is the extent to which, after 1985, the terms of the Document Retention Policy, and the implementation of a programme of destruction of documents, were the product of advice, decision and supervision by an army of litigation lawyers, from several countries, and being both retained private practitioners and in-house lawyers … The long-standing and very close association between in-house lawyers and private practitioners had the potential for blurring the roles and responsibilities of the lawyers.')

70 See K. Kirkland, 'Ethics in large law firms: The principle of pragmatism', *The University of Memphis Law Review*, 2005, vol. 4, 631. See also R. Nelson, 'The discovery process as a circle of blame: Institutional, professional and socio-economic factors that contribute to unreasonable, inefficient, and amoral behaviour in corporate litigation', *Fordham Law Review*, 1998, vol. 67, 773.

71 D. Hess, R. McWhorter and T. Fort, 'The 2004 amendments to the Federal Sentencing Guidelines and their implicit call for a symbiotic integration of business ethics', *Fordham Journal of Corporate and Financial Law*, 2006, vol. 11, 725, p. 754, citing R. Dunbar, *Grooming Gossip and the Evolution of Language*, Cambridge, MA: Harvard University Press, 1996.

72 For US examples, see S. Koniak, 'Corporate fraud: See, lawyers', *Harvard Journal of Law and Public Policy*, 2003, vol. 26, 195; M.C. Regan, 'Teaching Enron', *Fordham Law Review*, 2005, vol. 74, 1139; W. Simon, 'Wrongs of ignorance and ambiguity: Lawyer responsibility for collective misconduct', *Yale Journal on Regulation*, 2005, vol. 22, 1; E. Wald, 'Lawyers and corporate scandals', *Legal Ethics*, 2004, vol. 7, 54. For Australian examples, see B. Mescher, 'The business of commercial advice and the ethical implications for lawyers and their clients', *Journal of Business Ethics*, 2008, 81, 913; Parker and Evans, *Inside Lawyers' Ethics*, pp. 221–22.

73 P. Margulies, 'Lawyers' independence and collective illegality in government and corporate misconduct, terrorism, and organized crime', *Rutgers Law Review*, 2006, vol. 58, 939, p. 973 (arguing that Enron's outside lawyers had such a close relationship with their client that they were less able to resist client pressure and see issues objectively); Regan, 'Teaching Enron'; D. Rhode and P. Paton, 'Lawyers, ethics and Enron', *Stanford Journal of Law, Business & Finance*, 2002, vol. 8, 9.

74 See G. Haigh, *Asbestos House: The Secret History of James Hardie Industries*, Melbourne: Scribe, 2006; S. LeMire, 'The case study: James Hardie and its implications for the teaching of ethics', in B. Naylor and R. Hyams (eds), *Innovation in Clinical Legal Education: Educating Lawyers for the Future*, Melbourne: Legal Services Bulletin Cooperative, 2007, p. 25; Parker and Evans, *Inside Lawyers' Ethics*, pp. 237–41. Note that in the end Slater and Gordon, among others, helped to negotiate a deal that overcame the effects of the scheme and guaranteed compensation for James Hardie's asbestos victims.

75 W. Pue, 'Moral panic at the English Bar: Paternal vs commercial ideologies of legal practice in the 1860s', *Law & Social Inquiry*, 1990, vol. 15, 49.

76 See *Harvard Law Review* note, 'Collective Sanctions and Large Law Firm Discipline', *Harvard Law Review*, 2005, vol. 118, 2236; Schneyer, 'Professional discipline'.

77 But note that two US jurisdictions (New York and New Jersey) have introduced the possibility for discipline of law firms: see Transcript, 'How should we regulate large law firms? Is a law firm disciplinary rule the answer?', *Georgetown Journal of Legal Ethics*, 2002, vol. 16, 203. And as we see below, incorporated legal practices (but not other legal practices) have some regulatory requirements and monitoring in Australia.

78 ASX Corporate Governance Council, *Corporate Governance Principles and Recommendations*, Australian Securities Exchange, August 2007.

79 At least two United Kingdom-based global law firms (SJ Berwin and Freshfields Bruckhaus Deringer) have even gone to the extent of having formal corporate social responsibility programmes and reports: see G. Westcott, 'SJ Berwin puts corporate social responsibility high on its agenda', *The Lawyer*, 18 December 2006, p. 5.

80 Slater and Gordon, *Prospectus*, p. 84. Slater and Gordon also point out a further risk to its business that the firm's reputation 'could also be damaged through Slater & Gordon's involvement (as an adviser or as a litigant) in high profile or unpopular legal proceedings'. In other words, investors are on notice that Slater and Gordon will not give up its role as a zealous advocate, even if the case it takes on is unpopular. There is also a statement in the Integrated Legal Holdings prospectus about its duties as 'officers of the court'.

81 Mark, 'Corporatisation of law firms', p. 8.

82 Clause 3.2 of the Slater and Gordon Constitution states: 'The Company and the Directors must procure that, where possible, the Company fulfills its duty to the Shareholders, to the clients of the Company and to the court. In the case of an inconsistency or conflict between those duties of the Company, that conflict or inconsistency shall be resolved as follows:

(a)    the duty to the court will prevail over all other duties; and

(b)    the duty to the client will prevail over the duty to Shareholders.'

Clause 16 gives the Board power to not register a share transfer to a person who is a 'disqualified person' under the *Legal Profession Acts* or to require such a person to dispose of their shares.

83 See above n. 6.

84 See J. Flood, 'Partnership and professionalism in global law firms: Resurgent professionalism?', in D. Muzio, S. Ackroyd and J. Chanlet (eds), *Redirections in the Study of Expert Labour: Established Professions and New Expert Occupations*, Basingstoke: Palgrave Macmillan, 2007; A. Pinnington and T. Morris, 'Archetype change in professional organizations: Survey evidence from large law firms', *British Academy of Management Journal*, 2003, vol. 4, 85. There is evidence that medium and large Australian law firms have been particularly quick to embrace bureaucratized management practices, at least compared with their counterparts in the United Kingdom: A. Pinnington and J. Gray, 'The global restructuring of legal services work? A study of the internationalisation of Australian law firms', *International Journal of the Legal Profession*, 2007, vol. 14, 147.

85 Cf. S. Mayson, 'Your capital: Building sustainable capital: A capital idea', in L. Empson (ed.), *Managing the Modern Law Firm*, Oxford: Oxford University Press, 2007, pp. 141, 157.

86 S. Fortney, 'Fortifying a law firm's ethical infrastructure: Avoiding legal malpractice claims based on conflicts of interest', *Saint Mary's Law Journal*, 2002, vol. 33, 669, pp. 689, 697.

87 In 2002, Kim Cull, President of the Law Society of New South Wales, encouraged law firms to introduce 'ethics partners' and for the legal profession to protect whistleblowers within the legal profession: K. Cull, 'Ethics and law as an influence on business', *Law Society Journal*, 2002, vol. 40, 4. In the same year, the Law Institute of Victoria launched a programme for law firms to appoint 'a partner or senior consultant to be the designated ethics practitioner' as a point of first contact for all solicitors in the firm with an ethical question or problem: J. Cain, 'Good ethics requires constant vigilance', *Law Institute Journal*, 2002, vol. 76, 4; see also F. Shiel, 'Push for ethics advisers at law firms', *The Age*, 6 September 2002, p. 7; K. Towers, 'Ethics standards under attack', *Australian Financial Review*, 7 March 2003. The Law Institute of Victoria through its Ethics Committee said it would provide ongoing training for the ethics practitioners and started an Ethics Liaison Group as a direct result of that.

88 Chambliss, 'Nirvana fallacy', pp. 129–30. See also E. Chambliss, 'The professionalization of law firm in-house counsel', *North Carolina Law Review*, 2006, vol. 84, 1515; E. Chambliss and D. Wilkins, 'The emerging role of ethics advisors, general counsel, and other compliance specialists in large law firms', *Arizona Law Review*, 2002, vol. 44, 559.

89 Parker et al., 'Ethical infrastructure'.

90 B. Pheasant, 'Clayton Utz to run ethics audit', *Australian Financial Review* (Sydney), 24 April 2004, p. 3.

91 Model Laws ss. 2.7.9 to 2.7.11. See also Parker, 'Law firms incorporated', p. 372.

92 Note that individual practitioners in each firm continue to have their normal obligations to have a practising certificate if they are practising law, and to have mandatory professional liability insurance.

93 See Part 5 and Schedule 11, *Legal Services Act* 2007 (UK).

94 Model Laws s. 2.7.22. Note that there is no provision for the ILP as an entity to have or need a practising certificate, only individuals who provide legal services. Provision is also made in the legislation for cooperation between the general corporate regulator, the Australian Securities and Investments Commission and the legal profession regulators. The legal profession regulators generally only have authority in relation to professional obligations. Note also that while it was intended that these obligations on legal practitioner directors and incorporated legal practices will over-ride directors' other obligations to the company in the case of conflict, there is some doubt about whether this is legally the case.

95 Available at New South Wales Office of the Legal Services Commissioner website, www.lawlink.nsw.gov.au/lawlink/olsc/ll_olsc.nsf/pages/OLSC_tenobjectives (accessed 18 July 2008). These 10 objectives have also been adopted and developed by the Queensland Legal Services Commissioner. Available from www.lsc.qld.gov.au/24.htm (accessed 18 July 2008).

96 The Office of Legal Services Commissioner, 'Self-assessment and audits for incorporated legal practices', *Without Prejudice*, February 2004, pp. 1–2. The five scale items are: 'The Objective has not been addressed'; 'The Objective has been addressed but management systems are not fully functional'; 'Management systems exist for the Objective and are fully functional'; 'Management systems exist for the objective and are fully functional and regularly assessed for effectiveness'; 'The Objective has been addressed, all management systems are documented and all are fully functional and all are assessed regularly for effectiveness plus improvements are made when needed'.

97 See J. Briton and S. McLean, 'Incorporated legal practices: Dragging the regulation of the legal profession into the modern era', *Legal Ethics*, 2008, vol. 11, 241; S. Mark and T. Gordon, 'Innovations in regulation – responding to a changing legal services market', *Georgetown Journal of Legal Ethics*, 2009, vol. 22, 501.

98 C. Parker, T. Gordon and S. Mark, *Research Report: Assessing the Impact of Management-based Regulation on NSW Incorporated Legal Practices*, Sydney: Office of the New South Wales Legal Services Commissioner, 2008. Available from www.lawlink.nsw.gov.au/lawlink/olsc/ll_olsc.nsf/vwFiles/Research_Report_ILPs.pdf/$file/Research_Report_ILPs.pdf (accessed 1 January 2009). C. Parker, T. Gordon and S. Mark, 'Regulating law firm ethical infrastructure: An empirical assessment of the potential for management-based regulation of legal practice', *Journal of Law and Society*, 2010, forthcoming.

99 Schneyer, 'A tale of four systems'; Schneyer, 'Professional discipline'. See also M.C. Regan, 'Risky business', *The Georgetown Law Journal*, 2006, vol. 94, 1957.

100 See E. Chambliss, 'MDPs: Towards an institutional strategy for entity regulation', *Legal Ethics*, 2002, vol. 4, 109; Chambliss and Wilkins, 'New framework'.

101 G. Dwyer, 'The business of ethics', *Law Society Journal*, 2003, vol. 41, 38, p. 38 ('in a report issued in November 2002 the NSW Attorney-General recommended that the power of the OLSC [Office of the Legal Services Commissioner] to audit the

management systems of ILPs should be extended to any legal practice in NSW, including barristers and MDPs [multidisciplinary practices]').

102 See above n. 3.
103 This approach can be labelled 'meta-regulation', the regulation of self-regulation, or 'management-based regulation': C. Coglianese and D. Lazer, 'Management-based regulation: Prescribing private management to achieve public goals', *Law & Society Review*, 2003, vol. 37, 691; C. Parker, *The Open Corporation: Effective Self-Regulation and Democracy*, Cambridge: Cambridge University Press, 2002; and C. Parker, 'Law firms incorporated', pp. 367, 368.
104 The Australian regulators are still working on extending and improving the assessment and monitoring of ILPs: see above n. 97.
105 See R. Nelson, 'The discovery process'.
106 See Parker et al., 'Ethical infrastructure'.
107 See Chambliss and Wilkins, 'New framework'.
108 Model Laws s. 2.7.24.
109 P. Pursey, R. Heugens, M. Kaptein and J. van Oosterhout, 'Contracts to communities: A processual model of organizational virtue', *Journal of Management Studies*, 2008, vol. 45, 100.
110 Ibid.

# 8 Carnegie's missing step: prescribing lawyer retraining

*Lawrence K. Hellman[1]*

## 8.1 Introduction

The Carnegie Foundation's 2007 report on legal education has triggered a re-examination of the purposes and methods of legal education around the world. It proposes reforms calculated to produce graduates who are better prepared for practice and more strongly committed to perform responsibly in practice. Its recommendations are intended to lead law schools to develop lawyers who have a confident and constructive sense of professional identity and purpose so they will pursue their careers with a deeper commitment to the highest possible values of the legal profession – higher values than are currently observed among practitioners. While the Carnegie Foundation's recommendations are sound, the law schools' efforts to develop a more ethical legal profession will be limited if there is not a concomitant effort on the part of the leaders of the profession and regulators to secure broader adherence to the profession's ideals by those who are already licensed to practise. This is because one's legal education and professional formation continue into one's practice years, and they are impacted by the practising Bar during and after law school. The lessons taught in the law schools can be diluted by what law students and new lawyers observe in practice and how they see incidents of misconduct treated by the organized Bar and the more experienced lawyers with whom they come into contact. Therefore, building a more responsible legal profession requires a more focused commitment not only of law faculty, but of practising lawyers as well.

The Carnegie Foundation for the Advancement of Teaching issued a report[2] on legal education in 2007 that has proved to be very influential.[3] *Educating Lawyers: Preparation for the Profession of Law* (the Carnegie Report) makes two overarching recommendations: (1) preparation for the practice of law should be understood to involve three distinct but related 'apprenticeships' (cognitive, practical and ethical-social);[4] and (2) the three apprenticeships should be administered in an 'integrated' manner.[5] To implement the integrated model of legal education, the Carnegie Report encourages law schools to provide students with more lawyering experiences under the supervision of the law schools. This may be through clinics, externships or simulations.[6] One goal of this integrated approach to legal education is to persuade law schools to introduce strategies that will develop lawyers who have a confident and constructive sense of professional identity and purpose so that they will pursue their careers with a deeper commitment to the highest possible values of the legal profession – higher values than are currently observed among many practitioners.[7]

The Carnegie Report's recommendations have been praised widely.[8] However, in addition to any practical training they receive in law school, most law students gain legal experience through internships that take place outside of the curriculum and pedagogy offered by law faculty.[9] Beyond that, it is well understood that a fledgling lawyer's legal education and professional formation continue after they have graduated from law school and entered the profession.[10] The learning that takes place outside of law school is powerful,[11] and it can be especially influential in terms of the absorption of professional values and the formation of one's professional identity.[12] Unfortunately, the Carnegie Report does not take account of those forces that are beyond the ability of the law schools to control or influence. This chapter reviews the formative impact of non-law school professional experiences of emerging lawyers and addresses the need to engage the practising Bar if the legal profession is to be moved in the direction that the Carnegie Report advocates.

## 8.2 Placing the Carnegie Report within the MacCrate Report's 'legal education continuum'

Legal education has been a much-studied enterprise.[13] The 2007 Carnegie Foundation Report, *Educating Lawyers*, is only the latest in a string of studies that have sought to influence the educational experiences of those entering a profession whose performance is critical to the fairness of the legal system and the public's acceptance of the rule of law. One study that has had an enduring impact on the content of legal education is the report of an American Bar Association task force published in 1992, known as the 'MacCrate Report' in honour of Robert MacCrate, who chaired the task force. The task force was created to address what many viewed as a growing gap between legal education and the legal profession.[14] The MacCrate Report's title describes its key insight: *Legal Education and Professional Development: An Educational Continuum*.[15] It made the point that legal education 'neither begins nor ends with three years of law school study'.[16] Rather, it takes place along a 'continuum' that includes one's educational and life experiences before coming to law school,[17] as well as learning experiences that take place after admission to the Bar.[18] Consequently: 'It is the responsibility of law schools *and the practising bar* to assist students *and lawyers* to develop the skills and values required to complete the journey [to becoming a responsible professional].'[19] In short, the MacCrate Report recognized that both the law schools *and the practising Bar* have roles to play 'in assisting prospective lawyers as they move along the continuum from applicant to student to qualified lawyer'.[20]

The MacCrate Report articulated a 'Statement of Fundamental Lawyering Skills and Professional Values' that the educational continuum should seek to develop in each lawyer.[21] The Carnegie Report relies heavily on the MacCrate Report's Statement of Fundamental Skills and Values, and accepts the Statement's appropriateness in defining the objectives of legal education.[22] Indeed, in many ways the Carnegie Report can be viewed as an attempt to improve the process through which the fundamental skills and values identified in the MacCrate Report are developed in emerging lawyers. The Carnegie Report's 'integrated' approach for developing professional skills and values is proposed as a method that is superior to the MacCrate Report's 'additive' approach to legal education.[23] However, the Carnegie Report focuses exclusively on the law schools and how they can perform better with respect to developing the fundamental lawyering skills and values that were identified in the MacCrate Report. The Carnegie Report gives no attention to the existence of the educational continuum that was emphasized in the MacCrate Report.[24] This omission, though perhaps understandable,[25] is significant.

Like the MacCrate Report,[26] the Carnegie Report acknowledges that part-time and summer professional employment experiences during one's law school years have educational potential, offering a fertile environment for the development of professional skills and values.[27] Both reports encourage law schools to seek to harness that educational potential through the adoption of courses or seminars within the formal law school curriculum that would be linked to the students' working experiences.[28] But neither report offers specific recommendations on how law schools can do this effectively, particularly with respect to professional ethics, nor do they confront the significant challenges law schools will encounter in attempting to do so. Further, neither report comes to grips with the *post*-law school portion of the continuum. When the MacCrate Report turned its attention to this phase of a lawyer's development, it limited itself to considering formal 'transition to practice' or 'continuing legal education' programmes.[29] Even a section regarding 'on-the-job and in-house training' conceptualized organized training programmes in the CLE mould, avoiding consideration of the influence that practitioners outside of such formal programmes can have on students/trainee lawyers.[30] The Carnegie Report simply fails to acknowledge that professional value formation continues after new lawyers have left their law schools behind and that practitioners significantly influence that process through mentoring (formal and informal) that takes place in the practice environment. It also fails to appreciate that some of the influences experienced in practice may be decidedly negative.

While law schools play a vital role in educating future lawyers, it needs to be recognized that the lessons learned are not confined to the classroom – the character and values of future lawyers are influenced and formed throughout the educational continuum process. The successful implementation of the Carnegie Report's recommendations will only be achieved if the practising Bar supports and reinforces the efforts of the law schools.

## 8.3 The relative influence of law school instruction and practice on the formation of professional values: power and direction

Before the publication of the MacCrate Report in 1992, several sociological studies of the legal profession had established that the practice experiences of lawyers are more important than law school instruction in determining how they resolve questions of legal ethics.[31] The MacCrate Report accepted the accuracy of these findings:

> [A] young lawyer's ethical standards are likely to be shaped far more by his or her mentors in the early years of practice than by the experiences one acquires in the limited practice settings available in law school. Too often, practicing lawyers fail to appreciate their own responsibilities in this area ... Law schools can, and should, teach [the fundamental professional] values in clinical and traditional courses and should instill in students the desire to achieve them in the course of their professional careers. The efforts of the law schools, however, will mean little if the practicing bar shuns its own responsibilities for inculcating professional values. Practicing lawyers can teach by the power of example. Practicing lawyers influence students during their law school years, through contact in part-time work or through summer jobs. Later, in a young lawyer's early years of practice, partners, associates, other mentors, and adversaries may be more significant than law teachers in teaching these professional values.[32]

Numerous more recent studies demonstrate that the practice experience of newly graduated lawyers in both small and large firm contexts is a much stronger determinant of professional behaviour than legal education.[33]

Not only is the influence of practising lawyers more powerful than the influence of law school when it comes to the absorption of professional values, but unfortunately it can also be a powerfully negative experience. An empirical study I published as the MacCrate Report was being completed examined the experiences of several cohorts of law students who were working part time in law offices while they attended law school.[34] These employment placements were not associated with a law school externship programme. Through the analysis of journals maintained by these working law students, the study documented in painful detail that (1) the law students were frequently exposed to poor role models,[35] (2) for a substantial proportion of the students in the study, such exposure was more powerful than what the law school was teaching about professional responsibility,[36] and (3) such exposure had an undesirable effect on some students' formation of professional values:[37]

> This study demonstrated that a student's practice environment quickly supersedes law school as a source of reference for demarcating professionally acceptable behavior. Unfortunately, the reference points provided by the

students' mentors and other lawyers to whom they are exposed frequently falls substantially below the standards projected by the law schools and the ethical codes as the profession's ideals.[38]

It may be possible for the law schools to mitigate the negative influences that law students encounter in practice environments while they are still in law school. For example, the MacCrate Report encouraged law schools to offer 'supporting seminars' to better guide their students who work in law offices during the academic year or in summer internships.[39] The Carnegie Report offers a similar recommendation.[40] But how far can such efforts go, given the power of the practice environment to shape the professional formation of young lawyers?

The major premise of the Carnegie Report is that, through a more purposeful and integrated approach to the formation of professional identity and purpose, the law schools can have a lasting effect on the ethical decision-making of their students long after they have graduated.[41] The authors of the Carnegie Report were encouraged to believe that law schools can achieve this worthy goal on the strength of studies that 'have shown that moral identity and ethical commitment can change quite dramatically well into adulthood'.[42] But if moral development continues into adulthood, it will also continue *after* law school. Moreover, the moral development that takes place *during* law school will be affected by the professional experiences of law students *outside* the auspices of the law schools. Both during law school and afterwards, lawyers-in-training will encounter pressures that cut against conformity with the articulated values of the legal profession. Can the law schools effectively combat those pressures? Can they 'inoculate' law students against the negative influences of unprofessional conduct they may observe in the practice world and find to be condoned or tolerated by more experienced lawyers?[43]

We can only speculate at the potency and endurance of any 'vaccination' sought to be administered by the law schools against the potentially adverse influences of unprofessional conduct to which new graduates/lawyers-in-training will be exposed. Such efforts certainly cannot hurt, but there is reason for scepticism as to their effectiveness. Even when the working students in my study were attending a seminar designed for the purpose of supporting their resistance to inappropriate mentoring and role-modelling encountered in their practice situations, noticeable disillusionment and a retreat from idealism toward pragmatism were observed in about 20 per cent of the sample.[44] The potentially deleterious influence of experiences in practice on professional development has been corroborated by a number of more recent studies.[45]

Both the MacCrate Report[46] and the Carnegie Report,[47] as well as much of the literature of clinical legal education,[48] posit that well-designed clinical instruction is best calculated to 'inoculate' students against a postgraduate retreat from professional ideals. But the Carnegie Report also recognizes the vulnerability of law students to unintended and unconstructive messages that permeate the 'hidden curriculum' of the law school experience.[49] If the law schools have difficulty 'inoculating' students against the perceived negative effects of the law school experience itself,[50] there is reason to doubt their ability to protect their graduates from the frequent and powerful negative influences to which they are likely to be exposed when they leave the law school environment behind. Negative role-modelling is surely as prevalent in the practice situations encountered by law school graduates as it is in practice situations encountered during law school.

## 8.4 The extent of negative role-modelling encountered in practice

It is difficult to overstate the extent to which the students in my study were subjected to inappropriate professional conduct that appeared to be condoned by those with whom they practised. Over 60 per cent of the working students were exposed to at least one instance of flagrant professional misconduct, often within the very offices where they worked.[51] Many students saw a lawyer lie, cheat, steal or disserve a client, frequently doing so as if this were 'business as usual' in the legal profession:[52]

> Perhaps the most disturbing fact to be drawn from the tabulation of these episodes is that the most frequently reported types of violations involved some of the rankest forms of professional misconduct: dishonesty (29 apparent violations), breaches of confidentiality (19), excessive fees (21), and neglect (18). Disregard for the conflict of interest rules was surprisingly widespread (40 apparent violations). Though fewer in number, the frequency of some other categories of gross misconduct is also alarming: frivolous claims and defenses (10 apparent violations), abuse of prosecutorial discretion (8), candor to tribunal (7), bribery (2), and destruction of evidence (2). A total of 296 apparent violations were observed by the 66 students who participated in the [study].[53]

Students clearly recognized that compliance with the legal profession's self-regulatory ideal was rare.[54]

This is not to suggest that most lawyers are irresponsible and unethical, or that unwholesome conduct is the norm in practice. There were many exemplary episodes reported in the students' journals. But the sheer volume of inappropriate conduct to which the working law students were exposed cannot be ignored. A number of more recent studies have observed the prevalence of professional misconduct in practice and its potentially adverse impact on lawyers-in-training as they develop their sense of professional responsibility.[55] The following comment from a later study is illustrative:

> Our professional experience and the observations of the participants in this study ... demonstrate the power of the students' and new graduates' early experiences in shaping their professional attitudes ... [N]ew law graduates are more concerned with learning ways to master, to succeed, to stand out, and to win the next case than in responding to the ethical tensions that are

inherent in a professional practice. For many new [law school] graduates, reflection and ethical considerations seem to be abstract distractions that are better-suited for the life of the academic. Frequently under considerable pressure, new practitioners generally have little time to consider the conflicting values and tension inherent in the role of the good professional because they are in 'the real world, not law school'.[56]

## 8.5 The adverse impact of negative role-modelling on the formation of professional values

For many lawyers-in-training, an unmistakable dissonance arises because of the apparent disparity between what is taught in law school and what is observed among practitioners. Not infrequently, the impact of this dissonance is disillusionment and the devaluation of the professional values espoused by the law schools. The influence of inappropriate role-modelling was summarized in my earlier study as follows:

> Fifteen of the 81 journals (almost 20%) contained entries depicting a student whose expectations about the standards of lawyers were being disappointed and, hence, downgraded ... Comments in seven journals explicitly acknowledged that the writer sensed a reduction in his own commitment to lead a professional life that would be utterly irreproachable. These students were consciously lowering their expectations of themselves with regard to their level of conformity to professional ideals. For this group, it was beginning to be acceptable to knowingly depart from the articulated rules of the profession, and they were growing comfortable in making excuses for their willingness to make these compromises ... Besides these explicit acknowledgements of a shift from idealism to relativism, it was quite common to find entries which revealed students who were reacting to perceived misconduct in a disturbingly tolerant way. Dozens of episodes were recorded in which a student simply went along with or accepted misconduct by a lawyer. Some went along reluctantly. Others went along more easily, rationalizing that 'everyone does it' or that economic considerations justified the misconduct. Many students apparently went along with or accepted the misconduct because they did not recognize it as such.[57]

One of the most unfortunate effects of negative role-modelling on lawyers-in-training can be the erosion of commitment to the legal profession's system of self-regulation:

> Twenty-eight entries in 18 different journals [out of a total of 66] stated that either the writer or a lawyer or other [student] intern known by the writer would not take action with respect to observed misconduct because of some sort of fear.[58]

Fear for job security, fear of gaining a reputation as a troublemaker and fear of retribution led many students in my study to adopt 'the tolerant "live and let live" attitude to which they were so frequently exposed'.[59] Without a viable system of self-regulation, adherence to the rules of the profession – not to mention the profession's highest ideals – can be thrown into jeopardy.

More recent studies have produced similar findings regarding the adverse impact on new lawyers that often flows from the observation of unethical behaviour that appears to be condoned or tolerated in the workplace.[60]

Given the frequency and severity of professional misconduct to which students are exposed during and after law school, there is serious potential for erosion of new lawyers' commitment to the principles espoused by the law schools and the professional codes of conduct. Just as working students are exposed to the sub-par performance of more experienced lawyers, many find themselves adrift in a supervisory gulf where no mentor is available or willing to confirm the inappropriateness of the conduct being observed.[61] In fact, a survey administered during my study revealed that no more than 1 per cent of working students' time in the field is spent discussing questions of legal ethics.[62] In such circumstances, it must be expected that a not insignificant portion of new lawyers will, consciously or unconsciously, stretch the distance between their idealized and pragmatic visions of what constitutes acceptable professional conduct. Two journal entries clearly displayed the path toward rationalization that a neophyte lawyer can travel when adjusting to the pressures of practice:

> We all seem to be letting our ideals and in some instances morals regarding the legal system deteriorate. We are getting involved with the practical aspect of the law so much that the idealistic aspect is lost ... I don't believe this transformation is purposeful, but it certainly has occurred ... [63]
>
> I still believe attorneys must hold on to the idealistic goals as much as possible, but I have got to lower mine somewhat to prevent being a doormat for opposing parties.[64]

## 8.6 Carnegie's missing step: prescribing lawyer retraining

The Carnegie Report does not take account of the impact of professional misconduct that lawyers-in-training observe during law school and when they enter practice, while they are still forming their professional identities. No matter how diligently the law schools pursue the Carnegie Report's recommendations in seeking to develop in their students a strong and constructive sense of professional identity and purpose, they will be fighting against the influences of the 'real world'.

What lawyers do and how they conduct themselves is part and parcel of the education of new lawyers. Every practitioner must think of himself or herself as a 'professor of legal ethics', regardless of whether he or she is serving formally as a supervisor of a student intern or newly licensed lawyer. Any lawyer, at any moment, may be teaching lessons of professional responsibility to observant law-yers-in-training. Those lessons have the potential to reinforce or undermine what the law schools seek to do to form the professional identity of their students. Unfortunately, we know that a substantial percentage of those lessons are of the undermining variety.

Law schools do not operate in a vacuum. While some developing lawyers can be inspired by positive role models that they encounter in practice, many will be adversely influenced by sub-standard behaviour that they see tolerated by the profession. Without a redoubling of the Bar's efforts in the realm of self-regula-tion, the best efforts of the law schools will be diluted by the actions of the prac-tising Bar. For the work of the law schools to be optimally effective, serious misconduct of the practitioners to whom law students are exposed will either have to stop or be reported and disciplined more regularly than is presently the case. This is a necessary precondition before we can credibly implore law students to pursue aspirations that will take them beyond the minimal standards of professional conduct.

How ready are practising lawyers to contribute constructively to the profes-sional development of new lawyers? If the Carnegie Report's assessment of the state of legal education is correct, then it must follow that many practising lawyers are ill-equipped for the role they inevitably play in the development of new law-yers. Only if practising lawyers are expressly trained to appreciate their influence and to use that influence productively can the Carnegie Report's objectives be fully achieved. How the Bar should be retrained to support the work of the law schools is not addressed by the Carnegie Report. This is Carnegie's missing step.

## Notes

1 The author expresses grateful appreciation to Allesan Armstrong and Kindra Dotson, OCU LAW Class of 2009, and Associate Library Director Lee Peoples for their valu-able research assistance in the preparation of this chapter for publication.
2 W.M. Sullivan, A. Colby, J.W. Wegner, L. Bond and L.S. Shulman, *Educating Lawyers: Preparation for the Profession of Law*, San Francisco: John Wiley & Sons, 2007. Hereafter 'Carnegie Report'.
3 See, for example, N.H. Rogers, 'Law schools to discuss possible major changes', *National Law Journal*, 11 September 2007, available at www.law.com/jsp/article.jsp?id=1189450985191 (accessed 7 September 2009). Vesna Jaksic, 'School's third-year program overhauled to teach practice of law', *National Law Journal*, 13 March 2008, available at www.law.com/jsp/nlj/PubArticleNLJ.jsp?id=1205322356908 (accessed 7 September 2009); Washington & Lee University curriculum announcement, available at http://law.wlu.edu/THIRDYEAR (accessed 16 March 2009); Stanford University curriculum announcement, available at www.law.stanford.edu/news/pr/47/A%20%C3%A2%E2%82%AC%C5%933D%C3%A2%E2%82%AC%C2%9D%20Stanford @ 20Law%220Law%20School%20Announces%20New%20Model%20for%20Legal%20 Education (accessed 7 September 2009); M. Lore, 'Balancing law school curriculums: Report on state of legal education causes stir among academics', *Minnesota Lawyer*, 29 October 2007; 'Symposium: The opportunity for legal education', *Mercer Law Review*, 2007, vol. 59, 821; J.D. Glater, 'Training law students for real-life careers', *New York Times*, 31 October 2007, p. 9.

4 Carnegie Report, pp. 27–28.

5 Ibid., pp. 194–97.

6 Ibid., p. 115.

7 Ibid., pp. 52–53.

8 See, for example, E. Chemerinsky, 'Radical proposals to reform legal pedagogy', *Harvard Civil Rights-Civil Liberties Law Review*, 2008, vol. 43, 595; E. Mertz, 'Inside the law school classroom: Toward a new legal realist pedagogy', *Vanderbilt Law Review*, 2007, vol. 60, 483; R. Stuckey, 'Teaching with purpose: Defining and achieving desired outcomes in clinical law courses', *Clinical Law Review*, 2007, vol. 13, 807; C.M. Bryce, 'Teaching justice to law students: The legacy of Ignatian education and commitment to justice and justice learning in 21st century clinical education', *Gonzaga Law Review*, 2007, vol. 43, 577; L.S. Kreiger, 'Human nature as a new guiding philosophy for legal education and the profession', *Washburn Law Journal*, 2008, vol. 47, 247; H.N. Katz, 'Evaluating the skills curriculum: Challenges and opportunities for law schools', *Mercer Law Review*, 2008, vol. 59, 909.

9 D.B. Wilkins and G.M. Gulati, 'What law students think they know about elite law firms: Preliminary results of a survey of third year law students', *University of Cincinnati Law Review*, 2001, vol. 69, 1213, p. 1214 ('By the time they graduate, most law students have worked for at least one legal employer … '); D.N, Zillman and V.R. Gregory, 'Law student employment and legal education', *Journal of Legal Education*, 1986, vol. 36, 390, p. 400 ('With the large majority of any graduating class clerking, the clerkship becomes one of the common experiences of law school. No other experience, besides the mandatory first-year classes, is shared by more members of a law school class.')

10 ABA Section of Legal Education and Admissions to the Bar, *Legal Education and Professional Development: An Educational Continuum, Report of The Task Force on Law Schools and the Profession: Narrowing the Gap* (MacCrate Report), July 1992, available at www.abanet. org/legaled/publications/onlinepubs/maccrate.html (accessed 7 September 2009). Hereinafter 'MacCrate Report'.

11 E.W. Myers, '"Simple truths" about moral education', *American University Law Review*, 1996, vol. 45, 823; I.D. Miller, 'Preventing misconduct by promoting the ethics of attorneys' supervisory duties', *Notre Dame Law Review*, 1994, vol. 70, 259.

12 R.L. Nelson and D.M. Trubek, 'Arenas of professionalism: The professional ideologies of lawyers in context', in R.L. Nelson, D.M. Trubek and R.L. Solomon (eds), *Lawyers' Ideals/Lawyers' Practices: Transformations in the Legal Profession*, New York: Cornell University Press, 1992, 177, p. 184 ('The workplace is the crucial determinant of lawyer behavior.').

13 See L.K. Hellman, 'The effects of law office work on the formation of law students' professional values: Observation, explanation, optimization', *Georgetown Journal of Legal Ethics*, 1991, vol. 4, 537, pp. 538–39 (providing citations to numerous studies); Carnegie Report, pp. 18–19 (additional citations). For a recent review of the major studies of legal education over the past century, see J.O. Sonsteng, D. Ward, C. Bruce and M. Petersen, 'A legal education renaissance: A practical approach for the twenty-first century', *William Mitchell Law Review*, 2007, vol. 34, 303, pp. 363–89.

14 See, for example, H. Edwards, 'The growing disjunction between legal education and the legal profession', *Michigan Law Review*, 1992, vol. 91, 34.

15 MacCrate Report.

16 Ibid., p. 8.

17 Ibid., pp. 225–32.

18 Ibid., pp. 285, 305–17.

19 Ibid., p. 8 (emphasis added).

20 Ibid., p. 8.

21 Ibid., pp. 135–221.

22 Carnegie Report, pp. 93, 113, 136, 173–74.

23 Ibid., p. 190.

24 The Carnegie Report does refer to 'a continuum of teaching and learning'. Carnegie Report, p. 147. However, this is a reference to the continuum of the law school experience itself (typically three years), not the MacCrate Report's continuum that looks backwards and forwards from the law school years.
25 One reason why the Carnegie Report gives little attention to the influence of practitioners on the formation of new lawyers may be that the Carnegie Foundation's mission is focused more on educational institutions than the professions *per se*. After all, the official name of the organization is the Carnegie Foundation for the Advancement of Teaching. *Educating Lawyers* is one of a series of reports that have been published or are in development by the Foundation to examine the education of a range of professionals – lawyers, engineers, doctors, nurses and clergy. Carnegie Report, p. 15. Thus the Foundation's work is directed most explicitly at educators of professionals, not the professionals themselves.
26 MacCrate Report, pp. 268–72.
27 Carnegie Report, p. 88.
28 Ibid., p. 88; MacCrate Report, pp. 270–72.
29 Ibid., pp. 285–317.
30 Ibid., pp. 314–16.
31 F.K. Zemans and V.G. Rosenblum, *The Making of a Public Profession*, Chicago: American Bar Association, 1981, pp. 171–72; D.L. Rhode, 'Moral character as a professional credential', *Yale Law Journal*, 1985, vol. 94, 491, p. 559 (citing J. Carlin, Lawyers' *Ethics: Survey of the New York City Bar*, New York: Russell Sage Foundation, 1966 and J.F. Handler, *The Lawyer and the Community: The Practicing Bar in a Middle-Sized City*, Madison, WI: University of Wisconsin Press, 1967.): J. Law, 'Articling in Canada', *Texas Law Review*, 2002, vol. 43, 449; N.B. Rapoport, 'Presidential ethics: Should a law degree make a difference?', *Georgetown Journal of Legal Ethics*, 2001, vol. 14, 725; P.J. Schiltz, 'Legal ethics in decline: The elite law firm, the elite law school, and the moral formation of the novice attorney', *Minnesota Law Review*, 1998, vol. 82, 705; U.H. Weigold, 'The attorney–client privilege as an obstacle to the professional and ethical developments of law students', *Pepperdine Law Review*, 2006, vol. 33, 677; J. Jenkins, 'The American Inns of Court: Preparing our students for ethical practice', *Akron Law Review*, 1993, vol. 27, 175, p. 182; C. O'Grady, 'Preparing students for the profession: Clinical education, collaborative pedagogy, and the realities of practice for the new lawyer', *Clinical Law Review*, 1998, vol. 4, 485, p. 501.
32 MacCrate Report, pp. 235–36. The MacCrate Report later cited a study that found 90 per cent of law students clerked in a law office during their law school years and these clerkship experiences were more influential than law school in terms of the development of lawyering skills. MacCrate Report, pp. 268–69, citing Zillman and Gregory, 'Law student employment and legal education'.
33 See, for example, L.C. Levin, 'The ethical world of solo and small law firm practitioners', *Houston Law Review*, 2004, vol. 41, 309, p. 362 ('New lawyers entering practice learn to resolve ethical problems by looking to other lawyers.') and p. 376 ('[T]he lawyers I interviewed rarely spoke of lessons learned in law school when they described their ethical decision-making. Instead, they seemed to form their conclusions about how to resolve certain ethical questions during their early years in practice. Colleagues and mentors often affected their decision-making when first confronted with ethical issues.'); R. Granfield and T. Koenig, '"It's hard to be a human being and a lawyer": Young attorneys and the confrontation with ethical ambiguity in legal practice', *West Virginia Law Review*, 2003, vol. 105, 495, p. 522 ('Most of the attorneys we interviewed had absorbed the ethical code of their workplace – a set of values that allowed them to make the compromises necessary to be professionally successful while viewing oneself as a moral individual.'); L.C. Levin, 'Preliminary reflections on the professional development of solo and small law firm practitioners', *Fordham Law Review*, 1998, vol. 70, 847, p. 888 ('It is clear even from this preliminary study that office colleagues and mentors

contribute in important ways to the ethical acculturation of these lawyers'); A. Sarat, 'Enactments of professionalism: A study of judges' and lawyers' accounts of ethics and civility in litigation', *Fordham Law Review*, 1998, vol. 67, 809, p. 835 ('study of professionalism (civility and honesty) in litigation, concludes, "unless firms muster the will to adapt … in ways that are supportive of so-called professional values, little progress can be made" '). D.L. Rhode, 'The professional responsibilities of professional schools', *Journal of Legal Education*, 1999, vol. 49, 24, p. 34.

34  Hellman, 'The effects of law office work'.
35  Ibid., pp. 601–5.
36  Ibid., pp. 596–600.
37  Ibid., pp. 605–8.
38  Ibid., p. 611.
39  MacCrate Report, pp. 270–71.
40  Carnegie Report, p. 88.
41  Ibid., p. 133: '[I]f law schools would take the ethical-social apprenticeship seriously, they could have a significant and *lasting* impact on many aspects of their students' professionalism' (emphasis added).
42  Ibid., pp. 134–35 (citations omitted).
43  The notion of 'inoculation' was suggested to me by Professor Clark Cunningham of Georgia State University School of Law.
44  Hellman, 'The effects of law office work', pp. 605–7.
45  See generally, L. Corbin, 'How "firm" are lawyers' perceptions of Professionalism?', *Legal Ethics*, 2005, vol. 8, 239; Chapter 12 in this volume. K. Kirkland, 'Designed and de facto implementation of ethical norms in large law firms', unpublished paper delivered at Third International Legal Ethics Conference, Griffith University and the University of Queensland, Brisbane, 13–16 July 2008; J. Palermo, A. Evans and W. Lang, 'Ethical climate and ethical behaviour: Individual and organisational factors for Australian lawyers', unpublished paper delivered at Third International Legal Ethics Conference, Griffith University and the University of Queensland, Brisbane, 13–16 July 2008.
46  MacCrate Report, p. 235.
47  Carnegie Report, pp. 120–22.
48  See, for example, Weigold, 'The attorney–client privilege as an obstacle', p. 685; O'Grady, 'Preparing students for the profession'; L.F. Smith, 'Designing an extern clinical program: Or as you sow, so shall you reap', *Clinical Law Review*, 1999, vol. 5, 527; M.A. Milleman and S.D. Schwinn, 'Teaching legal research and writing with actual legal work: Extending clinical education into the first year', *Clinical Law Review*, 2006, vol. 12, 441.
49  Carnegie Report, pp. 29, 150.
50  Some perceive that the paradigmatic law school experience (at least in the United States) influences students to abandon idealism for commercialism. See, for example, Carnegie Report, p. 150; D.L. Rhode, 'Professionalism in professional schools', *Florida State University Law Review*, 1999, vol. 27, 193; J.S. Auerbach, *Unequal Justice: Lawyers and Social Change in Modern America*, New York: Oxford University Press, 1976, pp. 275–77, 295–96; A.S. Watson, 'The Watergate lawyer syndrome: An educational deficiency disease', *Journal of Legal Education*, 1974, vol. 26, 441.
51  Hellman, 'The effects of law office work', p. 611, n. 296.
52  Ibid., pp. 574–75, nn. 134 and 135.
53  Ibid., pp. 604–5 (footnotes omitted).
54  Ibid., pp. 582–88.
55  See, for example, M.L. Girth, 'Facing ethical issues with law students in an adversary context', *Georgia State University Law Review*, 2005, vol. 21, 593; Levin, 'Preliminary reflections on the professional development', p. 893 ('one [interviewed] lawyer recounted stories about an early employer, a sole principal, from whom he "learned how to break every rule in the universe". Another [interviewed] lawyer who had

worked in a large Manhattan firm, recalled how a partner mentored him in unethical billing practices.'), p. 890 (novice attorney reported he was mentored in 'unethical billing practices'); P.A. Joy, 'Evolution of ABA Standards relating to externships: Steps in the right direction?', *Clinical Law Review*, 2004, vol. 10, 681; P.A. Joy, 'The ethics of law school clinic students as student-lawyers', *Texas Law Review*, 2004, vol. 45, 815; N.B. Rapoport, 'Enron, Titanic, and the perfect storm', *Fordham Law Review*, 2003, vol. 71, 1372; L.G. Lerman, 'Professional and ethical issues in legal externships: Fostering commitment to public service', *Fordham Law Review*, 1999, vol. 67, 2295, p. 2999 (neglect; failure to reveal knowledge of false testimony), p. 2304 (neglect; failure to supervise), p. 2306 (unauthorized practice of law), p. 2307 (billing fraud); L.G. Lerman, 'Scenes from a law firm', *Rutgers Law Review*, 1998, vol. 50, 2153, pp. 2158–61, 2176–78 (young associates recount senior lawyers' unethical billing practices and pressures for novice attorneys to conform to the firm's practice); Sarat, 'Enactments of professionalism', p. 833 ('hiding documents was a daily occurrence'); M.R. Ramos, 'Legal law school malpractice: Confessions of a lawyer's lawyer and law professor', *Ohio State Law Journal*, 1996, vol. 57, 863; B. Bedzer, 'Reconstructing a pedagogy of responsibility', *Hastings Law Journal*, 1992, vol. 43, 1159; J.R. Elkins, 'The moral labyrinth of zealous advocacy', *Capital University Law Review*, 1992, vol. 21, 735; O'Grady, 'Preparing students for the profession'; Jenkins, 'The American Inns of Court', p. 175; Levin, 'Ethical world', p. 335 (many small and solo lawyers (who may employ law students) fail to recognize ethical issues that arise in practice); C. Menkel-Meadow and R.H. Sander, 'The "infusion" method at UCLA: Teaching ethics pervasively', *Journal of Law and Contemporary Problems*, 1995, vol. 58, 129; Miller, 'Preventing misconduct by promoting the ethics of attorneys'; S.L. Pepper, 'Counseling at the limits of the law: An exercise in the jurisprudence and ethics of lawyering', *Yale Law Journal*, 1995, vol. 104, 1545; M.R. Ramos, 'Legal malpractice: The profession's dirty little secret', *Vanderbilt Law Review*, 1994, vol. 47, 1657.

56 R.J. Uphoff, J. Clark and E.C. Monahan, 'Preparing the new law graduate to practice: A view from the trenches', *University of Cincinnati Law Review*, 1997, vol. 65, 381, pp. 406–8 (footnotes omitted). For similar findings in more recent studies, see Granfield and Koenig, 'It's hard to be a human being and a lawyer', pp. 516–18 (revealing that many young attorneys engage in questionable ethical practices out of a desire to be a team player and preserve their careers); Wilkins and Gulati, 'What law students think they know about elite law firms', pp. 1245–47 (stating that young attorneys prioritize fitting in to the firm's culture and building 'relationship capital' over ethical obligations).

57 Hellman, 'The effects of law office work', pp. 605–7 (footnotes omitted).

58 Ibid., p. 587 (footnote omitted).

59 Ibid., p. 588.

60 See Granfield and Koenig, 'It's hard to be a human being and a lawyer', pp. 513–18 (revealing that many young attorneys engage in questionable ethical practices out of a desire to be a team player and preserve their careers, and outlining the various techniques young lawyers use to rationalize their behaviour), pp. 1245–47 (stating that young attorneys prioritize fitting in to the firm's culture and building 'relationship capital' over ethical obligations); Lerman, 'Scenes from a law firm', p. 2164 (new associate confesses to padding billing 'enough that I felt I wasn't going to get fired'). The latest work of Kath Hall and Vivien Holmes at the Australian National University describes, from a social psychological perspective, how the 'power of rationalization' often leads to inappropriate behaviour. See K. Hall and V. Holmes, 'The power of rationalization to influence lawyers' decisions to act unethically', *Legal Ethics*, 2008, vol. 11, 137.

61 Hellman, 'The effects of law office work', pp. 571–81, especially 579–80: '53 of the 81 journals (about two-thirds) … contained evidence of supervisory deficiencies'. For a more recent study with similar findings, see L.G. Lerman, 'Professional and ethical

issues in legal externships: Fostering commitment to public service', *Fordham Law Review*, 1999, vol. 67, 2295, pp. 2304–5.
62 Hellman, 'The effects of law office work', p. 564.
63 Ibid., p. 606, quoting Journal SP86–20 – concluding entry.
64 Ibid., p. 607, quoting Journal SU86–87 – concluding entry. The power of rationalization to 'justify' inappropriate conduct is examined in Hall and Holmes, 'The power of rationalization to influence lawyers' decisions'.

# 9 Professionalism and Pro Bono publico

*Lorne Sossin*[1]

## 9.1 Introduction

The relationship between work that lawyers call by the shorthand tag 'pro bono publico' and the public interest is at once simple and complex. It is simple in the sense that lawyers are key guardians of the rule of law, which in a democracy is a cornerstone of the public interest. There is a clear public-interest benefit for lawyers to ensure access to the rule of law, especially on the part of the vulnerable. It is complex because lawyers seek not only to ensure access to the rule of law but also, in many cases, to serve clients, run a business and seek to profit from the provision of legal services. For example, one of the few reasons for which it is ethically permissible to turn away a potential client is if they cannot pay their legal fees.[2] Thus lawyers at once uphold the public interest and pursue their own interests (often through advancing the interests of their clients). These objectives, of course, will not always be in alignment.

In this chapter, I suggest that the current approach to the public interest dimension of pro bono is not coherent. The current approach views pro bono as a public good notwithstanding who is providing the service or why, and notwithstanding who is receiving the service or for what problem. In my view, pro bono should be viewed from two distinct perspectives – that of the lawyer and that of the client. If viewed from the perspective of the lawyer, the important question to ask is why the lawyer is engaging in pro bono. Some lawyers will seek out pro bono opportunities because they see this work as a public duty. Other lawyers, however, may work for partial or no compensation for any number of self-interested reasons – for example, to assist in enhancing their reputation or marketing their services, or as a loss leader for an important client, to impress someone more senior or for other idiosyncratic motives. If the point of pro bono is to reflect the best public service traditions of the legal profession, some of these reasons for acting seem antithetical to this goal. If, however, the interests of the client are considered paramount, then meeting the client's needs is the point of pro bono, irrespective of the lawyer's reasons for providing the service. But will a well-served litigant necessarily be concerned why their lawyer takes on a case pro bono?

Conversely, should a pro bono lawyer care about their client's real reasons for seeking legal services? A client's subjective needs will not always advance the public interest. While pro bono services to prevent an eviction or deportation may be easily justified on public-interest grounds, obtaining free legal advice to launch dubious litigation against a neighbour or to escape a debt can pose challenges to the public-interest rationale for pro bono.

The current approach to pro bono lacks coherence because we embrace the lawyer and client perspectives but seem unable to provide a satisfying account of how existing pro bono policies and programmes advance the public interest under either. While this analysis will focus on the situation of pro bono in Canada, and particularly in Ontario, I believe the issues addressed are of broader application, particularly to common law jurisdictions where access to justice in civil litigation settings is regulated foremost by the monopoly position of lawyers in the market. That said, while a public interest perspective on pro bono is relatively novel in Canada, it is a well-established paradigm in other common law jurisdictions, particularly Australia.[3]

Through an analysis of pro bono activities,[4] this chapter seeks to show that the simple relationship between the legal profession and the public interest is in fact more complicated than it looks. Both the reason why lawyers take on pro bono work, and the reason why clients seek their assistance matter, but neither on its own provides a complete justification for pro bono in the public interest. Despite this complexity (or perhaps because of it), I argue that a public-interest approach allows for both lawyer and client perspectives to inform an understanding of pro bono publico. And, understood in a public interest paradigm, I believe pro bono serves a vital and necessary role in the legal profession and the legal system. In short, I argue that pro bono is a fundamental component of justifiable lawyering.

The analysis is organized into two sections. First, I examine the public-interest justifications of pro bono activities. Second, in light of these justifications, I consider the relationship between pro bono and professionalism.

## 9.2 Pro Bono and the public interest

Typically, a discussion of pro bono activities begins with the idea (and ideal) that pro bono activities reflect a public good – hence the full term, pro bono publico.[5] It is unclear, however, why pro bono is assumed to be in the public interest. Pro bono represents, in most cases, a lawyer donating her time to provide services free of charge to clients involved in the civil justice system.[6] While definitions of pro bono publico may vary, most contemplate legal assistance provided for no charge to low-income or disadvantaged members of the community, legal assistance provided for non-profit organizations or law-reform initiatives involving low-income or disadvantaged members of the community, or legal assistance which otherwise could be said to advance the 'public good'.[7]

There is no doubt that low-income people have a wide range of legal needs, most of them unmet by even the most generous legal aid system.[8] There is also little doubt that the gap between the people who qualify for legal aid, on the one hand, and those who can afford to meet their legal needs through the private Bar, on the other, represents a significant access to justice barrier. In many civil justice settings (family law dealing with custody of children, housing, employment, immigration, consumer protection, and so on), the stakes could not be higher for the individuals involved. Still, it remains less than obvious how volunteering to help someone sort out their private relationships, disputes and legal entanglements serves the *public* interest. In this sense, pro bono services lack the clear connection between, for example, the provision of legal aid to accused persons in the criminal justice system and the public interest.

While this connection may be tenuous, it is certainly an enduring feature of the legal landscape in the common law world. The origins of pro bono publico remain contested. Some historians have linked the modern concept of pro bono to the medieval practice of bishops compelling lawyers in Europe to provide legal services for spiritual rather than worldly compensation.[9] The full history of pro bono publico in Canada has yet to be written. Certainly, lawyers who came of age prior to the rise of legal aid plans internalized the expectation that taking on clients in need was a part of their professional responsibility. This was usually an *ad hoc* arrangement, which focused in particular on the indigent accused facing criminal prosecution. Indeed, the precursor to legal aid in Ontario was a service developed in 1951 by the Law Society to match those facing criminal prosecution and unable to afford a lawyer with available lawyers willing to take their case. In the 1960s, the sense that voluntarism by the Bar was unable to meet the legal needs of the poor led the government and the Law Society to collaborate on the creation of the Ontario Legal Aid Plan in 1967. By the 1990s, providing legal aid had come to be seen more as a responsibility of government than the profession, and it is perhaps no coincidence that the rejuvenation of pro bono as an element of legal professionalism coincides with the demise of the profession's stewardship over legal aid.

While the history of pro bono and legal aid are intertwined in Canada, increasingly pro bono has come to be seen as relevant only where legal aid coverage is unavailable. Given the tremendous need and scarce resources which characterize provincial legal aid schemes, access to justice advocates might question whether pro bono efforts undercut efforts to attract more public funding to expand legal aid. Indeed, some legal aid lawyers point to the irony that, in their view, they contribute more pro bono services than any other sector since they are so rarely compensated for all of the work they undertake on a file.

Legal aid and pro bono thus have tended to exist in tension with one another in Canada. Legal aid schemes arose in the 1960s and 1970s in Canada primarily as a reaction to the failure of traditional pro bono practices to meet the growing needs of the poor.[10] As Jack Major explains, the result of the establishment of legal aid schemes across Canada has been a false assumption that such schemes excuses lawyers as a profession from the burden of ensuring access to justice:

> The present legal aid system grew out of the profession's acknowledged obligation to help the poor, but was in no way intended as a replacement for its over-riding obligations, nor as a full and complete response by the

profession. Legal aid as it exists today was the direct result of lawyers' attempts to fulfill their obligation to serve the needy.[11]

Ironically, the failure of legal aid schemes to meet the growing needs of the poor may be seen as a catalyst for the rise of organized pro bono programmes and organizations in the late 1990s and early 2000s.[12] Legal aid and pro bono, for all of their different ethos and characteristics, both find their public-interest rationale from the same set of principles – that law is a helping profession, and that rights-bearing individuals should be able to assert their rights to the full benefit of the law, notwithstanding their lack of means.

While there is a live (and lively) debate in the United States as to whether pro bono or state-run legal aid is a preferred means of addressing the needs of the poor, there are no credible voices advocating pro bono as a substitute for or as preferable to legal aid in Canada (at least in the criminal law settings where legal aid is most active). Rather, legal aid remains the gold standard for those committed to principles such as the rule of law, access to justice and social justice. Scarce state resources for legal aid, and the limited scope of legal aid coverage, have instead become the point of departure for any assessment of pro bono. It is in civil justice settings, where legal aid coverage is scarce and inconsistent across the country, that the rise of pro bono programmes has been the most apparent and has had the most significant impact. Pro bono in Canada begins from the motto that 'the good should not be the enemy of the best'. It should come as no surprise, then, that pro bono organizations in Canada have looked to the legal aid system for sustenance, just as the legal aid community has been wary at the rise of pro bono.[13]

If there is a public 'good' being served by pro bono in the civil justice system, it arguably flows from one or more of three related principles: the rule of law, access to justice and social justice.

### 9.2.1 The rule of law

The first principle justifying pro bono on public interest grounds is the rule of law. All should be subject to similar legal rules and have similar legal rights. It is unfair and unjust that some are unable to enforce legal rules and unable to assert legal rights simply because they lack the financial means to retain a qualified lawyer. By providing pro bono services, lawyers fill this gap and ensure the rule of law governs all. In its recent report, the Law Society of Upper Canada's Task Force on the Rule of Law and the Independence of the Bar noted:

> It is when a person is most vulnerable, that his or her lawyer can make the difference between a just and an unjust outcome, or fair or unfair treatment. An independent Bar means that everyone is entitled to have their position presented fearlessly and zealously by an independent lawyer within the limits of the law; that no one should be denied the benefit of the law; and that no one may escape the consequences of the law. This

commitment underscores the code of professional conduct that governs lawyers; it is also the essence of the lawyer's role in the administration of justice.[14]

In *Christie v British Columbia*,[15] the Supreme Court, while holding that no one should be denied the benefit of the law, also held that the rule of law does not necessarily require access to legal representation:

> The issue, however, is whether *general* access to legal services in relation to court and tribunal proceedings dealing with rights and obligations is a fundamental aspect of the rule of law. In our view, it is not. Access to legal services is fundamentally important in any free and democratic society. In some cases, it has been found essential to due process and a fair trial. But a review of the constitutional text, the jurisprudence and the history of the concept does not support the respondent's contention that there is a broad general right to legal counsel as an aspect of, or precondition to, the rule of law.[16]

Thus the rule of law as a principle underlying the public benefit of pro bono cuts both ways. If the rule of law requires the independence of the Bar but not access to it, then pro bono appears to be more of a personal choice than a public duty; however, if the rule of law is to truly provide equal benefit to the law, in the absence of constitutionally mandated legal aid it will fall to pro bono activities and the leadership of the Bar to realize this right.

### 9.2.2 Access to justice

The second public-interest principle is related to the first, and it is that the courts should be open to all who have legal disputes that require judicial resolution. Access to justice, in other words, is a public good, and explains why the public bears the cost of court administration, from building and maintaining courthouses to judicial salaries. The public rationale for this expenditure is compelling on the criminal side of the justice system, where the state threatens individuals with a loss of their liberty. Access to civil justice is a more complex issue.

Some kinds of civil justice, such as family law or consumer protection law, provide as compelling a public rationale for the provision of legal services as criminal justice. But other areas of civil justice seem built on idiosyncratic and individual choices, which poor and wealthy citizens alike may make. For example, some people may feel wronged by unfounded rumours that assail their reputation. Some people may believe an oral agreement did not amount to a contract. Some people may believe they were dismissed from employment without goo' grounds. In all of these settings, the civil justice system may provide a remedy, ⊦ it is not clear that the same question of the public good and access to justice a' in each. We may conclude that the loss of employment to wrongful cond' more serious, and that it would be a public harm if vulnerable employees ' access to a forum in which to assert their rights, as would be the ca' context of the adverse impact of a rumour on an individual's reputation. If one is committed to access to justice, however, is one also committed to respecting the choices which individuals make and, by corollary, to ensuring legal representation to advance individual interests on public-interest grounds? This question is taken up in more detail below. For now, suffice to conclude that access to justice as a public-interest principle ought not to encompass everyone's access to all forms of civil justice.

The justice system includes not just civil and criminal justice but also an important third sphere of administrative justice. It is appropriate to address the access to justice issues that are distinctive to the sphere of administrative justice. The legal needs of the poor are implicated not only in private litigation contexts such as employment law, family law and consumer protection law, but also, importantly, in public litigation – involving disputes in areas such as social welfare, health benefits, immigration and refugee protection, public housing, and so forth. Pro bono is less associated with these areas of law, in part because some provincial legal aid schemes in Canada provide limited coverage in these areas, and thus unmet needs are more likely to be seen as deficits of legal aid than as opportunities for pro bono. In some tribunal settings, paralegals provide the lion's share of legal services, and the focus has been on the quality and reliability of service, rather than access to them. The lack of scrutiny of access in the administrative justice sphere, however, may be changing.[17]

Access to administrative justice relates to myriad public agencies, boards, commissions and tribunals that are established by statute with specific public-interest functions, including but not limited to the adjudication of disputes. Some parties in administrative justice settings without the means to retain lawyers will have access to state-run legal aid programmes (refugee claimants, tenants with claims before a rental housing board, welfare recipients, university students defending against academic discipline), or other forms of legal assistance (unionized employees accessing union counsel, for example). Most parties to administrative justice will, however, be unrepresented. This does not necessarily suggest a failure in the system of administrative justice. One of the goals of administrative justice, after all, was to provide accessible forms of dispute resolution where public duties and obligations were at stake.[18] Many of these tribunals were established by statute with a mandate to provide accessible and expeditious dispute resolution for which legal representation would not be needed. For this reason, while access to civil justice may be a matter of public interest, access to administrative justice will in almost every case engage the public interest.

### 9.2.3 Social justice

A third public-interest rationale for pro bono, related to the first two, is that pro bono may facilitate social justice through redressing imbalances of power in the courtroom where one party is self-represented. Where a party cannot understand or meet the case against them, and cannot give voice to their legal rights, this presents a critical challenge to the egalitarian values of a liberal democracy. This

principle also suggests that the public interest in pro bono will reside in those cases where the lawyer's role is one of empowerment.

There is another dimension to the social justice rationale for pro bono, which relates to the legal profession's monopoly on the provision of legal representation. The profession, through the statutory authority granted to provincial law societies, is able to regulate entry to the profession and prohibit non-lawyers from entering this market.[19] As a result, the price of legal services is much higher than it would be in an unregulated market. The result of this has been to price a significant swathe of the population out of being able to access legal services. In recognition of this situation, the legal profession has internalized the ethic of pro bono service – as a kind of *quid pro quo* for the privileges lawyers enjoy.

This attitude may be rooted in *nobless oblige*, but it is said to lead to tangible benefits for lawyers. Lawyers gain a better understanding of the role of law in a democratic society through pro bono; they learn valuable skills regarding how to represent vulnerable individuals and they gain a sense of fulfilment by making a positive contribution to justice. Further, these lawyers learn about the effects and implications of poverty. As Rob Atkinson explains: 'Along the same lines, it is suggested that, once one sees how badly off the needy really are, one will want to pitch in even more. If one does, presumably, one will then receive even more of the blessedness that is the giver's primary entitlement and reward.'[20]

Social justice thus includes the idea that, through pro bono activities, lawyers will establish meaningful connections to and insights about their communities. For this reason, a lawyer's pro bono obligations could not adequately be addressed through a lawyer simply donating money to a worthy cause (including a public-interest legal organization).[21] On this view, it is through personal commitment, involvement and individual relationships that social justice is pursued.

The principles of the rule of law, access to justice and social justice each (or in combination) provide a justification for the public interest in pro bono. The spectre of the unrepresented litigant poses a danger when looked at from any one of these perspectives. While there seems to be a general recognition that the problem of self-represented litigants in the civil justice system is a public problem, there is no consensus that the solution must come from the state or the public purse. This was the subject of a constitutional challenge launched by the Canadian Bar Association (CBA) in British Columbia. The CBA alleged that the exclusion of civil matters from legal aid coverage violated the Constitution.[22] The CBA took this step as the culmination of a significant campaign to highlight access to justice in civil matters. The CBA described its efforts in the following terms:

> The CBA has been fighting for more than a decade to expand civil legal aid services for those who do not have the means to access our legal system … Unfortunately, our submissions have fallen on deaf ears. In fact, rather than increase, civil legal aid funding – particularly in this province – has been severely reduced. The result is tragic. Every single day in British Columbia the rights of people who cannot afford legal services fall by the wayside. They

cannot access the justice system. Often their shelter, health, safety, sustenance and livelihood are at stake.[23]

The CBA's constitutional challenge was dismissed by the British Columbia Supreme Court on grounds that the CBA did not merit public-interest standing. It should be litigants, the court reasoned, not lawyers, who challenged the lack of access to justice. The likelihood of legal aid making a dent in the problem of the unrepresented litigant in non-criminal matters in the short term appears slim.

The unmet legal needs of the middle class have increased dramatically over the past decade.[24] Access to justice for the middle class as a policy initiative has concentrated on pro bono projects. The development of these projects has been facilitated by the creation of public-interest organizations such as Pro Bono Students Canada (1996), Pro Bono Law Ontario (2002), Pro Bono Law BC (2002) and Pro Bono Law Alberta (2007). Together, these have served as catalysts for pro bono profile and activities throughout the country. This has also come, not coincidentally, at a time of increasing competition for legal talent, and increasing disaffection on the part of younger lawyers with private legal practice. Can pro bono solve all these problems?

The claim that pro bono allows lawyers to discharge a public duty by upholding the rule of law, providing access and promoting social justice is intuitively appealing, but does it withstand scrutiny? Why should we not see all charitable activity as public? Is activity undertaken in the context of religious institutions or private clubs and societies somehow different? I would suggest that for pro bono to be properly characterized as being in the public interest, there must be a link between the subject matter or circumstances of the litigation (and/or the litigant) and a public-interest value. Thus, the case for pro bono as public activity is more attractive in settings where lawyers take on constitutional challenges on behalf of vulnerable groups than settings where two small business owners believe they were cheated by a supplier. Whether a lawyer acts pro bono for a tenant or a landlord matters in terms of the public interest. While the impetus behind a lawyer's engagement in pro bono may be lauded notwithstanding the kind of client seeking their services, not all civil matters should be seen as similarly and equally advancing a public good. Indeed, a survey from the 1970s disclosed that many lawyers reported working on pro bono activities, but two-thirds of this work turned out to consist of free legal services for friends and relatives.[25] Once again, here the lawyer's reasons for engaging and the client's reasons for seeking pro bono may not be aligned.

A possible model, adopted by the Law Council of Australia in 1992, approaches the scope of pro bono publico in the following terms:

1.  A lawyer, without fee or without expectation of a fee or at a reduced fee, advises and/or represents a client in cases where:

    (i)   a client has no other access to the courts and the legal system; and/or
    (ii)  the client's case raises a wider issue of public interest; or

2. The lawyer is involved in free community legal education and/or law reform; or

3. The lawyer is involved in the giving of free legal advice and/or representation to charitable and community organizations.[26]

If all civil matters may be transformed into a public good through pro bono representation, how is pro bono distinct from other access-related initiatives, such as contingency fees under which a lawyer is permitted to contract with a client to receive a portion of a settlement or damages in lieu of fees? In contingency fee arrangements, lawyers only receive compensation when the client is successful, and clients who could not otherwise afford to litigate gain access to civil justice. Ontario, the last jurisdiction to maintain a ban on contingency fees (outside of the class actions context), relented in 2004 and finally enacted legislation to permit these arrangements. Ontario lifted the ban explicitly on access to justice grounds.

While contingency fees may have an access to justice rationale, they reflect an expressly market-based approach to the provision of legal services. For this reason, they are sometimes criticized as preying on vulnerable litigants with strong cases. In these settings, litigants end up paying far more based on contingency fees than they would have if paying for lawyers by the hour, while at the same time risk-averse lawyers who are paying upfront for the litigation eschew difficult, novel or less clear cases, leaving the most vulnerable without any effective representation at all. Unlike lawyers engaging in contingency fee arrangements, in which rational self-interest is harnessed to serve access ends, lawyers engaging in pro bono can claim to be advancing the public good *per se*.

The relationship between pro bono services and the financial interest of the lawyers providing these services merits greater attention. The claim of pro bono to be doing public interest work raises the issue of whether these lawyers should disclose the nature of this representation to court, and also whether the clients of these lawyers should be entitled to costs if successful.

Ontario – like all Canadian jurisdictions – adopts a cost-shifting regime in which, as a general matter, unsuccessful parties in civil actions must reimburse successful parties for a significant share of their legal expenses. Cost-shifting is intended to serve multiple rationales, including acting as a deterrent on parties litigating matters which ought not to be litigated, an incentive to encourage settlement or, failing settlement, expeditious litigation, and finally, compensating a winning party for expenses incurred to vindicate their position. If costs were not made available where a case was taken on a pro bono basis, then a losing party would enjoy an unwarranted windfall. By contrast, if costs were made available, they would be based on a fictitious claim, since the winning party was not, in fact, out of pocket as a result of the litigation.

The costs question also gives rise to a further dilemma for the pro bono lawyer. If a case is taken on with the idea that a victory will bring compensation for costs, is it truly pro bono (i.e. work done without compensation for the public good), or does it start to look like a closer cousin to contingency fee arrangements (i.e. where a lawyer expects to be compensated if successful but bears the financial risk if unsuccessful)? Contrariwise, if pro bono is a public good, what is wrong with courts making available costs as an incentive to encourage more lawyers to take on such files? While this issue may not have much traction among the 'megafirms' in downtown Toronto, in smaller centres and rural areas, taking on a significant case pro bono without the hope of recovering costs may prove prohibitive.

All these issues were canvassed by the Ontario Court of Appeal in the *Cavalieri* case.[27] *Cavalieri* involved a corporate proceeding before the Court of Appeal in which the appellant was successful in setting aside a default judgement, and after which the appellant sought costs. The respondent objected on the grounds that the appellant's counsel was acting on a pro bono basis. Neither Rule 57 of the Ontario *Rules of Civil Procedure* nor section 131 of the *Courts of Justice Act*, which together govern the awarding of costs in civil matters in Ontario, addressed the pro bono issue.

The Court of Appeal had a separate hearing on the costs question, highlighting the fact that the case at Bar did not engage public law or Charter issues and was a purely private law dispute. Pro Bono Law Ontario (PBLO), the Ontario Trial Lawyers' Association and the Advocates' Society, intervened to address this question. All the interveners agreed that costs in some circumstances should be available to parties represented by pro bono counsel.[28] The PBLO also encouraged the court to consider that parties or their counsel may wish to donate costs in pro bono cases to charitable organizations on a *cy-pres* basis.[29]

In its decision, the Court of Appeal accepted that costs should be available, at least in some circumstances, for parties represented by pro bono counsel, and adopted 'access to justice' as a newly recognized costs criterion in Ontario.[30] The court openly accepted that allowing pro bono counsel to seek costs would enhance access to justice by attracting more counsel to take on such cases.

Although the court determined that the application of this criterion to particular contexts would be sorted out on a case-by-case basis, the court added that it would more likely be available in public law or public-interest cases, and in those settings could even be available to a losing party if the circumstances warranted.[31] In *Cavalieri*, which raised no public-interest issue, the court held that costs would be available. The court's analysis in *Cavalieri* nicely captures the ambivalence to which the search for the public benefit in pro bono for civil matters gives rise.

An even starker tension emerges from the jurisprudence relating to advance costs. In *British Columbia (Minister of Forests) v Okanagan Indian Band*,[32] the Supreme Court recognized that interim costs could be available in advance of the determination of litigation if three conditions were met. These conditions are:

1.  The party seeking interim costs genuinely cannot afford to pay for the litigation, and no other realistic option exists for bringing the issues to trial – in short, the litigation would be unable to proceed if the order were not made.
2.  The claim to be adjudicated is *prima facie* meritorious – that is, the claim is at least of sufficient merit that it is contrary to the interests of justice for the opportunity to pursue the case to be forfeited just because the litigant lacks financial means.

3. The issues raised transcend the individual interests of the particular litigant, are of public importance and have not been resolved in previous cases.

The court held that these criteria were met in the litigation before it. The aboriginal band seeking interim costs was impecunious, and could not proceed to trial without an order for interim costs. The case was of sufficient merit that it should go forward. The issues sought to be raised at trial were considered by the court to be of profound importance to the people of British Columbia, both aboriginal and non-aboriginal, and their determination would be a major step towards settling the many unresolved problems in the Crown–aboriginal relationship in that province.

In *Little Sisters Book and Art Emporium v Canada (Commissioner of Customs and Revenue)*,[33] the court had an opportunity to revisit the application of the *Okanagan* approach. The court held that it was only a 'rare and exceptional' case that was special enough to warrant an advance costs award. With respect to demonstrating that litigation could not proceed absent interim costs, it would also be necessary to show that no lawyer would be willing to take on the case on a pro bono basis; if a lawyer could be found willing to do so, presumably the *Okanagan* threshold would not be met. As the court stated in *Little Sisters*: 'The impecuniosity requirement from *Okanagan* means that it must be proven to be impossible to proceed otherwise before advance costs will be ordered. Advance costs should not be used as a smart litigation strategy; they are the last resort before an injustice results for a litigant, and for the public at large.'[34]

Thus the court's desire to facilitate pro bono activities has been rooted in a concern for injustice through lack of representation, particularly where the nature of the litigation or the litigant engage rule of law, access to justice and social justice considerations. The court also has expressed anxiety, however, as to how individual choices by lawyers may distort public interest priorities. It is to the lawyer's reasons for engaging with pro bono as a public good that the analysis now turns.

## 9.3 Pro Bono and professionalism

Deborah Rhode, in a recent paper entitled, 'Where is the public in lawyers' public service? Pro bono and the bottom line', argues that the commitment to pro bono has become increasingly justified on pragmatic and business grounds, which in turn has marginalized the premise that pro bono represents the fulfilment of a lawyer's social responsibility.[35] She writes:

In principle, the Bar's commitment to provide unpaid service 'pro bono publico' implies concern for the public; it has also been about what is good for lawyers. What would enhance their reputation, experience, contacts and relationships?[36]

Is pro bono a matter of marketing, or a matter of legal ethics?

From law societies to the courts to professional associations to law schools, the legal community holds out pro bono activities as reflecting the best aspirations of the legal profession. Jack Major, then a Justice of the Supreme Court of Canada, claimed that: 'The concept of service pro bono publico is found at the very core of the profession. In fact, it distinguishes the practice of law as a profession.'[37] Gavin McKenzie has written that the first principle which ought to animate codes of professional conduct for lawyers 'should be the reinforcement of the public service orientation of the practice of law'.[38] On a more personal level, former Chief Justice McMurtry has observed: 'I have come to believe that any lawyer's career that does not include a significant component of public service could ultimately lead to a real degree of dissatisfaction.'[39]

As indicated above, pro bono may be seen as part of a bargain by which the legal profession is permitted to enjoy the fruits of being a self-regulating mono-poly, but must in return commit itself to addressing the needs of those who have been priced out of the market. On this view, pro bono serves to transform lawyers from guns for hire to guardians of social justice. Those more sceptical by nature might see the growing popularity of pro bono among the private Bar as simply a marketing or public relations tool, akin to large polluters investing in 'carbon offsets' to demonstrate their commitment to improving the very environmental conditions their for-profit activities imperil.

David Tanovich, in his article, 'Law's ambition and the reconstruction of role morality in Canada',[40] argues that the legal profession in Canada is in the midst of a 'role-morality' reconstruction, shifting from an ethic of zealous advo-cacy on behalf of the client to an ethic of pursuing justice. The rise of pro bono within the Canadian legal profession both reproduces and reflects this ethic. Even lawyers working in corporate settings devoted primarily to protecting and aug-menting private wealth may give expression to a desire to serve the public interest through pro bono activities. Indeed, large corporate-oriented firms have in many cases led the way in developing pro bono policies, and pioneering pro bono initiatives.[41] Regardless of whether lawyers practise on their own or in large firms, pro bono has been touted as the elixir for the spiritual crisis of the 'lost lawyer'.[42]

Here too, however, the relationship between pro bono and the public interest is anything but obvious. We should be wary of equating access to lawyers with access to justice.[43] It is clear that representation matters, and in some settings the presence or absence of counsel may be determinative of whether justice or injus-tice results. This is precisely why we see legal aid as a sphere of public interest and entitlement for the vulnerable. However, access to justice may also mean access to a qualified paralegal or access to the means to effective representation (e.g. public legal information, self-help centres, etc.).

As Pascoe Pleasance's study in the United Kingdom has demonstrated, access to justice may also mean access to the means to solve problems, many of which have both a legal and a social dimension.[44] Advice bureaux, referral centres and community centres with a legal advice-giving component are all more consistent with this approach than simple legal representation; simply settling the legal matter while leaving the underlying social problems unaffected may represent a superficial and temporary band-aid.

If a core public interest in pro bono is access to justice, and if access to justice at least includes as one of its components access to lawyers, then it is appropriate to look to the legal profession for leadership in advancing access to justice in this sense. Pro bono activity is not, however, a requirement for lawyers in Canada. Neither do provincial law societies require lawyers or firms to disclose the number of hours or kinds of activities devoted to pro bono.[45]

Allan Hutchinson has persuasively chronicled the ways in which the legal profession generally, and law societies in particular, have failed to follow through on their rhetorical commitment to providing equal access to justice.[46] He concludes that if the profession is to have any real chance of matching its rhetoric of service to the reality of social need, lawyers must begin to take seriously the obligation to provide their service at reduced rates, to take legal aid clients and to engage in pro bono work. In other words, he suggests that it is not enough to heap praise on those lawyers who undertake such work. The obligation must be built into the basic ethical fabric of professional responsibility.[47]

Perhaps most significantly, law societies have been reticent even to define the nature or scope of pro bono activity. In Ontario, for example, the Law Society's Rules of Professional Conduct refer to pro bono only in a Commentary to the Rules (2.08) relating to 'Reasonable Fees and Disbursements'. That Commentary states:

> It is in keeping with the best traditions of the legal profession to provide services pro bono and to reduce or waive a fee where there is a hardship or poverty or the client or prospective client would otherwise be deprived of adequate legal advice or representation. A lawyer should provide public interest legal services and should support legal organizations that provide services to people of limited means.

The Canadian Bar Association's Code of Professional Conduct echoes a similar theme, although without mentioning pro bono activities *per se*:

> Lawyers should make legal services available to the public in an efficient and convenient manner that will command respect and confidence, and by means that are compatible with the integrity, independence and effectiveness of the profession.[48]

Unlike legal aid, which is demand driven (as many people who qualify for legal aid certificates will receive them), pro bono is understood by the profession principally as supply driven (only as many people can be served as there are lawyers willing to volunteer to help them). For this reason, as suggested in the *Cavalieri* decision above, the concern has been to encourage more lawyers to volunteer more of their time and expertise. As the recent British Columbia Civil Justice Reform Working Group Report observed:

We believe that, consistent with the altruistic reasons many lawyers had for deciding to enter law school, most lawyers want to volunteer and mandatory requirements are therefore not necessary at this time … *it will be a matter of encouraging them to volunteer (at the firm and professional level) and rewarding them for doing so.* (emphasis added)[49]

As in British Columbia, Ontario's most recent foray into civil justice reform has featured a more prominent role for pro bono representation in civil matters. In November 2007, former Justice Coulter Osborne released an interim report as part of the government-commissioned Civil Justice Reform Project.[50] Osborne recognized the ambivalence of the legal profession towards pro bono in the following terms:

I agree that pro bono services cannot adequately respond to all of the needs of unrepresented litigants. I do not think that imposing mandatory pro bono quotas or greater regulation of fees charged by lawyers is the solution. Market forces and the lawyers' sense of public duty will drive the amount of pro bono services that any one lawyer can offer and the fees he or she may charge. A recommendation to regulate these areas would have a chilling effect on the spirit of volunteerism that appears to be growing among the bar. I prefer to leave it to the Law Society of Upper Canada to examine these issues, should it see fit to do so. However, I encourage Ontario lawyers to continue to offer pro bono services and innovative billing options to enhance access to justice.[51]

The courts have lent their support to the rise of pro bono as well. The recently published *Principles on Self-Represented Litigants*, prepared by the Canadian Judicial Council, states that members of the Bar are 'expected to participate in designing and delivering legal aid and pro bono representation to persons who would otherwise be self-represented'.[52]

As Hutchinson has observed, the legal profession is quick to laud pro bono but equally quick to resist the notion that it is a professional requirement. The United States has witnessed a number of embryonic initiatives to regulate a minimum commitment to pro bono on the part of all lawyers. The ABA's 1983 Model Rules of Professional Conduct, as amended, proclaim that: 'A lawyer should aspire to render at least fifty (50) hours of pro bono publico legal services per year.'[53] At a minimum, pro bono advocates seek to create reporting requirements on pro bono activities for all lawyers. Interestingly, the closer the possibility of regulation appears, the greater the desire becomes on the part of the profession to broaden the definition of pro bono itself.[54]

In 2005, for example, the New York State Bar Association voted to expand the scope of activities covered under the pro bono publico umbrella, as part of an effort to give lawyers credit for the wide range of public services they perform and to allow those activities to form part of what could be counted for regulatory purposes. Along with supporting a definition of pro bono that includes providing

legal services to the poor, the New York Bar voted to include service to individuals, civic groups or government agencies 'seeking to secure or protect civil
rights, civil liberties or public rights, or to meet the basic needs of individuals of
limited means ... where payment of standard legal fees would significantly
deplete the recipient's economic resources', participation in 'activities for
improving the law or the legal system' and financial contributions to 'groups
or organizations whose principal purpose is to address the legal needs of
individuals of limited means, and of not-for-profit organizations'.[55] When push
comes to shove (or, more to the point, when indifference comes to push),
lawyers appear more comfortable with a focus on the lawyers' reasons for engaging with pro bono rather than a focus on the needs of those priced out of legal
services.

The sense that pro bono is defined by 'doing good' and not necessarily by
addressing the unmet legal needs of the poor is exemplified by the following
remarks of a sole practitioner in New York who participated in the debate to
expand the definition of pro bono described above:

> Michael Miller, a solo practitioner and past president of the New York
> County Lawyers' Association, said, 'there are many ways to do good' other
> than by providing direct services to the poor. He said the state bar and the
> Office of Court Administration should recognize the broad range of services
> lawyers can and do provide for the public good. Mr. Miller noted that he
> devoted six weeks to providing legal services after the Sept. 11, 2001, terror
> attacks and served as an elections observer in a war zone – and neither
> activity fit [fits?] within the current pro bono structure.[56]

Importantly, the spectre of regulatory involvement in pro bono in the United
States has served as a catalyst for discussion (and dissention) as to what kind of
public commitment legal ethics requires of lawyers.

The profession's ambivalence is also reflected in the approach of private law
firms (and, as discussed below, within government as well). Some firms have opted
to show their commitment to pro bono activities by allowing lawyers to bill the
time they spend on such files. A recent story in the Ontario *Lawyers Weekly*
explains the rationale for this approach:

> Young lawyers like Ian Collins are very conscious of the cost of legal services,
> the plight of the impoverished and the importance of giving back to the
> community. Burns says, 'New lawyers are looking for firms that value pro
> bono work and treat it as billable time. Firms are smart to pay attention to
> what young associates want. Some firms now use the fact that they do pro
> bono work to recruit students.'
> Collins agrees: 'Associates are looking for a connection to the public
> interest. They go into law because of that. Students want firms who live up to
> their advertising and do pro bono work. It creates good relations within the
> community, to know that we're not just sitting in our tower.'

Collins goes on to say that Fasken Martineau has a policy of treating the first 50 hours of pro bono work as billable time, with the possibility of extending that number upon approval. Collins is enthusiastic about the expansion of the pro bono project to Superior Court, and anticipates that more experienced associates will want to become involved after they've worked with the small claims court program.[57]

As in the case of costs for pro bono counsel discussed above in the context of *Cavalieri*, the trend towards rewarding pro bono activities in order to demonstrate a firm's commitment to public service further blurs the distinction between lawyers undertaking pro bono as a public duty and lawyers undertaking pro bono as a matter of individual choice and/or as a response to market incentives and pressures. Or, as Rhode laments, pro bono has become a bottom-line calculation rather than a matter of discharging an ethical obligation.[58] In her view, 'some measure of altruism is what makes the pro bono tradition so important to sustain.'[59]

Not only is there murkiness on the question of benefit for the lawyer providing pro bono, there is also anxiety with respect to the genuineness of client needs. Members of the Bar have expressed concern that pro bono legal services should not grow to such an extent that they actually take away paying clients from lawyers. In other words, where pro bono services are provided, these lawyers argue that those services be limited to those demonstrably in need and not be provided to those with means who could afford to pay for a lawyer. For this reason, Pro Bono Law Ontario programmes, such as the Small Claims Duty Counsel project or the new self-help-oriented Law Help Centre in Toronto, are available only to those who meet a specified income threshold.

My perspective here is similar to that outlined above. I think the scrutiny regarding income thresholds is misplaced. Pro bono is distinct, based on its claim to advance the public interest. The public interest, as discussed, turns on the link between pro bono and core principles such as the rule of law, access to justice and social justice. Where these links can be demonstrated, either because of the unmet needs at issue and/or the public duty being discharged by the lawyer, pro bono ought to be expressly recognized through the regulatory process. Whether this occurs in the form of public reporting requirements, rules of professional conduct or other means is an important question, but one that lies outside the scope of this chapter.

The fact of regulatory involvement of any kind is likely to lead to the nature and scope of pro bono to become contested – this is also, in my view, a potentially good thing. It will lead to more refined and well-conceived accounts of the public interest in a particular lawyer, firm or organization's approach to pro bono and will serve as a catalyst for more legal practice to include policies and programmes that express a lawyer, firm or organization's commitment to pro bono.

What is inconsistent both with a needs approach and a public duty approach to pro bono is the current regime, whereby a lawyer's engagement in pro bono activities is entirely discretionary, and any activity in which a lawyer seeks to engage for no compensation is treated similarly.

## 9.4 Conclusion

As I have explored in this chapter, I believe the provision of legal services to the poor is unquestionably a matter of public interest. Providing legal services free of charge to those not in need, or those whose needs are matters of private preference alone, is less clearly so. Further, providing legal services free of charge in high-profile matters as part of a marketing or public relations campaign to advance a firm's status or success with recruitment and retention also appears less clearly tied to an ethical norm. Pro bono publico, in this sense, is less of a threshold and more of a spectrum.

What would the spectrum of pro bono look like if these contextual considerations were taken into account? While a full account of the evaluative criteria which might play a role in such a determination is beyond the scope of this chapter, based on the analysis above, I believe that at least the following four such considerations should guide this determination:

1.  Client need (including the complexity and gravity of the matter) and client vulnerability (including any power imbalance between the party benefiting from pro bono services and other parties to the dispute) should be the most important considerations.
2.  The nature of the dispute must also be taken into account – purely private disputes between parties of equal resources such as civil claims between small business owners would be less significance than disputes involving public agencies (immigration, public housing and social welfare disputes come to mind) or disputes where a party's lack of resources exacerbates the vulnerability inherent in the dispute (family law disputes and landlord–tenant matters might be the clearest examples). The nature of the dispute and the nature of the client are closely connected. For example, family law and landlord/tenant disputes are characterized both by the vulnerability of the parties in need of pro bono services and the power imbalance which often characterizes the dispute.
3.  The reasons of the individual lawyer involved in providing pro bono services (billable hours, marketing, and so on) would be next on my hierarchy of considerations. Even if a lawyer might receive recognition for pro bono time, or enhanced reputation and profile as a result of taking on such cases, the public-interest dimension of pro bono is incompatible with a primarily instrumental rationale on the part of the lawyer. Here again, the analysis needs to be contextual rather than categorical, and the perspective should be that of the reasonable observer rather than the subjective perspective of the individual lawyers involved.
4.  Finally, the reasons of the law firm or employer matter too, as well as the regulatory perspective – especially where pro bono is incented or mandated

through regulatory standards or the activities of the regulator. The perspective of the employer or regulator may include enhancing skills, building professional identity, improving the public perception of lawyers or particular firms, but in my view the public interest turns most on addressing the unmet legal needs of vulnerable individuals.

The purpose of an evaluative framework like the one sketched above is to make comparative assessments on pro bono that is at the high end of the public interest, and pro bono that is at the low end. Such a framework facilitates assessing performance, setting benchmarks and ensuring that pro bono activities are effective and accountable.

I have argued that the relationship between pro bono activities and the public interest merits closer attention. First, I expressed the need for a conceptual framework capable of justifying the public interest principles advanced by pro bono activities, notably the rule of law, access to justice and social justice principles. Second, I emphasized the lack of coherence between the lawyer-centred view and the client-centred view of pro bono. I focused on the emerging tensions within the relationship between professionalism and pro bono – for example, while pro bono is seen as, by definition, the delivery of legal services without compensation, the Ontario Court of Appeal in *Cavalieri* justified the availability of costs for pro bono lawyers on the grounds that lawyers may need financial incentives to take on pro bono cases.

I have argued that without elaborating on the meaning of publico, pro bono is adrift and rudderless. Too often, pro bono has been invoked in Canada, as in other jurisdictions, as a way of avoiding important and difficult debates about the public interest in access to civil justice. I believe, by contrast, that pro bono should be the catalyst for such debates. The result, in my view, will be a culture and a system of pro bono capable of addressing both the unmet needs of the poor and the unfulfilled public duties of the legal profession.

## Notes

1  The Osgoode Hall Law Journal has granted Routledge/Cavendish permission to reprint this chapter. An earlier version of 'Professionalism and Pro Bono Publico' was originally published in a special 50th anniversary issue of the Osgoode Hall Law Journal devoted to Legal Ethics and Professional Responsibility. 'The public interest, professionalism, and pro bono publico', *Osgoode Hall Law Journal*, 2008, vol. 46, 131. I am grateful for the comments received at the Gold Coast, Australia where the paper on which this chapter was based was presented as part of the Third International Legal Ethics Conference in July 2008, and at the University of Glasgow, where the paper was presented as part of the Centre for Applied Ethics and Legal Philosophy Workshop Series in November of 2008. I am grateful to those who attended these talks for their comments and ideas.
2  The 'cab rank rule' suggests lawyers should simply take the next client in the queue, but allows for an exception where the next client cannot afford to pay. See G. MacKenzie, *Lawyers and Ethics*, Toronto: Carswell, 1998, Ch. 4; see also E. Cherniak and S. Austin, 'Standing for justice: The lawyer's role in client selection', paper prepared for

the CJO Advisory Committee on Professionalism, Seventh Colloquium. Online. Available from www.lsuc.on.ca/media/seventh_colloquium_cherniak.pdf (accessed 7 September 2009).

3 See, for example, National Pro Bono in Australia, *Mapping Pro Bono in Australia*, Sydney: National Pro Bono Resource Centre, 2007, pp. 3–5. The Queensland Public Interest Law Clearinghouse is a good example of an Australian pro bono initiative tied expressly to legal problems defined as involving the public interest – 'public-interest' matters are defined as those that affect a large number of people, raise matters of public concern, require legal intervention to avoid an injustice, or particularly impact disadvantaged or marginalized groups – see www.qpilch.org.au/01_cms/details.asp? ID=2#40 (accessed 7 September 2009).

4 There is no definition of pro bono with which everyone would agree. At its broadest, pro bono publico may be defined as legal work carried out without compensation for the public good. Many would define the term more narrowly, to cover legal representation on behalf of the poor.

5 See Justice J.C. Major, 'Lawyers' obligation to provide legal services', *Alberta Law Review*, 1995, vol. 33, 493; R. Atkinson, 'Pro bono publico representation of the poor: The good as enemy of the best', *American University Journal of Gender, Social Policy & Law*, 2001, vol. 9, 129; and T. Rostain, 'Colloquium: What does it mean to practice law "in the interests of justice" in the twenty-first century? Lawyering and the possibility of integrity', *Fordham Law Review*, 2002, vol. 70, 1811.

6 In light of the provincial legal aid schemes that are required to provide legal assistance to those unable to afford a lawyer in criminal matters, pro bono has come to be associated in Canada primarily with the civil justice system.

7 This definition formed the basis of a recent survey undertaken by the Pro Bono Resource Centre in Australia. See M. Twomey and J. Corker, 'Pro bono at work: Report on the pro bono legal work of 25 large Australian law firms', *Legal Ethics*, 2008, vol. 11, 255, pp. 256–57.

8 Data from the United Kingdom suggest existing resources do not even scratch the surface of need. While over one-third of those surveyed in 2004 had experienced a legal problem in the past year, only 13 per cent of that group received any advice from a lawyer. See P. Pleasance, *Causes of Action: Civil Law and Social Justice*, Norwich: TSO, 2006. The Canadian Forum on Civil Justice is now undertaking an ambitious needs assessment in Alberta to determine both the incidence and the impact of unmet legal needs in that Province. See http://cfcj-fcjc.org/research/mapping-en.php (accessed 7 September 2009).

9 See J.A. Brundage, 'Legal aid for the poor and the professionalization of law in the Middle Ages', *Journal of Legal History*, 1998, vol. 9, 169.

10 See P. Monahan and F. Zemans, *From Crisis to Reform: A New Legal Aid Plan for Ontario*, North York, Ontario: York University Centre for Public Law and Public Policy, 1997.

11 Major, 'Lawyers' obligation', p. 724.

12 Supporters of legal aid have reacted to this recent rise in pro bono programme with skepticism. See, for example, A. Go, 'Pro bono can't replace legal aid', *Toronto Star*, 13 May 2004. The connection between cuts to legal aid schemes and the rise of pro bono is documented in peer jurisdictions outside Canada as well – see, for example, F. Regan, 'Legal aid without the state: Assessing the rise of pro bono schemes', *University of British Columbia Law Review*, 2000, vol. 33, 343.

13 Legal Aid Ontario, for example, is one of the largest funders of Pro Bono Law Ontario. See www.pblo.org/about (accessed 7 September 2009).

14 See Task Force on the Rule of Law and the Independence of the Bar, *Protecting the Public: The Report of the Law Society of Upper Canada's Task Force on the Rule of Law and the Independence of the Bar*, Toronto: Irwin, 2007.

15 *Christie v British Columbia* [2007] SCC 23.

16 Ibid. at 21.

17 Pro Bono Students Canada, for example, has established a 'Courts and Tribunals' initiative under which law students are providing public legal education and other services for administrative tribunals, including the Ontario Health Professions Appeal and Review Board, which lies outside the coverage of legal aid.

18 This point is developed further in L. Sossin, 'Access to administrative justice', in L. Sossin and C. Flood (eds), *Administrative Law in Context*, Toronto: Emond Montgomery, 2008.

19 In 2007, the regulation of paralegals in Ontario has now opened up a market for legal services to non-lawyers. The regulation of notaries in British Columbia and Quebec may also be seen as a qualification to this assertion. The point remains, however, that lawyers are in a monopoly position with respect to most areas of legal representation.

20 Atkinson, 'Historical perspective', p. 140.

21 This issue is explored in S. Lubet and C. Stewart, 'A public assets theory of lawyers' pro bono obligations', *University of Pennsylvania Law Review*, 1997, vol. 145, 1245.

22 See *Canadian Bar Association v British Columbia* (2006) BCSC 1342 ('CBA'), upheld on appeal to the British Columbia Court of Appeal at *Canadian Bar Association v British Columbia* (2008) BCCA 92. For a discussion of this litigation, see L. Sossin, 'The justice of access: Who should have standing to challenge the constitutional adequacy of legal aid?', *University of British Columbia Law Review*, 2007, vol. 40, 727. For the argument in support of a constitutional right to civil legal aid, see P. Hughes and J. Arvay, 'A constitutional right to civil legal aid', in Report of the Canadian Bar Association, *Making the Case: The Right to Publicly Funded Legal Representation in Canada, Report of the Canadian Bar Association*, Ottawa: Canadian Bar Association, 2002, pp. 331–44, 345–65.

23 See   www.cba.org/CBA/News/2005_Releases/2005-06-20_remarks.aspx   (accessed 7 September 2009).

24 A legal needs assessment was commenced in 2008 for Ontario as a collaborative venture between the Law Society of Upper Canada, Legal Aid Ontario and Pro Bono Law Ontario. See www.lsuc.on.ca/media/civil_legal_needs_en.pdf (accessed 7 September 2009).

25 J.F. Handler, *Lawyers and the Pursuit of Legal Rights*, New York: Academic Press, 1978, p. 100. See also Z. Macaluso, 'That's OK, this one's on me: A discussion of the responsibilities and duties owed by the profession to do pro bono publico work', *University of British Columbia Law Review*, 1992, vol. 26, 65.

26 National Pro Bono Resources Centre, 'Government lawyers and pro bono', Sydney: National Pro Bono Resource Centre, 2004, available from www.nationalprobono.org. au/documents/NPBRCGovtlawyerspaper.doc (accessed 7 September 2009).

27 *1465778 Ontario Inc v 1122077 Ontario Ltd* Docket C43533 (released 25 October 2006) (Ont. C.A.) (*Cavalieri*).

28 While the costs remain the entitlement of the parties, not counsel, the court recognized that counsel would typically make arrangements with clients to recover any costs if available; otherwise, the clients who expended no funds on the litigation would receive an unjustified windfall. See *Cavalieri* at para. 36.

29 The term *cy-pres* is derived from the term *cy-pres commé possible*, meaning 'as near as possible'. The concept allows for distribution of residual damage awards, particularly in class action litigation, where it is not possible to determine each plaintiff's actual damages or when plaintiffs fail to collect their portion of the award. Under the *cy-pres* doctrine, courts may order residual funds to be put to the 'next best compensation use, for the aggregate, indirect, prospective benefit of the class (aggregate *cy-pres* distribution)'. See H.B. Newberg and A. Conte, *Newberg on Class Actions*, 3rd edn, St Paul, MN: Thomson/West, 1992, § 10.17. In April of 2007, the PBLO itself was the recipient of a $19,500 *cy-pres* award where certain settlement funds from concluded litigation had not been claimed. See www.lsuc.on.ca/media/apr1807_cy_pres_award.pdf (accessed 7 September 2009).

30 Access to justice thus has been added to the four other recognized criteria: indemnification, encouraging settlement, discouraging frivolous and vexatious litigation, and discouraging unnecessary steps in litigation.
31 *1465778 Ontario Inc v 1122077 Ontario Ltd* Docket C43533 (released 25 October 2006) (Ont. C.A.) at 20, 45.
32 *British Columbia (Minister of Forests) v Okanagan Indian Band* [2003] SCC 71.
33 *Little Sisters Book and Art Emporium v Canada (Commissioner of Customs and Revenue)* [2007] SCC 2.
34 Ibid., at 71.
35 D.L. Rhode, 'Where is the public in lawyers' public service? Pro bono and the bottom line', paper presented at the Private Lawyers and the Public Interest: The Evolving Role of Pro Bono in the Legal Profession Conference, Baldy Centre, University of Buffalo, 24–26 April 2008.
36 Ibid., p.1.
37 Major, 'Lawyers' obligations', p. 721.
38 G. MacKenzie, 'The Valentine's Day card in the operating room: Codes of ethics and the failing ideals of the legal profession', *Alberta Law Review*, 1995, vol. 33, 859, p. 874.
39 R. McMurtry, 'The legal profession and public service', paper delivered to the Third Colloquium of the Chief Justice's Advisory Committee on Professionalism, University of Ottawa, 2004, p. 3.
40 D. Tanovich, 'Law's ambition and the reconstruction of role morality in Canada', *Dalhousie Law Review*, 2005, vol. 28, 267.
41 The Blakes firm, for example, is one of the first to designate a pro bono partner and to organize a pro bono division within the firm. See www.blakes.com/english/probono.html (accessed 7 September 2009).
42 See A. Kronman, *The Lost Lawyer: Failing Ideals of the Legal Profession*, Cambridge, MA: Harvard University Press, 1995.
43 R. MacDonald, 'Access to justice: Scope, scale and ambitions', in J. Bass et al. (eds), *Access to Justice for a New Century: The Way Forward*, Toronto: Irwin, 2005.
44 See P. Pleasance et al., *Causes of Action: Civil Law and Social Justice*, London: Legal Services Commission, 2004. Available from www.lsrc.org.uk/publications/Causes%20of%20Action.pdf (accessed 7 September 2009).
45 Mandatory pro bono has been debated in the US context – see, for example, R.E. Loder, 'Tending the generous heart: Mandatory pro bono and moral development', *Georgetown Journal of Legal Ethics*, 2001, vol. 14, 459; and Atkinson, 'Historical perspective' – but has not been considered seriously in Canada. That said, in 2008, for the first time, the mandatory reporting form issued by the Law Society of Upper Canada included a section asking members to indicate the level of their pro bono activity.
46 See A. Hutchinson, *Legal Ethics and Professional Responsibility*, Toronto: Irwin, 1999.
47 Ibid.
48 CBA Code of Professional Conduct, Rule XIV, Ottawa: Canadian Bar Association, 1988, available from www.cba.org/CBA/activities/pdf/codeofconduct06.pdf (accessed 7 September 2009).
49 British Columbia Justice Review Task Force, 'Effective and Affordable Civil Justice', 2006, p. 19, available from www.bcjusticereview.org/working_groups/civil_justice/cjrwg_report_11_06.pdf (accessed 7 September 2009).
50 At www.attorneygeneral.jus.gov.on.ca/english/about/pubs/cjrp/080_unrepresented.asp (accessed 7 September 2009).
51 Ibid.
52 See www.cjc-ccm.gc.ca/english/news.asp?selMenu=1061212 (accessed 7 September 2009).
53 Model Rules of Professional Conduct (1983), R. 6.1.
54 For a discussion of this debate, see Atkinson, 'Historical perspectives'.

55 J. Caher, 'Bar group expands pro bono definition', *New York Lawyer*, 5 April 2005, available from www.nylawyer.com/display.php/file=/probono/news/05/040505a (accessed 7 September 2009).
56 Ibid.
57 V. Mutton, 'Provincial pro bono initiatives get a helping hand from firms', *The Lawyers Weekly*, 18 December 2007.
58 *Little Sisters Book and Art Emporium v Canada (Commissioner of Customs and Revenue)* [2007] SCC 2 at 71.
59 Ibid. at 3.

# 10 The psychology of good character: the past, present and future of good character regulation in Canada

*Alice Woolley and Jocelyn Stacey*

## 10.1 Introduction

Imagine this. Justice O'Halloran, a justice of the British Columbia Court of Appeal in the late 1940s meets Dr Klassen, a forensic psychiatrist working in Toronto, Ontario in the 1990s. They meet to discuss an application for admission to a law society by an applicant who has disclosed that he falsified his résumé and transcripts in applying for an articling position. In particular, they are there to determine whether the applicant is of 'good character' for the purposes of admission. To begin the discussion, each makes an opening statement about what they think is primarily relevant to a determination of that kind:

> *Justice O'Halloran:* The law student's training is not manual training, but is training of the mind, not only in law, but if he wishes to be something more than a mere legal mechanic, he must study logic, history, in particular constitutional history, political science and economics, a certain amount of philosophy and acquire a reasonable familiarity with English literature, and know something at least of the literature of other countries ... The object of law training is to attract young men of high character, and to train them in a manner that they will be trustworthy, honourable and competent in the performance of their legal duties, and will use such influence as they have to maintain and improve but not destroy our Canadian constitutional democracy.[1]
>
> *Dr Klassen:* 'Behaviour flows from character. In 1994, the applicant displayed bad behaviour from which an inference could be drawn about bad character. In 1999, the applicant displayed good behaviour. The question ... [is] whether this was the result of a conscious decision on the part of the applicant to change his behaviour without an underlying change in character (in which case, his earlier behaviour was related to transient factors), or whether that good behaviour flowed from the applicant's bad character as yet unchanged.[2]

This (artificial) exchange indicates the shifting ground on which rests the requirement[3] that applicants to Canadian law societies be of 'good character'.

Regulation of the 'character' of prospective Canadian lawyers has, as these quotations indicate, partially shifted from concern with an applicant's moral character – deciding 'who an applicant is' – to concern with an applicant's psychological personality – deciding how the applicant will act in the practice of law. Historically, the point of the good character requirement was to assert the significance of lawyers' moral character as part of a broader 'cultural project'[4] of professionalism. Today, by contrast, the emphasis also includes assessment of psychological personality; evidence of past bad acts leads to an assessment by a law society of whether an applicant's current character is such that the applicant represents a future risk to the public. Adoption of a psychological conception of character has been only partial, however; regulatory faith in the significance of moral character persists, and remains influential in admission decisions. Current regulation of lawyer character is neither fully moral nor fully psychological, but a hybrid, with emphasis on applicants' morals as well as on their likelihood of future misconduct.

This chapter considers the legitimacy of preclusion of applicants from the practice of law on either ground. It argues, first, that continued exclusion of applicants on the basis of moral character is not justifiable. Moral character is not empirically measurable and does not predict an applicant's future conduct as a lawyer. Further, emphasis on applicants' moral character tends to valorize a particular concept of the 'good lawyer', without recognizing the multiple ways in which lawyers can be 'good' in a pluralist society.

Second, it argues that considering character in a purely psychological sense is also problematic. To adopt a psychological conception of character would require emphasis on psychological evidence with respect to an applicant's 'personality', and a clinical assessment of the applicant's likelihood of misconduct should they be admitted to the Bar. While psychological evidence is used in a variety of legal contexts to predict future behaviour, numerous studies indicate that it is not in fact a reliable source of information. We conclude that there is no reason to believe that a purely psychology-based approach will lead to more coherent and fair decision-making in good character cases.

## 10.2 The changing conception of character

### 10.2.1 The 'cultural project' of good character

The requirement that Canadian lawyers be of 'good character' has existed since the advent of formal professional regulation. For example, the first legal standards for those seeking to act as lawyers within the North-West Territories were established in December 1885 by the Lieutenant-Governor. Individuals seeking enrolment as an advocate who were not already admitted to the Bar or who had not practised in another of the 'Queen's Dominions' had to demonstrate 'good character'. In 1888, these rules were expanded to require anyone seeking enrolment as an advocate to establish his good character.[5] When the Law Society of Alberta was created in 1907, 'A letter of good character was the entrance fee.'[6]

Determining the precise meaning of 'good character' in its historical context is challenging. The only published Canadian decisions prior to 1989 are a 1922 decision restricting judicial jurisdiction over character determinations[7] and the *Martin* decision, in which the British Columbia Court of Appeal affirmed the Law Society's refusal to admit an applicant with communist beliefs. Some assessment as to the meaning of good character in this time period can, however, be drawn from Wes Pue's extensive analysis of this early period of Canadian legal professionalism. Pue argues that the creation of the structures of lawyer professionalism in Canada was a deliberate act, a response by lawyers to cultural and social conditions, to their sense of Canada (especially western Canada) as a fundamentally egalitarian society, but also one threatened by disruptive forces of social change and radicalism.[8] To those lawyers, professionalism – especially professionalism as it was developing in the United States – was 'a social vision which held forth the promise of founding a better world on terrain mid-way between the Bolshevik abyss and a sort of *ancien regime* repression'.[9]

Professionalism in this sense had three components: directing lawyer education, towards creating a better kind of person; establishing admission standards to ensure only the right kind of people became lawyers; and setting standards of lawyer behaviour and disciplining those lawyers who breached them.[10] A common thread ran throughout: the emphasis was never on technical competence, it was on the type of person the lawyer was. As indicated by the quotation from Justice O'Halloran's judgement in *Martin*, legal education was designed to take men of 'high character' and to develop them into individuals who were 'trustworthy, honourable and competent'. Admission focused on 'centrally important questions regarding what sort of person from what sort of background could properly embody law in a new British dominion'.[11] And finally, discipline and conduct were oriented in part at behaviours which were undesirable, but more fundamentally at ridding the profession of 'bad' people. As dramatically expressed in 1927 by Sir James Aikins, president of the Canadian Bar Association: 'If the legal profession refuses to ruthlessly rid itself of its barnacles and fungus, how can the public be expected to extend to the profession, as a profession, the high honor, the dignity and revenue which that profession rightly deserves.'[12]

When viewed in this context, it seems likely that a lawyer in 1920, when asked about good character and its identification, would have drawn some connection between bad acts and bad character, and between good acts and good character. But that connection would not have been an exercise in psychological prediction. Sir James Aikins would not have viewed bad conduct as empirically or probabilistically relevant to whether the person engaging in that conduct was at heightened risk of behaving badly in the future (although he probably would have thought it quite likely); he would have viewed bad conduct as evidence of a bad nature, indicating that a person was fundamentally unworthy of admittance to the profession. Moreover, as evidenced by the historical association in the United States of the good character requirement with denial of admission to whole groups of people, including women and minorities,[13] good character was to some extent entirely unrelated to how an applicant had lived their life. Character was general and related to the essential 'truth' of a person, rather than to any particular acts he had committed (or might commit in the future).

### 10.2.2 The good character requirement today

The good character requirement continues to apply to all prospective Canadian lawyers. All applicants for admission to a provincial law society must provide some documentation in support of their good character (for example, letters of reference) and must also disclose information related to past 'bad acts' that might, in the law societies' view, be indicative of bad character.[14]

Information as to what regulators understand 'good character' to mean today can be drawn from published law society decisions, guidelines, stated purposes and a governing definition. Based on that information, it appears that the current understanding of the meaning and significance of good character is somewhat confused. On the one hand, orientation of the inquiry is towards a psychological concept of character: character is inferred from past and present conduct, and its relevance is its predictive value relative to future conduct. Thus justification for the requirement is said to relate fundamentally to protection of the public; it is through character screening that the 'high ethical standards' of the profession will be maintained.[15] Character is viewed as the 'well spring of professional conduct in lawyers',[16] and the general test for determining character is whether the applicant's conduct, in the past and currently, indicates an absence of good character. The applicant must demonstrate that he or she is of good character taking into account:

> a. the nature and duration of the [prior] misconduct; b. whether the applicant is remorseful; c. what rehabilitative efforts, if any, have been taken, and the success of such efforts; d. the applicant's conduct since the proven misconduct.[17]

On the other hand, the inquiry into character remains focused in significant part on a notion of moral character similar to the requirement's historical antecedents. The definition of character adopted by the law societies is highly generic:

> Character is that combination of qualities or features distinguishing one person from another. Good character connotes moral or ethical strength, distinguishable as an amalgam of virtuous or socially acceptable attributes or traits which undoubtedly include, among others, integrity, candour, empathy, and honesty.[18]

It may be that this definition is distinct from the description of character given by Justice O'Halloran in *Martin*; however, it is similar in that it differs significantly from how a psychologist would understand character (or, more accurately, 'personality') insofar as it emphasizes character traits as good or bad, rather than merely as predictive of conduct. As noted by Meissner, psychological assessments of character 'circumvent ... any ethical connotations, [such] as [those which arise] when we speak of someone as a person or character, or allude to someone's good or bad character'.[19]

Further, the lack of enthusiasm for a purely psychological approach to character can be seen in several cases where the Law Society of Upper Canada has strongly rejected any suggestion that an applicant must demonstrate that she is a low risk to the public.[20] In addition, in only two reported cases was significant weight placed on psychological evidence with respect to the applicant.[21] In most cases, no psychological evidence is introduced, and no significance is given to that fact by the decision-maker.[22]

This suggests some uncertainty surrounding what is meant by good character. Decision-makers appear (largely) to recognize that, in the modern era, excluding applicants on the basis of a moralized and contestable notion of moral character such as that described by Justice O'Halloran in *Martin* is not justified. They also (at least sometimes) explain character empirically, as derived from past and present conduct and as predictive of future conduct. At the same time, however, decision-makers have not embraced a fully psychological concept of character. The generic definition of character, the express refusal to specifically address the likelihood of misconduct in the future and the lack of reliance on psychological evidence about the character of the applicant suggest that law societies still view character, at least in part, from a moral perspective. That is, the law societies no longer talk solely in terms of a moral conception of character. But the way in which they search for character amounts, in most cases and most of the time, to a search for moral character.

### 10.2.3 Moral character versus psychological personality

At this point, before considering the appropriateness of regulating either moral or psychological character, it is necessary to digress slightly to clarify the distinction between them. If a regulator adopts either a fully moral understanding of character, or a fully psychological understanding of character, what does that look like?

The differences between moral and psychological character can be illustrated through comparing the moral concept of 'character' with the psychological concept of 'personality'.[23] For the purposes of this comparison, we will adopt perhaps the best-known articulation of moral character, that of Aristotelian virtue ethics. This is not because legal regulators are committed to virtue ethics as a philosophical proposition. Neither is it because the concept of moral character employed by law societies matches perfectly with Aristotelian articulation of the virtues. And neither is it because Aristotelian virtue ethics is the only possible way to identify or consider character in a moral sense. We adopt virtue ethics because, first, it is a purely normative and philosophical articulation of the significance of a person's character, and thereby provides a useful comparator to psychological character. Second, virtue ethics is the theory of ethics that accords with the idea of character as ethically significant; deontological and consequentialist ethics, for example, make no similar claim. Third, virtue ethics arguably offers a 'best-case' version of a philosophical concept of character. If regulation of moral character is to be justified it will be through something like the concept articulated by virtue ethics.

What, then, is 'character' as understood by virtue ethics? Virtue ethics posits that the combination of an individual's virtues with the exercise of practical judgement will shape that individual's decisions and result (ultimately) in *Eudaimonia* (flourishing).[24] Character in this sense necessarily involves moral distinction, identification of aspects of character as good (virtues) or bad (vices). Further, those aspects of character are seen as something that runs deep within the individual who possesses them: 'A virtue is an acquired human quality the possession and exercise of which tends to enable us to achieve those goods which are internal to practices and the lack of which effectively prevents us from achieving any such goods.'[25] Thus a person possessed of the virtue of honesty will consistently view honesty as a reason for acting (or not acting), albeit one which operates in complexity with other reasons, circumstances or facts relevant to a particular decision. Character as understood by virtue ethics has been criticized as lacking empirical validity, but its orientation is normative, not empirical.[26] Further, virtue ethics understands behaviour as a combination of a person's character and her exercise of practical judgement, so that the correlation between virtues and conduct are necessarily analytically complex. As noted, a person who lies may or may not have the virtue of honesty; it depends what other virtues were implicated by the situation, and how the individual assessed what the facts required. Virtue ethicists also recognize that very few people possess a virtue perfectly, and that the reasons of action arising from a virtue may be counterweighed by non-rational considerations like, for example, embarrassment at admitting to a mistake even where honesty suggests that one should do so.[27]

Personality, by contrast, is a concept of behavioural psychology, a discipline that expressly rejects the relevance of character:

> Gordon Allport, the main personality trait theorist in 20th century United States psychology, explicitly banished the term *character* from academic discourse concerning personality. He argued that character was the subject matter of philosophy not psychology. The traits he urged psychologists to study were presumably objective entities (Allport dubbed them *neuropsychic structures*) stripped of moral significance and linked to 'adjustment' but not imbued with inherent value.[28]

Personality constitutes, loosely, the empirically identified and measured dispositions of individuals, dispositions identified through assessment of individual behaviour, how individuals are perceived by others, and how individuals perceive themselves.[29] There are five 'big' (i.e. broad) character traits: extraversion, agreeableness, conscientiousness, neuroticism and openness to experience.[30] There is no necessary moral judgement associated with the possession of one personality trait over another.[31] The relevance of personality traits is their

correlation to certain patterns of conduct: patterns of conduct indicate personality,[32] and personality is predictive of patterns of conduct.[33]

Given these distinctions, if a regulator is to base admission decisions on moral
character, its focus should be on the regulator's assessment of the applicant as a
possessor of virtues (or vices). This includes looking at an applicant's past conduct
as indicative of character, but could also include the regulator's measure of the
applicant (for example, her demeanour as a witness), and general subjective
assessment of the 'type of person' the applicant appears to be. By contrast, if a
regulator is to base admission decisions on psychological character, its focus
should be on assessing the applicant's personality traits[34] and connecting those
traits to a prediction of the likelihood of an applicant behaving in accordance
with ethical standards[35] in practice.

## 10.3 Is basing Bar admission on moral character justifiable?

### 10.3.1 Introduction

There are a number of criteria against which to justify regulatory actions – for
example, economic efficiency, internal coherence and consistency with democratic norms.[36] For the purposes of this analysis, we use two measures. First, when
assessed empirically, can the regulation fulfil its stated goals? Second, are the
goals of the regulation consistent with democratic norms? This section will suggest
that, when assessed in this way, regulation of applicants' moral character is not
justified. Specifically, the stated goal of regulating the character of applicants to
Canadian law societies is to protect the public interest. Fulfilment of this goal
requires that character be both identifiable and predictive. Character in a moral
sense is, however, neither of these things. It is not reliably identifiable and neither,
as identified, is it reliably predictive of future conduct. As a consequence, no
measurable protection for the public is likely to arise from attempts to regulate
lawyers' moral character. Further, the democratic norms of Canadian society
include a commitment to pluralism, to permitting the pursuit of multiple conceptions of the good. Regulating admission to the profession based on a particular
moral perspective on what constitutes the 'good' lawyer is not consistent with
those norms.

### 10.3.2 Identifying moral character

Humans tend to err in their assessment of the character of others. They do so
because they identify character too quickly and based on too little evidence. In
what psychologists call the 'fundamental attribution error',[37] humans tend to
assess individuals based on limited information – we decide that a person who
told a lie is dishonest, or that a student who does no work for a class is lazy. Such
assessments err because, while individuals possess significant local consistency in
behaviour (a person who acts one way in a particular situation is likely to act in

the same way if in that situation again), they possess relatively little cross-situational consistency in behaviour.[38] A person who is scrupulously honest in returning excess change at the grocery store will likely be honest if given excess change on another occasion but might lie to his wife about how much the groceries cost. As a consequence, a single observation of a person – or multiple observations within a single context – will not necessarily provide information about the 'character' of that person in other contexts.

This difficulty is compounded by moral ambiguity in actions. Assessing the morality of a person doing an act requires some prior assessment of the morality of the act – it is the moral character of the action that justifies conclusions about the moral character of the actor. But where the morality of the act is ambiguous, drawing such conclusions becomes more difficult. This is illustrated by the following example, in which the virtue ethicist Christine Swanton attempts to relate the conduct of individuals participating in the Milgram experiment, in which research subjects were instructed to administer electric shocks to a person giving incorrect answers to a test, to their character:

> Admittedly, Milgram's experiments show that a remarkable number of subjects administer electric shocks of considerable severity, in experimental situations of a certain type. The tendency to perform beneficent acts is arguably not as robust as one might hope. However, there was considerable variation in the mental states of those prepared to administer such shocks, and those differences may point to character traits of, for example, compassion, benevolence, respect for authority and commitments, which manifest themselves in various ways in dilemmatic situations.[39]

This observation may be descriptively valid from the vantage point of an ethical concept of character, but it does not empirically explain the character of the individuals in the experiment, who are identified as at once potentially lacking in benevolence but also as potentially having benevolence and compassion. This inconsistency is possible because Swanton has to characterize the behaviour in some moral way – 'cruelty' or 'obedience' – and then identify the relevant virtue that the behaviour may reflect; yet Swanton recognizes that the morality of the action is not straightforward, at least as perceived from the perspective of actor. Once that is the case, the conclusions about the morality of the actor become by necessity contingent and uncertain.

These problems with the identification of moral character are probably not well understood by those assessing the character of applicants for law society admission. It is observably the case, however, that those decision-makers have struggled in developing a basis on which to assess an applicant's character. In fact, a review of Canadian law society decisions reveals that it is very difficult to correlate the outcome of character decisions to any measurable benchmark, such as the severity of the past misconduct, the availability or type of psychological evidence, the existence of positive character references or, in one instance, even almost identically presented fact patterns.[40] Instead, law society determinations of character have tended to turn largely on decision-makers' impressionistic assessment of an applicant as a witness. Decisions appear to be based on whether the applicant provides evidence which is 'unsatisfactory'[41] or lacking in 'candour',[42] whether the applicant 'displays a certain caginess bordering on arrogance'[43] or by contrast is not 'wishy-washy',[44] provides self-reporting that is 'full and frank'[45] or speaks 'clearly, eloquently and without qualification state[s] that her actions were wrong'.[46]

### 10.3.3 Moral character as predictive of future conduct

The importance of circumstances in influencing behaviour makes moral character difficult to identify. It also creates the related problem that character as identified from behaviour in a particular situation is largely non-predictive of future conduct in different situations.[47] Or, to put it slightly differently, the overwhelming evidence of social psychology is that the best predictor of human behaviour is circumstances. People will in general tend to respond to situations in similar ways, and as the situation changes the response of most people will also change.[48] Situations do not determine conduct – it is rare to find uniform and universal responses to a situation – but in statistical terms the best correlation with behaviour is situation.

The social psychology experiments demonstrating this point are numerous and various.[49] For the purposes of this discussion, three brief examples illustrate the point. The previous section referenced the Milgram experiment. In that experiment, 63 per cent of research subjects instructed to administer electric shocks to a person giving incorrect answers to a test were willing to do so to the point where the test-taker was apparently suffering severe pain that could have led to death. This aspect of the Milgram experiment is relatively well known. What is less well known is that modifications in the experimental circumstances will produce radical variations in this number. Where the research subject is paired with a confederate apparently also participating in that experiment (but who is actually one of the researchers), and the confederate does so enthusiastically, compliance jumps from 63 per cent to 90 per cent; if the confederate refuses to participate, compliance falls from 63 per cent to 10 per cent.[50]

In the Princeton theological seminary experiment, theology students were told that they were required to make a presentation. As they walked to the presentation, they came across an individual in apparent physical distress. The only reliable predictor of whether students would stop and help the individual was what the students had been told about the time they had to get to the presentation: students who believed that they were late were consistently far less likely to assist than students who believed they had time to spare. Of those students who were in a great hurry, 10 per cent stopped to help; of those who were in a moderate hurry, 45 per cent stopped to help; of those with no need to hurry, 63 per cent stopped to help.[51] Information about students' underlying moral commitments – as might be indicated, for example, by their reasons for attending a theological seminary – were in no way predictive of whether or not they would engage in helping behaviour.

Finally, there is the 'mood effect' dime experiment.[52] A 1972 study observed individuals leaving a phone booth who either 'found' a dime in the phone or who did not. As the individual left the phone booth, one of the researchers would drop a folder, scattering papers across the individual's path. The researchers then observed whether the individual leaving the phone booth helped pick up the papers. Helping behaviour was materially affected by whether or not the individual had found a dime. Of the 16 people who found a dime, 14 stopped to help. Of the 25 who did not find a dime, only one stopped to help.[53]

What these experiments suggest is that even if conclusions about the character of an applicant for law society admission can be drawn from the limited information about that applicant's past conduct, which is unlikely, those conclusions will not necessarily indicate anything much at all about how that applicant will behave in the varying circumstances of law practice. The change in circumstances that results is significant to the extent that no meaningful prediction can be made.

### 10.3.4 Moral character and pluralism

As noted above, one of the challenges in identifying moral character is that it not only requires the drawing of inferences about a person's character from that person's conduct, but also that the conduct itself be subject to moral evaluation. While in some instances doing so may not require stepping outside the publicly agreed on morality of a particular society – where, for example, an applicant's actions were attended with criminal sanction – in other instances it may. The 'immorality' or 'morality' of the conduct may lie in the eyes of the beholder. The most obvious examples are the historical cases in which lawyers were denied admission because of their political convictions. However, it is also the case that the moral values emphasized by Canadian law societies include contested values such as honour,[54] integrity[55] and civility.[56] Further, the definition of 'character' endorsed by the law societies is general enough to allow the law societies to incorporate those contested values within character decisions. There are no clear standards of conduct which an applicant must have met, and which failure to meet will automatically result in disqualification. It is notable in this respect that applicants for admission have more frequently been judged wanting in character where their immoral acts were plagiarism[57] and alteration of transcripts[58] than where their immoral acts gave rise to criminal convictions for assault,[59] perjury[60] and election fraud.[61]

Pluralism is a key democratic value, and the ability of individuals to pursue their own conception of the good within legal bounds is recognized constitutionally in the Canadian Charter of Rights and Freedoms[62] and numerous other Canadian laws. Prospective lawyers should be permitted to conduct themselves in ways that are reasonably justifiable, even if they are not universally acceptable. While plagiarism and alteration of transcripts may not be reasonably justifiable actions, a political commitment such as communism is. Further, given the willingness of law societies to discipline lawyers for relatively minor incivility,[63] and the breadth of the definition of good character adopted by the law societies, there is some reason to be concerned about the regulatory reach of the good character requirement.

### *10.3.5 Conclusion*

The stated purpose for the requirement that applicants to Canadian law societies be of good character is 'protection of the public'. If that requirement continues to focus on applicants' moral character, this purpose will not be fulfilled. Moral character cannot reliably be identified – and is not, in any event, predictive of how applicants will behave once they are practising. Statistically speaking, the circumstances of professional practice will be the single most important influence – for good or for ill – on how individuals conduct themselves. If protection of the public is the goal, then it is on those circumstances, rather than on the moral character of applicants, that the law societies' regulatory aim should be focused. Excluding applicants on the basis of their moral character (or absence thereof) provides no meaningful public protection.

Further, focusing on applicants' moral character continues the law societies' pursuit of the cultural project of professionalism without sufficient recognition that there are numerous ways in which a lawyer can be 'good' in the practice of law. Applicants are not provided with clear standards of conduct that they must have met; the definition given to character is broad and allows for the incorporation of contested values such as civility; and the good character requirement is enforced in a way that is inconsistent, impressionistic and unpredictable. This approach does not sufficiently accord with the democratic norm of pluralism, and the legal recognition that individuals should not be unduly burdened in their pursuit of a good way to live.

## 10.4 Is basing Bar admission on psychological character justifiable?

In 2007, Woolley argued that if the good character requirement was to be retained, it needed to focus on protection of the public from applicants whose past conduct indicated a propensity to unethical conduct in the practice of law.[64] She argued that the inquiry should be directed at identifying conduct in circumstances similar to law practice that raised a legitimate question about how that applicant would act in practice, on psychological evidence about the applicant and, in general, about the applicant's fitness for legal practice:

> the focus needs to be less on an applicant's 'character' writ large than on her 'fitness' for the ethical rigours of legal practice. A bar applicant should only be denied admission if his 'past misconduct ... is rationally connected to his fitness to practice law,' and fitness needs to be carefully defined based on the 'standards imposed upon persons who actually practice law'.[65]

The recommendation was that law societies abandon the emphasis on moral character and focus instead on something closer to psychological personality, on whether an applicant's personality is such that she presents an increased risk to the public if admitted to legal practice.

In this section, we consider the practicality of this recommendation. In particular, through analysis of the success (or failure) of using psychological evidence in other legal settings to make predictions about future conduct, we consider the possibility of making realistic predictions about whether an applicant for law society admission poses a risk to the public in the practice of law. Based on this review, we conclude that while the empirical problems related to use of psychological evidence are different from those related to moral character, they are equally significant. Psychological evidence appears unable to provide reliable predictions of future conduct in specific cases.

This section begins with a review of the use of psychological evidence in good character cases, and a look at the extent to which decision-makers have struggled to make that evidence effective. It will then examine the use of such evidence in custody and dangerous offender proceedings, and the empirical studies demonstrating its predictive inaccuracy. Finally, it will assess what those materials indicate about the empirical validity of using a psychological standard to determine whether a particular applicant should be admitted to the Bar. Here, in distinction from our critique of the search for applicants' moral character, we do not dispute the normative validity of adopting a psychological perspective on character. If it is possible to predict accurately that a particular applicant is likely to violate the ethical norms and standards applicable to the practice of law, we do not dispute the legitimacy, in accordance with the regulator's public protection mandate, of excluding that applicant from legal practice. The question is whether, empirically, that prediction is possible.

### 10.4.1 Psychological evidence in good character proceedings

As noted, good character hearings have not widely embraced the use of psychological evidence in assessing character. Only two of the published cases have involved the consideration of significant psychological evidence, and in those cases the decision-makers appeared not to have a clear sense of how to use the evidence. The first case, *Re P(DM)* considered the application for admission of DMP, who had been convicted of offences related to paedophilic sexual assault. DMP lodged a plea of guilty to sexual assault and having sexual relations with a minor, and was sentenced to eight months in jail and three years of probation. The justification for this relatively light sentence was, in the judge's view, to give DMP an opportunity to turn his life around and to succeed in law school.[66] DMP did attend law school, obtained and completed articles, and applied for admission to the Law Society of Upper Canada.

His application was rejected on the basis that he was not of good character. A central issue for the panel was whether DMP was rehabilitated. The panel found that when he committed the crimes, DMP was clearly not of good character; the question was whether, in the intervening five years, his character has 'so changed that he can now be said to be of good character'.[67] To answer this question, the panel considered a variety of psychological evidence. The conclusion of DMP's treating psychologist in the first instance was that DMP would require significant therapy to form better relationships with adult women. However, less than a year later the treating psychologist was of the view that DMP was cured. The other psychologists who provided evidence to the panel (most of whom had not met DMP, but had reviewed the record) disagreed with the treating psychologist on his prognosis. The panel accepted the evidence of these other psychologists, and rejected that of the treating psychologist.

While the panel appears to have been careful and thoughtful in its consideration of how to balance this evidence, the use that it makes of it is inconsistent with the adoption of a rigorously psychological perspective on character. Given the stated purpose of the good character requirement, the question should be whether, given the psychological evidence, DMP posed a risk to the public if he was admitted to the Bar. Yet the focus of the hearing was not on this issue, but was rather on the general question of whether DMP was at risk of recidivism. It appears that while this decision uses psychological evidence, it does not do so because of a psychological explanation of the importance of character (or personality) as a predictor of behaviour as a lawyer. It uses psychological evidence to substantiate an ethical view of character: since DMP did these horrific acts, and the possibility of him doing them again cannot be ruled out, he is in general a man of bad character who ought not to be admitted to the profession.

The other case to include extensive psychological evidence was *Re Preyra*, in which the Law Society of Upper Canada twice heard the application for admission of Preyra, who falsified his résumé and transcripts when applying for articles. Preyra was denied admission after the first hearing in 2000, and admitted after the second hearing in 2003. In both hearings, extensive psychological evidence was presented. In deciding not to admit Preyra after that hearing, the panel did not expressly refer to the psychological evidence.

In the second hearing, more psychological evidence was introduced. A new psychiatrist testified based on his treatment of Preyra for the intervening three years, and Dr Klassen was asked by the Law Society to reassess Preyra. In reaching the decision to admit him, the panel noted the favourable psychological evidence and appeared to rely on it, although the panel was uncertain as to how to incorporate the evidence, given the stated irrelevance of predictions of future conduct:

> Good character is determined at the date of the hearing. Both section 27 and the case law under this section are clear that no speculation as to Mr. Preyra's future behaviour is permitted. It is presumably for this reason that restrictions or conditions cannot be placed on the admission of a member. Despite [the fact] that, Dr. Klassen testified that he could not predict Mr. Preyra's future behaviour, Mr. Preyra is not required to demonstrate that the risk of future dishonesty is unlikely or non-existent. It is necessary,

however, to ensure that, on a balance of probabilities, Mr. Preyra's change from bad character to good character is *bona fide*.[68]

These cases thus provide little meaningful guidance as to how psychological evidence, and a psychological concept of personality, could be used to reform the good character requirement. Decision-makers were not able to incorporate that evidence into a fact-based consideration of the likelihood that a particular applicant poses an increased risk to the public. The emphasis, even here, was on the moral aspect of character.

### *10.4.2 The use of psychological evidence*

The use of psychological evidence in Canadian courts is prolific. One author estimates that such evidence is introduced in over 100,000 judicial or quasi-judicial proceedings every year.[69] Specifically, courts rely on psychological evidence when the legal issue requires a determination regarding a person's future behaviour. For example, the legal test for custody in Canada is the 'best interests of the child'.[70] In determining custody matters, the court has to answer questions – 'Who is a better parent?' and 'What situation is in the best interests of the child?' – the answers to which are psychological, not legal. In addition, the answers are prospective and predictive; they turn on what will be, not on what was. The test is significantly indeterminate,[71] and remains so even though legislation gives judges a list of factors to consider in awarding custody;[72] the factors are undefined and are not placed in priority, leaving them substantially subjective.[73] To address the psychological and prospective nature of the inquiry, and its fundamental indeterminacy, judges rely heavily on psychological evidence in most child custody hearings.[74] Psychological evidence allows the court to bridge the gap between the ascertainable facts (for example, that a parent behaved in a particular way) and the proper outcome given those facts and the ephemeral target of the current and future 'best interests' of the child.[75]

Psychological evidence is also fundamental for dangerous offender proceedings.[76] The rationale for a dangerous offender designation is to prevent the reoccurrence of further criminal acts in the future; it thus requires some type of forecasting about whether such criminal acts are likely to occur. Legislation requires that psychological evidence be used to determine the risk posed by the offender, and the penal sanction necessary to address that risk.[77] Courts, in turn, rely on and accept recommendations by psychologists on these questions.[78] Psychological evidence is the cornerstone of dangerous offender proceedings; the designation is not made without it.

There is, however, significant academic consensus that judicial confidence in the use of psychological evidence in these contexts is misplaced. Indeed, the empirical data and its academic analysis suggest that the evidence is deeply suspect. Psychological evidence does not do what it is supposed to do: it does not reliably measure future dangerousness or future parenting. In fact, the main approach used by psychologists to predict behaviour – that is, clinical assessments of individual patients – has been empirically questioned. Studies in a variety of circumstances, but most notably of offenders classed as dangerous whose circumstances of incarceration change due to legal challenge, indicate that such assessments are little more accurate than flipping a coin, and in some circumstances may even be less so.[79] Psychologists appear unable to determine with accuracy whether a person who has committed dangerous acts in the past will do so again in the future. With respect to actuarial predictions, the general consensus appears to be far more positive;[80] despite this, however, there has been reluctance to adopt actuarial prediction techniques for use in the courtroom. Actuarial prediction does not provide information about individuals, but only about categories to which individuals belong, and is thus problematic for judicial decision-making targeted at individuals.

Overall, the results of the empirical studies testing the validity of predictions of violence and with respect to custody decisions[81] are not encouraging. This provides reason to doubt the reliability of psychological predictions as to future conduct by prospective lawyers, despite the widespread reliance on these predictions in judicial proceedings.

### 10.4.3 Should good character be 'psychologized'?

If understood psychologically, as a set of personal dispositions that in certain circumstances lead to a greater likelihood of wrongful conduct, regulation of the character of applicants for law society admission appears facially justifiable. Exclusion of applicants more likely to harm the public is, *eo ipso*, to ensure the public's protection. But then the question becomes how character in this sense is established. How can a law society determine whether an applicant for admission has a personality trait that has manifested itself in circumstances sufficiently similar to legal practice to warrant the prediction that the individual poses a greater risk to the public should they be admitted to practice?

At first blush, psychological evidence seems to provide an answer to this problem. In both the custody and dangerousness contexts, psychologists provide the court with exactly this type of analysis: based on the current information about a particular individual – their personality and how they have acted in various circumstances – what is the likely outcome going forward? If this evidence were reliable, the judicial and legislative recognition of its legitimacy would be sufficient reason for its adoption in the context of character review, and would provide a modern justification for the retention of what is essentially a historical anachronism.

The glaring problem, however, is the doubtful reliability of this evidence. The academic consensus is that the predictions of future conduct are largely inaccurate. Moreover, this inaccuracy could well be compounded in the context of good character proceedings. In dangerousness cases, the individuals in question have committed a serious personal injury offence and repeated criminal offences. There is a pattern of behaviour that the psychologist can assess.[82] By contrast, in the context of good character, the behaviour that gives rise to the inquiry is highly variable, there may be no repeated pattern of behaviour to assess and, as noted below, there is no actuarial model against which to judge the clinical assessment.

In the custody contexts, there is an important level of situational variability. This variability is, however, still less significant than in the context of law society admission. In the custody context, you have circumstances that may change, but they at least have some relationship to each other: this parent parenting this child now and this parent parenting this child in the future. This consistency of circumstances may provide some reason to think, at least some of the time, that the predictions have merit. In the good character context, there may be little temporal or situational relationship between the pre-application conduct and the situations in which applicants will find themselves as lawyers.

In the context of dangerousness, there is also the ameliorating effect that arises from the potential availability of actuarial evidence, which can either be used on its own or to buttress clinical assessments. It is almost certain that no actuarial calculations could be done with respect to the relationship between past conduct by applicants for admission to the Bar and future conduct as a lawyer. To generate an actuarial model would require information about lawyers who violate the ethical norms and rules of the legal profession, information about those lawyers' age, gender, background and upbringing. It would also require information about the circumstances in which those lawyers practise. That information would then need to be compared to information about applicants to the Bar to determine whether they are likely to fall into the high-risk group if admitted. Finally, the information would need to be significant enough to create statistical accuracy – it would need to relate to a large number of lawyers over a significant period of time. Either such information is unlikely to be available or, if it is available, it is unlikely to be especially helpful. What we do know about lawyers who get into regulatory difficulties in Canada is that they are older, male and practising in solo or small firm private practice.[83] However, that information unfortunately tells us nothing about the likelihood of a young applicant, whose future practice circumstances are as yet unknown, being a risk to the public in the future.

With respect to the argument that there is some reason to use the evidence in good character hearings because of judicial recognition of its legitimacy elsewhere, it needs to be noted that courts making determinations on dangerousness or custody have little choice about whether to rely on psychological evidence. Once an individual has been incarcerated repeatedly for violent offences, society has to make some determination about the consequences for that individual, and how to manage the future risk that person potentially presents. And once parents separate, or once a parent has demonstrated an apparent incapacity to care for a child, some determination as to what should happen to that child needs to be made. In making those arguably unavoidable decisions, the legislature has articulated defensible legal standards on which to make them – prevention of future violence and protecting the best interests of the child. It is the function of courts to apply those standards. Thus judicial determination of the empirical foundation to which to apply those legal principles is almost impossibly difficult but is also inescapable; the decision has to be made and the principles have to be applied. Whatever the flaws of psychological evidence, it may assist a judge in making those determinations, and its use can be justified on that basis.

This perspective was recognized by the Supreme Court of Canada in *R v Lyons*,[84] in which the court considered the constitutionality of the dangerousness provisions. Lyons argued that one of the problems with the provisions was the reliance on psychological evidence, given the essential invalidity of that evidence. The Supreme Court rejected this argument. It did not disagree that the evidence was problematic, but simply asserted that, in a balance between a 'risk of harm to innocent persons at the hands of an offender who is judged likely to inflict it'[85] and the rights of that offender, the weight should be placed on avoiding harm to the innocent. The fallibility of the evidence may warrant greater procedural protections, but did not invalidate the entire exercise.

A similar argument could be made about the good character requirement. Arguably, a law society faced with an applicant who has behaved badly has to make a decision about whether to admit that applicant. Doing so on the basis of whether the applicant presents a risk to the protection of the public is a legitimate legal principle to apply in making that admission decision. Determining the empirical foundation against which to apply that principle involves a psychological question: given what this person has done – their personality traits, the circumstances of the prior conduct and the circumstances of law practice – do they pose a greater risk to the public or to the profession's ethical standards? If so, the person should not be admitted. Since a law society is almost certainly ill-suited to make this determination, and could benefit from the assistance of psychological evidence, psychological evidence should be relied on in making this decision.

On closer examination, this argument is flawed. We agree that if law societies are going to continue to scrutinize applicants' 'character', they need to be more cognizant of the essentially psychological nature of the standard they are imposing, and be more rigorous in considering the application on that basis, including appropriately critical use of psychological evidence. But this begs the question of whether the scrutiny of applicants' character is warranted. As noted, if the psychological evidence was first rate and reliable, not much in the way of reasons would be needed to justify using it to assess applicants' character. But the evidence is neither first rate nor reliable. As such, it should only be used if there is little other option, if the decision has to be made and the evidence provides some grounds to assist the competent authority making it. That is arguably the case for dangerousness and certainly the case for custody, but is not the case for character scrutiny.

## 10.5 Conclusion

The current approach to character screening in Canada is incoherent. It retains its historical commitment to the significance of an applicant's moral character, while simultaneously incorporating psychological concepts of measurability and predictive significance in assessing whether an applicant should be admitted. This chapter separated these two strands concerning good character to determine whether either can be used as a justifiable requirement for applicants for law society admission.

It argued that neither can be justified, albeit for somewhat different reasons. The problem with 'moral character' is both empirical and normative. Empirically, it suffers because moral character cannot be reliably identified and neither is it meaningfully predictive as to a person's future conduct. As a consequence, consideration of an applicant's moral character will not result in fulfilment of the requirement's stated purpose of protecting the public. Normatively, the problem with emphasizing moral character is that it embroils law societies in the project of defining what constitutes 'good' in the practice of law, and does not permit sufficient respect for the multiplicity of ways in which lawyers can be good.

The problem with psychological character is that it is empirical. If psychological character could be reliably measured and used to make predictions about conduct, it would be a legitimate consideration in determining whether to admit an individual to the law society. The law society could justifiably exclude from admission an individual whose personality created a material risk of future violations of the rules governing the practice of law, and hence to the protection of the public. The problem, however, is that the theoretical possibility of making such decisions with accuracy is not matched by the practical reality. The best evidence is that clinical predictions as to future behaviour are largely unreliable. Actuarial predictions are much better but are not possible in the context of law society admissions because of the paucity and non-comparability of data about law society applicants and the relationship between the profile of those applicants and lawyers who later violate the profession's rules.

What, then, can be said about the future of the good character requirement in Canada? Given the difficulties identified here with both a moral and a psychological approach to assessing character, and given the relatively minor impact the requirement has had in practice, our recommendation is that it be abandoned. Once an applicant has successfully completed the necessary academic training, articles and the Bar admission course or examinations, that applicant should be admitted to legal practice. Scrutiny of their character serves no purpose and is not justified.

## Notes

1 *Martin v Law Society of British Columbia* [1950] 3 D.L.R. 173:189.
2 *Law Society of Upper Canada v Preyra* [2000] L.S.D.D. No. 60 (Q.L.), para. 33.
3 See, for example, *Law Society Act R.S.O.* 1990, c. L-8 s. 27(2): An Act respecting the Barreau du Quebec R.S.Q., c. B-1 s. 45(2); *Legal Profession Act* 1990 S.S. 1990–91, c. L-10.1 s. 24(1)(b). Similar requirements exist in all Canadian provinces.
4 W.W. Pue, 'Cultural projects and structural transformation in the Canadian legal profession', in W.W. Pue and David Sugarman (eds), *Lawyers and Vampires*, Oxford: Hart Publishing, 2003, p. 389.
5 L. Knafla, 'Frontier lawyers: Origins of the Alberta Law, 1882–1914', in Law Society of Alberta, *Just Works: Lawyers in Alberta 1907–2007*, Toronto: Irwin Law, 2007, pp. 17–18.
6 Ibid., p. 22.

7 *Hagel v Law Society of British Columbia* [1922] 31 B.C.R. 75.
8 Pue, 'Cultural projects', p. 375.
9 Ibid.
10 Ibid., pp. 375–94.
11 Ibid., p. 379.
12 Ibid., p. 394.
13 D. Rhode, 'Moral character as a professional credential', *Yale Law Journal*, 1985, vol. 94, 491, p. 499. The good character requirement does not appear to have a similar history in Canada, presumably because the existence of an articling requirement allowed for informal forms of social exclusion. (Rhode notes that when there was an apprenticeship system this was the primary means of social exclusion.) The Ontario legislature passed a special Bill allowing the enrolment in the Law Society of Upper Canada of a black man, Delos Rogest Davis, after he was unable to obtain articles. Famously, in 1937, Bora Laskin, the first Jewish member of the Supreme Court of Canada and ultimately Chief Justice, was unable to find a job after graduating from Harvard Law School. Upon returning to Toronto, 'the brilliant legal scholar with two master's degrees had to write headnotes for a law publisher at fifty cents a note'. It was not until 1960 that a black woman was admitted to the Law Society of Upper Canada and not until 1976 that the first First Nations woman would 'graduate from law'. C. Backhouse, *Petticoats and Prejudice: Women and Law in Nineteenth-Century Canada*, Toronto: The Osgoode Society, 1991, pp. 300 (re Davis), 324 (re Laskin) and 326 (re late admissions).
14 See, for example, *Law Society Act R.S.O.* 1990, c. L-8 s. 27(2): An Act respecting the Barreau du Quebec R.S.Q., c. B-1 s. 45(2); *Legal Profession Act*, 1990 S.S. 1990–91, c. L-10.1 s. 24(1)(b). Like requirements exist in all of the Canadian provinces. The legislative regimes and administrative practices of each provincial law society are summarized in detail in A. Woolley, 'Tending the Bar: The "good character" requirement for law society admission', *Dalhousie Law Journal*, 2007, vol. 30, 27, pp. 31–35.
15 *Re Rajnauth and Law Society of Upper Canada* (1993), 13 O.R. (3d) 381 at 384.
16 G. MacKenzie, *Lawyers and Ethics: Professional Responsibility and Discipline*, Toronto: Thomson Carswell, 2007, pp. 23–24.
17 *Law Society of Upper Canada v Birman*, 2005 ONLHP 6, [2005] L.S.D.D. No. 13 (Q.L.), para. 6.
18 *Re P (DM)*, [1989] O.J. No. 1574 (Q.L.), p. 22. Please note that page references to this case are based on a 10 point Times New Roman PDF downloaded from Quicklaw.
19 W.W. Meissner, *The Ethical Dimension of Psychoanalysis: A Dialogue*, New York: Suny Press, 2003, p. 267.
20 *In the Matter of an Application for Admission to the Law Society of Upper Canada by Joseph Rizzotto, Reasons of Convocation*, 14 September 1992 at 32 and also *Law Society of Upper Canada v Preyra* [2000] L.S.D.D. No. 60 (Q.L.).
21 *Re P (DM)*, [1989] O.J. No. 1574 (Q.L.) p. 22; *Law Society of Upper Canada v Preyra* [2000] L.S.D.D. No. 60 (Q.L.), and also *Law Society of Upper Canada v Preyra* [2000] L.S.D.D. No. 60 (Q.L.). In two cases, the panel took note of the fact that the applicant had had psychological counselling – *Miller v Law Society of Upper Canada*, 2004 ONLSHP 4 and *Law Society of Upper Canada v Birman* 2006 ONLSHP 32 – and in one case the panel noted that it would have been helpful to have had the assistance of psychological evidence – *Burgess v Law Society of Upper Canada* 2006 ONLSHP 66.
22 *In the Matter of an Application for Admission to the Law Society of Upper Canada by Joseph Rizzotto, Reasons of Convocation*, 14 September 1992; *Law Society of Upper Canada v Schuchert* [2001] L.S.D.D. No. 63 (Q.L.); *Law Society of Upper Canada v D'Souza* [2002] L.S.D.D. No. 62 (Q.L.); *Law Society of Upper Canada v Levesque* [2005] L.S.D.D. No. 38 (Q.L.); *In the Matter of an Application by Michael John Spicer for Admission to the Law Society of Upper Canada, Reasons of Convocation*, 1 May 1994; *Law Society of Upper Canada v Shore* 2006 ONLSHP 55.

23 The distinction between character and personality is one used in the academic literature. For example, Christine McKinnon explains the concept of ethical character by
distinguishing it from the concept of personality. Some of the points made here – for
example, with respect to the moral neutrality of personality traits – are also made by
McKinnon. C. McKinnon, *Character, Virtue Theories and the Vices*, Peterborough: Broad-
view Press, 1999, pp. 59 – 61. See also R. Stagner, *Psychology of Personality*, 3rd edn,
Toronto: McGraw-Hill, 1961. Although it also should be noted that there is some
inconsistency in this usage: see Meissner, *The Ethical Dimension of Psychoanalysis*.

24 McKinnon, *Character, Virtue Theories and the Vices*, p. 61.

25 A. MacIntyre, *After Virtue: A Study in Moral Theory*, Notre Dame IN: University of Notre
Dame Press, 1981, p. 178. See also: R. Hursthouse, 'Virtue ethics', in E. Zalta (ed.),
*Stanford Encyclopedia of Philosophy*, Stanford, CA: The Metaphysics Research Lab. Avail-
able from http://plato.stanford.edu/entries/ethics-virtue (accessed 7 September 2009).

26 J.W. Perkins, 'Virtues and the lawyer', *Cath Law*, 1998, vol. 38, 185, p. 198.

27 Hursthouse, 'Virtue ethics'.

28 Citations omitted. C. Peterson and M.E.P. Seligman, *Character Strengths and Virtues:
A Handbook and Classification*, Oxford: Oxford University Press, 2004, p. 55.

29 Various studies measuring character are discussed in J.M. Digman, 'Personality structure: Emergence of the five-factor model', *Annual Review of Psychology*, 1990, vol. 41, 417,
pp. 418–22. Note that the number of 'factors' or 'traits' that should be associated with
psychological personality is the subject of ongoing academic discussion. See, for example, N.G. Waller, 'Evaluating the structure of personality', in C.R. Cloninger (ed.),
*Personality and Psychopathology*, St Louis, MS: American Psychopathological Association,
1999.

30 Digman, 'Personality structure', p. 420. See also B. De Raad, *The Big Five Personality
Factors: The Psychological Approach to Personality*, Seattle, WA: Hogrefe & Huber, 2000. For
a discussion of the complexity of linking behaviour with character, see W. Fleeson and
E.E. Noftle, 'Where does personality have its influence? A supermatrix of consistency
concepts', *Journal of Personality*, 2008, vol. 76, 1355.

31 Peterson and Seligman, *Character Strengths and Virtues*. McKinnon, 'Character, virtue
theories and the vices', p. 61: 'We judge character along ethical dimensions ... Pre-
ferences among personality-types are much more context-sensitive and have much less
to do with ethical considerations than do judgments about character.'

32 I. Ajzen, *Attitudes, Personality and Behavior*, 2nd edn, Toronto: McGraw-Hill, 2005, p. 2.

33 ' ... it is assumed by all trait theorists (despite their critics) that personality traits,
however assessed have their links to behavior, a basic level is the specific response to a
specific situation': Digman, 'Personality structure', p. 424. The correlation between
assessed personality and future conduct is imperfect. Personality operates along with a
multiplicity of other factors related to the individual and to the situation, to determine
how an individual will act. See: D. Matsumoto, 'Culture, context, and behavior', *Journal of Personality*, 2007, vol. 75, 1285.

34 As noted by Matsumoto, 'Culture, context, and behavior', other psychological factors
such as intellect and emotion also relate to how individuals will act in the future. These
are not questions of 'character' *per se*, but would be relevant to a character requirement
if that requirement were exclusively orientated towards predictive accuracy.

35 Ethics would need to be a defined term – a psychological assessment cannot determine
a likelihood of generalized goodness.

36 For a longer discussion of the criteria that should be used to assess regulation of lawyers, see A. Woolley, 'Legal ethics and regulatory legitimacy: Regulating lawyers for
extra-professional misconduct', in R. Mortensen, F. Bartlett and K. Tranter (eds),
*Alternative Perspectives on Lawyers and Legal Ethics: Reimagining the Profession*, New York:
Routledge, 2010, forthcoming.

37 The FAE arises from the tendency of people to 'seriously and routinely under-
estimate ... both the number of observations and the distribution within them that is

required to warrant the attribution of … character traits such as honesty'. G. Sreeni-vasan, 'Errors about errors: Virtue theory and trait attribution', *Mind*, 2001, vol. 111, 47.

38 See J.M. Doris, 'Persons, situations, and virtue ethics', *Noûs*, 1998, vol. 32, 504; J.M. Doris, *Lack of Character: Personality and Moral Behavior*, Cambridge: Cambridge University Press, 2002; L. Ross and R.E. Nisbett, *The Person and the Situation*, New York: McGraw-Hill, 1991; P. Zimbardo, *The Lucifer Effect: How Good People Turn Evil*, New York: Random House, 2007; G. Harman, 'Moral philosophy meets social psychology: Virtue ethics and the fundamental attribution error', *Proceedings of the Aristotelian Society*, 1999, vol. 99, 315. G. Harman, 'The nonexistence of character traits', *Proceedings of the Aristotelian Society*, 2000, vol. 100, 223.

39 C. Swanton, 'Virtue ethics', in N.J. Smelser and P.B. Baltes (eds), *International Encyclopedia of the Social and Behavioral Sciences*, New York: Elsevier, 2001, p. 16222.

40 In Woolley, 'Tending the Bar', pp. 48–53, I reviewed all of the published Canadian decisions on good character and attempted to correlate outcomes to each of these grounds but was unable to do so.

41 *Law Society of Upper Canada v D'Souza* [2002] L.S.D.D. No. 62 (Q.L.) at 42.

42 *Re P (DM)* [1989] O.J. No. 1574 (Q.L.) at 5.

43 *In the Matter of an Application for Admission to the Law Society of Upper Canada by Joseph Rizzotto, Reasons of Convocation*, 14 September 1992 at 32.

44 *Law Society of Upper Canada v Levesque* [2005] L.S.D.D. No. 38 (QL) at 23.

45 *Law Society of Upper Canada v Schuchert* [2001] L.S.D.D. No. 63 (Q.L.) at 21.

46 *Law Society of Upper Canada v Shore* 2006 ONLSHP 55 at 50.

47 It should be noted that to some extent the empirical data underlying this point are the same as the empirical data underlying the inability to identify character and the problem of the fundamental attribution error. In essence, social psychologists point out the influence of circumstances on conduct, and from that conclude (a) that character cannot be identified from isolated instances of conduct; and (b) that character does not predict conduct – circumstances do. The points are separated here largely for clarity in explaining the problem.

48 See note 38.

49 Ibid.

50 D. Luban, *Legal Ethics and Human Dignity*, New York: Cambridge University Press, 2007, p. 266.

51 C. Miller, 'Social psychology and virtue ethics', *The Journal of Ethics*, 2003, vol. 7, 365, p. 370.

52 The point of this experiment is to demonstrate that even minor changes in mood can radically affect conduct. The situation is viewed by writers such as Doris as making the situationalist point, because the mood change, and ultimately the behavioural change, are brought about by a minor change in the situation.

53 Doris, 'Persons, situations and virtue ethics', p. 504.

54 For a critique of honour, see W.B. Wendel, 'Nonlegal regulation of the legal profession: Social norms in professional communities', *Vanderbilt Law Review*, 2001, vol. 54, 1955.

55 For a critique of integrity, see Luban, *Legal Ethics*, Ch. 8. The significance of integrity as a core ethical value of Canadian lawyers is discussed in A. Woolley, 'Integrity in zealousness: Comparing the standard conceptions of the Canadian and American lawyer', *Canadian Journal of Law and Jurisprudence*, 1996, vol. 9, 61.

56 There have been numerous Canadian cases in which lawyers have been disciplined for incivility. For a discussion of these cases and a critique of, see A. Woolley, 'Does civility matter?', *Osgoode Hall Law Journal*, 2008, vol. 46, 175.

57 *Law Society of Upper Canada v Preyra* [2000] L.S.D.D. No. 60 (Q.L.) at 33.

58 *Law Society of Upper Canada v D'Souza* [2002] L.S.D.D. No. 62 (Q.L.).

59 *Law Society of Upper Canada v Schuchert* [2001] L.S.D.D. No. 63 (Q.L.).

60 *Law Society of Upper Canada v Levesque* [2005] L.S.D.D. No. 38 (Q.L.) at 23.

61  *In the Matter of an Application for Admission to the Law Society of Upper Canada by Joseph Riz-zotto, Reasons of Convocation,* 14 September 1992 at 32.
62  *Constitution Act* 1982.
63  See, for example, *Law Society of Alberta v Pozniak* [2002] L.S.D.D. No. 55 (Q.L.), where a lawyer was disciplined for calling another lawyer 'clueless'.
64  Woolley, 'Tending the Bar'.
65  Ibid. at note 152 and accompanying text, quoting from M.K. McChrystal, 'A structural analysis of the good moral character requirement for Bar admission', *Notre Dame Law Review,* 1984, vol. 60, 67, p. 101.
66  *Re P (DM)* [1989] O.J. No. 1574 (Q.L.) at 11.
67  *Re P (DM)* [1989] O.J. No. 1574 (Q.L.) at 24.
68  *Law Society of Upper Canada v Preyra* [2000] L.S.D.D. No. 60 (Q.L.) at 99.
69  R. Nichwolodoff, 'Expert psychological opinion evidence in the courts', *Health Law Journal,* 1998, vol. 6, 279, para. 2.
70  See, for example, *Family Law Act* (SA) 2003, c. F-4.5 at s. 18(1).
71  B. Walter, J. Isenegger and H. Bala, '"Best interests" in child protection proceedings: Implications and alternatives', *Canadian Journal of Family Law,* 1995, vol. 12, 367, para. 17; T.J. Hester, 'The role of mental health professionals in child custody determinations incident to divorce', *Women's Rights Law Report,* 1992, vol. 14, 109, p. 109; D.W. Shuman, 'What should we permit mental health professionals to say about "the best interests of the child?" An essay on common sense, Daubert, and the rules of evidence', *Family Law Quarterly,* 1997–98, vol. 31, 551, p. 567.
72  *Family Law Act* (SA) 2003, c. F-4.5 at s. 18(2)(b). The list includes factors such as the child's physical, psychological and emotional needs, the child's cultural, linguistic, religious and spiritual upbringing and heritage, and any plans proposed for the child's care and upbringing.
73  Walter Isenegger and Bala, 'Best interests', para. 18.
74  T.R. Litwack, G.L. Gerber and C.A. Fenster, 'The proper role of psychology in child custody disputes', *Journal of Family Law,* 1979–80, vol. 18, 269, p. 271.
75  *C(G) v T.V-F* [1987] 2 S.C.R. 244.
76  And is required by the Criminal Code (R.S.C. 1985, c. C-46 at ss. 752.1(1) and 753(1)).
77  Ibid. at s. 753(1).
78  See, for example, *R v Otto* [2006] S.J. No. 303 (CA) at para. 19 and *R v Berikoff* [2007] B.C.J. No. 218 (CA) at para. 16. There is so much reliance on expert evidence in this arena that there is some indication that the lines between the expert and the decision-maker have become blurred. Experts in a few cases have felt comfortable crossing the evidentiary-legal line, giving not just behavioural predictions but also legal designation recommendations. See *R v F.E.D.* [2007] O.J. No. 1278 at para. 25; *R v Allen* [2007] O.J. No. 2226 at para. 30; *R v Haug* [2008] S.J. No. 100 at para. 118.
79  The accuracy of clinical studies was most notably cast into considerable doubt by two broad studies in the 1970s of inmates who had been predicted to be dangerous but were transferred to civil hospitals following legal changes arising from the infamous decisions in *Baxstrom v Herold* 383 U.S. 107, 1966 and *Dixon v Attorney General of the Commonwealth of Pennsylvania* 325 F. Supp. 966, 197. The first of those studies revealed that, of the inmates labelled as dangerous, only 20 per cent committed an assault during the four years subsequent to the transfer. Further, in that four-year period, only 3 per cent of these 'dangerous offenders' were considered dangerous enough to be sent back to the hospital for the criminally insane. Subsequently, when 121 of these patients were additionally released from the civil hospital into the community, only nine of the 121 were convicted of a crime in a two and a half year period, and only one of those convictions was for a violent offence. The results of the studies are summarized in J. Monahan, *The Clinical Prediction of Violent Behaviour,* Rockville, MD: US Department of Health and Human Services, 1981, pp. 45–48. Subsequent studies have confirmed these problems with clinical prediction. See J.J. Cocozza and H.J. Steadman,

'Prediction in psychiatry: An example of misplaced confidence in experts', *Social Problems*, 1977–78, vol. 25, 265, p. 274 and J. Monahan, 'Clinical and actuarial predictions of violence: The scientific status', in D.L. Faigman, D.H. Kaye, M.J. Saks and J. Sanders (eds), *Modern Scientific Evidence: The Law and Science of Expert Testimony*, Eagan, MN: West Publishing, 2009, p. 141.

80 One author summarizes three of the most notable actuarial models used for predicting violence, and reviews literature assessing the accuracy of each model. Each model categorizes subjects into several risk categories ranging from low to high. The literature review indicated that for each model there was a considerable degree of accuracy. Overall, where application of a model generated the lowest predicted likelihood of future violence, between 1 and 11 per cent of subjects were actually violent; where the application of a model generated the highest predicted likelihood of future violence 75 to 100 per cent of the subjects were actually violent. J. Monahan, 'A jurisprudence of risk assessment: Forecasting harm among prisoners, predators and patients', *Virginia Law Review*, 2006, vol. 92, 391, pp. 409–13. For a direct comparison of clinical and actuarial predictions, see also W.M. Grove and P.E. Meehl, 'Comparative efficiency of informal (subjective, impressionist) and formal (mechanical, algorithmic) prediction procedures: The clinical-statistical controversy', *Psychology, Public Policy and Law*, 1996, vol. 2, 293.

81 Clinical predictions about parenting arrangements have also been subject to heavy criticism, although empirical studies specifically examining the validity of predictions in this context are rare. Critics rely on data showing the unreliability of predictions of violence, buttressed by observing the significant additional complicating factors that exist in custody cases, to argue that predictions of what outcome will be in the best interests of the child are fundamentally unreliable. See A.R. McBurney, 'Bitter battles: The use of psychological evaluations in child custody disputes in West Virginia', *West Virginia Law Review*, 1995, vol. 97, 773, pp. 776–78; Litwack, Gerber and Fenster, 'The proper role of psychology', p. 272.

82 This is also the case in custody hearings where the state has apprehended the child; in almost all these cases, there is not a single incident motivating the state decision, there is a repeated pattern of neglect or abuse, and also repeated attempts on the part of the agency to assist the parent in properly caring for the child.

83 H. Arthurs, 'The dead parrot: Does professional self-regulation exhibit vital signs?', *Alberta Law Review*, 1995, vol. 33, 800, p. 805 and H. Arthurs, 'Why Canadian law schools do not teach legal ethics', in Kim Economides (ed.), *Ethical Challenges to Legal Education and Conduct*, Oxford: Hart, 1998, pp. 112–16.

84 *R v Lyons* [1987] 2 S.C.R. 309.

85 Ibid. at para. 100.

# 11 The 'self-regulation' misnomer

*Fred C. Zacharias*

The US legal profession presents itself as self-regulating. In the most recent version of the Model Rules of Professional Conduct (Model Rules), the American Bar Association (ABA) proudly states: 'Although other professions also have been granted powers of self-government, the legal profession is unique in this respect.'[1] Judges routinely refer to self-regulation of the Bar,[2] academics rely on it[3] and lawyers accept it as a given.[4]

This internal understanding of the profession sometimes functions as an ideal, leading to exhortations for lawyers to exercise self-restraint or to impose strict behavioural standards on themselves. At other times, the understanding serves as a euphemism for protecting the guild; the ABA, in the preamble to its Model Rules, suggests that self-regulation can obviate 'the occasion for [external] government regulation'.[5] In practice, the characterization of law as self-regulated has subjected the profession to criticism, because the characterization carries with it the implication of self-serving norms. The oversight of lawyer behaviour frequently has been questioned on that basis.

But is the standard depiction of law as a self-regulated industry actually true? This chapter will suggest that the label oversimplifies the reality, with unfortunate consequences. Ultimately, because the term 'self-regulation' has many meanings and is frequently misused, the chapter concludes that it has become a misnomer that should be avoided.

The first two parts of the chapter address two main respects in which observers who present the Bar as self-regulated have failed. First, they have not adequately considered what the self-regulation characterization means. Because the characterization alludes to various possible aspects of regulation, it often is misunderstood. Second, observers who present the Bar as self-regulated in the broad senses of the term typically do not take adequate account of the real state of attorney regulation. In the United States, at least, the legal profession is subject to numerous external constraints, some of which are rigorous. The broad self-regulation label thus represents an overstatement. The third part of the chapter discusses ramifications of continuing to employ the label.

This chapter will leave most of the related questions for separate treatment, including the history of how the conception of the self-regulated profession developed, its consequences for regulators and other participants in the legal system, and the best mechanisms for remedying its adverse effects.[6] It is worth noting at the outset, however, that the image of a self-regulated Bar has influenced the work of the ABA and the manner in which courts and commentators have responded to professional standards of behaviour. The meaning and accuracy of the self-regulation characterization – whether it is a misnomer – therefore has significance for the way in which these actors operate, or should operate, in the future.

Critics of attorney regulation in the United States often leap from an assertion that the profession self-regulates to a suggestion that lawyers are free of external oversight – a status that some observers approve and others decry. Susanna Kim, for example, notes that 'lawyers have the power of self-regulation. In comparison to all other professions, the legal profession is the most free of external government control.'[7]

This conception of self-regulation leads proponents of strong legal ethics standards to demand that the Bar pre-empt outside influence. Thus, in the wake of the Enron scandal, one commentator argued that: 'As a group that self-regulates, lawyers must address [the post-Enron issues], formulate policy, and draft rules and regulations with effective enforcement.'[8] In the Model Rules, the ABA clings to the notion that effective drafting of the professional rules and lawyer self-restraint will foreclose external regulation of the profession.[9]

Many observers, however, assume that self-regulation means self-interested regulation. David Barnhizer states that: 'There is a *universal law* that tells us that no one is capable of fairly judging themselves.'[10] Benjamin Barton argues that 'because the legal profession is basically self-regulating, most regulations governing lawyers are self-serving and aimed at increasing lawyer profits and protecting the monopolistic nature of the legal profession'.[11] Such assertions may reflect literary licence, but they are certainly exaggerations. Many aspects of the professional codes are designed to serve client, systemic and public interests. The active modern disciplinary process, though arguably not adequate, targets lawyer misconduct.

These observations are not intended to defend the existing regime of lawyer regulation. The point is simply that the term 'self-regulation' lends itself to logical leaps. The term contains suggestions of exclusive control, self-interest and the absence of alternative regulation that do not accurately describe the contemporary regulatory scheme. As a result, regulators or critics who rely on the term without having a specific definition in mind (or without spelling out their definition) risk misconceptions that can be counter-productive. The following pages scrutinize the self-regulation label, consider the realities of attorney regulation in the United States and note a few areas in which reference to a broad but undefined notion of a self-regulated Bar has had, or can have, negative effects.

## 11.1 The meaning of self-regulation

The term 'self-regulation' has been used to embody various conceptions of regulation, particularly when applied to the legal profession.[12] At one extreme, self-regulation means 'self-restraint'. Professionals, including lawyers, typically are expected to 'regulate' their own conduct by desisting voluntarily from inappropriate behaviour. To facilitate this process, standards developed by peer groups often guide the behaviour of members of a 'self-regulated' profession. Cooperative mechanisms for peer review may also help inform the profession and enable the members to learn from the experiences of others, without intending to punish them.

At the next level, self-regulation refers to 'self-monitoring' – the profession's development of formal substantive behavioural norms. It suggests a profession that establishes its own enforceable standards of conduct. The observation that a profession is self-regulated in this sense may imply that the norms the profession has adopted are comprehensive and supplant the need for other forms of regulation. Even under this broad conception, however, the professional standards sometimes are state-approved or state-enforced through certification boards, licensing agencies or disciplinary authorities.

Used in its most emphatic sense, the term 'self-regulation' signifies that a profession is 'self-policing' – perhaps entirely self-policing. It other words, the profession itself controls the behaviour of its members by establishing and enforcing standards of conduct on terms set by the members themselves. Commentators who warn of the dangers of the 'guild regulating the guild' or the 'fox guarding the chicken coop' typically envision this state of affairs.[13] When a profession is self-policing, the risk that self-interest will infect the governing standards and enforcement decisions is at its peak. If the profession does not minimize the effects of self-interest, external regulators eventually may choose to intervene.

The term 'self-regulation' is self-contained in that it looks exclusively to how a profession acts in constraining its members' behaviour. But a realistic evaluation of the degree to which a profession is self-regulating necessarily depends on the presence and engagement of external regulators. This is true whatever form, or level, of self-regulation one refers to. If one conceives of the self-restraint form of self-regulation, the conduct and the substance of the standards resulting from self-regulation will be influenced by external regulation. A professional's decision to exercise self-restraint by avoiding criminal behaviour, for example, necessarily is affected by the degree to which the pertinent criminal law is enforced.[14] Conversely, the external use that can be made of peer assessments will inevitably define the impact of peer review on individual lawyers and on the nature of the peer review itself; as in the medical profession, when a finding of error can be used as a predicate for civil liability, the reviewers usually will become more hesitant to issue such a finding.[15]

The existence and nature of external regulation is equally pertinent to the intermediate, self-monitoring conception of self-regulation. The fact that a profession adopts a formal code of behaviour does not alone mean that members of the profession will accept the standards as gospel. That depends, at least in part, on whether the standards are enforced and are consistent with external regulation – particularly enforced external regulation.[16] Thus, if a code approves of (or insists on) conduct that criminal or other statutory law forbids, the members of the profession might be tempted to violate the professional norm. Assume, for instance, that a reporter's professional code requires the maintenance of sources' confidentiality but criminal law requires reporters called before grand juries to testify about their sources. The impact of the code clearly will be influenced by the existence and enforcement of the external law.

When a profession controls both the promulgation of professional standards and their enforcement, the risk of self-interested regulation is at its peak. Yet the force of even this emphatic form of self-regulation varies with the behaviour of potential alternative regulators. If the profession's self-policing occurs in tandem with other regimes regulating the profession's members, three possibilities present themselves. The self-regulation can become meaningless because the external regulators force inconsistent behaviour. The self-regulation and external regulation may be harmonized, so that the standards do not compete. Or the self- and external regulation can each be operative but only at different times or in different contexts, in a way that makes it possible for members to live with substantive inconsistencies.

This elementary discussion of the variable meaning of self-regulation provides the background for an important observation. Where the US legal profession is concerned, lawyers, courts, commentators and lay observers often conflate the various conceptions. Sometimes the observation that law is a self-regulated industry refers to a form of self-regulation that is conceptually plausible in light of modern realities; sometimes it hearkens back to an archaic vision of the profession.

The most recent version of the Model Rules of Professional Conduct, for example, adverts to a somewhat outdated vision of self-restraint and influential peer standards; it opines that lawyers self-regulate and warns that a failure to do so prudently will invite external regulation.[17] Many contemporary critics of the self-regulated legal profession focus instead on the perceived monopoly of the Bar in promulgating the substantive constraints on lawyers; they assert the inherently self-interested nature of particular rules monitoring the profession.[18] Other critics, emphasizing the self-policing view of self-regulation, seem to argue that enforcement of professional standards fails because judges who control disciplinary enforcement are lawyers protecting their own.[19] Almost universally, current observations about the nature or effects of lawyer self-regulation do not acknowledge the second half of the self-regulation equation – namely, the existence of multiple forms of regulation that constrain legal practice in modern times.

The remainder of this chapter will briefly identify the realities of today's regulatory regime governing US lawyers and explain what those realities mean for the different conceptions of self-regulation. The chapter will suggest that it is important for observers to be clear in their own minds about the precise characteristic of the regulatory regime that they are criticizing. Because of its multiple meanings, the term 'self-regulation' gets in the way of such clarity, so the chapter argues that the term has become a misnomer that should be replaced with more accurate alternatives.

## 11.2 Modern regulation of lawyers

For purposes of discussion, let us divide the regulation of lawyers into three parts: (1) regulation by institutions external to the Bar and judiciary; (2) judicial regulation other than implementation of the disciplinary codes; and (3) professional codes, with discipline based on the codes. In the United States, each of these aspects of lawyer regulation has evolved – with external non-judicial regulation increasing over time and disciplinary codes being a relatively recent phenomenon. This chapter will leave description of the historical evolution of lawyer regulation to other fora, focusing exclusively on the actual state of regulation today.[20]

It is worth noting that many forms of regulation – over lawyers or other professionals – represent the composite work of multiple regulators. One institution will set the law or professional norms, but another may institute enforcement, while a third may provide or oversee the process by which the legal standards are interpreted and enforcement is administered, and still another may be the ultimate decision-maker on the facts. Except in situations in which courts establish the law and enforce it themselves (as when they impose sanctions upon lawyers for in-court behaviour), regulation of the US legal profession almost always has some composite elements. To determine whether a particular form of regulation governing lawyers can fairly be characterized as self-regulation, one therefore must first identify who controls which aspects of the regulating process.

### *11.2.1 Regulation by non-judicial institutions external to the Bar*

State and federal legislatures play an ever-increasing role in setting behavioural standards that govern the legal profession. Observers, and sometimes even lawyers themselves, tend to forget that lawyers are subject to most statutes governing businesses and ordinary citizens – including corporate and partnership law, prohibitions against fraud and deceit, and consumer protection statutes. Criminal statutes, too, cover lawyers who violate them or conspire with their clients to do so.

In one respect, criminal laws seem less applicable to the Bar than to laypersons. Because lawyers defending clients charged, or potentially chargeable, with a crime inevitably are privy to information about their clients' activities, courts and prosecutors have taken care not to hold lawyers liable merely for knowing that information.[21] Lawyers are, however, forbidden to personally encourage or participate in their clients' criminal acts.[22] Starting in the late twentieth century, prosecutors increasingly targeted members of the profession, particularly in connection with securities and other white-collar crimes that provided lawyers with personal financial incentives to participate.[23] Prosecutors also began to call lawyers to testify against their clients before grand juries, on the theory that the clients' use of lawyers to further their crimes nullified any claim of attorney–client privilege.[24]

During the same period, another form of external lawyer regulation developed: administrative regulation. The most prominent instance of an agency's effort to impose standards of behaviour on the practice of law that arguably conflicted with the profession's own asserted standards involved the federal Office of Thrift Supervision's regulation of banking lawyers. In the notorious *Kaye, Scholer* case,[25] OTS threatened the very existence of a major national law firm for presenting client information to the agency in a 'misleading' fashion, which the firm thought appropriate because the firm viewed itself as an advocate under the legal ethics codes.[26] The OTS regulations, however, were not the first agency rules that constrained lawyers. The US Patent Office long has claimed the ability to determine the qualifications of, and to regulate, persons appearing as advocates before the agency.[27] Many other agencies have adopted standards governing lawyers as well.[28] Most recently, the United States Congress adopted legislation requiring the Securities and Exchange Commission to promulgate independent regulations governing lawyers in the Securities Bar.[29]

Can these many forms of regulation plausibly be characterized as self-regulation? No professional organization of lawyers controls them. With respect to statutory law, legislatures promulgate the standards. Criminal law is enforced in part by prosecutors who screen cases and institute proceedings, in part by judges who preside over the criminal process and in part by juries who implement the law. Civil statutes are sometimes enforced in court at the behest of lay plaintiffs and at other times require the involvement of government bureaucracies.

Administrative regulation of lawyers may be prompted by state or federal agencies themselves (as with the OTS standards at issue in *Kaye, Scholer*) or by the legislature (as in the case of the recent *Sarbanes-Oxley Act*). In either event, agency personnel eventually establish the professional standards, interpret them and apply them to lawyers. Enforcement of those standards ordinarily starts with an agency, but the agency action may be reviewable in the courts.

Each of these regulatory mechanisms can fairly be conceived as self-regulation only in a very limited way: lawyers are involved as participants in the standard-setting or enforcement processes in roles other than being a defendant. Many legislators and employees of regulating agencies, for example, are attorneys. Moreover, both legislatures and agencies typically accept comments from the Bar before promulgating their standards, just as they accept lobbying efforts or public comments from other potential targets of their regulations. With respect to criminal regulation, all prosecutors are required to be members of a Bar. Judges who administer criminal and civil statutes and oversee agency regulation are lawyers as well.

Does this mean the foxes are guarding the chicken coop? Only if the lawyers working as legislators, bureaucrats, prosecutors or judges do not perform their jobs objectively. One can surmise that lawyers in these positions might understand the predicaments in which practising lawyers find themselves, and sympathize with the difficult choices these lawyers sometimes must make, but that can render the regulators more informed and more able to discard specious explanations for misbehaviour just as much as it can bias the regulators in lawyers' favour. The question of whether the resulting regulatory regime serves the Bar thus is an empirical one. To date, there are no studies showing that modern prosecutors, agencies or courts charged with enforcing particular statutes or regulations against lawyers are particularly sympathetic to those targets.[30] Neither have recent studies shown that lawyer-legislators or lawyer-bureaucrats are more prone to adopting lawyer-friendly standards than their lay counterparts.

The more important point is that, as a practical matter, lawyers' involvement in the various processes described above is unavoidable if the Bar is to be regulated at all. The participation of lawyers stems from the fact that legal training is what qualifies a government official to be a regulator – to set legal standards, enforce them in administrative or judicial proceedings, or act as arbiter. The observation that lawyers self-regulate by participating in the regulatory process thus is tautological. It may justify observers in analyzing whether a particular regulatory regime works in its intended fashion or whether additional lay participation would be fruitful, but the self-regulation label alone has little substantive force.

### 11.2.2 Judicial regulation other than implementation of disciplinary codes

As Bruce Green and I have described elsewhere,[31] courts oversee lawyers' professional behaviour in many ways other than implementing the disciplinary codes. Let us consider two of these mechanisms here: judicial implementation of civil law targeting lawyers and direct judicial regulation of lawyers.

US lawyers are subject to a variety of civil causes of action, including malpractice, breach of fiduciary duty, fraud or deceit, malicious prosecution and abuse of process, among others.[32] As with all common-law remedies, judges establish the prevailing legal standards. In some cases, however, lay juries share in the standard-setting process. In most jurisdictions, for example, the malpractice standard (i.e. the reasonably prudent attorney) is so vague that juries can interpret it in almost any way.[33] Some jurisdictions leave the determination of breaches of fiduciary duty to flexible jury decision-making as well.[34]

Whether the standards are clear or not, juries clearly play a role in enforcing civil liability against lawyers. More importantly, the potential for civil liability causes insurers to regulate the Bar as well; risk-management policies of malpractice insurers require lawyers to limit the clients they represent, the subject matters they take on and their practices in the handling of cases.[35] The implementation of civil remedies therefore is the result of a shared enterprise among judges, lay jurors and insurers. By any measure, the frequency of civil verdicts against lawyers and their influence on lawyers' behaviour has exploded over the past 30 years.[36]

One cannot fairly conceptualize the civil liability remedies as lawyer self-regulation, at least not in the pejorative sense. Lawyer-judges help establish the standards, but do so in an adversarial setting in which advocates on opposite sides urge divergent positions. The judges draw on legal concepts (e.g. negligence, fiduciary duty) that apply to non-lawyers as well. Lay participation in the application of those standards is significant. Insurers, though they may employ lawyers to devise risk-management policies, are economic enterprises that have as their goal the avoidance of the types of conduct that might prompt sanction. In short, the overall civil liability regime governing lawyers seems no less objective than civil liability regimes governing other professions, and the presence of lawyer-judges in the process does little to change that.

In contrast to judicial regulation of lawyers through oversight of the civil liability system, which has become significant only in relatively recent times, direct judicial regulation of lawyers is as old as the US legal system. Early US courts established standards for lawyer behaviour on a case-by-case basis, using their authority to control who could practise before them (i.e. the admissions power), the inherent power to administer judicial proceedings and the so-called supervisory authority to regulate lawyers as officers of the court.[37] Modern courts continue to exercise these powers in tandem with, or parallel to, the disciplinary codes.[38] For example, judges determine when conflicts of interest disqualify lawyers from appearing – sometimes adverting to the professional codes, sometimes not. Judges individually and local courts as institutions set rules governing lawyer behaviour in the discovery and trial processes. In some circumstances, judges administer lawyers' fees. They also sanction lawyers for what they perceive to be misconduct.

In the direct regulation context, judges select the standards governing lawyers and enforce them. But the judiciary is not always the driving force for lawyer constraint. Rarely will a judge act unless the adversary – a lawyer committed to his client's ends – raises the issue of misconduct and urges punishment or redress.

Does this constitute lawyer self-regulation under any meaningful understanding of the term? Only if judges feel sufficient sympathy for lawyers that they hesitate to sanction them as aggressively as they otherwise might, or if adversaries are reluctant to pursue sanctions against their brethren. The anecdotal modern history, however, does not bear those possibilities out.[39]

Judges, in their opinions, in-court comments and publicly, have been critical of lawyer conduct.[40] When courts have been provided with harsh tools for punishing lawyer behaviour, as in the 1983 amendments to Federal Rules of Civil Procedure 11, judges have applied those tools vigorously – so vigorously that their zealousness in regulating the Bar has been criticized.[41] Likewise, in applying supervisory power, courts have not been particularly deferential to the Bar's professional standards, relying on the ethics codes only in haphazard fashion.[42] And lawyers pressing for sanctions against other lawyers in litigation have become ever more active; adversaries have incentives to aggressively encourage judges to impose sanctions for misconduct.[43]

### 11.2.3 Professional codes and professional discipline

The above discussion suggests that the notion that lawyers self-regulate is misguided, or is misleading, when applied to the mechanisms for constraining behaviour that are external to the professional codes. The argument that lawyers regulate themselves through the codes seems more appealing because, as the codes and enforcement of the codes initially developed, they *were* controlled by the practising Bar. The first generally accepted code, the ABA's 1908 Canons of Ethics, was written by a private organization of lawyers – in part to influence judicial regulation – and was enforced, if at all, through voluntary committees of lawyers.[44]

A fair analysis of the participants in the adoption and enforcement of modern legal ethics codes, however, casts doubt on the proposition that the profession is self-policing. The ABA's model codes do set the framework for discussions of contemporary lawyer standards. But catalysts for changes to the standards can also come locally in response to recurring issues in the state (e.g. sex with clients), public issues (e.g. lawyer involvement in corporate fraud) or the work of active local Bar committees. The ultimate standards are determined within each state.

Moreover, state Bar associations do not themselves control the rules. Typically, state supreme courts do, exercising their alleged inherent power over the legal system.[45] The process of amending the codes consists first of a review of proposed changes by a committee charged with studying the issues and receiving public comments. These comments usually come from lawyers, but interested observers are free to contribute their positions. Committee membership often includes academics or practising lawyers who have a track record of involvement in, and some objectivity about, professional responsibility matters. The committees offer their own proposals to the state Supreme Court, which independently decides whether to adopt a new professional standard as law.

Virtually all of the participants in the process of setting these standards *are* lawyers, although that does not have to be the case. The Supreme Court justices, however, make their judgements not in their capacity as lawyers, but in their capacity as judicial lawmakers. The degree to which they defer to Bar proposals varies with the jurisdiction and the issues involved. As a practical matter, state Supreme Courts sometimes do seem to have been captured by the Bar.[46]

Not so much in the disciplinary process, however. At one time, discipline typically was committed to state disciplinary systems that were staffed by lawyer volunteers and were ineffective in sanctioning misconduct. After the ABA commissioned a report exposing this ineffectiveness[47] and adopted Model Rules in 1983 that were subjected to public scrutiny, states became more serious about their disciplinary processes. Virtually all states now fund professional disciplinary agencies, staffed with full-time prosecutors.[48] Systems for imposing discipline vary, but all operate under the rubric of the courts.[49] Once past the investigation stage, adversarial proceedings commence, with final review of disciplinary decisions usually belonging to the state Supreme Courts. Some states, such as California, include lay participation in the screening process and provide for an independent court to evaluate disciplinary matters.[50]

Because the evolution of the modern disciplinary regimes is of recent vintage, there have been no serious studies of their effectiveness. But at least two conclusions are indisputable. First, the process of discipline is far better funded and far more professional than in the past. Moreover, discipline of lawyers has become a field of legal practice, with the development of an association of disciplinary pro-secutors[51] and a significant cadre of lawyers who specialize in defending disciplinary cases.[52] Lawyers may continue to self-regulate in the sense that lawyers are involved as lobbyists, standard setters and judges, but they also now self-prosecute; far more lawyer behaviour is subjected to serious review than in previous eras.

As for the lawyer-judges who are involved in defining and enforcing the codes, the evidence is at best ambiguous. The question of whether Supreme Court jus-tices can, and should, take a more active role in setting standards for lawyers remains open.[53] To the extent that some state Supreme Courts are captured in the standard-setting process, that probably stems from the justices' discomfort with making law in the abstract, in the absence of concrete facts and adversarial presentation of the issues.

In the enforcement process, in contrast, the justices exercise their traditional role of deciding factual disputes and applying pre-existing law. One cannot simply *assume* that the justices will act partially to a particular set of litigants just because they share some characteristics with them, any more than they act partially on the basis of gender, race or other demographic criteria. Judicial opinions from the disciplinary context suggest that courts bend over backwards to avoid any appearance of alliance with the Bar, precisely because of the public's perception that the legal profession self-regulates. In *State ex rel. Oklahoma Bar Ass'n v Giger*, for example, the court approved the suspension of a lawyer's licence, noting that: 'The public must have confidence that the legal profession, which is self-regulated, will not look the other way when its members break the law.'[54]

### 11.2.4 Ramifications of the regulatory scheme for the self-regulation conception

This chapter's summary of attorney regulation in the United States suggests sev-eral initial conclusions. First, law is a heavily regulated industry, with regulation coming from many sources. Second, overall, only a few forms of lawyer regula-tion can plausibly be characterized as self-regulation, and even these can be so characterized only to a limited extent. Third, in instances in which the potential dangers of self-monitoring and self-policing arguably are present, one cannot assume those dangers exist in the absence of empirical evidence to that effect. To date, that evidence has not been developed.

In general, therefore, one should not rely on the self-regulation label itself as a basis for concluding that the whole enterprise of lawyer regulation is corrupt. It may well be that the participation of lawyers in the regulatory process has an adverse effect in some respects or that particular regulations are self-serving; I myself have questioned particular rules and orientations of the various reg-ulators.[55] However, the assumption that lawyer participation warrants condemnation of the entire scheme of regulation overlooks the synergistic impact of external standards. It also inadequately considers the relative institutional qualities of the various potential regulators.

More importantly, to the extent criticism of contemporary regulation rests primarily on lawyers' participation in the process, one needs to acknowledge that such participation may be inevitable, whatever regime is adopted in its place. Probably, the most that an observation of self-regulation can reasonably suggest is that a particular part of the regulatory scheme is *prone* to biased or self-interested decision-making. This, in turn, may justify a call to measure the objectivity of the particular decision-makers empirically, or to consider mechanisms for making that aspect of the system more effective.

## 11.3 Effects of the self-regulation misnomer

So far, the chapter has suggested several ways in which labelling the US legal profession as self-regulated inaccurately describes the profession's authority and power. The classic notion that the ABA monopolizes the development of professional standards simply is wrong. The assumption that the Bar dominates the sanctioning process is equally overblown. Although there may be fair questions about lawyer or judicial participation in some aspects of the regulatory regime, the global notion that US lawyers control their own oversight should by now have been relegated to the past.

At one level, this reality seems to present a purely semantic problem: the concept of self-regulation has multiple dimensions, but the term 'self-regulation' fails to distinguish which dimension is in play. Thus use (or misuse) of the term as shorthand can falsely encourage a belief that the inherent dangers of the broadest forms of self-regulation – self-monitoring and self-policing – are universally present. This explains why the characterization of law as a self-regulated industry typically has had pejorative connotations even though self-regulation can encompass admirable qualities.

Yet there also are substantive ramifications of conceptualizing the US legal profession as self-regulated. It is beyond the scope of this chapter to detail all of the adverse consequences or to propose remedies. The following pages, however, briefly note some of the ways in which persistent use of the self-regulation misnomer can cause inappropriate responses by laypersons, lawyers, professional code drafters and external regulators alike.

For example, when legitimate references to narrow aspects of lawyer self-regulation (such as lawyer self-restraint) are not defined, they reinforce some observers' mistaken belief that the broader aspects (such as self-policing) are prevalent or are the regulatory norm. Consider lay perceptions of the disciplinary process. Told that legal ethics codes implement self-regulation, lay observers naturally assume that the codes monitor the totality of lawyer behaviour and that enforcement of the codes is the over-arching mechanism for policing misbehaviour. They thus expect that misconduct, negligence that harms clients and incompetence all will be punished by disciplinary regulators. As a consequence, when particular lawyers avoid suspension or disbarment for their actions, laypersons routinely conclude that the disciplinary system has failed and that the failure must be a result of the self-regulatory model – lawyers protecting their own.[56]

The flaw in this analysis should by now be obvious. The professional codes are neither comprehensive nor pre-emptive; complementary forms of regulation exist. More importantly, enforcement of the codes, as part of the lawyer licensing process, does not have as its primary function punishing lawyers or providing remedies for client injuries. Discipline's main goals are to make sure that lawyers who continue in practice – the targeted lawyer and others potentially aware of the disciplinary case – are competent and familiar with their professional obligations.[57] Disciplinary regulators may decline to suspend or disbar a negligent lawyer or a lawyer who has misunderstood their obligations because they are confident the lawyer can be competent in the future, leaving the issue of whether other sanctions are appropriate to the civil liability and criminal law regimes.

However, one cannot dispel lay criticism simply by asserting that the underlying claim of self-regulation is wrong. That is because a charge of 'self-regulation' also may encompass the narrower notion that lawyer-judges administer discipline in a lawyer-friendly way. This specific accusation might be refutable on an empirical basis, but it is not a non-starter. Its semantic association with the less viable broad claims regarding the Bar's failure to fulfil comprehensive self-monitoring or self-policing functions keeps the misconceptions underlying the broad claims alive. In short, the failure to disaggregate the various aspects and potential defects of self-regulation perpetuates myths about the US legal profession.

The upshot is twofold. First, the unchallenged, undiluted perception of laypersons that lawyers self-regulate undermines respect for the regulation of lawyers as a whole; laypersons both expect too much of the disciplinary process and undervalue other regulation of the Bar. Second, to the extent that the Bar disregards the criticisms of the disciplinary process because of the underlying flaws of the self-regulation claim, the profession ignores the potentially valid aspect of the claim that needs to be addressed empirically – namely the objectivity of judges in the disciplinary process.

Like laypersons, lawyers also conflate the multiple conceptions of self-regulation, with adverse consequences. Consider this scenario:

> An attorney with a potential conflict of interest must decide whether to accept the representation of a client. The attorney consults the professional code, because it is there to provide guidance. The code suggests that the conflict is consentable.

At this point, many lawyers will (if the case is potentially profitable) ask the client to consent to the representation and will assume that consent ends the matter. Why? Because of the lawyers' intuition that the profession is self-regulating. That intuition is accurate insofar as lawyers are expected to exercise self-restraint and the Bar provides guidelines (e.g. the codes) to help them do so.

But in the hypothetical scenario, the lawyer's reliance on the codes is simultaneously prompted by a less accurate assumption about the self-regulating profession – namely, that the Bar-promulgated legal ethics code monitors the totality of lawyers' conduct and, when it provides an answer, pre-empts the regulatory field. In fact, once litigation commences, a trial or administrative court may disqualify the lawyer despite the client's consent. Alternatively, a jury may find in a subsequent malpractice or breach of fiduciary duty case that the lawyer had no business seeking and accepting the client's consent. The reality is that many forms of regulation govern the same conduct of the lawyer. He errs in assuming that the Bar self-regulates, in the global standard-setting sense.

The broader Bar suffers from a similar conceit, with a different set of consequences. When professional rules are proposed, they often are supported most vociferously on the basis that the Bar should self-regulate in order to avoid external oversight of the conduct in question. The ABA, theorizing that the Bar is in the best position to judge appropriate legal practice, has made the pre-emption goal a principle justification for its model codes. The Model Rules, like the earlier version, state:

> To the extent that lawyers meet the obligations of their professional calling, the occasion for government regulation is obviated. Self-regulation also helps maintain the legal profession's independence from government domination.[58]

Does the ABA position make sense? Perhaps, if all the ABA means is that voluntarily self-restraint by lawyers will produce optimal behaviour and may lessen the need for external regulators to target lawyers actively. Yet the statement in the Model Rules also seems to refer to self-regulation of a more significant ilk, apparently envisioning the Bar's standards as the exclusive form of monitoring and constraining lawyer behaviour. If so, this vision reflects wistful longing at best because, as we have seen, the professional codes have not pre-empted the regulatory field for many years.

In practice, the ABA's failure to define precisely the role self-regulation plays diverts the organization from effective code-drafting. It extends the myth that the ABA is in control, preventing the membership from confronting the reality that modern ethics codes reflect co-regulation rather than a regulatory monopoly. If the ABA were to acknowledge that reality, it could begin to consider more explicitly how the various regulatory mechanisms should interact. As I have discussed elsewhere, the legal ethics codes and disciplinary process are not always an appropriate, and certainly not always the best, method for addressing particular aspects of lawyer behaviour.[59]

The persistent image of emphatic self-regulation also serves to mislead members of the rule-making Bar into believing, more generally, that the Bar is able to control external regulation. Thus, for example, when it became clear in the wake of the Enron scandal that the SEC would impose some responsibility on corporate lawyers to prevent or reveal corporate misconduct, an ABA Task Force sought to prevent such regulation, rather than helping the SEC to formulate its position.[60] When the SEC adopted regulations of securities under the *Sarbanes-Oxley Act*, the California and Washington Bars challenged it as an unconstitutional abrogation of state professional rules.[61] Both of these efforts cast the Bar in a bad light, as being devoted to turf protection rather than consumer protection. The ABA's unrealistic conception of self-regulation as pre-emptive of external oversight ultimately caused the external regulators to disregard the Bar's input.

These are not isolated phenomena. The image of the self-policing legal profession has continually spurred the Bar to develop rules based on a vision of lawyering at odds with other law. Attorney–client confidentiality fits uncomfortably with legal attorney–client privilege principles. Advocacy rules sometimes contradict administrative regulations governing the role of lawyers, as in the *Kaye, Scholer* case. Rather than attempting to align the disparate approaches or providing lawyers with guidance on how to reconcile their behaviour under the ethics codes and other law, the Bar's tendency has been to push its own vision – typically with little hope of winning the day when the codes and other law conflict.[62]

The self-regulation misnomer – the use of a label that includes potentially inaccurate characterizations or conceptions of professional standards – has had unfortunate impacts on co-regulators of the Bar as well. A misperception about how the profession self-regulates can undermine the manner in which the co-regulators interact with each other and the Bar. This can make it difficult to harmonize intertwined regulation and to inform targets of the regulation of how they must conduct themselves.

In our previous scenario, for example, the attorney with a possible conflict of interest is potentially governed by the ethics code's conflict rules (adopted by the state Supreme Court), a trial court's disqualification standards, and a jury's application of malpractice law. The trial court must implement its own supervisory standards governing disqualification, but must have some understanding of how the Supreme Court's conflict rule and the substantive malpractice law should influence the supervisory standards. The attorney needs to know how to reconcile the multiple standards – or, if they conflict, which to obey.

Here is the problem. Suppose that a state Supreme Court conceives of the profession as self-regulated because the justices believe in the notion of lawyer self-restraint. The court's characterization of the Bar as self-regulated may cause the court to defer to the ABA and local Bar committees on the substance of the codes.[63] In other words, by failing to internalize the limits of its self-regulation conception (i.e. that the codes suggest ways in which lawyers should restrain themselves), the court may allow a more emphatic conception of self-regulation to become the norm (i.e. that lawyers are entitled to monitor themselves and set their own standards). Supreme Courts captured in this way default on their responsibility to co-regulate – to make objective determinations when they convert the professional standards into law.

By the same token, suppose that a state Supreme Court, in adopting the professional rules, avoids the profession's control. It treats the Bar as self-regulating only in the limited sense of offering suggestions for self-restraint or suggesting standards for implementation by the court or external regulators. Lower court judges, however, may nonetheless assume that the Supreme Court defers to Bar self-monitoring. These judges therefore may give insufficient weight to a standard the Supreme Court has carefully selected.

To illustrate the point, consider again the hypothetical lawyer with a potential conflict of interest. The trial judge exercising supervisory authority needs to determine whether to disqualify the lawyer despite the fact that the lawyer has obtained a waiver in accordance with the conflict-of-interest rule. Alternatively, the court must determine whether to allow the lawyer who has proceeded without consent (in violation of the ethics code) to remain in the case. If a judge, because of their understanding of lawyer self-regulation, assumes the Supreme Court has deferred to the Bar's expertise in promulgating conflict-of-interest rules, the judge may treat the Supreme Court standard as non-judicial, non-controlling law even though the Supreme Court actually has given the issues thorough consideration.

It is important to understand why the results in these two scenarios are attributable to the self-regulation misnomer. As noted above, the characterization of the self-regulated Bar encapsulates several possible assumptions about the regulation of lawyers, some of which are false and others of which are unproven. In the first example, the state Supreme Court that allows itself to be captured is adopting the ABA's misconception that the profession is exclusive (or always superior) in its ability to identify appropriate standards and monitor itself. The self-regulation misnomer causes the court to ignore the reality that law is a regulated industry in which the court is supposed to serve as an independent co-regulator. In the process, the court fails to adequately evaluate the rules – and particularly, potential self-interest inherent in the rules.

In the second scenario, the trial judges who treat the professional rules adopted by the Supreme Court as weak law also are influenced by a conception of self-regulation that may not be accurate. They assume that the Supreme Court allows the Bar to self-monitor and, as a consequence, treat the resulting standards as universally self-interested (or not deserving of respect) – whether or not that is the case. The trial judges, in effect, are driven to act entirely independently in implementing their supervisory authority, even though it might be more appropriate to defer to, or reconcile their standards with, the Supreme Court's rule.

In the best of all possible worlds, of course, the scheme of interlocking co-regulation would leave decision-making in each instance in the hands of the institution best qualified to make the particular determination. Presumably, the Bar has valuable insights into the appropriate substance of professional standards. The state supreme court has important decision-making attributes as well – including independence, the ability to create uniformity in judicial decision-making and the ability to harmonize professional standards with those in civil law. The lower courts have better capacity to perceive how general standards apply in concrete settings and to analyze the effects of applying professional standards strictly on particular affect litigation. In the scenario just discussed, however, the consequence of the different actors' reactions to the concept of self-regulation prevents each from realistically determining their own relative institutional strengths, and on that basis determining who should control the standards in which circumstances.

At root, the ABA probably is most responsible for these effects of the self-regulation misnomer. It has long pressed the notion that it should establish the standards governing lawyer conduct and that those standards should, in large measure, pre-empt the field. Because it has not been realistic about the pervasiveness of external regulation, the ABA has never sought to analyze how regulation should be allocated – in other words, when the work of which kind of regulator should become most prominent. Absent this kind of analysis, it becomes inevitable that the standards implemented by various co-regulators overlap and sometimes contradict one another.

## 11.4 Conclusions

What conclusions can one draw from the phenomenon of the self-regulation misnomer? The first is that it is the term 'self-regulation' rather than the concept itself that is problematic, because the term embodies multiple processes (including self-restraint, self-monitoring and self-policing) and multiple possible dynamics (including the goals of guiding lawyers, benefiting the guild, shaping public policy and pre-empting external regulation). An observer's use of the term in a particular context may be intended to claim the existence of all aspects of self-regulation, but more typically reflects a focus on a single characteristic.

The fairest characterization of the regime governing the legal profession is that it consists of co-regulation administered by a variety of institutions and personnel. Lawyers may participate in the regulatory process, but do not always control it. When lawyers are the decision-makers, they sometimes act in capacities that require them to act objectively or in contexts, such as adversarial trials, in which there are safeguards assuring their objectivity. In other situations, in contrast, lawyer-regulators may be in a position to press the interests of the Bar if they are inclined to do so.

The second conclusion suggested by this chapter's analysis, therefore, is that the terminology 'self-regulation' should be avoided – without pre-empting observers' ability to assert the benefits of self-regulation through other terms (e.g. 'self-restraint') or to question those aspects of lawyer self-monitoring or self-policing that may reflect bias. Critics should acknowledge that law is a heavily regulated industry and that the totality of the regulatory regime reflects co-regulation. The ABA and state code-drafters likewise should remove references to self-regulation from the codes, instead focusing directly on the questions of how lawyers should restrain themselves, which professional standards should pre-empt external law, when lawyers should look to external law for guidance, and when co-regulators should consider themselves responsible for developing and enforcing the primary constraints on particular types of lawyer misbehaviour.

Third, sharpening the terminology should help critics identify which aspects of lawyer regulation are problematic. If a critic's concern is his perception that particular standards, enforcement mechanisms or disciplinary decisions are weighted too heavily in the Bar's favour, expressing that concern will focus the debate on specific needed reform, rather than producing wholesale distrust of the regulatory enterprise. If, in contrast, a critic perceives that the regulatory process itself is flawed because lawyer participation in it (e.g. as judges or regulatory personnel) produces biased decision-making, stating that claim in non-conclusory terms should lead to an empirical analysis of the merits of the claim and, if the evidence bears out the claim, re-evaluation of the entire system.

Finally, this chapter's analysis suggests that the various co-regulators of the profession need to take stock of their own institutional strengths and determine how their decision-making should interact with that of the other co-regulators. Replacing the term 'self-regulation' with the term 'co-regulation' makes clear that the many forms of lawyer constraints are intertwined. The term 'co-regulation' makes it more difficult for the various regulators (e.g. code drafters, supervisory judges) to envision particular standards as operating in limited spheres and as bearing no relationship to regulation in other spheres. Changing regulators' thinking in this way can only be beneficial because it requires serious attention to institutional choice – determinations of which regulators can best address which aspects of lawyers' behaviour.

This chapter began with the question 'What does the term "self-regulation" mean?' The chapter's implicit answer to that question is that the term in theory has many meanings, which in practice amount to none. By conflating the many conceptions of self-regulation and using a shorthand characterization of the legal profession as self-regulated to draw conclusions, observers and regulators alike have avoided serious analysis of potentially serious issues plaguing the regulatory scheme. In the process, they have undermined trust in the regulatory process and the possibility of correcting those deficiencies that do exist. Eliminating reliance on the term would be an important first step in the development of better, and more comprehensive, standards governing the behaviour of the Bar.

## Notes

1 American Bar Association, *Model Rules of Professional Conduct*, Chicago: American Bar Association.
2 For example, *Matzkin v Delaney, Zemetis, Donahue, Durham & Noonan*, 39 Conn. L. Rptr. 627 (2005); *Horn v. New York Times* 100 N.Y.2d 85, 94 (2003); M. Greenberg, 'Beyond confrontation: A holistic approach to the practice of law', *New England Law Review*, 1996, vol. 30, 927, p. 934; D. Young and L. Hill, 'Professionalism: The necessity for internal control', *Temple Law Review*, 1998, vol. 61, 205, p. 206.
3 For example J. Macey, 'Occupation code 541110: Lawyers, self-regulation, and the idea of a profession', *Fordham Law Review*, 2005, vol. 74, 1079; J. Sahl, 'The public hazard of lawyer self-regulation: Learning from Ohio's struggle to reform its disciplinary system', *University of Cincinnati Law Review*, 1999, vol. 68, 65; T. Schneyer,

'From self-regulation to Bar corporatism: What the S& L crisis means for the regulation of lawyers', *South Texas Law Review*, 1994, vol. 35, 639.

4 For example A. Blumenthal, 'Attorney self-regulation, consumer protection, and the future of the legal profession', *Kansas Journal of Law & Public Policy*, 1994, vol. 3, 1; T. Byerley, 'Lawyer self-regulation and the Client Protection Fund', *Michigan Business Journal*, 1996, vol. 75, 538; D. Richmond, 'The duty to report professional misconduct: A practical analysis of lawyer self-regulation', *Georgetown Journal of Legal Ethics*, 1999, vol. 12, 175.

5 American Bar Association, *Model Rules of Professional Conduct*.

6 These issues are discussed in F. Zacharias, 'The myth of lawyer self-regulation', *Minnesota Law Review*, 2009, vol. 93, 1147.

7 S.M. Kim, 'Dual identities and dueling obligations: Preserving independence in corporate representation', *Tennessee Law Review*, 2001, vol. 68, 179, p. 255.

8 K. Ourednik IV, 'Multidisciplinary practice and professional responsibility after Enron', *Florida Coastal Law Journal*, 2003, vol. 4, 167, p. 193.

9 American Bar Association, *Model Rules of Professional Conduct*.

10 D. Barnhizer, 'Profession deleted: Using market and liability forces to regulate the very ordinary business of law practice for profit', *Georgetown Journal of Legal Ethics*, 2004, vol. 17, 203, p. 255 (emphasis added).

11 B. Barton, 'The ABA, the rules, and professionalism: The mechanics of self-defeat and a call for a return to the ethical, moral, and practical approach of the canons', *North Carolina Law Review*, 2005, vol. 83, 411, p. 419; see also B. Barton, 'Do judges systematically favor the interests of the legal profession', *Alabama Law Review*, 2008, vol. 59, 453, p. 454.

12 For example, F. Marks and D. Cathcart, 'Discipline within the legal profession: Is it self-regulation', *University of Illinois Law Forum*, 1974, 193, pp. 194–95 ('two tasks are involved in the process of self-regulation: the task of monitoring conduct and the task of maintaining the quality of performance'); E. Steele and R. Nimmer, 'Lawyers, clients, and professional regulation', *American Bar Foundation Research Journal*, 1976, 917, pp. 921–22 (discussing self-regulation in terms of bar control of admission requirements and the substance of the disciplinary codes).

13 For example, J. Coffee Jr, 'The attorney as gatekeeper: An agenda for the SEC', *Columbia Law Review*, 2003, vol. 103, 1293, p. 1316 ('private self-regulation of attorneys through bar associations means the continued government of the guild, by the guild, and for the guild'); K. Ostberg, 'The conflict of interest in lawyer self-regulation', *Professional Lawyer*, 1989, 6, p. 7 ('Because trade associations [like the ABA and state Bar associations] do not represent the public, they should have ... no role in deciding who enters the profession or in deciding conflicts between its own members and the public.').

14 For example, see G. Becker, 'Crime and punishment: An economic approach', in G. Becker and W. Landes (eds), *Essays in the Economics of Crime and Punishment*, New York: Columbia University Press, 1974, pp. 40–41 (discussing the effectiveness of public efforts to discourage offences).

15 See generally I. Moore, J. Pichert, G. Hickson, C. Federspiel and J. Blackford, 'Rethinking peer review: Detecting and addressing medical malpractice claims risk', *Vanderbilt Law Review*, 2006, vol. 59, 1175 (discussing the pros and cons of statutory privileges maintaining the secrecy of peer review proceedings).

16 For example, see D. McGowan, 'Why not try the carrot? A modest proposal to grant immunity to lawyers who disclose client financial misconduct', *California Law Review*, 2004, vol. 92, 1825, p. 1830 (discussing the likely effects of enforcing, or not enforcing, a whistleblower rule for corporate lawyers through discipline or civil liability); F. Zacharias 'Integrity ethics', *Georgetown Journal of Legal Ethics*, 2009, vol. 22, 541 (discussing the effects of enforced and unenforced external standards on lawyer behaviour).

17 American Bar Association, *Model Rules of Professional*.

18 For example, Barton, 'The ABA, the rules, and professionalism', p. 419 (arguing that 'most regulations governing lawyers' are self-serving products of self-regulation); A. Davis, 'Professional liability insurers as regulators of law practice', *Fordham Law Review*, 1996, vol. 65, 209, p. 231 ('the bar has proved itself to be supremely self-serving in regulating itself').

19 For example, R. Lee, 'The state of self-regulation of the legal profession: Have we locked the fox in the chicken coop?', *Widener Journal of Public Law*, 2003, vol. 11, 69, p. 73 ('judicial regulation of lawyers remains lawyers regulating lawyers'); N. Moore, 'The usefulness of ethical codes', *Annual Survey of American Law*, 1989, 7, p. 15 (noting that, because supervising courts 'are comprised of judges, who are not only members of the broader legal profession, but also former (and potentially future) practicing lawyers ... the legal profession has achieved a degree of self-regulation far beyond ... the expectations of any other professional group').

20 The historical development of professional regulation is discussed in Zacharias, 'The myth of lawyer self-regulation'.

21 For example, see *United States v Beckner* 134 F.3d 714, 721 (5th Cir. 1998) ('an attorney to be convicted for aiding and abetting a client's fraud, that attorney must have had actual knowledge of the fraud and must have taken an active role in advancing the wrongdoing'); *Greenberg Traurig of New York, P.C. v Moody* 161 S.W.3d 56, 82 (Tex.App. 2004) ('Mere knowledge and silence are not sufficient to establish conspiracy. Instead, because of the attorney's duty to preserve client confidences, there must be some indication that the attorney agreed to the fraud.').

22 For example, see *United States v Dolan* 120 F.3d 856, 869 (8th Cir. 1997) (affirming conviction of an attorney for conspiring with a client to conceal property from a bankruptcy court); *United States v Vaughn* 797 F.2d 1485, 1490–91 (9th Cir. 1986) (upholding conviction of an attorney who helped a client purchase an airplane, knowing it would be used in narcotics trafficking); *Kentucky Bar Association v Rorrer* 222 S.W.3d 223, 229 (Ky. 1997) (disbarring an attorney convicted for using his professional skills to further a conspiracy involving his client and the attempted laundering of drug money); cf. Model Rules, Rule 1.2(d) (forbidding lawyers to assist or participate in illegal conduct).

23 See F. Zacharias 'The humanization of attorneys', Symposium Issue of *The Professional Lawyer*, 2002, 9, p. 30 (providing authorities supporting the proposition that prosecutors 'have targeted lawyers more directly, as potential criminal suspects or facilitators of crime').

24 For example, see M. Stern and D. Hoffman, 'Privileged informers: The attorney subpoena problem and a proposal for reform', *University of Pennsylvania Law Review*, 1988, vol. 136, 1783, pp. 1787–89 (characterizing the phenomenon as an 'explosion' of attorney subpoenas); F. Zacharias, 'A critical look at rules governing grand jury subpoenas of attorneys', *Minnesota Law Review*, 1992, vol. 76, 917, p. 919 (cataloguing cases in which prosecutors increasingly 'resorted to the tactic of subpoenaing lawyers to appear as witnesses before the grand jury').

25 *Salvatore v Kumar*, NY Slip Op 08435 (2007).

26 For example, see D. Curtis, 'Old knights and new champions: Kaye Scholer, the Office of Thrift Supervision, and the pursuit of the dollar', *Southern California Law Review*, 1993, vol. 66, 985, pp. 988–96 (describing the history of the *Kaye, Scholer* case and the nature of the competing claims).

27 See Changes to the Representation of Others Before the U.S. Patent and Trademark Office, 69 Fed. Reg. 35452, 37 C.F.R. pt. 11 (June 24, 2004); see also *Sperry v Florida ex rel. Fla. State Bar*, 373 U.S. 379 (1963) (upholding the pre-emptive effect of the US Patent Office's regulations governing who could practise before it).

28 See generally F. Zacharias, 'Recent trends in federal regulation of lawyers', *Professional Lawyer*, 2003, vol. 15, 1.

29 *Sarbanes-Oxley Act* of 2002, Pub. L. No. 107–204, 116 Stat. 745 (2002).

30 The ABA's Clark Report and an extensive study by Raymond Marks and Darlene Cathcart did provide empirical information regarding the previous generation of disciplinary enforcement before the adoption of the Model Rules. See Special Committee on Evaluation of Disciplinary Enforcement, *Problems and Recommendations in Disciplinary Enforcement (Clark Report)*, Chicago: American Bar Association, 1970, p. 19; Marks and Cathcart 'Discipline within the legal profession'. These studies, however, have not been updated to take into account modern realities. But see Commission on Evaluation of Disciplinary Enforcement, *Lawyer Regulation for a New Century (McKay Report)*, Chicago: American Bar Association, 1992; Zacharias, 'The myth of lawyer self-regulation', p. 1147 (discussing changes in disciplinary enforcement in modern times).

31 F. Zacharias and B. Green, 'Rationalizing judicial regulation of lawyers', *Ohio State Law Journal*, 2009, vol. 70, 73.

32 The various causes of action are detailed in R. Mallen and J. Smith, *Legal Malpractice Vol. 1*, St Paul, MN: West Books, 2008, pp. 1–5.

33 See G. Munneke and A. Davis, 'The standard of care in legal malpractice: Do the Model Rules of Professional Conduct define it?', *Journal of the Legal Profession*, 1998, vol. 22, 33, pp. 56, 58–60 (noting that, in most American jurisdictions, juries may be informed or instructed about the mandates in the prevailing professional code, but that the professional standards do not control juries' determinations of whether the standard of care was breached).

34 See M. Duncan, 'Legal malpractice by any other name: Why a breach of fiduciary duty claim does not smell as sweet', *Wake Forest Law Review*, 1999, vol. 34, 1137, pp. 1165–66 (noting that courts sometimes employ juries in breach of fiduciary duty cases against lawyers); C. Wolfram, 'A cautionary tale: Fiduciary breach as legal malpractice', *Hofstra Law Review*, 2006, vol. 34, 689, p. 693 (arguing against a growing trend in the courts of treating breach of fiduciary duty claims as malpractice claims).

35 See Davis, 'Professional liability insurers as regulators of law practice', pp. 212–22 (discussing ways in which insurers regulate lawyer behaviour).

36 For example, see Mallen and Smith, *Legal Malpractice*, pp. 24–25 (providing statistics regarding the explosion of legal malpractice litigation); M. Ramos, 'Legal malpractice: No lawyer or client is safe', *Florida Law Review*, 1995, vol. 37, 1, p. 3 (discussing the exponential growth in 'the frequency and severity of legal malpractice').

37 See Zacharias, 'The myth of lawyer self-regulation', pp. 1155–60 (discussing ways in which early American judges 'could forbid lawyers to appear, sanction lawyers for litigation misconduct, or punish them in more indirect ways').

38 See Zacharias and Green, 'Rationalizing judicial regulation of lawyers', p. 73 (discussing modern courts' methods of supervising lawyer behaviour).

39 For a dissenting viewpoint, see Barton, 'Do judges systematically favor', pp. 454–55.

40 For example, see M. Aspen, 'A response to the civility naysayers', *Stetson Law Review*, 1998, vol. 28, 253, p. 253, n 1 (citing six Supreme Court justices' criticisms of the professionalism of lawyers); R. Katz, 'Ethical concerns: Ad hominem attacks', *American Law Institute-American Bar Association Continuing Legal Education*, 1991, vol. C695, 351, p. 372 (cataloguing surveys of judges reflecting 'nearly universal lament [over attorney incivility and lack of professionalism in] discovery').

41 See Fed. R. Civ. P. R. 11 (as amended 1983) (providing for sanctions for lawyers filing pleadings for any improper purpose). See generally L. Marshall, H. Kritzer and F. Zemans, 'The use and impact of Rule 11', *Northwestern University Law Review*, 1992, vol. 86, 943, p. 948 (evaluating the impact of the 1983 amendments to Rule 11 and noting that, although criticisms of judges' over-use of the rule may be overblown: 'Unquestionably, these amendments led to a dramatic increase in Rule 11 activity.').

42 See F. Zacharias, 'Are evidence-related ethics provisions "law"?', *Fordham Law Review*, 2007, vol. 76, 1315, pp. 1320–23 (discussing areas in which courts have not deferred to standards in the professional codes).

43 See D. Hart, 'And the chill goes on – federal civil rights plaintiffs beware: Rule 11 vis-à-vis 28 U.S.C. 1927 and the court's inherent power', *Loyola of Los Angeles Law Review*, 2004, vol. 37, 645, p. 662 (finding that, with the reduction in Rule 11 sanctions after the 1993 amendments, sanctions under 28 U.S.C. 1927 and other judicial sanction authority increased).

44 See J. Altman, 'Considering the ABA's 1908 Canons of Ethics', *Fordham Law Review*, 2003, vol. 71, 2395, pp. 2492–95 (detailing the promulgation of the 1908 Canons).

45 See American Law Institute, *Restatement of the Law Governing Lawyers (Third)*, Philadelphia, PA: American Law Institute, 2000 ('The highest courts in most states have ruled … that their power to regulate lawyers is inherent in the judicial function.'); C. Wolfram, *Practitioner's Guide to Modern Legal Ethics*, St Paul, MN: West Publishing, 1986, pp. 24–25, 31–32 (describing state Supreme Courts' assertion of 'inherent powers' over the Bar).

46 For example, see B. Barton, 'An institutional analysis of lawyer regulation: Who should control lawyer regulation – courts, legislatures, or the market?', *Georgia Law Review*, 2003, vol. 37, 1167, p. 1186 (discussing state Supreme Courts' propensity for being captured by the Bar).

47 See generally Clark Report.

48 McKay Report (noting that 'almost all states' had a professional disciplinary staff).

49 See American Law Institute, *Restatement of the Law* ('regulating the system of lawyer discipline [is a function] reserved in most states to the highest court of the state').

50 *The State Bar Court of California*. Available from www.calbar.ca.gov/state/calbar/sbc_generic.jsp?cid=13469 (accessed 18 December 2008) (describing the California disciplinary process and the State Bar Court).

51 See National Organization of Bar Counsel, available from www.nobc.org (website of 'The National Organization of Bar Counsel (NOBC) … a non-profit organization of legal professionals whose members enforce ethics rules that regulate the professional conduct of lawyers who practice law in the United States, Canada and Australia').

52 See Association of Professional Responsibility Lawyers, available from www.aprl.net (website of an organization of 'lawyers concentrating in the fields of professional responsibility and legal ethics' and consisting in significant part of 'counsel for respondents in disciplinary hearings … [and] legal malpractice litigators').

53 See Zacharias and Green, 'Rationalizing judicial regulation of lawyers', p. 73 (arguing that state Supreme Courts should take a more active role in establishing the professional standards and harmonizing them with other judicial regulation of lawyers).

54 *State ex rel. Oklahoma Bar Ass'n v Giger* 37 P.3d 856, 864 (Okla. 2001).

55 For example, see B. Green and F. Zacharias, 'Permissive rules of professional conduct', *Minnesota Law Review*, 2006, vol. 91, 265, pp. 285–87 (discussing self-interested professional rules).

56 D. Margolies, 'Commentary: Neal case adds to negative perception of lawyers', *Missouri Lawyers Weekly*, 17 December 2007 (discussing the failure to discipline a lawyer as 'reinforc[ing]' the widely held, if erroneous, public perception that lawyers are more interested in protecting their own than in meting out justice').

57 See F. Zacharias, 'The purposes of lawyer discipline', *William and Mary Law Review*, 2003, vol. 45, 675, pp. 685–89 (discussing the licensing and client-protection goals of professional discipline).

58 American Bar Association, *Model Rules of Professional Conduct*.

59 For example, see Zacharias, 'The humanization of attorneys', pp. 26–30 (discussing areas in which the Bar should encourage external regulation and other areas in which it should change the direction of its own efforts).

60 See Green and Zacharias, 'Permissive rules of professional conduct', p. 319, n. 193 (discussing the ABA response to the SEC proposal).

61 Ibid., p. 290 (outlining Washington's response); Letter from State Bar of Cal. to Securities & Exchange Comm'n, 13 August 2003. Available from www.calbar.ca.gov/

calbar/pdfs/sections/buslaw/corporations/2003-10-08_SEC.pdf (arguing that the SEC could not constitutionally pre-empt state ethics rules governing attorney–client confidentiality).

62 This phenomenon is discussed in F. Zacharias, 'Harmonizing privilege and confidentiality', *South Texas Law Review*, 1999, vol. 41, 69, pp. 72–73.

63 For example, Barton, 'An institutional analysis of lawyer regulation', p. 1204 ('State supreme courts have … delegat[ed] virtually all of their regulatory authority under the vaunted system of 'lawyer self-regulation.').

# 12 Why good intentions are often not enough: the potential for ethical blindness in legal decision-making

*Kath Hall*

Getting rid of a delusion makes us wiser than getting hold of a truth.

*Ludwig Borne*

## 12.1 Introduction

This chapter takes as its starting point the question of how otherwise experienced and principled lawyers can make blatantly unethical decisions. As recent research has shown, lawyers can become involved in legitimizing inhuman conduct, just as they can in perpetuating accounting fraud or hiding client scandal.[1] To an outsider looking at these circumstances, it invariably appears that the lawyers involved *consciously* acted immorally. Within the common framework of deliberative action, we tend to see unethical behaviour as the result of conscious and controlled mental processes.

While awareness is always part of our actions, this chapter challenges the pervasiveness of assumptions about the power of conscious processes in ethical decision-making. Drawing on a range of psychological research, it focuses on two important findings: first, that automatic mental processes are far more dominant in our thinking than most of us are aware; and second, that because we do not generally have introspective access to these processes, we infer from their results what the important factors in our decision-making must be. These findings challenge the notion that individuals can be fully aware of what influences them to act ethically or unethically. It also suggests that we need to concentrate on those conscious processes that we do know influence decision-making in deepening our understanding of how to improve ethical awareness.

As this chapter argues, one of the most important cognitive processes in the context of ethical awareness is rationalization. Not only is rationalization part of how we consciously reason about our ethical decision-making, but it also has the capacity, when used over time, to become an automatic mental process. This tendency can be increased by situational factors that encourage rationalization, and by professional and organizational justifications that mask unethical conduct. As such, rationalization is important to consider in the context of legal decision-making. If reasons such as 'It is just my job', 'I was told to do it' or 'Everyone else is doing it' become deeply embedded in how lawyers think about their behaviour, and this thinking is reinforced by workplace or professional norms, ethical blindness can result. In particular, lawyers may not 'see' the moral components of their behaviour – not because they are morally uneducated or lack good intentions, but because rationalization processes remove the ethics from view.

## 12.2 Ethical awareness in decision-making

Rest, in his influential framework on the steps that lead to ethical behaviour, identifies the first part as requiring individuals to recognize that a moral problem exists or a moral principle is relevant to a particular situation.[2] This is seen as a conscious cognitive and interpretive step, and as a necessary precursor to ethical judgement and behaviour.[3] Embedded in Rest's characterization is the implication that moral awareness is a reliable and stable part of the ethical decision-making process.[4]

Yet there is now significant evidence about the power of unconscious processes in decision-making.[5] Over a century ago, Freud claimed that a large portion of human thinking was affected by unconscious biological influences.[6] Since that time, academic understanding of the role of unconscious processes has expanded significantly through the work of cognitive, social and neurobiological psychologists.[7] In particular, in the context of developing models of the ways in which people comprehend language, process information, utilize memory, develop judgements, make decisions and evaluate behaviour, it has become increasingly clear that large parts of these mental processes occur outside of the view of the individuals involved.[8] Thus, while contemporary psychology now generally accepts the influence of both conscious and unconscious processes in human thinking, increasingly researchers have argued that unconscious mental processes account for a significant majority of mental acts.[9]

*Conscious* mental acts are defined as those about which we are aware, which are started by an act of will, which require effort and which we can control.[10] Because we have limited access to *unconscious* mental processes, they are by definition difficult to define. However, they have generally been characterized as either those that involve perceptual analysis or the encoding of environmental events (such as human memory), and those that begin as intentional, goal-oriented processes and over time operate without conscious guidance (such as learning a musical instrument or driving a car).[11] Unconscious processes can therefore include not only lower-level processing such as perceptual functions, but also higher-order psychological processes such as developing feelings, forming motives and making judgements.[12]

These findings seem to contradict the preference many people have for believing in their ability to increase their self-awareness and influence their own thinking. What must be remembered, however, is that despite the widespread influence of unconscious processes on our thinking, significant aspects of our mental activities remain reserved for conscious thought. Indeed, the primary reason that the mind relies so heavily on unconscious and automatic processes is to free our conscious mental capacity for other functions.[13] Researchers have long noted that it would be impossible for humans to function effectively if conscious, controlled and aware mental processes had to deal with every aspect of life.[14] Instead, it appears that the sophistication of our minds has developed alongside human evolution so that over time more aspects of our daily tasks have been assigned to the realm of unconscious acts.[15] The result is that:

> the adaptive unconscious [holds] a lot of interesting stuff about the human mind … [It] occurs outside of awareness for reasons of efficiency, and not because of repression … The mind is a well-designed system that is able to accommodate a great deal in parallel, by analyzing and thinking about the world outside of awareness while consciously thinking about something else within it.[16]

A second point to emerge from the research on unconscious mental processes is that because we are unable to observe large parts of our own thinking processes, we tend to focus on the results of these processes in analyzing our behaviour.[17] This finding has helped researchers to explain how it is that people can provide reasons for their decisions, but have no recollection of the perceptual or mental processes that they went through in making those decisions.[18] Nisbett and Wilson suggest that the mind uses *a priori* theories about the causal connection between stimulus and response to reason about behaviour.[19] They note that people tend to experience this process as an authentic and accurate process of introspection. Because we are not able to consult a memory of our decision-making processes, we unconsciously draw on theories that are based on cultural or subcultural explanations of events, experiences and observations to explain our actions. As they write:

> if we ask a person why he [sic] enjoyed a particular party and he responds with 'I like the people at the party,' we may be extremely dubious as to whether he has reached this conclusion as a result of anything that might be called introspection. We are justified in suspecting that he has instead asked himself Why People Enjoy Parties and has come up with the altogether plausible hypothesis that in general people will like parties if they like the people at the parties. Then, his only excursion into his storehouse of private information would be to make a quick check to verify that his six worst enemies were not at the party. If not, he confidently asserts that people-liking was the basis for his party-liking.[20]

What these two findings suggest for ethical decision-making is that we may need to rethink the extent of deliberative reasoning involved in the chain of moral judgement. It is probable that people *unconsciously react* first to situations, and then *consciously reason* through their decisions and behaviour in relation to those situations. This process can happen so fast that it is all perceived as being part of an authentic and conscious act of evaluation. Yet, because the reactive part of the process happens almost exclusively at the unconscious level, the reasoning that follows is based on those aspects of the process that reach conscious awareness. This idea is also consistent with Haidt's work on moral intuitions. He argues that ethical judgements usually reflect immediate *intuitive* reactions which individuals justify post hoc by recourse to socially acceptable reasons:[21] 'Individuals do not engage in moral reasoning to arrive at a conclusion, but rather engage in moral reasoning to justify a conclusion already reached.'[22]

Finally, psychological research suggests that ethical decision-making is influenced by a strong unconscious bias towards maintaining our self-interest. There is evidence from cognitive, social and evolutionary psychology that self-interest is an automatic egocentric default in our thinking.[23] Perceptions, judgements and behaviours are generally shown to be biased towards promoting our self-interest and maintaining a positive self-image: 'individuals view themselves as moral, competent and deserving and this view obstructs their ability to see and recognise [ethical issues] when they occur'.[24] As a result, Epley and Caruso suggest that: 'Automatic evaluations produce moral reasoners who are not empiricists reasoning dispassionately about a particular issue, but motivated partisans seeking justification for a pre-existing intuition.'[25]

## 12.3 The importance of rationalization

In the context of such a discussion on awareness in ethical decision-making, rationalization assumes great importance. This is because it is the central cognitive process by which we evaluate our decisions and find convincing and rational reasons for our behaviour. Rationalization is also an egocentric process.[26] We rationalize behaviour in ways that serve our self-interest and preserve our self-esteem. Indeed, research suggests that we are highly resistant to both the thought of our wrongdoing and to the negative feelings that can result.[27] Common rationalizations for wrongdoing include: 'I was told to do it'; 'It wasn't so bad'; 'They deserved it'; 'Everyone else was doing it'; 'No one got hurt'; and 'I didn't know that what I was doing was wrong.'[28]

As rationalization also generally involves shifting responsibility for a negative decision or action to an outside source (such as another person, an institution or to external pressures) it can work to significantly reduce the threat to a person's self-esteem from acknowledging they did something wrong.[29] This externalizing is also done in a way that is automatic and reflexive, rather than laboured and conscious; it can result in the person not being aware of the effect of rationalization on the accuracy of their perceptions or on the ethical blindness that can result.

It is also useful to note that rationalization is at the heart of the concept of *cognitive dissonance*.[30] When we experience conflict between our actions, beliefs and experiences, cognitive dissonance theory suggests that we are likely to use common psychic mechanisms to reduce the discomfort caused by this dissonance. The most fundamental mechanism we can use in this context is rationalization. It enables us to create consistency within our thoughts by allowing us to develop justifications for why our actions were necessary and appropriate. Rationalization allows our minds to think: 'If I said it, I must believe it … if I did it, I must think it's right.'[31]

Finally, rationalization is one of the conscious mental processes that can be affected by repeated use. To the extent that the same or similar circumstances are involved in a decision, awareness of the process of rationalization can be decreased.[32] In particular, the more we develop and use particular rationalizations, the more they can become a habitual and seemingly valid part of our thinking processes. However, as the process of automation is itself unconscious, our awareness of both this process and the original issues that motivated our rationalizations can easily be hidden from view.[33]

Examples of the link between poor legal decision-making and rationalization are provided by recent studies into lawyer misconduct. In his book *Eat What You Kill: The Fall of a Wall Street Lawyer*, Milton Regan analyzes the internal and external forces that affected John Gellene, a partner with Milbank, Tweed, Hadley and McCloy, who was sentenced to fifteen months' jail for failing to declare a conflict of interest in a large bankruptcy proceeding.[34] Regan focuses on what may have led Gellene to believe that his unethical conduct was acceptable. He suggests that Gellene unduly focused on the standards of practice commonly used within the bankruptcy section of the firm and on his own reputation as an experienced and intelligent lawyer. In particular, Regan notes that different sections of the firm developed their own understandings of the ethical obligations that applied in their area and that ethical issues were often marginalized or ignored as a result.[35] Of relevance in the context of Gellene's decision-making was that the bankruptcy section applied implicit understandings which encouraged lawyers to focus on the ambiguities in the laws on conflict of interest rather than on the significant ethical issues often involved in these cases.[36]

As a result, Regan argues that Gellene may have unconsciously drawn on the flexible and ambiguous standards that were seen to apply to conflicts of interest, and on his own self-interest in wanting to retain the work of such a large client, to reason that the conflict in the particular case did not pose a threat to his client loyalty or independence.[37] As he writes:

> Gellene's possible belief that [the facts of this case] gave rise to only a technical conflict of interest in turn [might have] permitted him to rationalize that withholding information about these connections was not freighted with moral significance … The important point is … that corporate bankruptcy culture may [have made] this rationalization seem plausible in situations in which a lawyer would prefer not to make full disclosure.[38]

Regan notes that personal motives may have also encouraged Gellene to rationalize his behaviour. By all accounts, Gellene was a loner, a hard worker and a perfectionist.[39] As Gellene said in testimony:

> not just for my adult life but before that I've been recognised as a person with gifts in terms of my intellect and my ability to deal with problems, and

I've been very good and very competent at the kinds of problems presented [by] my clients in the practice of law and in academics and so on.[40]

It is therefore arguable that Gellene was motivated both by his image of himself as a good lawyer and by the pressure for success within the firm to draw on 'moral understandings' different from those expressed in the bankruptcy law. This he did by focusing on the common practices adopted within the firm and the specific facts of the case before him, with the result that a distortion occurred in his appreciation of the ethical issues involved. Rather than acting out of fraud or conscious deceit, Gellene's behaviour could have arisen from a combination of automatic mental processes (rationalization), motivated cognitions (self-interest) and situational factors (such as the ambiguous legal rules).

The idea that legal decision-making can be influenced deeply by processes of rationalization is also reflected in Richard Abel's book *Lawyers in the Dock: Learning from Attorney Disciplinary Proceedings*.[41] In this book, Abel analyzes seven cases involving disciplinary proceedings against lawyers. One of the common themes he identifies in almost all of these cases is the inability of the lawyers to admit to their error. As Abel writes:

All but one of the lawyers were convinced that they had done nothing wrong. Few could have been identified as potential rule violators in advance: indeed, all but one had practiced law successfully, some for many decades.[42]

Abel also notes a common pattern in these cases: once the lawyers committed themselves to an unethical course of action, they found it difficult to change. They seemed to construct 'an alternative reality, which made their conduct acceptable, laudable, even imperative'.[43] Most of the lawyers sought to shift responsibility for their actions to others, such as uncooperative clients and unsympathetic judges. They also focused on other lawyers who engaged in similar unethical practices to them. As Abel concludes, the common picture that emerged was of lawyers who had a deeply entrenched capacity to develop rationalizations or schemas that hid or denied their unethical action.[44]

Abel's conclusions are consistent with research suggesting that people in complex environments often rely on 'mental scripts' to organize their experiences.[45] These scripts tend to derive from an individual's unconscious processing of their prior experience to form 'knowledge' that, once learnt, does not need to be considered actively again. As Gioia notes, such scripts can be influenced by professional or organizational understandings of what is acceptable behaviour, and often include no ethical component in their cognitive content.[46]

In the context of legal practice, common scripts can include meeting a client's desired ends, zealous advocacy, generating firm income, career progression and creative interpretation of the rules.[47] It is arguable that lawyers begin developing these scripts in law school when they are introduced to abstract legal reasoning, impartial/zealous advocacy, competitive success, excessive workloads and interpretive approaches to law. Legal practice then reinforces these ideas to the extent that lawyers continue to operate in a highly competitive and morally ambiguous world. Wasserstrom describes the issue in this way:

> Ironically, lawyers' self-conception as advocates for the client, as neutral, non-judgmental facilitators of transactions, or as professionally trained to make 'arguments' on either side of an issue, can allow a high degree of rationalization of their complicity in conduct that is ultimately not in their ... client's interest, certainly not in the public interest and often immoral, if not illegal.[48]

Lawyers can also be encouraged in their tendencies to rationalize unethical behaviour by commercial justifications.[49] As Luban notes, lawyers inhabit a world of 'inevitable righteousness' where seemingly objective and commercial reasons can be used again and again to support ethically questionable behaviour.[50] This enables lawyers to think of themselves as 'rational, blameless and consistent decision makers',[51] while at the same time engaging in a process of rationalized self-deception about the true nature of their behaviour.

Finally, Wasserstrom argues that lawyers' conception of their role is fundamental to their willingness to rationalize ethical misconduct.[52] When deciding whether they have acted appropriately, lawyers often overly emphasize the needs of their clients, and argue that what they have done is commonly required, expected or demanded in their professional role. 'Such reasoning is often used to deflect or defuse potential moral criticism by explaining that the role constitutes a sufficient reason for doing or not doing something that would otherwise be objectionable, criticizable, or morally wrong.'[53]

This idea that unconscious rationalizations can influence unethical conduct is challenged in two related decisions of the Supreme Court of Queensland. In both these cases, the court adopted the approach that lawyers' professional misconduct could be only accidental or deliberate. In the case of *Janus v Qld Law Society Inc*,[54] Chief Justice de Jersey used the term 'ethical blindness' to describe the behaviour of a lawyer who had applied for readmission 14 years after being struck off the roll.[55] In the original action, the lawyer was found to have engaged in serious misdealings with clients' moneys, and to have unlawfully maintained legal proceedings.[56] In the application for readmission, the court unanimously considered it relevant that the applicant continued to assert that he should be exonerated or partly excused for his earlier behaviour. All judges considered that this approach reflected 'ethical blindness' on the part of the applicant, as it showed that he was unable to appreciate that his earlier conduct was wrong.[57] Furthermore, the majority of the court considered that such 'ethical blindness' was central to assessing the applicant's intrinsic character.[58] As de Jersey CJ stated in the context of one of the three acts of misconduct:

> The grounds on which the applicant relied to reduce his ethical culpability in relation to this matter were technical in nature, and largely concerned with peripheral or irrelevant aspects. That he raised them in the course of these

proceedings hardly did him credit. Rather, it suggested he lacked proper insight into the relevant ethical considerations.[59]

This approach, of treating a lack of full comprehension of wrongdoing as a reflection of the intrinsic character of the individual involved, was again applied in the case of *Barristers' Board v Young*.[60] Here, the Supreme Court of Queensland found that a barrister's failure to acknowledge the full extent of her previous wrongdoing was relevant in its decision to remove her name from the Roll of Barristers. In this case, the barrister falsely gave evidence to the Queensland Criminal Justice Commission's Inquiry on Electoral Fraud by failing to admit that she had enrolled at an address at which she did not live for the purposes of voting in a plebiscite for the Australian Labor Party. After giving the false evidence, the barrister voluntarily returned to the Inquiry to correct her statements, claiming that her earlier evidence had been motivated by her fear of the consequences and her confusion over the actual events. She also contacted the Queensland Barristers' Board to explain her incorrect evidence, and stated in a letter to the Board that she considered she had not committed any wrongdoing at the time of the Inquiry as her recollection of events was not then very clear.

In deciding that the barrister's name should be removed from the roll, Chief Justice de Jersey again expressed his concern about individuals who were not prepared to admit to their own wrongdoing. He considered that the barrister's explanation of her conduct to the Inquiry, and to the Barristers' Board, displayed 'a lack of insight into the repugnancy of her conduct'.[61] The court also found that her claim to the Barristers' Board reflected clear evidence of her lack of moral awareness.[62] This was despite the fact that a psychiatrist gave evidence on the barrister's behalf suggesting that at the time of the Inquiry she was suffering from acute depression and that her evidence may not have been as deliberately untruthful as it later seemed. However, de Jersey CJ rejected this evidence. As he stated:

> [I] should mention in particular Dr Reddan's view that the respondent 'was not being quite as deliberately untruthful as she later seemed to suggest'. It is difficult to understand the precise purport of that view. *A lie is always deliberate, and the respondent has admitted she lied.* (emphasis added)[63]

These cases suggest that, in line with much of the academic writing on ethical misconduct, Australian courts seem to treat claims of a lack of ethical awareness as evidence of either character flaw or moral weakness in the individual concerned. While it is not suggested that the individuals in these cases should be absolved of their responsibility, it is suggested that the courts need to develop a more sophisticated understanding of the relevant psychological processes in the context of legal misconduct. They also need to consider making use of a broader range of strategies and responses to deal with lawyers' failure to comply with professional standards. Finally, the legal profession needs to recognize that an over-reliance on rationalizations can significantly undermine a lawyer's ethical awareness, with potentially serious results.

## 12.4 Reducing ethical blindness

As indicated above, lawyers would benefit from specific training on the way rationalization processes influence their decisions. As Argyris notes:

> People can be taught how to recognize the reasoning they use when they design and implement their actions ... They can face up to the fact that they unconsciously design and implement actions that they do not intend. Finally, people can learn how to identify what individuals and groups do to create organizational defenses and how these defenses contribute to an organization's problems.[64]

This process of training could include consideration of the extensive psychological research on cognitive biases, motivational and group factors and the effect of social influences on the quality of decision-making. It could also include a consideration of practical examples where rationalizations might influence legal decisions with negative results. Connecting the theory of ethical decision-making with practical problems is particularly important in any training aimed at raising awareness of the consequences of unreflective decision-making. In the context of legal training, it could also contribute to the development of a more sophisticated understanding of the many contexts in which rationalization can undermine well-intentioned behaviour by lawyers.

It is also important to consider whether lawyers' unconscious decision-making processes can be influenced. As Milkman and colleagues acknowledge, up until now psychological research on decision-making has focused primarily on identifying and understanding the conscious and unconscious processes that negatively affect decisions.[65] Although this focus has resulted in a strong body of knowledge on what these processes are, it has largely left unanswered the question of what strategies might work to influence and improve automatic decision-making practices.

Some researchers have suggested ways to influence automatic cognitive processes.[66] For example, in one study researchers used a targeted cue to trigger conscious awareness of the hindsight bias (the unconscious tendency of individuals to exaggerate the extent to which they could have anticipated a particular outcome).[67] Because the researchers considered that the mechanism producing the hindsight bias was the failure of individuals to take account of uncertainty in the knowledge that was available at the time a particular outcome occurred, they conducted a test in which research subjects were reminded of contrary evidence in a case they were asked to consider. What they found was that, by countering the mechanism which had produced the distortion, they could trigger a more conscious process of reflection by the individuals involved. This also appeared to make them significantly more resistant to the hindsight bias by broadening the information they used in their decision-making.

If, as this chapter has argued, rationalization undermines ethical decision-making, then focusing on what motivates people to rationalize behaviour may help to identify ways in which to reduce ethical blindness. In particular, it may be useful to concentrate on the link between rationalization and self-esteem. For example, Bersoff suggests that if people can be challenged around the validity of their rationalization process, they may be less likely to rely on it.[68] In particular, based on a study that he conducted where students received an overpayment for work done, he noted that rationalizations only tended to facilitate unethical behaviour to the extent that people believed, in good faith, that their justificatory reasoning was valid: 'Any realization that one [is] purposely cutting corners or biasing the judgment process [can] ruin the air of legitimacy surrounding the rationalized action.'[69] This led Bersoff to conclude that specific manipulations could be used to challenge the objectivity or integrity of a person's process of rationalization. To the extent that these interventions create a conflict between a person's image of themselves as a good person/decision-maker and the actions/decisions they are considering taking, they could create a more conscious process of evaluation of the validity of the rationalizations that may possibly be used.[70]

## 12.5 Conclusion

In reflecting on the question of how experienced and principled lawyers can make blatantly unethical decisions, this chapter has argued that recognizing the influence of unconscious processes on ethical decision-making is essential. In particular, understanding how and why the mind facilitates ethical blindness is a necessary part of identifying when ethical weaknesses can occur. Most lawyers are not poor decision-makers. However, many are fallible thinkers who fail to recognize the power of rationalization on the quality and ethicality of their decisions. As ethical issues are often not prominent in the cognitive, workplace and professional norms that drive the legal profession, lawyers need to be encouraged to be aware of the ways rationalization can remove these issues from view.[71]

It is also important to remember that, for most of us, it is difficult to acknowledge that common aspects of our decision-making practices are risky or unreliable. Particularly where good decision-making is central to our self-concept, we can be resistant to suggestions that common mental processes are maladaptive. Research also suggests that we are generally prone to being overly positive in our assessment of how we think we would act in unethical situations. We fail to realize that there is often a conflict between the standard of behaviour we think we exhibit and the way we actually behave. Argyris explains the situation this way:

> One of the paradoxes of human behaviour ... is that the master program people actually use is rarely the one they think they use. Ask people in an interview or questionnaire to articulate the rules they use to govern their actions, and they will give you what I call their 'espoused' theory of action.

But observe these same people's behavior, and you will quickly see that this espoused theory has very little to do with how they actually behave ... When you observe people's behavior and try to come up with rules that would make sense of it, you discover a very different theory of action – what I call the individual's 'theory-in-use'. Put simply, *people consistently act inconsistently*, unaware of the contradiction between their espoused theory and their theory-in-use, between the way they think they are acting and the way they really act.[72]

All of this suggests that even lawyers who consider themselves to be excellent decision-makers can benefit from training in the psychological dynamics of decision-making. For some lawyers, it may be necessary to create incentives for this training. These incentives could come from law firms emphasizing and rewarding lawyers who engage in training on their decision-making practices and thereby reduced the firm's exposure to liability for poor decisions. The legal profession could also stress the important role of lawyers as skilled and informed decision-makers, and the positive professional and reputational consequences that can come from enhancing and developing this role.

For such changes to be welcomed also requires debates on legal ethics to now go beyond common assumptions that unethical conduct results from character flaws, moral weakness or a lack of ethical insight. We need to recognize that unconscious mental processes can intervene early in the decision-making process and fundamentally distort ethical awareness. If a lawyer's initial response to a challenging situation fails to recognize that there are ethical issues involved, whether the lawyer continues to act on this response will, to an extent, depend upon their knowledge of how rationalizations can distort their decision-making. If lawyers have sufficient understanding of the risks of automatic rationalization, or there are external factors to encourage reflective decision-making, ethical behaviour is more likely to follow. If, on the other hand, workplace, professional or cognitive factors combine to reinforce a lawyer's immediate unconscious and often self-interested reasoning, then ethical blindness can easily result.

## Notes

1 See, for example, D. Luban, 'Torture and the professions', *Criminal Justice Ethics*, 2007, vol. 2, 58; A. Perlman, 'Unethical obedience by subordinate attorneys: Lessons from social psychology', *Hofstra Law Review*, 2007, vol. 36, 451; D.L. Rhode and P.D. Paton, 'Lawyers, ethics and Enron', in N. Rapoport and B. Dharan (eds), *Enron: Corporate Fiascos and Their Implications*, New York: Foundation Press, 2004; J.C. Coffee Jr, *Gatekeepers: The Role of the Professions in Corporate Governance*, Oxford: Oxford University Press, 2006; M.C. Regan Jr, 'Teaching Enron', *Fordham Law Review*, 2005, vol. 74, 1139; D.C. Langevoort, 'Where were the lawyers? A behavioural inquiry into lawyers' responsibility for clients' fraud', *Vanderbilt Law Review*, 1993, vol. 46, 75.
2 J.R. Rest, *Moral Development: Advances in Research and Theory*, California: Praeger, 1986.
3 See K.D. Butterfield, L.K. Trevino and G.R. Weaver, 'Moral awareness in business organizations: Influences of issue-related and social context factors', *Human Relations*, 2000, vol. 53, 981, p. 985.

4 J. Jordan, 'A social cognition framework for examining moral awareness in managers and academics', *Journal of Business Ethics* 2009, vol. 84, 237; D. Chugh, M.H. Bazerman and M.R. Banaji, 'Bounded ethicality as a psychological barrier to recognizing conflicts of interest', in D.A. Moore et al. (eds), *Conflicts of Interest: Challenges and Solutions in Business, Law, Medicine, and Public Policy*, Sydney: Cambridge University Press, 2005.

5 See, for example, D. Wegner, *The Illusion of Conscious Will*, Cambridge, MA: MIT Press, 2002; T.D. Wilson, *Strangers to Ourselves: Discovering the Adaptive Unconscious*, Cambridge, MA: Harvard University Press, 2002; T. Gilovich, D.W. Griffin and D. Kahneman (eds), *Heuristics and Biases: The Psychology of Intuitive Judgement*, Cambridge, UK: Cambridge University Press, 2002. For recent research on awareness in the context of ethical decision-making, see D. Chugh, 'Societal and managerial implications of implicit cognition: Why milliseconds matter', *Social Justice Research*, 2004, vol. 17, 203; D. Chugh and M.H. Bazerman, 'Bounded awareness: What you fail to see can hurt you', *Mind and Society*, 2007, vol. 6, 1; Chugh, Bazerman and Banaji, 'Bounded ethicality'; D. Narvaez and D.K. Lapsley, 'The psychological foundations of everyday morality and moral expertise', in D. Lapsley and C. Power (eds), *Character Psychology and Character Educational*, Notre Dame, IN: University of Notre Dame, 2005, p. 140; M.C. Regan, 'Moral intuitions and organizational culture', *St Louis University Law Journal*, 2007, vol. 51, 941; C.R. Sunstein, 'Moral heuristics', *Behavioral and Brain Sciences*, 2005, vol. 28, 531.

6 S. Freud, *The Psychotherapy of Everyday Life*, New York: Vintage, 1965 [1901].

7 See discussion in Wilson, *Strangers to Ourselves*, p. 5.

8 See, for example, S. Chaiken and Y. Trope (eds), *Dual-process Theories in Social Psychology*, New York: Guilford Press, 1999.

9 See G. Gigerenzer and D.G. Goldstein, 'Reasoning the fast and frugal way: Models of bounded rationality', *Psychological Review* 1996, vol. 103, 650; J.A. Bargh and T.L. Chartrand, 'The unbearable automaticity of being', *American Psychologist*, 1999, vol. 54, 462; Wilson, *Strangers to Ourselves*. Some researchers estimate that up to 80 per cent of all mental activities are unconscious: see R.F. Baumeister, E. Bratslavsky, M. Muraven and D. Tice, 'Ego depletion: Is the active self a limited resource?', *Journal of Personality and Social Psychology*, 1998, vol. 74, 336.

10 Bargh and Chartrand, 'The unbearable automaticity of being', p. 463.

11 ibid., p. 464. So, for example, when we engage in any complex task such as driving a car, we necessarily begin this process needing to give great attention to the act of driving. However, the more we drive, the more this process becomes automatic. It is also likely that we may reach a point where, because of our familiarity with driving, we increase the risks we are willing to take in performing that task. We drive faster or are willing to engage in other activities while we drive. We may also become less aware of signs on roads or changes in road conditions.

12 Wilson, *Strangers to Ourselves*, p. 8.

13 Bargh and Chartrand, 'The unbearable automaticity of being', p. 464.

14 See G. Bateson, *Steps to an Ecology of Mind*, San Francisco: Chandler, 1972.

15 As William James noted in 1890: 'The more of the details of daily life we can hand over to the effortless custody of automatism, the more our higher power of mind will be set free for [its] own proper work.' Quoted in Wilson, *Strangers to Ourselves*, p. 43.

16 Wilson, *Strangers to Ourselves*, pp. 8–9.

17 See, for example, D.J. Berns, 'Self-perception: An alternative interpretation of cognitive dissonance theory', *Psychological Review*, 1967, vol. 74, 183.

18 See R. Nisbett and T.D. Wilson, 'Telling more than we can know: Verbal reports on mental processes', *Psychological Review*, 1977, vol. 84, 231, p. 232.

19 Ibid., p. 249.

20 Ibid.

21 J. Haidt, 'The emotional dog and its rational tail: A social intuitionist approach to moral judgment', *Psychological Review*, 2001, vol. 108, 814. See also Regan, 'Moral

intuitions'; F. Cushman, L. Young and M. Hauser, 'The role of conscious reasoning and intuition in moral judgment', *Psychological Science*, 2006, vol. 17, 1082; M. Hauser, F. Cushman, L. Young, R. Jin and J. Mikhail, 'A dissociation between moral judgment and justifications', *Mind & Language*, 2007, vol. 22, 1; J.M. Darley, 'How organizations socialize individuals into evildoing', in D.M. Messick and A.E. Tenbrunsel (eds), *Codes of Conduct: Behavioural Research into Business Ethics*, New York: Russell Sage Foundation, 1996, p. 13.

22 Regan, 'Moral intuitions'.

23 As Moore and Loewenstein note, for obvious evolutionary reasons self-interest is naturally advantaged in terms of goals and outcomes in decision-making processes. See D. Moore and G. Loewenstein, 'Self-interest, automaticity, and the psychology of conflict of interest', *Social Justice Research*, 2004, vol. 17, 189, p. 195; S.T. Fiske and S.E. Taylor, *Social Cognition*, New York: McGraw-Hill, 1991; A.G. Greenwald, 'The totalitarian ego: Fabrication and revision of personal history', *American Psychologist*, 1980, vol. 35, 603.

24 Chugh, Bazerman and Banaji, 'Bounded ethicality', p. 3. Research also suggests that individuals are generally unaware of data that contradict this view of themselves. See Greenwald, 'The totalitarian ego'.

25 N. Epley and E.M. Caruso, 'Egocentric ethics', *Social Justice Research*, 2004, vol. 17, 171, p. 181.

26 Ibid.

27 D. Luban, 'Integrity: Its causes and cures', *Fordham Law Review*, 2003, vol. 73, 279, p. 281. See also Chugh, Bazerman and Banaji, 'Bounded ethicality'.

28 See Sykes and Matza's work on neutralizations in G.M. Sykes and D. Matza, 'Techniques of neutralization: A theory of delinquency', *American Sociological Review*, 1957, vol. 22, 664. Also see J. Haidt and F. Bjorklund, 'Social intuitionists answer six questions about morality', in W. Sinnott-Armstrong (ed.), *Moral Psychology Vol. 2: The Cognitive Science of Morality*, Cambridge, MA: MIT Press, 2008.

29 C.R. Snyder and R.L. Higgins, 'Excuses: Their effective role in the negotiation of reality', *Psychological Bulletin*, 1988, no. 104, 23.

30 See generally L. Festinger and J.M. Carlsmith, 'Cognitive consequences of forced compliance', *Journal of Experimental Social Psychology*, 1958, vol. 58, 203; E. Aronson, 'The return of the repressed: Dissonance theory makes a comeback', *Psychological Inquiry*, 1992, vol. 3, 303; Luban, 'Integrity'.

31 Luban, 'Integrity', p. 281.

32 B.E. Ashforth and V. Anand, 'The normalization of corruption in organizations', *Research in Organizational Behavior*, 2003, vol. 25, 1.

33 Bargh and Chartrand, 'The unbearable automaticity of being', p. 469.

34 M.C. Regan Jr, *Eat What You Kill: The Fall of a Wall Street Lawyer*, Ann Arbor, MI: University of Michigan Press, 2006.

35 Ibid., p. 152.

36 Ibid., p. 179.

37 Ibid., pp. 328, 334.

38 Ibid., pp. 334–35.

39 Ibid., p. 4. See also N. Rapoport, 'The Curious Incident of the Law Firm that Did Nothing in the Night-Time', *Legal Ethics*, 2007, vol. 10, 98, p. 108.

40 Rapoport, 'The Curious Incident', p. 114.

41 R.L. Abel, *Lawyers in the Dock: Learning from Attorney Disciplinary Proceedings*, New York: Oxford University Press, 2008.

42 Ibid., p. 491.

43 Ibid., p. 494.

44 Regan, 'Eat What You Kill', p. 498. Rationalization processes can create a distortion of moral and ethical reality in the context of legal decision-making. De Groot-van Leeuwen suggests this is partly because lawyers have an unending capacity to fashion

arguments to convince themselves that the strict legal rules do not apply to them. See L. de Groot-van Leeuwen, 'A window on lawyer misconduct', *Legal Ethics*, 2008, vol. 11, 107.

45 See V. Anand, B.E. Ashforth and M. Joshi, 'Business as usual: The acceptance and perpetuation of corruption in organizations', *Academy of Management Executive*, 2004, vol. 18, 39; D.A. Gioia, 'Pinto fires and personal ethics: A script analysis of missed opportunities', *Journal of Business Ethics*, 1992, vol. 11, 381.

46 Gioia, 'Pinto fires and personal ethics'. See also Regan, 'Moral intuitions', pp. 949, 965.

47 See K. Hall and V. Holmes, 'The power of rationalisation to influence lawyers' decisions to act unethically', *Legal Ethics*, 2009, vol. 11, 137; P.J. Schiltz, 'On being a happy, healthy, and ethical member of an unhappy, unhealthy, and unethical profession', *Vanderbilt Law Review*, 1999, vol. 52, 871.

48 R. Wasserstrom, 'Roles and morality', in D. Luban (ed.), *The Good Lawyer*, Totowa, NJ: Rowman & Allanheld, 1984, p. 26.

49 See generally Hall and Holmes, 'The power of rationalisation'.

50 See Luban, 'Integrity', p. 281. On the illusion of objectivity in decision-making, see N. Epley and E.M. Caruso, 'Egocentric ethics', *Social Justice Research*, 2004, vol. 17, 171.

51 Chugh, Bazerman and Banaji, 'Bounded ethicality'.

52 Wasserstrom, 'Roles and morality'. See also Hall and Holmes, 'The power of rationalisation'.

53 Wasserstrom, 'Roles and morality', p. 26.

54 *Janus v Qld Law Society Inc* [2002] QCA 180.

55 See the discussion of these cases in R. Mortensen, 'Lawyers' character, moral insight and ethical blindness', *The Queensland Lawyer*, 2002, vol. 22, 166.

56 The applicant also faced criminal charges over these offences and spent some in prison as a result. *See Janus v Qld Law Society Inc* [2002] QCA 180 at 5 and 8.

57 *Janus v Qld Law Society Inc* [2002] QCA 180 at 48.

58 *Janus v Qld Law Society Inc* [2002] QCA 180 at 12.

59 *Janus v Qld Law Society Inc* [2002] QCA 180 at 38.

60 *Janus v Qld Law Society Inc* [2002] QCA 180 at 56.

61 *Janus v Qld Law Society Inc* [2002] QCA 180 at 18.

62 See the discussion by Mortensen, 'Lawyer's character', p. 171.

63 *Janus v Qld Law Society Inc* [2002] QCA 180 at 20 and Mackenzie J at 41.

64 C. Argyris, 'Teaching smart people how to learn', *Harvard Business Review*, 1991, vol. 69, 99.

65 K. Milkman, D. Chugh and M.H. Bazerman, 'How can decision making be improved?', *Harvard Business School NOM Working Paper No. 08–102*, 2008.

66 See discussion in Milkman, Chugh and Bazerman, 'How can decision making be improved?'

67 P. Slovic and B. Fischhoff, 'On the psychology of experimental surprise', *Journal of Experimental Psychology: Human Perception and Performance*, 1977, vol. 3, 552.

68 D. Bersoff, 'Why good people sometimes do bad things: Motivated reasoning and unethical behavior', *Personality and Social Psychology Bulletin*, 1999, vol. 1, 25.

69 Ibid.

70 Ibid.

71 See Gioia, 'Pinto fires', p. 388.

72 Argyris, 'Teaching smart people'.

# Index

For Product Safety Concerns and Information please contact our EU
representative  GPSR@taylorandfrancis.com
Taylor & Francis Verlag GmbH, Kaufingerstraße 24, 80331 München, Germany

www.ingramcontent.com/pod-product-compliance
Lightning Source LLC
Chambersburg PA
CBHW061157220326
41599CB00025B/4516

* 9 7 8 0 4 1 5 6 3 1 5 5 6 *